Selected Writings

Chris Harman

Bookmarks Publications

Selected Writings – Chris Harman
First published July 2010 by Bookmarks Publications
Copyright © Bookmarks Publications
ISBN 9781905192694
Cover design by Mark Dunk
Typeset by Adam Di Chiara
Printed by Melita Press

Contents

Introduction	7
1: History and theory	
Time, tide and class struggle	15
Women's liberation and revolutionary socialism	21
Two Marxes or one?	56
Voice of the hanged	58
2: Party and class	
Party and class	65
Students and the movement	86
The workers' government	89
3: Russia and Eastern Europe	
How the revolution was lost	101
Hungary 1956	120
Dubcek's downfall: now it's back to "orthodox" repression...	127
The Eastern Bloc	130
State capitalism - the theory that fuels the practice	160
4: Economics	
The crisis of bourgeois economics	165
The rate of profit and the world today	219
5: The state we're in	
The new "new left" – a critique	239
The summer of 1981: a post-riot analysis	244
The urgent challenge of fascism	282
Climate change and class conflict	284
6: Imperialism and resistance	
Ho: he gave the Third World a heart	293
Defend Arab revolution	297
The prophet and the proletariat	301
Notes	365

Introduction

Colin Barker

When Marx died in 1883, Engels declared at his graveside that his lifelong comrade had been a man of science, but that before all else he was a revolutionist. The words might have been tailored as an epitaph for Chris Harman, whose tragically early death in Egypt in November 2009 brought to a sudden end a brilliant life in socialist politics.

Chris became a socialist while still at school in Watford. At Leeds University he joined the International Socialists (IS), forerunner of the Socialist Workers Party (SWP), and moved to the London School of Economics to begin postgraduate work. There he became centrally involved in the beginnings of the student movement in Britain, in the development of the Vietnam Solidarity Campaign, and became a regular contributor to both *Labour Worker* (predecessor of *Socialist Worker*) and *International Socialism*. He would go on to edit both of these publications – as well as *Socialist Review* – with great distinction, over many years.

Chris's was an immensely productive life. It was our good fortune that, early on, he was denied a full-time lectureship at Middlesex Polytechnic. Academia's loss was socialism's gain. Chris became a full-time revolutionary, and a permanent fixture in the leadership of the IS and then the SWP. In that role he toured the country, and indeed the world, speaking wherever a group of comrades was able to provide him with a platform. And he *wrote*. His output was phenomenal. As well as writing a whole number of important books and pamphlets, he produced a steady flow of commentary, journalism and major articles on a very wide range of topics – from economics to philosophy, from the contemporary state of the class struggle to cultural theory, from the history of world development to the history of the workers' movement in many parts of the world, from women's liberation and Islam to the defence and development of revolutionary strategy.

Chris acknowledged himself the pupil of two of the founding thinkers of the IS/SWP tradition: Tony Cliff and Michael Kidron. Both were very creative Marxists, insisting on the need to face up to the changed realities of capitalism in the post-war world, when most of the left believed it was necessary to choose between loyalty to Moscow or alliance with Cold War America. The only possible position for revolutionaries, Cliff and Kidron argued, was rejection of this choice in favour of working class power. The theories they developed of state capitalism and deflected permanent revolution allowed them to do this.

Chris made their theories his own, and then developed them further. The earliest article in this selection is his 1966 celebration of the tenth anniversary of the Hungarian Revolution. Here Chris not only identified the exploitative, anti working class character of the Hungarian regime, but recorded the inner dynamics of the uprising, pointing out the crucial role of the workers' councils. The article can be read as a prelude to his first book, *Bureaucracy and Revolution in Eastern Europe* (1974), in which he began to display his talents as a Marxist historian, reviewing the history of popular revolt in East Germany in 1953, Poland and Hungary in 1956, Czechoslovakia in 1968 and Poland in 1970-71. In 1984 he revised the whole work, as *Class Struggles in Eastern Europe 1945-83*, to include a brilliant account of the 1980-82 Solidarity movement in Poland.

Chris's article on the 50th anniversary of the 1917 Russian Revolution, "How the revolution was lost", provides a very clear account of the processes by which the Russian workers' and peasants' revolution, isolated internationally, first "degenerated" and was finally completely defeated from within by Stalin's counter-revolution.

His 1971 article "The Eastern Bloc" took the story forward, to show how the Five Year Plans involved the complete subordination of Russia's industrial and agricultural workforce to the demands of competitive accumulation with international imperialism. But if the harsh policies of the state capitalist regimes were successful for a period in producing a high-speed industrialisation of their economies, by 1971 tendencies to crisis were manifesting themselves. Falling growth rates and the irrationalities of rigid central direction were generating a vicious circle of stagnation, popular resistance and repression. Identifying the contradictions of reform that would, 20 years later, blow the Stalinist states apart, Chris insisted on the necessity of clarity about the real nature of the modern world, and the need to organise the real forces of opposition.

As Chris's analyses of Russia and Eastern Europe developed, they became more and more interwoven with a parallel development and deepening of his work on global political economy. The crises of state capitalism were, after all, only part of the larger and deepening crisis of world capitalism as a whole. His 1989 article "The myth of market socialism" (*International Socialism* 42, 1989)[1] wove together an account of the decay of state capitalism, a sharp critique of then fashionable arguments for a "market-based socialism", some brilliant observations on the ways competition actually works in contemporary "corporate capitalism" along with its savagery and waste, and a summary of the case for a genuine socialism based on a vast expansion of working class democracy.

That was only one article among many. Four of his essays from the early 1980s were collected together in the book *Explaining the Crisis* (1984), a work of considerable power, notable among other matters for Chris's exploration of the working of war economies as part of his ongoing analyses of the inter relations between states and capital. Chris's 1996 article "The crisis of bourgeois economics", would in a rational world be required reading in every economics department. As he shows, not one of the competing schools has any answers to a world in growing crisis. The best they can offer is "grin and bear it". Chris proposes the only feasible solution, working class revolution.

More articles followed, looking at "globalisation" and the size and character of the modern working class, tracking capitalism's booms and recessions and analysing modern imperialism – a series that culminated in his superb last book *Zombie Capitalism* (2009). Rereading all this work, it is striking how Chris was able always to do more than repeat old theories, but to bring them alive and develop them. He excelled at uniting an astounding mastery of rich empirical materials with an immense clarity of both understanding and expression. Chris wove together a sense of Marxism as a living tradition of thought and practice with an openness to what was new. It was never enough to repeat old truths, for the world changed in significant ways, and rarely repeated itself in any simple fashion.

This comes out very strongly in his "The summer of 1981: a post-riot analysis", which is a lesson in how socialists should think through something new. What has happened, who was involved, and how? In what ways do these events compare with similar events? What interpretations, and what solutions, have been offered? What sense should revolutionaries make of them, what can they hope for and what kinds of interventions should they make?

Three articles in this selection illustrate Chris's internationalism, and all raise important questions for socialists. When Chris delivered the substance of his obituary of Ho Chi Minh at a memorial meeting in the Conway Hall in London, he was fiercely attacked – not for his support for the anti-imperialist struggle of the Vietnamese, but for daring to remind the audience that "Uncle Ho" was a Stalinist, and that he had been responsible for the murder of numbers of Trotskyists. Chris was always clear that, first, you must decide which side you are on in any struggle (and no one should support US imperialism!) but, second, you must carefully evaluate your allies and maintain your political independence. Chris's report of his visit to the Palestinian camps in Jordan at the time of Black September catches such complexities and the weakness of any "nationalist" response: the Arab King Hussein was as cruel an enemy of the Palestinians as the Israeli, British or US governments.

The failures of Arab nationalism were among the factors that gave impetus to the rise of "Islamist" politics, the subject of Chris's masterly survey "The prophet and the proletariat" (1994). This offers a terrific materialist account of religion and of the politics of religion, with a due and documented sense of its inner contradictions. Sharply critical of those who accuse Islamism of being "fascist", it provides a characteristically rich empirical account of Islamism in a number of key states, ending with a serious view of the politics of Islamism, and outlining a Marxist stance towards its forms of expression.

All of Chris's writings are marked by a deep historical sense. As he developed as a writer, he became himself a notable historian. As well as his narratives of class struggle in Eastern Europe, he wrote a major history of the tragedy of German communism in *The Lost Revolution: Germany 1918 to 1923* (1982), while *The Fire Last Time: 1968 and After* (1988) remains the best single book on the significance of the movements of that time. His articles on a host of subjects are filled with historical materials, but his crowning achievement is the wonderful *A People's History of the World* (1999). In the present volume his historical work is represented by a short piece he wrote for *Socialist Review* on the publication of *A People's History* and by "Women's liberation" (1984), which both puts a detailed case for the origins of women's oppression in the rise of class society, and sharply takes on contemporary debates with feminism.

Chris Harman was, before all else, a revolutionary socialist, for whom there was only one possible solution to the world's ills – international working class revolution. This was an idea whose attempted realisation he documented in Russia, Germany, Spain, Portugal, Hungary, Poland, Argentina, Bolivia and elsewhere. It provided the standard against which he judged every kind of movement, every kind of idea, every kind of party. For him, Marx's slogan – "the emancipation of the working class is the act of the working class" – remained the core of everything he wrote and said.

To that idea he attached a vital codicil. Working class revolution is impossible unless revolutionary socialists develop a suitable form of party organisation. Not because it is the job of such a party to make the revolution, but because every real movement with the potential to achieve any kind of change – and especially a socialist revolution – is inwardly divided, made up of a whole set of contradictory tendencies and ongoing arguments about the nature of the world and what is possible and desirable. Movements, not parties, make revolutions, but they don't do so unless *within* them there are organised socialists arguing how best the movement can fight. As he wrote in his foundational article "Party and class" (1968), the issue is not a choice between a stress on the spontaneity and creativity of a workers' movement and the conscious interventions of a centralised, democratic socialist party, but how to combine the two. Chris returned again and again to this argument.

Three aspects appear here. The leaflet he drafted for the IS in April 1968, "The urgent challenge of fascism", states a simple case: the far right is on the rise, and revolutionary socialists need to unite to counter that threat. The leaflet sets out four principles on which unity is possible. There is an underlying assumption: there will be lots of differences among us, but we can and will debate them together and learn to act together. That one leaflet helped the IS more than double its membership in 1968.

In "The workers' government", written with Tim Potter in 1977, Chris takes issue with those who argue that socialists should focus their energies on forming a "left" government within the existing parliamentary set-up. What matters is that socialists maintain their independence within the workers' movement, urging that workers themselves must take matters into their own hands and seek their own solutions to pressing political problems. To forget this is to lead the movement into defeat. The argument is a modern repetition of Marx's case, in 1850, for the "revolution in permanence".

A few words on the man: Chris was a very modest person, and this comes across in his writing style. One of the most genuinely learned men most of us have ever known, he never showed off. He wrote with great clarity, always seeking to *persuade*. Chris became a very popular speaker in the SWP, but not because he could entertain. One comrade told me, "I always *learn* something at Chris's meetings: that's why I love hearing him speak."

The same was true of his writing. Read, and learn.

---

1. For simple reasons of length, this article – along with a whole number of others – could not be included in this collection. Plans are already afoot to bring out another volume in the near future. For those who can't wait – thanks to one of capitalism's real developments of the forces of production, a matter on which Chris was very eloquent – most of Chris's extraordinary output of articles is now available on the internet. For this we must thank those who set up and maintained the astonishing archive at www.marxists.org. See also Chris's own "blog" at www.chrisharman.blogspot.com, where he posted quite a few of his notes and articles, and the German site http://www.marxists.de, which also contains numbers of pieces by Chris.

1: History and theory

Time, tide and class struggle

Our hidden history

We have all been brought up on myths about the "superiority" of the West. These assume that there has been a single line of civilisation going back to Greece and Rome, involving over the last 2,000 years a "Judaeo-Christian inheritance" which has been more "civilised", more innovative or more "humane" than that to be found in the rest of the world. The notion of a continuous tradition, supposedly responsible for the rise of industrial capitalism in Europe, is still to be found today, for instance in David Landes's influential book *The Wealth and Poverty of Nations* and in Ellen Meiksins Wood's *Peasants, Citizens and Slaves*. Even some people who reject any notion of the "superiority" of the West accept the myth of continuity, but in a mirror image way. Edward Said's *Orientalism*, for instance, sees a single, iniquitous culture of contempt for the rest of the world as characterising European thought from the time of Aeschylus (5th century BC) through the rise of Christianity and the Crusades up to modern imperialism.

In fact, history has not developed like that at all. A thousand years ago north west Europe was one of the most backward parts of the world. It was made up of Iron Age societies with very few towns and no real cities. Homes and even castles were made of wood coated in mud, clustered together in villages separated by forests, wasteland or marshes. There were no proper roads between them, and any travel over land was along rough tracks, on foot, by mule, or sometimes on horseback. Most lords were as unable to read and write as the vast mass of peasants they exploited. What passed as literature was produced in monasteries, and mainly involved the copying by hand of old religious texts. Insofar as there was a "Graeco-Roman inheritance" in Europe, it amounted to a handful of texts in Latin which might be read, at any point in time, by an even smaller number of monks.

There was a huge contrast with this state of affairs if you looked eastwards to the Arab lands and China, or westwards to Central and South America. The biggest cities in the world were undoubtedly in China, followed by places like Baghdad and Cairo. Even 800 years earlier, when Rome was at its prime, Teotihuacan (outside present-day Mexico City) was as big as Rome, while in the 14th century Vijayanagar in southern India was bigger than Paris or London.

Merchant caravans made long overland journeys from northern China through Samarkand and Bukhara to northern India, Tehran, Baghdad and Constantinople. One set of sea routes connected southern China with southern India, the Persian Gulf, the Red Sea, down the eastern coast of Africa to Zanzibar, and beyond. Another maintained regular contact between Egypt, present-day Algeria and Morocco, right up into an Islamic civilisation in Spain that was to last more than 700 years.

The great mass of the population still lived in the often vast areas between the cities, working as peasants scratching the land to provide for a livelihood for themselves and paying rents and taxes to ruling classes. But within the cities there developed a level of literacy, artistic culture, and scientific and technical advance way beyond that even dreamt of in Europe. It was within the Indian and then the Arab civilisations of the first millennium that people pioneered our present numerical system, discovered the use of zero, advanced the calculation of pi, estimated the size of earth (more accurately than Columbus did five centuries later), and continued and enriched the philosophical traditions established in Greece and Greek Alexandria at a time when knowledge of these was minimal in Europe. China in these centuries was already deploying many thousands of water mills and manufacturing cast iron and steel in bulk, and went on to witness the invention of paper, gunpowder, the first clockwork clocks and the mass printing of books five centuries before Europe, as well as the development of shipbuilding and navigating techniques (the compass, for instance) that allowed long-distance ocean voyages.

How did such developments occur? And why were parts of Europe in the next millennium able to catch up, overtake and eventually conquer the heartlands of the older civilisations? There are currently fashionable explanations which see things in terms of the different "cultural" features of the different civilisations. This runs through, for instance, David Landes's account, and has been the rationale for the BBC's series on the millennium. But this does not explain where the different cultures came from. It does not explain why Hinduism, rather than, say, Buddhism, came to dominate the Indian Middle Ages, why Confucianism defeated rival ideological systems in China, or why medieval Islam differed in important ways from Islam at the time of the 7th century.

The different "cultures" were, in fact, the *product* of historical development, not its cause. And they were not separated off from each other. We can trace the spread across Eurasia and Africa (and, separately, across the Americas) of the great innovations which increased the ability of human beings to make a livelihood and transformed the societies they lived in. So wheat first domesticated in the Middle East made its way to the Atlantic coast of Europe, north Africa and the Pacific coast of China; rice from southern China reached west India; iron spread out from Asia Minor to the whole of Eurasia over a 1,500-year period; steelmaking from west Africa diffused down into the centre and east of the continent over a similar time span; the camel domesticated in Asia about 1000 BC opened the way to commerce through the Sahara and to the transformation of Arabia in Mohammed's time; horse harnesses from central Asia and gunpowder, compasses and paper from China were essential prerequisites for the development of late medieval Europe.

Civilisation and exploitation

Each culture arose as a transitory facet of a single process of world history (or possibly of two similar processes, one in the "old world" and one in the "new world", until they clashed in the time of Columbus and Cortes). At different times and in different parts of the world the development of human control over nature was accompanied by the concentration of wealth into the hands of ruling classes, and with this the growth of "civilisation" in the full meaning of the term – the growth of towns, the use of writing, the establishment of full-time groups of traders and artisans, the rise of organised religion. Humanity's level of material production was such that without an exploiting minority squeezing wealth out of the toiling majority there could he no concentration of the resources needed for civilisation to take off. This is why the successive civilisations and accompanying cultures to be found in Africa, Asia, Europe and North and South

America were all based on such exploitation.

But in every case a ruling class whose initial rise was associated with advances in the creation of wealth later became an impediment to further advance. Typically, civilisation expanded up to a certain point, but then began to go into reverse as the level of exploitation by the ruling class made it difficult for the mass of people to produce the things needed to keep society going. So the first great civilisations of Mesopotamia, the Indus Valley, Egypt, Crete and mainland Greece had all experienced "Dark Ages" of greater or lesser severity by 1400 BC. There followed the rise in the first millennium BC of the classical Greek, Roman, Indian and Chinese civilisations. But these in turn ran into great problems by 500 AD. Europe fell back into its "Dark Age", with virtually no industry, trade or literacy. In India trade and the towns declined, artisan production deprived of markets retreated into virtually self-contained village units, where it became organised by castes, and literacy became a virtual monopoly of Brahmans and entangled with superstition. It was at this point that Hinduism finally ousted Buddhism as the dominant religion and the fully formed caste system took root. China did not experience a relapse on anything like the same scale, but the empire fragmented in the 3rd century AD, and there was a 200-year gap before there was a revival of trade, urban life and learning.

In the Middle East and Mediterranean region the advance of civilisation was associated, for the best part of half a millennium, with the rise of a new religion, Islam. In the towns of the Arabian peninsula a new trading class had emerged, unencumbered by old parasitic classes. The prophet Mohammed had provided it with a worldview which enabled it to defeat the decaying empires around it and establish a new empire which encouraged trade, artisan industries and urban life. Literature, science, art and philosophy flourished here as nowhere else for several centuries, developing traditions established in ancient India, Egypt, Greece and Rome, and passing them on to subsequent civilisations.

The rise of the parasites

By 1000 AD the Islamic Empire was decaying at its heart. Mesopotamia had known the most fruitful agriculture anywhere in the world for some thousands of years, based upon a network of canals linking the Tigris and Euphrates rivers. The Islamic rulers had initially cleared and refurbished canals neglected by their predecessors. After three centuries, however, the Islamic ruling classes too had become bloated and parasitic, willing to ravage the countryside in order to provide for their own luxury consumption. The land around the old Islamic capital, Baghdad, became barren and desolate, and the Islamic world was torn apart by revolts and civil wars. Islamic culture, now centred in cities like Cairo, Cordoba in Spain, Bukhara in central Asia and Timbuktu in west Africa, remained in advance of any in Europe for some time, but had lost its old dynamism.

The revived Chinese civilisation was still very dynamic in 1000 AD. Under the Sung Empire, there was a growth of trade and industry such as humanity had never known and was not to know again until after the European Renaissance of the 16th century. Indeed, without the advance of Sung China, the Renaissance – and the rise of capitalism which it heralded – would have been impossible. But by 1200 AD Chinese civilisation too was beginning to be stifled by the sheer opulence of a parasitic ruling class. A Turkic people established a rival empire, the Chin, over northern China, leaving the Sung dynasty with the south alone until, in the 13th century, both were conquered by a former herding people, the Mongols.

The same centuries saw the Mongols tear into the vestiges of the Islamic Empire in Iran and Mesopotamia and ravage northern India and eastern Europe. The name of their leader, Genghis Khan, has become a byword for wanton savagery. Yet they too were the product of circumstances, not a cause. Living and herding on the edges of great civilisations, they could learn from them, especially when it came to military weaponry, and then use their learning to great effect against the bloated ruling classes of neighbouring states. Nor was the effect of the Mongol rampage from one end of Eurasia to the other wholly negative. It helped transmit knowledge of techniques developed in the civilisations of the East to the lands of the West.

The Mongols were not the only people whose past "backwardness" left them unencumbered by the parasitic baggage. A new chain of civilisations flourished in this period in Africa, stretching below the Sahara from the Nile westwards across the continent and putting the past advances of the Islamic civilisations to new uses. And in western Europe advances in agriculture learned from the East combined with a new way of organising exploitation, serfdom, to produce a couple of centuries of rapidly growing food output. This soon produced, in turn, traders, towns and urban classes capable of taking up the industrial as well as the agricultural practices of the older civilisations. By the 13th century cathedrals were being built where there had not even been stone houses 380 years before, and pioneering intellectuals were making the long trek to Toledo in Spain to get access to the writings of Islamic philosophers and mathematicians, along with Arabic translations of Greek and Latin classics.

Even then, however, Europe was still far short of leading the rest of the world. In the 16th century its technology was only at about the same level as that of the Mogul Indian Empire, of the Ottoman Empire that had arisen in Asia Minor to conquer the Middle East and most of eastern Europe, of the Islamic states along the Niger in Africa, and of the Ming Empire that ruled China. If it eventually overtook these to carve out world empires it was because its past backwardness made it easier for its merchant and artisan classes to transform the whole of society in their own image. They had the advantage over their Chinese, Arab and Indian equivalents of arriving late in the game of world history. Even so, it took more than 300 years of political, ideological and economic struggle before they could enjoy full success.

First published in *Socialist Review* 236, December 1999

Women's liberation

Revolutionary Marxists differ from all other people who stand for women's liberation in one important respect. We do not believe women's oppression is something that has always existed – either because of the biological differences between the sexes or because of something inherent in the male psyche.[1]

We hold that women's oppression arose at a particular point in history – at the point at which society began to divide in classes.[2]

In all class societies women are oppressed; the evidence suggests that in at least some pre-class societies there was no such oppression.

The reason why the oppression of women arises with the division of society into classes is simple enough. Class divisions began to occur once advances in the forces of production enabled human beings to produce a surplus over and above what was necessary for the bare subsistence of the whole of society. This surplus was not enough for everyone to live above the subsistence level, but it was great enough for *some* people to. And this then made possible the further development of the forces of production and with them the growth of civilisation, art and culture.

Hence the growth of the surplus was accompanied by an increasing split between an exploiting class and an exploited class.

The growth of the surplus was accompanied by a growing division of labour. It was those who occupied certain positions in this division of labour who developed into the controllers of the surplus – the first exploiting class.

At this point the biological differences between men and women took on an importance they had never had before. Weighed down with the burden of child bearing, women tended to be channelled towards certain productive roles and away from others – away from those which provided access to the surplus. So for instance when societies move from hoe cultivation, which can be done by women despite the burden of pregnancy, to the use of heavy ploughs or to cattle rearing, women tend to be displaced from key productive roles, and the surplus comes to be controlled by males.[3]

Where fully developed ruling classes developed, women members of that ruling class tended to play a subordinate role – to be treated virtually as the possessions of the male rulers. And very much the same situation prevailed in independent peasant and artisan households: one man (the patriarch) controlled the interaction of the household with the outside world, and his wife was as much his subordinate as were the children and servants (the exception proves the rule: where a widow took her dead husband's place she dominated all the other men and women in the household;[4] where situations arose in which the productive role played by women tended to produce a marketable surplus, the women tended to challenge some aspects of the stereotyped patriarchal household)[5].

So in pre-capitalist class societies women of all classes were under the domination of men. But they were not under the domination of all men. For certain *men* were oppressed also. The male slaves of antiquity and the male toilers of the patriarchal household had no more freedom than did the women (even if some of the males in the patriarchal household might hope one day to escape from servitude by taking the patriarch's place).

The oppression of women in every case arose out of the way the development of the forces of production necessitated certain relations of production. It was based in the material history of society.

Of course, once the relations of production led to the oppression of women, this found its expression ideologically. The inferiority of women and their subordination to men came to be regarded as part of the natural order of things, and was backed up by elaborate systems of beliefs, religious rituals, legal enactments, the mutilation of the female body and so on. But you cannot understand the origin of any of these things without understanding their origins in the development of the forces and relations of production.

Capitalism is the most revolutionary form of class society. It seizes hold of the institutions of previous class societies and reshapes them in its own image. It does not bow down to their hierarchies or their prejudices. Rather it creates new hierarchies in opposition to the old, and completely transforms old prejudices so as to use them in its drive to accumulate.

Hence it is with all the institutions it encountered at its birth – organised religions, monarchies, hereditary castes, land tenure systems, belief systems. Capitalism puts a straight alternative to all these: either be transformed in the interests of capital accumulation or be smashed.

It is exactly the same with the family. Capitalism does take hold of certain elements of the pre-capitalist family. But it does so in order to recast them completely and to adapt them to its needs.

Capitalism is not driven forward by a desire to maintain the family (and with it women's oppression) any more than it is driven forward by a desire to propagate religion, maintain monarchies, advance obscurantist beliefs, etc. It has only one driving force – the exploitation of workers in order to accumulate. The family, like religion, the monarchy, etc is only of use to capitalism in so far as it helps this goal.

Because of this, the capitalist family is not some fixed, unchanging entity. As Marx and Engels noted in the *Communist Manifesto*, the drive to accumulate means a continual recasting of the very institutions capitalism itself has created:

> The bourgeoisie cannot exist without constantly revolutionising the instruments of production, and thereby the relations of production, and with them the whole relations of society. Conservation of the old modes of production in unaltered form, was, on the contrary, the first condition of existence for all earlier industrial classes. Constant revolutionising of production, uninterrupted disturbance of all social conditions, everlasting uncertainty and agitation distinguish the bourgeois epoch from all earlier ones. All fixed, fast frozen relations, with their train of ancient and removable prejudices and opinions, are swept away, all new-formed ones become antiquated before they can ossify. All that is solid melts away into air, all that is holy is profaned...

The capitalist family

In its earliest phase industrial capitalism had a tendency not only to destroy the pre-capitalist patriarchal peasant and artisan household, but to destroy family ties completely among the new working class. It cared little that this conflicted with old belief systems. Thus Marx and Engels referred in the *Communist Manifesto* to "the practical absence of the family among the proletarians".

But the capitalist class as a whole soon found this was undermining the basis of further accumulation – the reproduction of the working class. There had to be some way of making sure workers were able to refresh themselves for further work and of bringing up the next generation of workers so they could meet the physical and mental requirements of paid labour.

Capitalism did not have the resources or technology to provide for socialised reproduction (through baby farms, nurseries, communal restaurants and so forth) and so the most far-sighted representatives of the capitalist class looked to creating a new family structure for the working class. This would both cater for the material needs of the existing generation of workers and take responsibility for the upbringing of the next generation.

Having destroyed the old patriarchal household, capitalism now took certain elements from it and recombined them into the new working class family and, of course, they used much of the ideology associated with the old patriarchal household (religious texts and rituals etc) in order to persuade both workers and individual capitalists to accept the new family. But it was not patriarchal ideology which motivated the capitalist class as a whole, but its material interest in ensuring supplies of labour power.

The new working class family was essentially the nuclear family of a man, a woman and their children. The man was expected to work full time and to earn a wage capable of providing a minimal living standard for the whole family. The woman was expected to take charge of refreshing the man's labour power as well as giving birth to children and bringing them up.

Of course, this ideal family was seldom realised in practice. Individual capitalists were rarely prepared to pay a "family wage" to their male workers. Working class wives were forced by economic pressures to get whatever jobs were available to them (seasonal work in the sweated trades, home work, etc) while bearing the burden of child rearing and housework. But there was a sense in which the ideal fitted in with the needs of long-term capital accumulation. These needs, rather than some patriarchal conspiracy between male employers and male workers, explains why it was the ideal.

The new working class family did have its ideological advantages for the system. Although the male worker differed from the old patriarch in that he did not control any surplus, he could imagine himself as the old patriarch: he controlled the funds which the whole family had to subsist on, and could imagine the wage was his to spend as he liked. He could believe he was master in his own home – although from the point of view of the system he was only master of the means to enable him and his children to be wage slaves.

The new family created a split in the working class, as it encouraged the male workers to identify with certain of the values of their exploiters.

At the same time, the isolation of women in the home could cut them off from wider social movements. Their oppression reduced their ability to struggle against the system much of the time, and so opened them up to conservative views of society. Institutions like the church exploited their situation in order to try to get them to oppose social change.

That was why Marx and Engels argued the precondition for the liberation of women was their incorporation into social production – albeit capitalist production under the conditions of the most extreme exploitation. Nevertheless it would be wrong to see either working class women or working class men as offering any massive resistance to the imposition of the new working class family.

There was some resistance by women to being displaced from relatively well paid jobs. But by and large the ideal of a family in which they would be maintained while bringing up their children was bound to appeal to women for whom the alternative was grim – dangerous abortions, repeated miscarriages, slaving 12 hours a day in a factory and then having to care for children, or self-enforced celibacy.[6]

The system created the ideal of the new working class family because it wanted the next generation of workers to be able to toil for it; but this at least implied some sort of concern for the health of the present generation of working class mothers. It was hardly surprising, then, that the resistance of working class women was not so much to the ideal as to the failure of reality to live up to the ideal.

Women were oppressed in the new family structure, in that they were forced into dependence on their husbands and cut off from the world outside. But the burden of suffering imposed by childbirth and child rearing was reduced.

For working class men too the new family was an advantage. They had to be responsible for the upkeep of the family, and often resented this. But in return they were provided with the bare physical inputs needed to keep fit and well.

For both working class men and working class women the family had one other advantage. It seemed to provide a haven from a world of loneliness and psychological alienation. As capitalism drew workers into the cities, it often tore them apart from old friends and relatives. The family seemed to provide a way of guaranteeing friendship and affection. Again, the failure of reality to measure up to the ideal did not stop people hankering after the ideal.

The new family was not, as some feminists claim, the result of a conspiracy between capitalist males and working class males. But it was a reform to the system's benefit which those workers, both male and female, who did not see the possibility of ending the system were likely to identify with. That was why the slogan of "defence of the family" was always one which reactionary forces could use in order to get support from workers – including women workers.

Women's oppression under capitalism

The way the nuclear family serves to reproduce the labour force is the material root of working class women's oppression under capitalism today. It is the burden of child rearing and housework which restricts working class women's contact with the world outside the home and makes them dependent on working class men.

That is why working class women's oppression cannot be ended short of the massive social change necessary to socialise housework and child rearing.

Of course, the oppression is not simply material. Material oppression is backed up by a whole barrage of ideological factors. So the oppression does not stop when women go out of the home, if they decide not to have children, or if their children have grown up. Material and ideological pressures combine, for instance, to persuade women to work for wages less than most men would accept.

When it comes to the ideology of oppression another factor also has to be taken into consideration. This ideology is not generated by the working class itself, but has to be imposed on it from above, by the representatives of the bourgeoisie. As Marx put it, "the ruling ideas are the ideas of the ruling class". How working class women and men see and relate to each other is determined not only by their own material conditions, but also by the ideology generated by the ruling class family.

Under capitalism there is an oppression of bourgeois women which parallels that of working class women, although it is quite different in its origin and content.

The classic bourgeois family was one in which women were relieved of much of the burden of child rearing (by the employment of numerous domestic servants), but were also denied any role in production. Their husbands had control of the surplus and they were regarded very much as commodities – as adornments to their husbands' homes, with marriage being virtually a form of trade between male-dominated families. Ruling class women were confined to their homes, but in idleness, not in toil as with working class women.

The ideology which corresponded to this state of affairs depicted women as having qualities quite different from those of "industrious", "confident", "aggressive" males – the passive, gentle, caring, emotional, frivolous, "feminine" female.

Such a view did not match at all the real position of working class women, toiling at home, in domestic service or in the factory. But it did provide the set of stereotyped images with which not only ruling class men and women, but also working class men and women, were expected to see each other. For, insofar as they take for granted existing society, workers are always under enormous pressure to accept their exploiters' definition of the world.

The working class man would fantasise about what he would do if only he could succeed in bourgeois society – and one of the things he could do would be to possess women as commodities. The working class woman would fantasise about "succeeding" if only she could cultivate the attributes of femininity allegedly possessed by upper class women (fantasies encouraged by magazine stories and soap operas featuring working class women who manage to marry above their class of origin).

All this served to idealise and sanctify the real situation of the working class family and so to perform a very real function for capitalism. It acted as a mechanism to hold the working class family together and to keep the system going. Religion, pornography, the soap opera, the women's magazine, the law, all acted together to make the family seem necessary and inevitable, the most stable of institutions in an ever changing world.

But under capitalism no institution can remain unchanged forever. Nothing is so sacred that it can avoid being revolutionised by the further advance of the forces of production.

Within a few decades of the establishment of the stereotyped working class family it began to be undermined by changes in the material condition of capitalist society.

In the mid 19th century, the reproduction of the labour force was only possible if the average working class wife had eight or ten pregnancies (in London nearly 60 percent of infants died by the age of five in 1850) and so spent virtually all her life after marriage either pregnant or nursing young children.

But the very expansion of the productive forces produced by capitalism had, as a by-product, the development of new technologies that radically reduced the effort that needed to be put into the reproduction of the labour force. Improvements in health care meant that fewer children died.

New methods of birth control became available that were vastly superior to the rough and ready methods available in capitalism's infancy – first the condom and the cap, then, in the early 1960s, the pill and the IUD. The birth rate could decline and working class women be relieved of some of the burden of child-birth. Yet the need of the system for labour power was not threatened.

At the same time, new technology began to be applied to the tasks of child rearing and of tending for the male workers. The washing machine, the vacuum cleaner, the refrigerator, the displacement of the coal stove by modern heating systems, all had the effect of reducing enormously the amount of sheer drudgery taking place in the home.

As many writers on housework have pointed out, this did not overcome the tedium and the alienation of the woman who continued to be stuck in the home, especially if she was responsible for small children. But it did mean she could begin to think in terms of getting employment outside the home, in a way which her mother or her grandmother could not. For, especially after the couple of children she had were five or six years old, she could earn enough by selling her labour power to pay for ways of reducing (although not eliminating) the tedium and the drudgery (paid baby minders, convenience foods, nappy services, service washes in the launderette, once a week expeditions to the supermarket instead of the daily round of the local shops, and so on).

From the point of view of capital accumulation, the old stereotyped family came to be very wasteful. Women were now expending more labour in the home than was strictly necessary to reproduce labour power for the system.

If the average number of children born to a family is eight or more, it is probably more economical for the system for virtually all the upbringing of the children to take place in the individual home. But once the number of children is down to two or so, things begin to be the other way round. An average nursery will have one adult looking after six children. So for every extra worker who has to be taken on to do paid childcare, two women more are freed for exploitation through the labour market. This is especially the case if the women have to pay for the childcare out of their own earnings: the system then gets surplus value out of them without having to worry itself about the cost of paying for socialised childcare!

From the point of view of ageing capitalism, a woman stuck in the home caring for only two children and her husband is a waste of potential surplus value. The fact that she labours all day is no consolation for the system; her labour is labour that could be done more efficiently, relieving her for wage slavery.

Hence there has been a longterm tendency for the number of women in paid labour to grow. In Britain today more than half of married women now work, as opposed to less than one in five in 1950; in the US the proportion of 20 to 25 year old married women who worked rose from 31 percent in 1957 to 43 percent in 1968. This rise has been taking place since the 1920s; the slump of the 1930s did not reverse it, nor has the slump of the last ten years.[7]

It is true that the vast influx of women into paid labour during the two world wars was followed by measures to replace them by men when the wars ended – but that experience could not stop a long-term rise in the proportion of married women working over more than half a century.

The capitalist state, charged with maintaining the underlying conditions needed for capital accumulation, has been forced in all countries to respond to this change. It has had increasingly to take measures itself designed to complement the family in the reproduction of labour power – the provision of welfare benefits, preschool education, and so on.[8]

The changes have been cumulative. The more working class women have entered the workforce, the more they have demanded the facilities to make this possible. As they have begun to gain independent sources of income they have begun to question the old assumptions of complete dependence on their husbands. They have begun to demand more effective contraception, safe abortions, to have fewer children, some shift of responsibility for household tasks onto the shoulders of their husbands. They have increasingly taken the initiative in bringing to an end unhappy marriages.

The system is experiencing today what Marx thought it would a hundred years ago – a tendency to undermine the family. However, this tendency can never come to fruition because of counter-factors:

i. The full socialisation of childcare would require a level of investment which the capitalist system is loath to make, even in periods of expansion.
ii. The ideology of the family continues to be very important for the stability of the system. Women's belief that looking after their children should be their primary concern leads them to work for less than men. Organisations like the church which exploit the isolation of women, using the slogan of the defence of the family, still can provide some valuable ideological ballast for the system. So you find that governments pass anti-abortion laws and are slow to liberalise divorce laws, even though such questions are not in themselves important to the economic needs of the system.
iii. Finally, the new period of economic crisis since the mid-1970s has reduced the pressures to increase the supply of labour power by getting more women into the workforce and has increased the dependence of the system on backward-looking forces which use the slogan of "defence of the family". This has not stopped some continued expansion of the number of women looking for work, but it has dissuaded the system from making the investment needed to help them in this.

The development of the forces of production has put pressure on the old social relations embodied in the working class family. But it has not been enough to smash them.

There can be no end to women's oppression under capitalism

There can be no end to women's oppression without an end to privatised reproduction. But that, in turn, is not possible without a complete revolutionising of social relations. This is only possible in two circumstances:

i. If capitalism were able to enter into a new period of virtually uninterrupted expansion of the productive forces. The system could then, undoubtedly, replace privatised reproduction with socialised, mechanised housework, and even the building of Brave New World type baby farms etc. But merely to pose the alternative like this is to see how impossible it is in practice. The system cannot enter such a new period of expansion. The

stagnation of ageing capitalism cuts off any road to women's liberation by reform of the system.
ii. If socialist revolution occurs. Some of the massive resources wasted under capitalism could then be devoted to providing the real material base for socialisation of childcare and housework. And an insurgent working class would see this as a first priority, since it would seem a great boon not merely to working class women, but to working class men as well. Of course, after such a revolution, the ideological heritage of capitalism would persist, and that heritage would include sexist attitudes. But it would be relatively easy to fight back against that heritage once its material base had been destroyed.

A comparison is possible between the social structures which produce women's oppression under capitalism and certain other oppressive structures which have been thrown up in the course of capitalist development, like the Jim Crow structures in the Southern US and Orangeism in Northern Ireland.

These structures discriminated against a certain section of the population on the basis of race or religion. They came to be seen as archaic by many supporters of the system during its long period of economic expansion in the 1950s and 1960s. Capital accumulation seemed to depend upon access to labour power, regardless of its race or religion. There was a general spread of ideologies which reiterated the old liberal doctrine that everyone should have equal access to the market. Movements grew up which pressed for bourgeois civil rights. The system seemed able to cope with these, even though they roused some of the most oppressed sections of the population to political action. But then, with the first signs of economic crisis in the late 1960s, it had to retreat from granting more than token equality to the oppressed sections.

The early women's liberation movement was very much an offshoot of this general agitation for the formal equality the system promises to all those who live under it. Its demands were pushed initially by middle class women who wanted freedom to lead the same sorts of lives as middle class men. But they fitted in with the changed attitudes of many working class women, who for the first time felt themselves to be lifetime members of capitalism's paid labour force. At this stage the demands seemed reconcilable with the system's need to reshape the family so as get access to women's labour.

However, the impediments to real equality for working class women were even greater than those facing American blacks or Ulster Catholics. The system could not face the full cost of socialisation of reproduction even in the 1960s, let alone in the crisis years after the mid 1970s. Limited changes to allow women to become wage slaves were possible (and necessary); an end to their oppression was ruled out by continued dependence on the nuclear family for privatised reproduction.

Capitalism and the crisis of the women's movement

The harsh reality that women's oppression cannot be ended under conditions of capitalist crisis has faced the women's movement with three alternatives:

i. To abandon the goal of liberation in favour of pursuing the very limited reforms that are possible within the present system. Effectively this amounts to demanding individual advancement for a few privileged women, while leaving the conditions of the mass of women completely untouched. This was the path chosen by the bourgeois women involved in the movement and by a very large section of middle class feminists.
ii. To try to cut itself off from existing society by creating separatist counter-institutions.
iii. To identify with working class challenges to existing society as the way of smashing the structures responsible for women's oppression.

Which of the options gained hegemony within the women's movement depended on concrete circumstances. Where there was an upturn in workers' struggles in the late 1960s and early 1970s (France, Italy, Spain, Britain, etc) there was a tendency for almost all sections of the women's movement to orient at least in part to the working class. Its demands tended to be those which had some immediate appeal to the mass of working class women (equal pay, 24-hour nurseries, abortion rights, etc). But where the working class movement was weak (the US) or where it went into decline (most other places) the women's movement came to be hegemonised by feminism on the one hand and separatism on the other.

In practice, reformism and separatism reinforced one another. The bourgeois feminist prejudice against the working class helped create a "common sense" within the movement which treated any talk of women's liberation through working class revolution as "crude workerism" and "old fashioned Leninism". And the separatist objection to collaboration with men meant, in practice, keeping well clear of rank and file workers' struggles – and this in turn meant rejecting involvement in the only struggles that could gain more than the most marginal things from the system.

The division of labour between separatism and reformism found its ultimate expression in calls for an alliance between bourgeois or reformist politicians, the trade union bureaucracy, "women" and "blacks" (the "broad democratic alliance" of Eurocommunism, the "rainbow coalition" in the US, the electoralist strategy of people like Benn and Livingstone in Britain).

The tendency towards reformism is not an accident. Under capitalism there is only one force capable of imposing real change – the working class. If you don't base yourself on working class struggle, then you are inevitably driven to compromise with the system. But those who preach separatism are rejecting the notion of effective working class struggle. Even if they try to relate to women workers, they are basing themselves on the belief that one section of the working class can win without the assistance of other (male) sections of the class. They are avoiding the total mobilisation of forces that alone can guarantee victories.

Like the civil rights movements in the US and Northern Ireland, the women's movement of the late 1960s and early 1970s began to mobilise people against oppresssion created by the system. To that extent it encouraged the beginnings of a struggle against the system. But, again like those movements, it could not carry that struggle forward beyond a certain point. From then on the choice was between a radically different sort of movement, or merely improving the lot of a few fortunate individuals while the mass of people remained as oppressed as ever.[9]

That is why, for us, there can be no talk of re-creating the sort of women's movement that existed then. It belongs to a period that is past.

Of course it is possible that the crisis of the system will lead to attacks on women's rights which will, in turn, produce upsurges of protest from women. We have seen such upsurges in Britain every time attempts have been made in recent years to restrict abortion rights. Such struggles have to be supported wholeheartedly, but it also has to be seen that those involved in them will rapidly polarise between supporters of reformism and separatism on the one hand and those who are won to a revolutionary working class perspective on the other.

Wrong theories of women's oppression

The women's movement of the 1960s and 1970s threw up its own theories of women's oppression. It is necessary to look at what was wrong with these, because this enables us to see more clearly what the revolutionary Marxist view is.

The dominant view in what remains of the women's movement in Britain is the theory of patriarchy.

This holds that the oppression of women is a result of male domination and is quite separate from the division of society into economic classes. It sees "men" as benefiting from the oppression of women in all societies[10] and maintaining that oppression even if socialist revolution takes place. It accuses attempts to explain women's oppression on the basis of the dynamic of class societies as "reductionist". From this it draws the conclusion that the struggle for women's liberation is something quite separate from (even if parallel to) the struggle for working class revolution and socialism.

The theory is "hegemonic" in that few feminists challenge it, and it has been adopted wholesale by sections of the reformist left outside the women's movement. Indeed, although a few figures in the women's movement (for instance, Sheila Rowbotham) used to oppose the use of the term "patriarchy"[11], today the concept is usually treated as unquestionable.

It has great appeal because, as Lindsey German has noted, "The joy of patriarchy theory is that it can be all things to all people. It thrives on the vague feelings so beloved by sections of the women's movement, rather than on material analysis".[12]

Yet its theoretical basis is very flimsy indeed. For, if women have always been oppressed by men, the question must arise as to why? How is it that the male sex has been able to subordinate the female sex in this way?

Unless patriarchy theorists can answer these questions, they cannot explain the oppression of women. Therefore they cannot say how it is to be overcome. They end up, not with a theory of women's liberation, but with a view that rules out any real liberation!

One attempt at an explanation lies in ascribing women's oppression to ideological factors. Now, certainly the fact that the prevailing ideology regards women as subordinate reinforces their subordination: men grow up to see themselves as the superior sex and many women grow up to accept this. But where does the ideology of women's subordination itself come from?

Adherents of the theory cannot explain this and usually end up abandoning any materialist explanation of anything – saying, for instance, that historical materialism is wrong, that ideologies exist in their own right as "different modes of discourse".

Other patriarchy theorists do attempt to explain women's oppression materialistically. But they resort to a materialism which abstracts from class society. All that then remains as the basis of women's oppression is the biological difference between them and men. It is this, it seems, that enables men to conspire successfully to subjugate women. According to one such theorist, Heidi Hartmann, men "control women's labour and restrict their sexuality".

Hartmann goes as far as to try to recruit Engels for her position.[13] She quotes a famous passage in the *Origins of the Family* where Engels writes:

> The determining factor in history is...the production and reproduction of immediate life...On the one side the production of the means of existence, of food, clothing and shelter and the tools necessary for that production; on the other side the production of human beings themselves, the propagation of the species. The social organisation under which people of a particular historical epoch live is determined by both kinds of production.

She sees the two "modes" of production as being of equal importance, and argues there is no necessary connection between changes in one "mode" and changes in the other.

Engels clearly thought otherwise. For he himself went on to say that as class society develops, it is less and less the case that the two modes of production coexist. A society arises in which "family relations are entirely subordinated to property relations."

In fact, it is absolutely confusing to talk of "two modes". The mode of production in any society is a coupling together of forces of production and relations of production. The first half of the couple is continually exercising pressure for change on the second half. Every increase in the ability of human beings to control nature produces new interrelations between the human beings themselves, and therefore begins to transform the pre-existing relations of production. Either society changes, or the new ways of controlling nature have to be abandoned. There is always a tension, a dynamic in the mode of production which determines the shape of human history.

There is no such tension inbuilt into the "mode of reproduction". Human beings are not continually finding new ways of reproducing themselves (cloning in one epoch, laying eggs in another, live birth in a third); these new ways of reproducing are not continually coming up against the barrier of the existing relations between people.

The way people reproduce themselves is relatively static.[14] If it is seen as shaping human history, then there can be no change to it, no development. If the "forces of reproduction" determine the "relations of reproduction" then women's oppression is indeed something which must always have existed – and which will always exist.

But "relations of reproduction" – i.e. family structures – do indeed change. They change, like the rest of human relations, as a result of what takes place in the sphere of material production.

As we have pointed out earlier, when in pre-capitalist societies the most important areas of material production can be carried out by women who are burdened by pregnancy and child rearing, then you find societies in which women have high prestige and equality or even superiority to men.

The relations of reproduction – the family – result from the material conditions of production, not from some "mode of reproduction".

Once you grasp this, you can see how capitalism prepares the ground for the abolition of women's oppression. It brings about such an immense development of productive forces that, on the one hand, production can be carried out by anyone, however much crude "biological realities" might be an impediment to them; on the other hand it creates, for the first time, the technology to transform human biology (control fertility etc). But capitalism itself prevents the full realisation of these potentialities.

Patriarchy theory refuses to recognise this. Indeed, it presents us with a picture of present-day society as shaped by two quite different things. One is the drive to accumulate capital through exploitation. The other is a conspiracy by men of all classes to hold down women of all classes.

The logic of patriarchy theory is that while the class struggle may be seen playing a certain role, it has nothing to do with women's oppression. This depends on a second struggle, that of all women against all men. So if you really want to end women's oppression, in practice you turn your back on the class struggle.

The theory fits in neatly with the needs of both the separatist and the reformist strands within the women's movement. The separatist trend can see themselves as the consistent appliers of the theory. They are the people who take seriously the view of history as a power struggle between the sexes. Whether it is a question of blaming all men for sex crimes, of opposing "male institutions" like the trade unions, of trying to form areas of liberated female sexuality, or of counterposing "female values" to the macho aggression that is said to cause nuclear wars, they are able to take the offensive against feminists who see collaboration with some men as being important.

But the reformist trend can also use the theory as well. For if there are two distinct terrains of battle, then you can fight on one terrain while compromising on the other. Hence the way that in Britain talk of "fighting patriarchal values" has been used to justify collaboration between union leaders and a future Labour government to hold down wages with a "feminist incomes policy". Hence the way in which women in the trade union bureaucracy can accept the idea of union officials being appointed from above, getting several times the average wage, not being subject to recall, etc – providing there is an "adequate career structure for women" within the bureaucracy.

Halfway theories

Some socialist feminists have seen the dangers and inconsistencies of the patriarchy theory approach, and have tried to argue against it. But they have often ended up half conceding to its arguments.

Thus Sheila Rowbotham rejects patriarchy theory. But she explains the persistence of the family with a version of the "two modes of production" argument. In *Women's Consciousness, Men's World*, she argues the family is a pre-capitalist mode of production existing inside the wider capitalist system.[15] But the logic of this position is the same as that of patriarchy theory – that there are two distinct struggles, which are not necessarily linked up in the here and now.

Even revolutionary socialists who have sought to oppose many of the arguments of the middle class women's movement have made the mistake of accepting many of its theoretical formulations.

A good example of this is to be found in an argument which took place some years ago in the pages of this journal between Joan Smith and Irene Bruegel.

Joan started off the discussion[16] with some very telling and important criticisms of the lifestyle politics which was then becoming prevalent in the women's movement. As against those politics, she insisted women's oppression persists because of the economic importance of the family for capitalism. But she then went on to base her own position on the two modes of production theory elaborated by Sheila Rowbotham, Shulamith Firestone and Heidi Hartmann, complete with the same (truncated) quote from Engels. The result is an argument that is absolutely confused, and confusing.

Joan's view was that the existing family was as much a defining feature of capitalism as the exploitation of workers at the point of production. It was "part of the base" – not part of the superstructure. She justified this by saying that capitalism depends on 'free labour' and that you could not have free labour unless labour was reproduced in privatised households.

The argument was tortuous in the extreme. What Marx meant by "free labour" was labour where (1) the worker did not have any control over the means of production, and (2) the worker did not belong to the individual capitalist and so could be discarded the moment his or her labour was no longer needed. It is quite easy to imagine a society in which such labour was reproduced in state-run institutions and then sent out into the wider world to sell itself or starve.

Such a society does not exist at present, as we have explained earlier, because it does not suit the economic needs of capital accumulation – because the economic "base" does not yet need such a transformation of the institutional superstructure. As Kath Ennis pointed out in *International Socialism* ten years ago, "In theory capitalism could do without the family... But in practice, this would require such fundamental changes in society it is hard to imagine them ever being carried out."

Irene Bruegel took up and elaborated Kath Ennis's point in her reply to Joan.[17] She showed how capitalism had an economic interest in socialising certain aspects of housework, so enabling women to be exploited through the labour market. Her economic argument was irrefutable. It undercut any claim that the family is essential to capitalism in the same way as exploitation and accumulation.

Once that is accepted the logical thing is to see the family as part of the superstructure – something created by the needs of accumulation at a certain point in capitalist development, which capitalism now begins to undermine, but which it is prevented from abolishing because of its own crisis-prone nature.

Irene herself rushes off in the direction of the analysis of women's oppression provided by Anne Foreman. This does not start from the economics of capitalist production at all, but from the psychological needs of working class men. The family exists, for Anne Foreman, because "men find relief from alienation through their relation with women; for women there is no relief".

Irene accepts this view in its entirety. Both of them inevitably end up moving away from the revolutionary socialist struggle against the system to the lifestyle politics of certain middle class feminists. Joan is quite rightly completely scathing about about such a conclusion. She insists:

> If we follow an Anne Foreman type analysis, then, it is the "gender attributes of femininity", the polarity masculine/feminine, that is oppressive of women, rather than these being the ideological manifestations of women's oppression. This is essentially an idealist analysis in which the ideological forms which oppress women are generated within the relationships women have with the men they live with.[18]

But Joan herself is no more capable than Irene of drawing the logical conclusion from the collapse of the view that the family is something which is at all times an economic necessity for capitalism. She drops the two modes of production theory in practice (using phrases like "the family system of reproducing labour power"). But she cannot drop the view that the family – and women's oppression – is as important for capitalism as exploitation and accumulation. So she clings ever more tenuously to the view that only the family can produce "free labour". She even goes so far as to argue this is true for all class societies. "The essential element of the family remains unchanged in all class societies, because the family is the only way of reproducing society which allows for essential differences in reproduction from class to class and which takes the burden of reproduction from society in general and places it upon individuals or groups in society."[19]

So Joan, who had previously been so critical of "patriarchal" talk of the family as invariant, is led to put forward a view very close to that of patriarchy theory. Indeed, she begins to use the phraseology of patriarchy theory herself when she claims, "The essential history of patriarchy and women's oppression is the history of the family system of reproduction..."

Joan takes another step beyond her initial starting point at the same time. This is to locate women's oppression in the state. Again using the terminology of middle class feminist analysis, she writes,

"The patriarchal control of women shifts from the patriarchal household to the patriarchal capitalist state with its infinite battery of laws to control women and to the capitalist market where women are always paid less than men..."

She even goes so far as to talk of "the male state"!

Some of the reasons she has for wanting to stress the role of the state are good ones. She is still trying to attack ideas that locate women's oppression in the relationships between individual men and women. Nevertheless, the formulation is both mystical and misleading. It is not the state which supplies the system with its dynamic, it is the drive to accumulate. The state is merely one of the mechanisms used by the system in this drive – it is part of the superstructure. The family is another such mechanism: it too is part of the superstructure.

It is simply not true that all the oppression of women comes from the state, or that the state simply oppresses women though keeping intact the existing family. The oppression of women comes, ultimately, from the drive to accumulate. The state helps sustain this drive, and so has to prop up the family. But it also steps in to replace certain family functions as the system's needs change – supplying (although not on nearly a big enough scale) nurseries and schools, welfare benefits, providing free contraceptives, legislating for equal pay (although leaving immense loopholes in the legislation), etc.

It is the system that oppresses women, not just the state. And the oppression often takes place in contradictory ways.

These points are important. For Joan is confused. And her confusion has served to direct people away from the revolutionary Marxist analysis of women's oppression towards that put forward by those who reject Marxism. She writes of her work:

> My articles in *International Socialism 100* and *International Socialism 104* [first series] attempted to bridge the argument over the nature of patriarchy with the concern of the domestic labour school over the relationship of women's oppression to capitalism. It was an attempt to argue the relationship between male domination (the patriarchy) with the capitalist mode of production.

Patriarchy, as we have seen, is the theoretical expression of the reformist and separatist wings of the women's movement. What Joan is attempting to do is to "bridge the argument" between them and Marxism. It was an attempt which was bound to lead to complete confusion.

There is practical confusion as well. Underlying all the stages of

Joan's argument is an attempt to prove that women's oppression, like workers' exploitation, leads to the beginnings of spontaneous rejection of capitalism.

This happens, she argues, because the capitalist system rests on two equally important planks – workers' exploitation and women's oppression. She argues it again when she shifts to putting the blame for all of women's oppression directly on the state.

In both cases, separate women's struggles are seen as automatically coming into conflict with capital and the state. The struggle against patriarchy then becomes, for Joan, an automatic ally of a separate workers' struggle against capitalism. The basis is laid for an alliance of "distinct but not separate" struggles.

The women's part of the alliance is made up, for Joan, of all women, although led by revolutionaries. As she puts it:

> We can argue and recruit women to revolutionary politics on the basis of their oppression as well as their exploitation. Many women have broken with middle class backgrounds, as with working class backgrounds, and as with students it is possible to organise these women around the revolutionary party. But to do this we need an organisation of women wider than the revolutionary party to take up the issues of women's oppression and women's exploitation… It is necessary to build a women's movement with its own paper which can unite all women – public sector women, factory workers, women at home. Because capitalism oppresses all women, the material base for such an organisation exists.[20]

Note Joan refers to "all women" as being the base of such a movement, not working class women. For in each of the three stages of her analysis, it is all women who are forced, by what she calls "patriarchy" or the "male state" to fight back. It is this which enables her to talk about organising 'all women' without reference to their class position (they give up their working class backgrounds as well as their middle class backgrounds!). Yet this movement will somehow be committed to a "socialist platform" and a "working class struggle for freedom".

Joan epitomises the muddle you get into when you marry together two contradictory views of the roots of women's oppression – that of middle class feminism and that of revolutionary Marxism. You end up shifting from one position to another, never ending up on the solid ground from which alone it is really possible to fight for women's liberation.

Arguments against the revolutionary Marxist position

A number of arguments are used both by outright opponents of the Marxist theory of women's oppression and by those who want to muddle it up with some other theory. Let's look at these one at a time.

> *"The Marxist view effectively denies the reality of women's oppression by reducing everything to a matter of class."*

If you read our first section you can see this contention simply is not true. We don't "reduce" the issue to one of class. Women of all classes are oppressed, just as ethnic minorities of all classes are oppressed in certain societies. What we do say, however, is that you cannot get rid of this oppression without challenging its roots in class society. There are not two struggles, one against class society, the other against "patriarchy". There is one struggle against the cause of all forms of exploitation and oppression.

And there are huge differences in the sorts of oppression women from different classes face. The wife of a slave owner may be oppressed, but her oppression is quite different to that of a slave (even of a male slave). The ruling class woman may protest at her oppression, but the overwhelming majority of them will side with the system that maintains that oppression against any serious revolutionary challenge to it. And so, when the chips are down, they will aid and abet not only exploitation, but oppression of other women. Ruling class women always insist that the women's movement is something separate from, and opposed to, the working class movement.

Working class women, on the other hand, need to view the whole question of separation differently.

The prejudices of male workers have often meant women workers have had little choice, if they are to organise at all, but to organise separately to men. But they have always had to fight against this enforced separation, because it has weakened the struggle of the working class as a whole, so making it easier for the ruling class to maintain their oppression.

Historically, it has been the economically more powerful and less oppressed groups of workers who have stood for separate, sectionalist forms of organisation. Women and ethnically oppressed groups of workers have organised separately (with women's trade unions etc) merely as a means of getting the strength to batter down the walls of sectionalism.

> "The Marxist view means that the inferior position women are forced to accept at present is perpetuated, with men leading women. It is not women's self-activity which is seen as ending their oppression, but something men do for them."

Oppressed people find the confidence to stand up and fight their oppression through struggle. But this does not mean that the only struggle which gives them this confidence is the struggle of the particular oppressed group to which they belong. Struggles against all sorts of aspects of class society can have the same effect.

It has, for example, been the experience of trade union struggles that has given many women the confidence to begin to challenge the traditional roles they have been expected to perform in the family.

Of course, the divisions between different sectons of the working class – male/female, black/white, skilled/unskilled, oppressed/less oppressed – mean that simple, homogeneous, unified struggles of all workers together often do not occur. So there are struggles which involve mostly male workers or mostly female workers, mostly white workers or mostly black workers, mostly skilled workers or mostly unskilled workers. However, the struggle of any one group of workers always has implications for the struggles of other groups of workers. No oppressed group can separate off its struggles off from the rest of the class.

It is disastrous for it to try to do so.

If a relatively powerful group of workers, like say the miners in Britain or the auto workers in the US, are successful in struggle, this is a stimulus to the struggles of all other groups of workers – even if the most powerful groups of workers are mostly male and the weaker groups mainly female. At other points it may be the resistance of a previously weak group of workers who are mainly female that stems an employers' offensive and so inspires other, stronger groups of mainly male workers to struggle.

In fact, the greatest struggles against women's oppression have always taken place during periods of wider, more generalised struggle – during the great French Revolution of 1789-94, in the period immediately before and after the First World War, in the late 1960s and early 1970s. The successes of these struggles have always depended on the successes of the wider struggles. Defeat for these wider struggles spelt defeat for the struggle for women's liberation as well – whether with Thermidor in the 1790s, Stalinism and Nazism in the inter-war years, or the drift to the right in the late 1970s.[21]

It could not be otherwise. Oppression is a product of class society. And the only effective way to challenge class society is through the united struggle of the working class, not through the separate, isolated struggle of this or that particular oppressed group.

This does not at all mean that "women follow men". The particular group of workers who are in the forefront of the struggle will sometimes be mainly female, sometimes mainly male and sometimes completely mixed.

What is necessary in either case is that the leading group of workers understand that their own struggle is a struggle on behalf of all workers, despite all the efforts of the ruling class to make them believe otherwise, and that there is an argument with all other groups of workers to back the struggle. This will not happen unless there is a relentless battle by socialists against the tendency of less oppressed workers to identify with the advantages they enjoy over more oppressed workers – and explain to the more oppressed workers that their real enemies are not the less oppressed, but the ruling class that exploits all workers. Thus it has to be explained to groups of male workers who are in struggle that they need the backing of female workers, but that they will not get this if they continue to hold the sexist view that women are sex objects whose real place is in the home, etc. It has to be pointed out that women who are forced to be passive and dependent on men cannot be real fighters in the struggle of their class against the system.

Oppression enables the ruling class to divide and rule the whole working class – the least oppressed as well as the most oppressed sections. Involvement in any struggle leads people to begin to challenge this oppression – and only by a challenge to this oppression can the struggle enjoy long-term success.

To put it another way: to take seriously the claim that women can only follow the lead of other women is to say they have no part to play in many major battles in the class struggle. In fact, of course, some of the most important examples of working class women's struggles have been those in support of male workers – for example, the Women's Emergency Brigade in the Flint sit-down of 1937.

It is because they understood this that none of the greatest women revolutionary socialists saw their job as just organising women. Whether you talk of Eleanor Marx, Rosa Luxemburg, Mother Jones or Elizabeth Gurley Flynn you are talking about fighters who dedicated their energies to intervening in whatever struggles were currently being waged, whether of male or female workers.[22]

Even those revolutionaries like Clara Zetkin or Alexandra Kollontai who concentrated on organising women never saw this as their only activity. Alexandra Kollontai was active in the general work of both the Bolshevik and Menshevik parties, while Clara Zetkin played a key role in all the debates of the German Communist Party between 1919 and 1923. Even Sylvia Pankhurst, who only came to a full revolutionary socialist position in the course of The First World War, drew the conclusion from this that the need was not for a women's paper, the *Women's Dreadnought*, and a women's organisation, the East London Federation of Suffragettes, but for a workers' paper, the *Workers Dreadnought*, and a mixed organisation, the Workers' Socialist Federation. This of course has not stopped some confused feminists claiming Kollontai, Zetkin and Sylvia Pankhurst for the cause of separatism!

They all adopted this position because they all understood there is not and cannot be any separate road to women's liberation, under whatever name it goes (socialist feminism, revolutionary feminism or whatnot) other than that of revolutionary Marxism. They understood there are not two traditions – one of fighting oppression, the other of fighting for workers' power – that had to be welded together, but a single tradition which tries to build a revolutionary working class movement as "the tribune of all the oppressed and exploited."

In such a united movement, the highest aspiration would be for revolutionary women to lead men and for revolutionary men to lead women, depending on the particular section of the class which was in struggle at any point in time.

> "*Working class men are involved in maintaining the oppression of women and benefit from it. So they can't be involved in the struggle to end it.*"

We have argued earlier that the real cause of women's oppression is not individual men but the needs of capital accumulation. However, it is true that those needs are only fulfilled insofar as they find an agency for enforcing them – people who will oppress others. Many men are certainly involved in the oppression of women. People like Anna Paczuska and Lin James seem to be making a valid comment when they insist:

> It isn't capitalism that beats wives, rapes women, hires prostitutes and degrades women in pornography – it's men.[23]

But they are only right up to a point. Firstly, not all men are involved in the activities they list – unless you accept the radical separatist claim that "all men are rapists". Secondly, their list of what constitutes the oppression of women is hopelessly inadequate. If you add other elements of the oppression of women – for instance, the denial of the right of abortion, unequal pay, etc – then you find it is not the men working class women live with who enforce these, but the state or the employer. And when it comes to the socialising of girls to accept subordinate "feminine" roles, the main agency, as often as not, is not the father but the mother. Some of the biggest campaigns against abortion rights have been led by women. Even in genuinely patriarchal societies, the oppression of younger women is enforced not only by the patriarch himself, but also by the older women!

When working class women begin to challenge their oppression they find themselves not only up against many men, but also many women. This is because capitalism, in its drive for accumulation, has found many agencies for controlling women, whether through coercion or ideological persuasion – not just the wife beater and the rapist.

But it will be argued, men benefit from the oppression of women in a way that other women don't.

In fact, however, the benefits working class men get from the oppression of women are marginal indeed. They do not benefit from the low pay women get – this only serves to exert a downward pressure on their own pay. Nor can it really be argued they gain from the treatment of women's bodies as commodities – the only men who can benefit in this way are the men with the wealth to buy and sell commodities!

The benefits really come down to the question of housework. The question becomes the extent to which working class men benefit from women's unpaid labour.

But in the stereotyped capitalist family this is impossible to measure. As Lindsey German has put it:

> The division of labour is, after all, a division of labour where men do different work both in the factory and in the home. But to say that welding is better or worse than housework is to look at things in completely subjective and unmeasurable terms. The same is true of leisure. Men have more rigidly defined leisure, which tends to be social (the pub, football), just as they have more rigidly defined working hours. But it cannot simply be said to be more. It is different.

Housework, by definition, is work which is not subject to the tempo imposed by capitalist exploitation in the factory or office. It does not involve intensive effort for a certain number of hours, followed by a period of recuperation in order to allow the application of another fixed spell of intensive effort. Therefore there is no way the amount of labour that goes into it can be measured against the amount of labour that goes into factory work...

The great disadvantage that (working class) housewives suffer, is not that they are somehow exploited by men, but that they are atomised and cut off from participation in the collective action that can give the confidence to fight back against the system...

In fact, the problem of "benefits" only really arises when there is a departure from the old stereotyped division of labour between the "male worker" and the female "housewife". As married women are increasingly drawn into the labour force, many women find themselves doing full-time paid labour, yet are still expected to run the home. They are left with much less time to recoup their labour power than their husbands as they have to combine work and housework. Yet even in these situations, it is doubtful if the husbands benefit more than marginally.[24]

What the working class male gains directly in terms of labour from his wife can be roughly measured. It is the amount of labour he would have to exert if he had to clean and cook for himself. This could not be more than an hour or two a day – a burden for a woman who has to do this work for two people after a day's paid labour, but not a huge gain for the male worker.

It is only when the question of the reproduction of the next generation of workers – the raising of children – arises, that the burden to women becomes unbearable, and the apparent gain to the husband immense.

But the labour devoted to bringing up children cannot be treated as something given by the wife to the husband. It is rather, something which the wife provides to the system, satisfying its need to renew the labour force. As Ann Rogers has put it, "the working class woman is tied to servicing children, not to servicing men."[25]

The main point, however, is that the key to the real liberation of working class women lies in the socialising of both components of housework. And this socialisation is no loss to the working class man. He does not lose out if good, collectively operated canteens begin to provide him with excellent meals. He does not suffer if a 24-hour nursery system takes away from his wife the sustained burden of worrying about the children.

Indeed, insofar as these changes free both women and men from having to live in constrained, often bitter relationships, they are a gain for men as well as women.

Certainly, when things are looked at in this light, it cannot be said that the working class man has any material stake in the oppression of women. Whatever advantages he might have within the present set-up compared with his wife, they are nothing to what he would gain if the set-up was revolutionised.

What about the other sort of gain he might be said to have, the "ideological stake" – the feeling that somehow he has control over the family, so that however insignificant he might be in the world at large, he is master in the home?

This will be a very big factor at times when workers are not challenging the system. Then their minds are full up with all the ideological crap at hand. But once they begin to fight back against the system, then they can begin to see there is an alternative – an alternative in which they exercise control over the whole of their lives, and so don't need the phoney feeling of control that comes from dominance inside the family.

The theorists of patriarchy and the socialist feminists who tail behind them do not see this, because they do not really have any notion of how ideas can be transformed in struggle. They generalise from points of downturn in the struggle, drawing the conclusion that the ideas which prevail now will always prevail. Just as some people draw the conclusion from the present period that the working class is finished, so patriarchy and socialist feminist theorists draw the conclusion that workers can never challenge privatised reproduction and the oppression of women.

> *"Experience shows that you can have a workers' revolution which leaves the oppression of women intact."*

This is a central component of all patriarchy theories. It follows from the view that countries like Russia, Cuba, Vietnam and China are somehow socialist. In these societies the oppression of women continues to exist, and so, it is said, socialism can coexist with women's oppression.

Socialist feminists like Sheila Rowbotham cannot argue against this position. For they too believe socialist societies already exist (one of the reasons Sheila left the International Socialists 13 years ago was because we deigned to argue that North Vietnam was not socialist!)

However, those of us who recognise that the rise of Stalinism established state capitalism in Russia do not need to draw this conclusion at all.

In fact, the experience of the Russian Revolution of 1917 proves the opposite of what both the patriarchy theorists and the socialist feminists argue.

The revolution took place in the most difficult of circumstances. It occurred in a country in which the working class was a small minority of the population, where most people were still peasants, organised on a genuinely patriarchal basis, living almost medieval lives and subject to the deepest superstitions and prejudices. Although there were substantial numbers of women in certain industries and factories, who played an important part in the February Revolution, male workers were in the great majority among conscious revolutionaries – only about 10 percent of the Bolsheviks were women.

Yet the revolution carried through a programme of women's liberation never attempted anywhere else – complete liberation of abortion and divorce laws, equal pay, mass provision of communal childcare, socialised canteen facilities and so on.

In fighting to emancipate their class, women workers did begin to challenge the traditions of subordination to men – and the most militant male workers did see the need to support and encourage this challenge.

This was because the revolution *was* a revolution – a massive upheaval in which those at the bottom of society rose up and fought to control their own destinies. They could not do so unless they shook apart every hierarchy and challenged every element of oppression that divided their class and held it down. Of course, there was again and again resistance from many, many male workers to their traditionally dominant role in the family. But what was most impressive was the way in which the advanced workers, organised in the Bolshevik Party, understood the need to break with such divisive, prejudiced behaviour, and how they were able to win the majority of the class to their standpoint.

Hence it was that after the conquest of state power, the party set up a special department aimed at involving more working class women in the revolutionary process. Inessa Armand was put in charge of this work, and after her death Alexandra Kollontai. But male revolutionaries were also expected to take part in its work, attending its conferences etc.

The experience of the Russian Revolution was quite different, then, to what later happened after the rise of Stalinism – with the reimposition of the stereotyped family, anti-abortion laws, restrictions on divorce, and so on. It was also quite different to what happened when state capitalism was established elsewhere, either by the Russian army or by revolutions carried through by guerrilla armies.

Russia showed what happens with working class revolution. These other cases show what happens without it!

The party, the class and women's liberation

Revolutionary socialists start from what we can learn from the high points in the history of the working class struggle – that the less oppressed sections of workers can join with the more oppressed sections in a joint struggle against all forms of exploitation and oppression. White workers can be won to support for the struggles of black workers, male workers can be won to support for the struggles of female workers, skilled workers can be won to support for the struggles of unskilled workers.

Our central contention – that the working class can emancipate itself and in the process emancipate all of society – flows from what happens in periods of upturn in the struggle, not from what happens as all the ideological crap comes to the fore in periods of downturn.

We do not, however, let things rest at that. We understand there has to be a fight within the working class for the principles of the upturn – for solidarity, for the unity of white workers with black, of male workers with female workers – in the gloomiest periods of downturn. Only in this way can we prepare a minority of the class for the tasks which face the class as a whole. Only then can we ensure that when the upturn comes, a leadership exists within the class which can carry the struggle forward to victory.

We aim, in short, to build the beginnings of a revolutionary party in the downturn.

We cannot do this if we fall into the mistaken belief that there is an easy alternative of leaving it to organisations of the oppressed to fight racism and sexism. The party itself has to struggle against oppression on grounds of race, sex, religion or ethnic origin. This is part of its task of fighting to unite the class as a whole in struggle.

The party members have to be seen as people who argue among white workers and male workers in support of the interests of black workers and female workers. They have to recognise that in a period of downturn this means they will often be in a small minority. But they also have to understand that their situation will change once a period of real struggle begins. They have to learn to operate both as eager participants in the struggles of workers, and as a minority known for their open support for the interests of the most oppressed sections of the class.

However, the argument about the unity of the class is not just an argument that has to be put among white workers and male workers. It also has to be put among the most oppressed sections of the class. So, for instance, it is necessary to argue among white women workers in support of the interests of black workers, and among male black workers in support of the interests of women workers. Above all there has to be a fight within each oppressed section of workers against bourgeois and petty bourgeois influences which would persuade them there can be no unity with the less oppressed white and male workers.

So every member of the revolutionary organisation has to understand how at high points of class struggle sections of white and male workers have fought in the interests of black and female workers. The aim is to build a party which encapsulates that experience.

The building of such a party is something which is needed even more by the oppressed sections of workers than by the rest. For capitalism cannot be smashed without such a party, and you cannot end oppression without smashing capitalism.

Those who reject the perspective of building such a party on the grounds that it means "men leading women" and "whites leading blacks", or that "it subordinates the fight against oppression to the fight against exploitation" are, in fact, abandoning any perspective of destroying the roots of oppression. At best they are talking about protest movements against oppression that can never bring it to an end.

Reformism, Stalinism and the party

Every time the question of the party is raised, we face a problem. People who have had experience of non-revolutionary parties easily draw the conclusion that all parties are wrong. So it was in the first two decades of the present century: anarchism got a boost from the bureaucratic gradualism of social democracy; in the 1940s and 1950s people who had been manipulated by pro-Russian Stalinism often acted by turning against any sort of socialist politics; in the 1970s the experience of Maoist Stalinism gave a boost to all sorts of "autonomist" and separatist currents.

But our response to such experiences cannot and must not be to abandon our own fight for a revolutionary party. It has to be to explain that these experiences are what happens when you do not have a genuine revolutionary Marxist organisation fighting the influence of social democracy and Stalinism.

Whenever revolutionary socialists put forward the argument about the party our opponents always argue, "but you forget about self-activity being a precondition for socialism". Eighty years ago this was the argument used by trade union activists (the "economists") opposed to the building of a centralised party in Russia. Today it is often used by black activists or feminists opposed to the building of a unified revolutionary organisation. Lenin replied to the "economists":

> Use fewer platitudes about the development of the independent activity of the workers – the workers display no end of independent revolutionary activity you don't notice – but see, rather, that you don't demoralise underdeveloped workers by your own tailism.

That has to be our attitude today. It is not a question of whether self-activity exists or not. It is rather, whether we try to develop this into self-conscious self-activity, to make people aware of the need to generalise their struggle if they are to win. This means telling women and black workers in struggle not only that they have to fight their own oppression – they usually know that once they are in struggle – but how they are to fight it, how to win. And you can't do that without putting the argument about unity with male workers or white workers.

All sorts of struggles arise "independently" of the revolutionary organisation. But it does not help the struggles at all for revolutionaries to say "these struggles are independent of us, therefore we must not argue with those involved in them what they need to do to win". It is our duty at all times to put such arguments. For, if such struggles are not influenced by our ideas, they will be influenced by the prevailing ideas in any society – the ideas of the ruling class.

"Independent" struggles are always arising. But there are no such things as "independent" ideas. There are ideas which are in support of existing society, and ideas which are for its revolutionary overthrow. Ideas which exist between these two polar positions are not "independent" but, simply, a muddle.

The downturn and the danger of movementism

We noted earlier that the downturn in the class struggle since the 1970s has led many activists in the women's movement to turn away from a working class orientation towards reformism and separatism. The downturn has also had an effect on the attitudes of activists within revolutionary organisations in many countries.

They have seen sudden upsurges in one-issue movements while the mass of workers have continued to retreat in the face of capitalist offensives. This was the case with the riots of the "*marginali*" in Italy in 1977, the growth of the anti nuclear power movements in France and Germany in the late 1970s, the anti-racist struggle in Britain in 1977 and 1978, the peace movement of the early 1980s. It has been easy to draw the conclusion that you can forget about the working class and just concentrate on these movements.

These movements have drawn into political activity new layers of people. But because the working class as a whole has not been fighting, winning these people to a revolutionary Marxist perspective has been very difficult.

Often, instead of the revolutionary left winning new people from these movements the reverse has happened – these movements have won members of the revolutionary left to their non working class approach. Revolutionaries have begun to make concessions to the idea that the movements' goals can be achieved without working class action.

The situation has been made worse by the inevitable pattern of such movements. They can rise very quickly, precisely because their participants are not rooted in production. But the same lack of roots means they do not have real power. And so the movements begin to go into terminal decline the moment they have reached their peak. They rise like a rocket and drop like a stick.

Revolutionary socialists who put their faith in such movements receive an initial boost, only then to suffer all the demoralisation that comes with the decline.

Then all the pressure is on the movements' activists to move to the right. They make concessions to existing society because they find they cannot achieve their goals by fighting it. Revolutionaries who have made concessions to the arguments of the movements get drawn along by this rightward pull.

It is bad enough dissolving your politics into a movement that is dynamic, enthusiastic and growing. It is even worse doing so in a movement that is tired, demoralised and increasingly inward looking.

This explains the connection between "movementism" and what we in the SWP call the "swamp" – the milieu of ex-leftists who have drifted to the right as they adapt to reformism, the trade union bureaucracy and the mysticism of feminist separatism.

You cannot resist the pressures driving former activists to the right unless you start off with a very clear understanding of the limitations of all one issue movements, however vital the issues they try to fight over. You have to be insistent that they cannot win their demands unless they connect with the struggles of the mass of workers. And that means arguing loudly and clearly for a revolutionary socialist organisation that makes such connections, in theory and in practice.

Theories that separate off any struggle, whether for peace, against women's oppression or against racism, from the wider class struggle, prevent these connections being made.

That is why the ideas of people like E P Thompson impede the struggle against nuclear war. That is why the arguments of patriarchy and socialist feminist theorists impede the struggle for women's liberation. That is why black nationalist and separatist ideas impede the struggle for black liberation.

Those propagating such ideas may well play an important role, for a period, in encouraging people to fight back against aspects of the system. But their ideas, if not challenged, will lead the struggle into a blind alley sooner or later.

Revolutionary socialists have to be very hard politically so that we can stop activists being led, blindfolded, into the swamp. Of course, we are on the side of the peace movement against the military establishment, but this does not mean we drop our very hard criticism of the ideas of E P Thompson. In the same way, we are on the side of all women who challenge their oppression, but we don't hold back from relentless struggle against the mistaken ideas of middle class feminism.

Nothing is more dangerous than to put forward verbal formulations that hide the difference between revolutionary Marxists and such people.

It is here that we in the British SWP disagree profoundly with revolutionaries who have put forward organisational formulae which, in our view, are designed to bridge the unbridgeable – the idea of a unified revolutionary party on the one hand and the separatist notions of much of the women's movement.

They speak of "an independent women's movement" which "must be part of the overall working class movement", of a movement which is "distinct but not separate" from the revolutionary party, so that "we organise independently but are part of the wider socialist movement".[26]

Such formulations are extremely obscure. Does "independence" mean independence from capitalist society, from reformism or from the ideas of revolutionary Marxism? If it doesn't mean independence from Marxist ideas, is the revolutionary party then allowed to intervene inside the "independent movement"? If not, how does it fight the influence on women's struggles of bourgeois and reformist ideas?

Does the formulation mean that revolutionary socialists have to organise working class *women* separately from working class men? If so, it is extremely dangerous indeed. For it means organising them separately from the main struggles of the working class – struggles which usually involve both women and men (although in different proportions in different industries).

First published in *International Socialism* 23, spring 1984.

Two Marxes or one?

Before writing the final version of *Capital*, Marx wrote more than a thousand pages of rough drafts (usually known as the *Grundrisse*). These were unknown until discovered and published (in German) in the 1930s, and only recently have fragments begun to appear in English.

In these writings Marx deals with topics he hardly mentions elsewhere. So scholars interested in Marx's views on Oriental societies, on the rise of capitalism or on the philosophical underpinning of his work have been fascinated by them. However, their real importance does not lie in such new insights, but in the light they cast on disputes as to how Marx's other writings should be understood.

In recent years it has become fashionable in certain academic circles which claim inspiration from Marx to make a distinction between the young Marx who wrote in Paris in the 1840s and the old Marx who wrote *Capital*. Writers like, say, Erich Fromm hold that the young Marx was correct as against the old Marx. Other writers, like the French Stalinist Althusser hold the reverse. Both are agreed, however, that it is possible to distinguish between two completely different approaches (or "problematics" in Althusser's pretentious terminology) to the understanding of social development.

According to Althusser, the "mature" Marx saw society as a set of structures, developing according to objective laws, with men as mere cogs within them, mere products of their circumstances, unable to play any conscious role in social transformations. So Althusser derides as residues of an outmoded approach the use of terms like alienation and reification which imply that men can dominate the products of their labours. Similarly, he opposes the idea of "Marxist humanism" because it argues that men can be more than cogs in machines. A further consequence of his standpoint is that the superiority of Marxism over bourgeois social science is not a result of its relationship to revolutionary proletarian practice, but because of a superior methodology of science that Marx developed, which could (logically) be adopted by non-revolutionaries. Indeed, the relationship between Marxism and the revolutionary movement is argued to inevitably lead away from "science" to ideology.

It is not difficult to link Althusser's ideas to his own social position. He is simultaneously a supporter of the Franch Communist Party and the various state capitalist regimes, and a French academic. His views on the independence of theory from practice (his solution of the hoary old problem of the relation of theory to practice is to rebaptise theory as "theoretical practice") must be very congenial to all academics. At the same time his view that under socialism as under capitalism men will be just as much dominated by social mechanisms over which they have no control makes it very easy to define the oppressive and exploitative regimes of Brezhnev or Mao as "socialist". After all exploitation takes place under a different structural arrangement (one is reminded of the old East European joke: "Under capitalism there is the exploitation of man by man. Under socialism it is the other way round").

The publication by Dr McLennan of extracts from the *Grundrisse* is to be welcomed because they show quite clearly that all the talk about "two Marxes" is nonsense. Although written only about five years before Marx started out on the final draft of *Capital*, they are clearly in continuity with his writings of the 1840s. Of course, Marx had developed enormously in the meantime. He had introduced a whole range of fresh concepts. Yet at the same time whole passages are more or less copied out from the Paris writings. The same terminology is often employed – as it is indeed, although more sparsely, in *Capital* itself.

For Marxists who have always understood the continuity between the simple examination of alienation in 1844 and the vastly extended and elaborated account of alienated labour in *Capital*, Marx's *Grundrisse* will not add much to what they know already. However, for those who have been misled by the Stalinist academicism of Althusser it will present a real problem. Either they will have to admit that the Althusserian position has nothing in common with the Marxism of Marx, or they will have to abandon their past positions and come to terms with revolutionary theory and practice.

First published under the name Colin Humphries in *International Socialism* 49 (first series), autumn 1971.

Voice of the hanged

I came across the novels of B Traven by accident – I saw a copy of *March to Caobaland* on a half-price bookstall and bought it out of curiosity over the strange name of the author. He is not one of those writers that older socialists usually recommend to younger ones. And when people do read him it is usually for a reason as accidental as mine – because he wrote, the original of the John Huston film, *The Treasure of Sierra Madre*.

Yet Traven's novels – especially *March to Caobaland* and *The Rebellion of the Hanged* – are marvellous reading for any socialist. They are exciting, very readable stories, which tell what it's like to be on the receiving end of imperialism.

March to Caobaland is the story of a Mexican Indian peasant, Celso, trapped into debt slavery in a mahogany (*caoba*) camp deep in the jungle, which he slowly realises he will never be able to get away from, earning barely enough to sustain his endless labours.

> For the 50 centavos which Celso was getting per day, 20 centavos were deducted for food... Occasionally Celso felt like smoking and so he had to buy tobacco leaves. He needed camphor to heal mosquito bites... Occasionally he had to buy tallow to be used on his back after a whipping.
>
> Celso spent for clothes less than 10 percent of what an American spinster spends on clothing for her lap dog.

At the beginning of the book Celso is still a peasant, incredibly naive about the world at large, taking it for granted that he has no choice but to cringe before white men. But as he treks to become a mahogany worker for the second time his attitudes change. He tells those who are new to the camps:

> Unless you become like *caoba*, hard like steel, then you will find your last resting place near one of the camps. Here you've got to fight tooth and nail against the *capataces* (gangers), against the whippings and hangings, and above all against the jungle that wants to devour you.

Yet he remains, in *March to Caobaland*, the victim of an imperialism he cannot begin to understand:

> If the *muchachos* had been taken to New York and been shown there the offices of Central American Hardwoods, Chicle and Fruit Corporations, they would never have believed that such a small army of amiable men, girls and office boys lounging around desks were the power which had condemned them to the inferno of monterias, chicle camps and coffee and fruit plantations... Everyone in this long chain of men who were interested in the mahogany business was, himself, only a link completely innocent of the cruelties, misery and suffering of the *caoba* workers. Everyone, had he been asked, would have replied, "I never knew anything like that could happen".

We encounter Celso again halfway through *The Rebellion of the Hanged*. The mahogany camps are more hellish than ever. In an effort to ward off bankruptcy, the owners have devised the spur to productivity of hanging Indians alive. The mood of the peasant-become-worker Celso is no longer acquiescent. A new worker is told of him, "he was among the first of us to rebel".

Yet, most of the Indians still hold back:

> None of these men had ever risen in rebellion in their lives. They had not even protected their faces when lashed with a whip. The masters, the descendants of the colonisers, the Spaniards, the white generally, all were gods against whom an Indian peon never dared to revolt. The Indians knew only two categories: gods and servants. And not being a god, one can only be a servant, a humble and submissive one.

But a wider perspective is provided by the arrival as workers at the camp of three fugitives from crushed rebellions elsewhere in the country.

In a moment of desperation a group of Indians kill one of the white bosses. Suddenly they can't turn back.

They rise in a bitter, bloody, brutal rebellion, murdering the bosses, the foremen, the whites who provide services for the camps, their wives and children.

For Traven:

> It was no fault of the rebels that they were animated by sentiments of death and destruction. They had never been allowed to express their rights. A blind obedience was inculcated in them by flogging until it became second nature. Hence it was not mere savagery which drove the Indians to kill and despoil. They gave proofs of cruelty only because their adversaries and oppressors were a hundred times more savage than they themselves...

In the act of rebellion:

> The Indians learned something of which until then they had not had the least idea: that they themselves were capable of giving orders. Until that moment they had always imagined that in order to command it was necessary to be a crafty white *ladino* or a ruling class *gachupin*. Now they saw it was not difficult to give orders. Anyone can do that, right down to the most backward Indian, the most illiterate. An idiot is capable of being dictator.

There is much more to *The Rebellion of the Hanged*. But for that you will need to read the book.

To my mind Traven's other novels (or at least the ones I've been able to get hold of) do not reach the same heights. *The Death Ship* – about deported immigrants compelled to spend their lives shuttling between ports doing the most arduous work on the most dangerous ships – is good, but drags on a bit. *The Treasure of Sierra Madre* contains some biting irony, but lacks the power of Traven's best works. *The Cotton Pickers* begins well, but degenerates into a sort of sentimental folksiness in places.

Traven's own identity was for long a mystery. But now it seems certain that he was originally Ret Marut, one of the anarchist *literateurs* involved in the Bavarian Soviet republic of April 1919. After its crushing, he made a near-miraculous escape from a death sentence to turn up a few years later in Mexico. Here he lived until his death in 1969 with the Indians and hoboes who provide the material for his novels.

The tone of the novels remains very much anarchist. But it is a powerful, insurgent, almost political anarchism which has learnt from Traven's own experiences of civil war in Germany and the Indians' experiences of fighting in the revolutionary armies of Villa and Zapata. There are faults in his anarchism. But it nevertheless enabled Traven to produce some of the best revolutionary novels of the 20th century.

First published in *Socialist Review* 7, July/August 1980

2: Party and class

Party and class

Introduction (1980)

This article first appeared in *International Socialism* late in 1968. At the time there was ferment within the revolutionary left internationally. The great French general strike of May 1968 had brought thousands of people in every country to see the possibilities of working class revolution. Revolutionary socialist organisations trebled in size in a matter of months.

In Britain the predecessor of the Socialist Workers Party (SWP), the International Socialists, was the main beneficiary of this growth, but growth also led to sharp political arguments. The explosion of working class militancy and creativity in May 1968 led many new revolutionaries and some old ones to question the need for a democratic centralist party. "Party and class" was an attempt to take up the arguments and reassert the relevance of the revolutionary Marxist tradition.

After 1968 the argument against the party and democratic centralism faded. The urgent needs of the day-to-day struggle tended to convince people, as much as any political debate, of the need for party organisation. But in the past three or four years the discussion has gained new life, partly because in countries such as Italy, Germany and Spain the model of the party generally adopted after 1968 was of a Stalinist sort, inherited from Maoism, and this model failed to cope with changes in the pattern of class struggle after 1975.

But partly also because, in several countries, and especially Italy, a lull in the class struggle in industry saw the growth of new movements of oppressed groups, which had only a limited working class content. Faced with the militancy, enthusiasm and creativity of these movements, many revolutionaries reacted as to the May events of 1968. They decided that the old notions of democratic centralism no longer fitted.

They have begun to elaborate theories about "new forms of organisation" based upon the "autonomy" of the different movements. In extreme instances they have even "theorised" the need for what are effectively separate "parallel" revolutionary parties for each section of the oppressed: one for white trade unionists, one for women workers, one for oppressed national minorities, and so on.

These "new" ideas have found their enthusiasts in this country. Recently, for instance, the book *Beyond the Fragments*, by three socialist feminists, Sheila Rowbotham, Lyne Segal and Hilary Wainwright, received acclaim from many non-affiliated revolutionaries. And even the ranks of the SWP have not avoided the influence of these ideas. Some have raised the idea of each oppressed group having its own independent revolutionary organisation, each with a different programme and policies.

It is absolutely correct to search for new mechanisms by which a party overwhelmingly based within the working class can become, in Lenin's words, "the tribune for all the oppressed and exploited", so drawing the best elements in these movements towards the party. But these "theories", in the guise of looking for such mechanisms, effectively dissolve the notion of the party.

This, then, is the justification for reprinting this pamphlet.

I feel that many of the arguments we used in 1968 still retain their validity. However, there are two points on which I myself think the argument is deficient. First, it does not begin to deal with the immense practical and political problems of building socialist parties in actual historical circumstances, of the twists and turns that are needed from time to time to ensure that the revolutionary organisation is combining principled politics with an organic connection with the most militant and active sections of the class. Here readers are advised to follow up this pamphlet by reading Volume I of Tony Cliff's biography of Lenin.

Second, sometimes the argument in the pamphlet becomes unduly "intellectualist"; it speaks of the need for the party "to make its newest members rise to the level of understanding of its oldest". In fact, old members, recruited during a period of weak class struggle, often have a weaker comprehension of what revolutionary struggle is really about than the members who join in a later period of working class militancy.

Again, the pamphlet speaks of "a limitation" on the party's membership "to those willing to seriously and scientifically appraise their own activity and that of the party generally". Much better to say that the party must avoid trying to inflate its numbers by recruiting people who are not prepared to fight the system from a revolutionary standpoint – and who will not therefore see the need for serious discussion of strategy and tactics – but that it must at all times try to draw to its ranks the most militant, revolutionary section of the class. A small party, on the margins of class struggle, cannot be "diluted" by an influx of revolutionary workers.

We have reprinted the text intact, despite these errors, because the central case it argues remains as valid today as 12 years ago.

Party and class

Few questions have produced more bitterness in Marxist circles than that of the relation between the party and the class. More heat has probably been generated in acrimonious disputes over this subject than any other. In generation after generation the same epiphets are thrown about – "bureaucrat", "substitutionist", "elitist", "autocrat".

Yet the principles underlying such debate have usually been confused. This despite the importance of the issues involved. For instance, the split between Bolsheviks and Mensheviks that occurred over the nature of the organisation of the party in 1903 found many of those who were to be on the opposite side of the barricades to Lenin in 1917 in his faction (for instance, Plekhanov), while against him were revolutionaries of the stature of Trotsky and Rosa Luxemburg. Nor was this confusion an isolated incident. It has been a continuous feature of revolutionary discussion. It is worth recalling Trotsky's remarks, at the Second Congress of the Comintern, in reply to Paul Levi's contention that the mass of workers of Europe and America understood the need for a party. Trotsky points out that the situation is much more complex than this:

> If the question is posed in the abstract then I see Scheidemann on the one side and, on the other, American or French or Spanish syndicates who not only wish to fight against the bourgeoisie, but who, unlike Scheidemann, really want to tear its head off – for this reason I say that I prefer to discuss with these Spanish, American or French comrades in order to prove to them that the party is indispensable for the fulfilment of the historical mission which is placed upon them... I will try to prove this to them in a comradely way, on the basis of my own experience, and not by

counterposing to them Scheidemann's long years of experience saying that for the majority the question has already been settled... What is there in common between me and a Renaudel who excellently understands the need of the party, or an Albert Thomas and other gentlemen whom I do not even want to call "comrades" so as not to violate the rules of decency?[1]

The difficulty to which Trotsky refers – that both social democrats and Bolsheviks refer to the "need for a party", although what they mean by this are quite distinct things – has been aggravated in the years since by the rise of Stalinism. The vocabulary of Bolshevism was taken over and used for purposes quite opposed to those who formulated it. Yet too often those who have continued in the revolutionary tradition opposed to both Stalinism and social democracy have not taken Trotsky's points in 1920 seriously. They have often relied on "experience" to prove the need for a party, although the experience is that of Stalinism and social democracy.

It will be the contention of this argument that most of the discussion even in revolutionary circles is, as a consequence, discussion for or against basically Stalinist or social democratic conceptions of organisation. It will be held that the sort of organisational views developed implicitly in the writings and actions of Lenin are radically different to both these conceptions. This has been obscured by the Stalinist debasement of the theory and practice of the October Revolution and the fact that the development of the Bolshevik Party took place under conditions of illegality and was often argued for in the language of orthodox social democracy.

The social democratic view of the relation of party and class

The classical theories of social democracy – which were not fundamentally challenged by any of the Marxists before 1914 – of necessity gave the party a central role in the development towards socialism. For this development was seen essentially as being through a continuous and smooth growth of working class organisation and consciousness under capitalism. Even those Marxists, such as Kautsky, who rejected the idea that there could be a gradual transition to socialism accepted that what was needed for the present was continually to extend organisational strength and electoral following. The growth of the party was essential so as to ensure that when the transition to socialism inevitably came, whether through elections or through defensive violence by the working class, the party capable of taking over and forming the basis of the new state (or the old one refurbished) would exist.

The development of a mass working class party is seen as being an inevitable corollary of the tendencies of capitalist development. "Forever greater grows the number of proletarians, more gigantic the army of superfluous labourers, and sharper the opposition between exploiters and exploited",[2] crises "naturally occur on an increasing scale",[3] "the majority of people sink ever deeper into want and misery",[4] "the intervals of prosperity become ever shorter; the length of the crises ever longer".[5] This drives greater numbers of workers "into instinctive opposition to the existing order".[6] Social democracy, basing itself upon "independent scientific investigation by bourgeois thinkers"[7] exists to raise the workers to the level where they have a "clear insight into social laws".[8] Such a movement "springing out of class antagonisms...cannot meet with anything more than temporary defeats, and must ultimately win".[9] "Revolutions are not made at will... They come with inevitable necessity." The central mechanisms involved in this development is that of parliamentary elections (although even Kautsky played with the idea of the general strike in the period immediately after 1905-06).[10] "We have no reason to believe that armed insurrection... will play a central role nowadays".[11] Rather, "it [parliament] is the most powerful lever that can be used to raise the proletariat out of its economic, social and moral degradation".[12] The uses of this by the working class makes "parliamentarianism begin to change its character. It ceases to be a mere tool in the hands of the bourgeoisie".[13] In the long run such activities must lead to the organisation of the working class and to a situation where the socialist party has the majority and will form the government. The Labour Party "must have for its purpose the conquest of the government in the interests of the class it represents. Economic development will lead naturally to the accomplishment of this purpose".[14]

Not only did this perspective lay the basis for most socialist action throughout western Europe in the 40 years prior to the First World War, it also went virtually unchallenged theoretically, at least from the left. Lenin's astonishment at the SPD's support for the war is well known. Not so often understood, however, is the fact that even left critics of Kautsky, such as Rosa Luxemburg, had not rejected the foundations of the theory of the relation of the party to the class and of the development of class consciousness implied. Their criticisms of Kautskyism tended to remain within the overall theoretical ground provided by Kautskyism.

What is central for the social democrat is that the party *represents* the class. Outside of the party the worker has no consciousness. Indeed, Kautsky himself seemed to have an almost pathological fear of what the workers would do without the party and of the associated dangers of a "premature" revolution. Thus it had to be the party that takes power. Other forms of working class organisation and activity can help, but must be subordinated to the bearer of political consciousness. "This 'direct action' of the unions can operate effectively only as an auxiliary and reinforcement to and not as a substitute for parliamentary action".[15]

The revolutionary left and social-democratic theories

No sense can be made of any of the discussions that took place in relation to questions of organisation of the party prior to 1917 without understanding that this social democratic view of the relation of party and class was *nowhere* explicitly challenged (except among the anarchists who rejected any notion of a party). Its assumptions were shared even by those, such as Rosa Luxemburg, who opposed orthodox social democracy from the point of view of mass working class self-activity. This was not a merely theoretical failing. It followed from the historical situation. The Paris Commune was the only experience then of working class power, and that had been for a mere two months in a predominantly petty-bourgeois city. Even the 1905 revolution gave only the most embryonic expression of how a workers' state would in fact be organised. The fundamental forms of workers' power – the soviets, the workers' councils – were not recognised. Thus Trotsky, who had been President of the Petrograd Soviet in 1905, does not mention them in his analysis of the lessons of 1905, *Results and Prospects*. Virtually alone in foreseeing the socialist content of the Russian Revolution, Trotsky did not begin to see the form this would take.

> Revolution is first and foremost a question of power – not of the state form (constituent assembly, republic, united states) but of the social content of the government.[16]

There was a similar omission in Rosa Luxemburg's response to 1905,

The Mass Strike. Not until the February Revolution did the soviet become central in Lenin's writings and thoughts.[17]

The revolutionary left never fully accepted Kautsky's position of seeing the party as the direct forerunner of the workers' state. Luxemburg's writings, for instance, recognise the conservatism of the party and the need for the masses to go beyond and outside it from a very early stage.[18] But there is never an explicit rejection of the official social democratic position. Yet without the theoretical clarification of the relationship between the party and the class there could be no possibility of clarity over the question of the necessary internal organisation of the party. Without a rejection of the social democratic model, there could not be the beginnings of a real discussion about revolutionary organisation.

This is most clearly the case with Rosa Luxemburg. It would be wrong to fall into the trap (carefully laid by both Stalinist and would-be followers of Luxemburg) of ascribing to her a theory of "spontaneity" that ignores the need for a party. Throughout her writings there is stress upon the need for a party and the positive role it must play:

> In Russia, however, the Social Democratic Party must make up by its own efforts an entire historical period. It must lead the Russian proletarians from their present "atomised" condition, which prolongs the autocratic regime, to a class organisation that would help them to become aware of their historical objectives and prepare them to struggle to achieve those objectives.[19]

> The task of Social Democracy does not consist in the technical preparation and direction of mass strikes, but first and foremost in the political leadership of the whole movement.[20]

> The Social Democrats are the most enlightened, the most class-conscious vanguard of the proletariat. They cannot and dare not wait, in a fatalistic fashion with folded arms for the advent of the "revolutionary situation".[21]

Yet there is a continual equivocation in Luxemburg's writings on the role of the party. She was concerned that the leading role of the party should not be too great – for she identified this as "the prudent position of Social Democracy".[22] She identified "centralism", which she saw as anyway necessary ("the Social Democracy is, as a rule, hostile to any manifestation of localism or federalism"[23]) with the "conservatism inherent in such an organ (i.e. the Central Committee)".[24] Such equivocation cannot be understood without taking account of the concrete situation Luxemburg was really concerned about. She was a leading member of the SPD, but always uneasy about its mode of operation. When she really wanted to illustrate the dangers of centralism it was to this that she referred:

> The present tactical policy of the German Social Democracy has won universal esteem because it is supple as well as firm. This is a sign of the fine adaptation of our party to the conditions of a parliamentary regime... However, the very perfection of this adaptation is already closing vaster horizons to our party.

Brilliantly prophetic as this is of what was to happen in 1914, she does not begin to explain the origins of the increasing sclerosis and ritualism of SPD, let alone indicate ways of fighting this. Conscious individualists and groups cannot resist this trend. For "such inertia is due to a large degree to the fact that it is inconvenient to define, within the vacuum of abstract hypotheses, the lines and forms of non-existent political situations".[25] Bureaucratisation of the party is seen as an inevitable phenomenon that only a limitation on the degree of cohesion and efficiency of the party can overcome.

It is not a particular form of organisation and conscious direction, but organisation and conscious direction as such that limit the possibilities for the "self-conscious movement of the majority in the interests of the majority".

> The unconscious comes before the conscious. The logic of history comes before the subjective logic of the human beings who participate in the historic process. The tendency is for the directing organs of the socialist party to play a conservative role.[26]

There is a correct and important element in this argument: the tendency for certain sorts of organisations to be unable (or unwilling) to respond to a rapidly changing situation. One only has to think of the Maximalist wing of the Italian Socialist Party in 1919, the whole of the "centre" of the Second International in 1914, the Menshevik-Internationalists in 1917, or the KPD in 1923. Even the Bolshevik Party contained a very strong tendency to exhibit such conservatism. But Luxemburg, having made the diagnosis, makes no attempt to locate its source, except in epistemological generalities, or looks for organisational remedies. There is a strong fatalism in her hope that the "unconscious" will be able to correct the "conscious".

Despite her superb sensitivity to the peculiar tempo of development of the mass movement – particularly in *The Mass Strike* – she shies away from trying to work out a clear conception of the sort of political organisation that can harness such spontaneous developments. Paradoxically this most trenchant critic of bureaucratic ritualism and parliamentary cretinism argued in the 1903 debate for precisely that faction of the Russian party that was to be the most perfected historical embodiment of these failings: the Mensheviks. In Germany political opposition to Kautskyism, which already was developing at the turn of the century and was fully formed by 1910, did not take on concrete organisational forms for another five years.

Considerable parallels exist between Luxemburg's position and that which Trotsky adheres to up to 1917. He too is very aware of the danger of bureaucratic ritualism:

> The work of agitation and organisation among the ranks of the proletariat has an internal inertia. The European socialist parties, particularly the largest of them, the German Social Democratic Party, hive developed an inertia in proportion as the great masses have embraced socialism and the more these masses have become organised and disciplined. As a consequence of this, social democracy as an organisation embodying the political experience of the proletariat may at a certain moment become a direct obstacle to open conflict between the workers and bourgeois reaction.[27]

Again his revolutionary spirit leads him to distrust *all* centralised organisation. Lenin's conception of the party can, according to Trotsky in 1904, only lead to the situation in which:

> the organisation of the party substitutes itself for the party as a whole; then the Central Committee substitutes itself for the organisation; and finally the "dictator" substitutes himself for the Central Committee.[28]

But for Trotsky the real problems of working class power can only be solved:
> by way of systematic struggle between...many trends inside socialism, trends which will inevitably emerge as soon as the proletarian dictatorship poses tens and hundreds of new...problems. No strong "domineering" organisation will be able to suppress these trends and controversies.[29]

Yet Trotsky's fear of organisational rigidity leads him also to support that tendency in the inner-party struggle in Russia which was historically to prove itself most frightened by the spontaneity of mass action. Although he was to become increasingly alienated from the Mensheviks politically, he did not begin to build up an organisation in opposition to them until very late. Whether he was correct or not in his criticisms of Lenin in 1904 (and we believe he was wrong), he was only able to become an effective historical actor in 1917 by joining Lenin's party.

If organisation does produce bureaucracy and inertia Luxemburg and the young Trotsky were undoubtedly right about the need to limit the aspirations towards centralism and cohesion among revolutionaries. But it is important to accept all the consequences of this position. The most important must be a historical fatalism. Individuals can struggle among the working class for their ideas, and these ideas can be important in giving workers the necessary consciousness and confidence to fight for their own liberation. But revolutionaries can never build the organisation capable of giving them effectiveness and cohesion in action comparable to that of those who implicitly accept present ideologies. For to do so is inevitably to limit the self-activity of the masses, the "unconscious" that precedes the "conscious". The result must be to wait for "spontaneous" developments among the masses. In the meantime one might as well put up with the organisations that exist at present, even if one disagrees with them politically, as being the best possible, as being the maximum present expression of the spontaneous development of the masses.

Lenin and Gramsci on the party and the class

In the writings of Lenin there is an ever-present implicit recognition of the problems that worry Luxemburg and Trotsky so much. But there is not the same fatalistic succumbing to them. There is an increasing recognition that it is not organisation as such, but particular forms and aspects of organisation that give rise to these. Not until the First World War and then the events in 1917 gave an acute expression to the faults of old forms of organisation did Lenin begin to give explicit notice of the radically new conceptions he himself was developing. Even then these were not fully developed. The destruction of the Russian working class, the collapse of any meaningful Soviet system (i.e. one based upon real workers' councils), and the rise of Stalinism, smothered the renovation of socialist theory. The bureaucracy that arose with the decimation and demoralisation of the working class took over the theoretical foundations of the revolution, to distort them into an ideology justifying its own interests and crimes. Lenin's view of what the party is and how it should function in relation to the class and its institutions was no sooner defined as against older social democratic conceptions with any clarity than it was again obscured by a new Stalinist ideology.

Many of Lenin's conceptions are, however, taken up and given clear and coherent theoretical form by the Italian Antonio Gramsci.[30] What is usually ignored by commentators on Lenin is that throughout his writings are two intertwined and complementary conceptions, which to the superficial observer seem contradictory. Firstly there is continual stress on the possibilities of sudden transformations of working class consciousness, on the unexpected upsurge that characterises working class self-activity, on deep-rooted instincts in the working class that lead it to begin to reject habits of deference and subservience.

> In the history of revolutions there come to light contradictions that have ripened for decades and centuries. Life becomes unusually eventful. The masses, which have always stood in the shade and therefore have often been despised by superficial observers, enter the political arena as active combatants... These masses are making heroic efforts to rise to the occasion and cope with the gigantic tasks of world significance imposed upon them by history; and however great individual defeats may be, however shattering to us the rivers of blood and the thousands of victims, nothing will ever compare in importance with this direct training that the masses and the classes receive in the course of the revolutionary struggle itself.[31]

> We are able to appreciate the importance of the slow, steady and often imperceptible work of political education which social democrats have always conducted and always will conduct. But we must not allow what in the present circumstances would be still more dangerous – a lack of faith in the powers of the people. We must remember what a tremendous educational and organisational power the revolution has, when mighty historical events force the man in the street out of his remote garret or basement corner, and make a citizen of him. Months of revolution sometimes educate citizens more quickly and fully than decades of political stagnation.[32]

> The working class is instinctively, spontaneously social democratic.[33]

The special condition of the proletariat in capitalistic society leads to a striving of workers for socialism; a union of them with the socialist party bursts forth with a spontaneous force in the very early stages of the movement.[34]

Even in the worst months after the outbreak of war in 1914 he could write:

The objective war-created situation...is inevitably engendering revolutionary sentiments; it is tempering and enlightening all the finest and most class-conscious proletarians. A sudden change in the mood of the masses is not only possible, but is becoming more and more probable.[35]

In 1917 this faith in the masses leads him in April and in August-September into conflict with his own party:

Lenin said more than once that the masses are to the left of the party. He knew the party was to the left of its own upper layer of "old Bolsheviks".[36]

In relation to the "Democratic Conference" he can write:

We must draw the masses into the discussion of this question. Class-conscious workers must take the matter into their own hands, organise the discussion and exert pressure on "those at the top".[38]

There is, however, a second fundamental element in Lenin's thought and practice: the stress on the role of theory and of the party as the bearer of this. The most well known recognition of this occurs in *What Is To Be Done?* when Lenin writes that "without revolutionary theory there can be no revolutionary practice".[39] But it is the theme that recurs at every stage in his activities, not only in 1903, but also in 1905 and 1917 at exactly the same time that he was cursing the failure of the party to respond to the radicalisation of the masses. And for him the party is something very different from the mass organisations of the whole class. It is always a vanguard organisation, membership of which requires a dedication not to be found in most workers. (But this does not mean that Lenin ever wanted an organisation only of professional revolutionaries.[39]) This might seem a clear contradiction. Particularly as in 1903 Lenin uses arguments drawn from Kautsky which imply that only the party can imbue the class with a socialist consciousness, while later he refers to the class being more "to the left" than the party. In fact, however, to see a contradiction here is to fail to understand the fundamentals of Lenin's thinking on these issues. For the real theoretical basis for his argument on the party is not that the working class is incapable on its own of coming to theoretical socialist consciousness. This he admits at the second congress of the RSDLP when he denies that he "takes no account whatever of the fact that the workers too have a share in the formation of an ideology" and adds that "the 'economists' have gone to one extreme. To straighten matters out somebody had to pull in the other direction – and that is what I have done".[40]

The real basis for his argument is that the level of consciousness in the working class is never uniform. However rapidly the mass of workers learn in a revolutionary situation, some sections will still be more advanced than others. To merely take delight in the spontaneous transformation is to accept uncritically whatever transitory products this throws up. But these reflect the backwardness of the class as well as its movement forward, its situation in bourgeois society as well as its potentiality of further development so as to make a revolution. Workers are not automatons without ideas. If they are not won over to a socialist world view by the intervention of conscious revolutionaries, they will continue to accept the bourgeois ideology of existing society. This is all the more likely because it is an ideology that flavours all aspects of life at present and is perpetuated by all media. Even were some workers "spontaneously" to come to a fully fledged scientific standpoint they would still have to argue with others who had not.

To forget the distinction between the vanguard and the whole of the masses gravitating towards it, to forget the vanguard's constant duty of raising ever wider sections to its own advanced level, means simply to deceive oneself, to shut one's eyes to the immensity of our tasks, and to narrow down these tasks.[41]

This argument is not one that can be restricted to a particular historical period. It is not one, as some people would like to argue, that applies to the backward Russian working class of 1902 but not to those in the advanced nations today. The absolute possibilities for the growth of working class consciousness may be higher in the latter, but the very nature of capitalist society continues to ensure a vast unevenness within the working class. To deny this is to confuse the revolutionary *potential* of the working class with its present situation. As he writes against the Mensheviks (and Rosa Luxemburg!) in 1905:

Use fewer platitudes about the development of the independent activity of the workers – the workers display no end of independent revolutionary activity which you do not notice! – but see to it rather that you do not demoralise undeveloped workers by your own tailism.[42]

There are two sorts of independent activity. There is the independent activity of a proletariat that possesses revolutionary initiative, and there is the independent activity of a proletariat that is undeveloped and held in leading strings... There are Social Democrats to this day who contemplate with reverence the second kind of activity, who believe they can evade a direct reply to pressing questions of the day by repeating the word "class" over and over again.[43]

In short: stop talking about what the class as a whole can achieve, and start talking about how we as part of its development are going to act. As Gramsci writes:

> Pure spontaneity does not exist in history: it would have to coincide with pure mechanical action. In the "most spontaneous" of movements the elements of "conscious direction" are only uncontrollable... There exists a multiplicity of elements of conscious direction in these movements, but none of them is predominant.[44]

Man is never without some conception of the world. He never develops apart from some collectivity. "For his conception of the world a man always belongs to some grouping, and precisely to that of all the social elements who share the same way of thinking and working." Unless he is involved in a constant process of criticism of his world view so as to bring it the coherence:

> He belongs simultaneously to a multiplicity of men-masses, his own personality is made up in a queer way. It contains elements of the caveman and principles of the most modern advanced learning, shabby prejudices of all past historical phases, and intuitions of a future philosophy of the human race united all over the world.[45]

The active man of the masses works practically, but does not have a clear theoretical consciousness of his actions, which is also a knowledge of the world insofar as he changes it. Rather his theoretical consciousness may be opposed to his actions. We can almost say that he has two theoretical consciousnesses (or one contradictory consciousness), one implicit in his actions, which unites him with all his colleagues in the practical transformation of reality, and one superficially explicit or verbal which he has inherited from the past and which he accepts without criticism... [This division can reach the point] where the contradiction within his consciousness will not permit any action, any decision, any choice, and produces a state of moral and political passivity.[46]

All action is the result of diverse wills affected with a varying degree of intensity, of consciousness, of homogeneity with the entire mass of the collective will... It is clear that the corresponding, implicit theory will be a combination of beliefs and points of view as confused and heterogeneous. [If practical forces released at a certain historical point are to be] effective and expansive [it is necessary to] construct on a determined practice a theory that, coinciding with and being identified with the decisive elements of the same practice, accelerates the historical process in act, makes the practice more homogeneous, coherent, more efficacious in all its elements.[47]

In this sense the question as to the preferability of "spontaneity" or "conscious direction" becomes that of whether it is:

preferable to think without having a critical awareness, in a disjointed and irregular way, in other words to "participate" in a conception of the world "imposed" mechanically by external environment, that is by one of the many social groups in which everyone is automatically involved from the time he enters the conscious world, or is it preferable to work out one's own conception of the world consciously and critically.[48]

Parties exist in order to act in this situation to propagate a particular world view and the practical activity corresponding to it. They attempt to unite together into a collectivity all those who share a particular world view and to spread this. They exist to give homogeneity to the mass of individuals influenced by a variety of ideologies and interests. But they can do this in two ways.

The first Gramsci characterises as that of the Catholic church. This attempts to bind a variety of social classes and strata to a single ideology. It attempts to unite intellectuals and "ordinary people" in a single organised world view. But it can only do this by an iron discipline over the intellectuals that reduces them to the level of the "ordinary people". "Marxism is antithetical to this Catholic position." Instead it attempts to unite intellectuals and workers so as to constantly raise the level of consciousness of the masses, so as to enable them to act truly independently. This is precisely why Marxists cannot merely "worship" the spontaneity of the masses: this would be to copy the Catholics in trying to impose on the most advanced sections the backwardness of the least.

For Gramsci and Lenin this means that the party is constantly trying to make its newest members rise to the level of understanding of its oldest. It has always to be able to react to the "spontaneous" developments of the class, to attract those elements that are developing a clear consciousness as a result of these.

> To be a party of the masses not only in name, we must get ever wider masses to share in all party affairs, steadily to elevate them from political indifference to protest and struggle, from a general spirit of protest to an adoption of social democratic views, from adoption of these views to support of the movement, from support to organised membership in the party.[49]

The party able to fulfil these tasks will not, however, be the party that is necessarily "broadest". It will be an organisation that combines with a constant attempt to involve in its work ever wider circles of workers, a limitation on its membership to those willing to seriously and scientifically appraise their own activity and that of the party generally. This necessarily means that the definition of what constitutes a party member is important. The party is not to be made up of just anybody who wishes to identify himself as belonging to it, but only those willing to accept the discipline of its organisations. In normal times the numbers of these will be only a relatively small percentage of the working class, but in periods of upsurge they will grow immeasurably.

There is an important contrast here with the practice in social-democratic parties. Lenin himself realises this only insofar as Russia is concerned prior to 1914, but his position is clear. He contrasts his aim – "a really iron strong organisation", a "small but strong party" of "all those who are out to fight" – with the "sprawling monster, the new *Iskra* motley elements of the Mensheviks".[50] This explains his insistence on making a principle out of the question of the conditions for membership of the party when the split with the Mensheviks occurred.

Within Lenin's conception those elements that he himself is careful to regard as historically limited and those of general application must be distinguished. The former concern the stress on closed conspiratorial organisations and the need for careful direction from the top down of party officials, etc.

> Under conditions of political freedom our party will be built entirely on the elective principle. Under the autocracy this is impracticable for the collective thousands of workers that make up the party.[51]

Of much more general application is the stress on the need to limit the party to those who are going to accept its discipline. It is important to stress that for Lenin (as opposed to many of his would-be followers) this is not a blind acceptance of authoritarianism. The revolutionary party exists so as to make it possible for the most conscious and militant workers and intellectuals to engage in scientific discussion as a prelude to concerted and cohesive action. This is not possible without general participation in party activities. This requires clarity and precision in argument combined with organisational decisiveness. The alternative is the "marsh" – where elements motivated by scientific precision are so mixed up with those who are irremediably confused as to prevent any decisive action, effectively allowing the most backward to lead. The discipline necessary for such a debate is the discipline of those who have "combined by a freely adopted decision".[52] Unless the party has clear boundaries and unless it is coherent enough to implement decisions, discussion over its decisions, far from being "free", is pointless. Centralism for Lenin is far from being the opposite of developing the initiative and independence of party members; it is the precondition of this. It is worth noting how Lenin summed up the reasons for his battle for centralism over the previous two years in 1905. Talking of the role of the central organisation and of the central paper he says that the result was to be the:

> creation of a network of agents...that...would not have to sit round waiting for the call to insurrection, but would carry out such regular activity that would guarantee the highest probability of success in the event of an insurrection. Such activity would strengthen our connections with the broadest masses of the workers and with all strata that are discontented with the aristocracy... Precisely such activity would serve to cultivate the ability to estimate correctly the general political situation and, consequently, the ability to select the proper moment for the uprising. Precisely such activity would train all local organisations to respond simultaneously to the same political questions, incidents and events that agitate the whole of Russia and to react to these "incidents" in the most rigorous, uniform and expedient manner possible.[53]

By being part of such an organisation worker and intellectual alike are trained to assess their own concrete situation in accordance with the scientific socialist activity of thousands of others. "Discipline" means acceptance of the need to relate individual experience to the total theory and practice of the party. As such it is not opposed to, but a necessary prerequisite of the ability to make independent evaluations of concrete situations. That is also why "discipline" for Lenin does not mean hiding differences that exist within the party, but rather exposing them to the full light of day so as to argue them out. Only in this way can the mass of members make scientific evaluations. The party organ must be open to the opinions of those it considers inconsistent.

> It is necessary in our view to do the utmost – even if it involves certain departures from tidy patterns of centralism and from absolute obedience to discipline – to enable these grouplets to speak out and give the whole party the opportunity to weigh the importance or unimportance of those differences and to determine where, how and on whose part inconsistency is shown.[54]

In short, what matters is that there is political clarity and hardness in the party so as to ensure that all its members are brought into its debate and understand the relevance of their own activity. That is why it is absurd, as the Mensheviks tried to do, and as some people still do, to confuse the party with the class. The class as a whole is constantly engaged in unconscious opposition to capitalism; the party is that section of it that is already conscious and unites to try to give conscious direction to the struggle of the rest. Its discipline is not something imposed from the top downwards, but rather something that is voluntarily accepted by all those who participate in its decisions and act to implement these.

The social democratic party, the Bolshevik party and the Stalinist party

We can now see the difference between the party as Lenin conceived it and the social democratic party simultaneously envisaged and feared by Rosa Luxemburg and Trotsky. The latter was thought of as a party of the whole class. The coming to power of the class was to be the party taking power. All the tendencies within the class had to be represented within it. Any split within it was to be conceived of as a split within the class. Centralisation, although recognised as necessary, was feared as a centralisation over and against the spontaneous activity of the class. Yet it was precisely in this sort of party that the "autocratic" tendencies warned against by Luxemburg were to develop most. For within it the confusion of member and sympathiser, the massive apparatus needed to hold together a mass of only half-politicised members in a series of social activities, led to a toning down of political debate, a lack of political seriousness, which in turn reduced the ability of the members to make independent political evaluations, increased the need for apparatus-induced involvement. Without an organisational centralisation aimed at giving clarity and decisiveness to political differences, the independence of the rank-and-file members was bound to be permanently undermined. Ties of personal affection or of deference to established leaders become more important than scientific, political evaluation. In the marsh, where no one takes a clear road, even if the wrong one, then there is no argument as to which is the right one. Refusal to relate organisational ties to political evaluations, even if done under the noble intention of maintaining a "mass party", necessarily led to organisational loyalties replacing political ones. This in turn entailed a failure to act independently given opposition from old colleagues (the clearest example of this tendency was undoubtedly Martov in 1917).

It is essential to understand that the Stalinist party is not a variant of the Bolshevik party. It too was dominated by organisational structures. Adherence to the *organisation* rather than to the politics of the organisation mattered. Theory existed to justify an externally determined practice, not vice versa. Organisational loyalties of the apparatus are responsible for political decisions (the former relate in turn to the needs of the Russian state apparatus). It is worth noting that in Russia a real victory of the apparatus over the party required precisely the bringing into the party of hundreds of thousands of "sympathisers", a dilution of the "party" by the "class". At best politically unsure of themselves, the "Lenin levy" could be relied upon to defer to the apparatus. The Leninist party does not suffer from this tendency to bureaucratic control precisely because it restricts its membership to those willing to be serious and disciplined enough to take *political* and *theoretical* issues as their starting point, and to subordinate all their activities to these.

But does this not imply a very elitist conception of the party? In a sense it does, although this is not the fault of the party, but of life itself, which gives rise to an uneven development of working class consciousness. The party to be effective has to aim at recruiting all those it conceives of as being most "advanced". It cannot reduce its own level of science and consciousness merely in order not to be an "elite". It cannot, for instance, accept that chauvinist workers are "as good as" internationalist party members, so as to take account of the "self-activity" of the class. But to be a "vanguard" is not the same as to substitute one's own desires, or policies or interests, for those of the class.

Here it is important to see that for Lenin the party is not the embryo of the workers' state – the workers' council is. The working class as a whole will be involved in the organisations that constitute its state, the most backward as well as the most progressive elements. "Every cook will govern." In Lenin's major work on the state, the party is hardly mentioned. The function of the party is not to be the state, but rather to carry out continual agitation and propaganda among more backward elements of the class so as to raise their self-consciousness and self-reliance to the pitch that they will both set up workers' councils and fight to overthrow the forms of organisation of the bourgeois state. The soviet state is the highest concrete embodiment of the self-activity of the whole working class; the party is that section of the class that is most conscious of the world-historical implications of this self-activity.

The functions of the workers' state and of the party should be quite different (which is why there can be more than one party in a workers' state). One has to represent all the diverse interests of all the sections – geographical, industrial, etc – of the workers. It has to recognise in its mode of organisation all the heterogeneity of the class. The party, on the other hand, is built around those things that unite the class nationally and internationally. It constantly aims, by ideological persuasion, to overcome the heterogeneity of the class. It is concerned with national and international political principles, not parochial concerns of individual groups of workers. It can only persuade, not coerce these into accepting its lead. An organisation that is concerned with participating in the revolutionary overthrow of capitalism by the working class cannot conceive of substituting itself for the organs of. direct rule of that class. Such a perspective is only available to the social democratic or Stalinist party (and both have been too afraid of mass self-activity to attempt this substitution through revolutionary practice in advanced capitalist countries). Existing under capitalism, the revolutionary organisation will of necessity have a quite different structure to that of the workers' state that will arise in the process of overthrowing capitalism.[55] The revolutionary party will have to struggle within the institution of the workers' state for its principles as against those with opposed ones; this is only possible because it itself is not the workers' state.[56]

This enables us to see that Lenin's theory of the party and his theory of the state are not two separate entities, capable of being dealt with in isolation from one another. Until he developed the theory of the state, he tended to regard the Bolshevik Party as a peculiar adaptation to Russian circumstances. Given the social democratic (and later the Stalinist) conception of the party becoming the state, it is only natural for genuinely revolutionary and therefore democratic socialists not to want to restrict the party to the most advanced sections of the class, even if the need for such an organisation of the most conscious sections is recognised. This explains Rosa Luxemburg's ambiguity over the question of political organisation and theoretical clarity. It enables her to counterpose the "errors committed by a truly revolutionary movement" to the "infallibility of the cleverest central committee". But if the party and the institutions of class power are distinct (although one attempts to influence the other) the "infallibility" of the one is a central component in the process by which the other learns from its errors. It is Lenin who sees this. It is Lenin who draws the lessons, not (at least until the very end of her life) Luxemburg. It is not true that "for Marxists in the advanced industrial countries, Lenin's original position can much less serve as a guide than Rosa Luxemburg's".[57] The need is still to build an organisation of revolutionary Marxists that will subject their situation and that of the class as a whole to scientific scrutiny, will ruthlessly criticise their own mistakes and will, while engaging in the everyday struggles of the mass of workers, attempt to increase their independent self-activity by unremittingly opposing their ideological and practical subservience to the old society. A reaction against the identification of class and party elite made by both social democracy and stalinism is very healthy. It should not, however, prevent a clear-sighted perspective of what we have to do to overcome their legacy.

First published in *International Socialism* 35 (1st series), winter 1968

Students and the movement

The wave of student insurgency that followed the discovery of files on political activists at Warwick was the largest yet seen in Britain. Although in the past there have been the beginnings of national action among students, it has been on nothing like the present scale. For instance, the solidarity actions taken in solidarity with the London School of Economics (LSE) last year were almost everywhere confined to an already radicalised minority. What developed this time was a movement embracing something approaching the majority of students in more than half a dozen different centres, as well as significant minorities in more than a dozen others.

Eighteen months ago, in "Capitalism, Education and the Student Revolution", we tried to analyse the structural factors in modern capitalism that make likely periodic outbursts of student discontent: the massive expansion of higher education in response to capitalism's needs for increased numbers of technologists, scientists, manipulators and ideologues, and the resulting changes in both the class background and class destinies of students; the sons of the ruling class become only a small proportion of the total. This new mass of students (or at least its arts and humanities component) is particularly sensitive to the increasing irreconcilability between the liberal ideology it is taught to learn and propagate and the illiberal practices of late capitalism.

The post-Warwick events have once again underlined the explosiveness of the tensions created. In university after university large numbers of previously quiescent students have been moved into action by the spectacle of the authorities breaking with the tenets of their own liberal orthodoxy.

Institutions are questioned and ideas discussed as never before. This development not only worries the vice-chancellors. It also provides new opportunities for the revolutionary left.

Yet there is the danger that many of these will not be taken. For much of the left still seems unable to understand the simple realities of the student movement. On the one hand there are still those who regard protesting students as upper class kids having a freakout. On the other are those who see student activism as a substitute for building a revolutionary working class organisation – whether through talk of "red bases", of students as a "new revolutionary class", of "strategic minorities" or of an "international youth vanguard". Here two quite different things are confounded: a movement around liberal or reformist demands in which revolutionaries can play a key role and a movement of revolutionaries.

The precondition for effective intervention by the left among students is an understanding of the gap between its own ideas and the concerns of the mass of students. The level of these can only be raised if demands are put forward that most students are willing to fight for. If the left are patient enough, this should not be too difficult. An important feature of student movements is that they tend themselves to throw up demands that are *transitional*. Although liberal in form (e.g. for a degree of student control, for "opening the files", for ending racialist links) these cannot be satisfied for any length of time under capitalist society at its present stage. In fighting to impose them students not only "expose" the authorities, but also have to come to terms with the contradictory ideas in their own minds. For, liberals, particularly the professional liberals who officially lead the students, are unable to fight for such liberal demands in anything like a consistent fashion. Hence their constant tendency to narrow down the significance of demands until the established structure is hardly challenged (for example, from opening *all* files so as to guarantee against academic spying and blacklists, to the inspection of specific innocuous ones). Such equivocation continually endangers the movement – but it also forces many students into a debate that can only be of advantage to revolutionary ideas.

But here again the left often fails to make the best use of the situation. The other side of believing that a movement of students round liberal issues is really a revolutionary movement is a failure by the left to make known its own distinct view of society in its totality (and hence to explain why it alone is capable of consistently leading the struggle for liberal democratic demands).

Yet this is an essential task. For despite the genuine enthusiasm and mass involvement of the early stages of student struggles, in the long run these come to an impasse. For students do not have real power to transform society. They can question its pretensions, they can irritate the ruling class, but they cannot threaten it. Because the frustrations that express themselves in an outraged liberalism cannot be dealt with by confrontations in the universities alone – even the most massive mobilisations confined here eventually disintegrate.

Such a prospect seems remote to many involved in the recent upsurge. It seemed equally remote to the tens of thousands involved in the Springer action of only two years ago, to those who manned the barricades of May '68, to thousands around the "non-ideological" American New Left, to the successive generations of Japanese students who have "ignited" without success. Nearer home it seemed no closer to those who struggled in LSE 18 months ago.

Yet the German Students for a Democratic Society (SDS) *has* just formally dissolved itself at a half-empty conference; the American SDS fragments and further fragments; the remnants of those who fought back the CRS [French riot police] in the Latin Quarter tragically confront one another as well as the right in Nanterre and Vincennes. Out of a unified movement emerge on the one hand those like the Maoist Spontaeists or the Weathermen who futilely try to recreate a moment of solidarity and victory out of their own isolated actions; on the other those who have become part of wider and more realistic revolutionary organisations. In between are the majority who have still to find a way through to meaningful action, or long since gave up the attempt.

There is a good deal of life yet in the present student upsurge. It can annoy the authorities a deal more, as well as bring many more of its participants to a true comprehension of the class realities of our society. The revolutionary left must participate in it, attempting to give guidance and leadership, seeing its victories as our victories. But we must also be aware of its limitations, continually pointing out that the only force for carrying through a real transformation of society lies elsewhere and that students who seriously want to solve their own problems can only do so by becoming part of a revolutionary organisation that relates to aspirations and struggles of that class.

First published in *International Socialism* 43 (first series), April/May 1970

The workers' government

Over the last three years, there has been a major revision of the concept of "left governments". This was sparked off by the disastrous conclusion of the Chilean experience. While some currents, e.g. the International Socialists, saw it as showing once again the impossibility of the reformist road to socialism, other groups, notably *il Manifesto* in Italy, saw the election of such a government as being a first crucial step towards socialism.

By 1976, the analysis was being applied to Italy itself. The election programme of Avanguardia Operaia (AO) and PdUP (*il Manifesto* being a component in the latter) had as its main slogan the formation of a left government composed of the Communist Party, the Socialist Party, and perhaps the revolutionary left as well. Mass pressure, it was claimed, could prevent "the left government from stabilising the situation in the interests of capitalism" and "open the road for the working class to exercise power".

Since then, both organisations have split and one of the main points in the debate has been the role and limits of such a government.

In France, with the Socialist and Communist parties looking set to win a majority in next year's general elections, the debate within the revolutionary left has again taken up the concept. Whilst they have avoided the reformist traps of the Italian far left, the French groups often tend to see the left government as being an end in itself. Thus two key issues have been raised: firstly, can a government within bourgeois democracy "open the way to workers' power" and second, what should be the strategy of revolutionaries as the traditional workers' parties move to power?

What is a "left" or "workers'" government?

A government of the traditional workers' parties does not gain power merely because the majority of workers have voted for it. It also depends upon being allowed take office by the bourgeoisie; in other words they feel they are forced to give up their governmental positions to the leaders of the parties with a base in the workers' movement. They do this either because they feel it would be counterproductive to destroy the myths of parliamentary democracy merely to prevent the temporary loss of power or because they feel compelled to retreat before a mass upsurge of the workers' movement (as in Germany in 1918 and the SPD-USPD government, or in Spain with the Caballero government of September 1936).

However, it is *only* governmental positions that the bourgeoisie give up. They maintain their control over the major sectors of the state machine, over the key areas of the economy and over most of the means of communication. In other words, they retreat from the "front line" of the state, which in any case has less and less importance as the concentration of capital proceeds, but instead consolidate their power in the hierarchies of the state machine and in the economy.

Thus the "left government" is not a revolutionary government formed by the smashing of the bourgeois state. Rather it exists with capitalism and its state still intact.

At a time of major social crisis the bourgeoisie is prepared to concede even major material reforms on condition that their main agency of control – the state machine – is left intact. Short-term concessions can be made as long as the bourgeoisie retain the means to perpetuate their long-term control. Reforms can always be repealed and fresh attacks launched when the workers' movement has declined. But once the state has been destroyed, the bourgeoisie have no instrument to counterpose to the power of the working class.

Thus the left government will face a choice – either to cooperate with the instrument of the bourgeoisie or to set about destroying the state machine and replacing it by a structure of workers' power through councils and militia. And this choice will be forced upon it almost immediately. After all, Allende was only allowed into power on condition that he would leave the army intact. Any left government would be subject to a whole number of measures aimed at forcing it to cooperate with the state.

Thus a left government would in fact leave the power of the state untouched unless it moved decisively against the existing structures from the beginning. For instance, in republican Spain in the two months after the partial defeat of Franco's coup of July 1936 the bourgeoisie had lost control over much of industry. The state machine was splintered almost beyond repair and the workers' militias had a near monopoly of armed power. The bourgeois liberals in government found themselves almost helpless.

Therefore in September 1936, governmental power was allowed to pass into the hands of Largo Caballero, the "left" socialist. Caballero could achieve for the bourgeoisie what the liberals alone never could – the reconstruction of the state machine, since he was trusted by the masses. He accepted that the only way a "constitutional" left government could function was through reliance upon the remnants of the old state machine and therefore used his ideological influence (along with that of the other workers' organisations) to rebuild the state. By May 1937 the job had been done so well that the state hierarchies could replace Caballero with someone much more acceptable to their interests. Caballero was thrown out by the state machine he had rebuilt; just as Allende was murdered by the same generals whose power he had promised to respect. Yet the Spanish working class in 1936 had the power to destroy the state and the will to construct their own. By relying on the old state, Caballero prevented the growth of the organs of workers' power, his only defence against the day when the bourgoisie decided to get rid of him, and any "leftism" that he represented.

Such a tendency to collaborate with the state machine is not *primarily* a consequence of the existence within such governments of bourgeois parties. Even a "pure workers' government" made up entirely of the traditional parties of the working class will still be in de facto coalition with the bourgeoisie through the state. The policies of Allende were not determined by the bourgeois component (the small Radical Party) in his government. What was far more important was the constitutional agreement of 1970 not to interfere with the hierarchies of the state and his insistence (like all reformists) that the state was a neutral instrument that could be used in the building of socialism.

Some tendencies in the left would say that the above analysis is "primitive" and mechanistic; that it crudely equates the mass Euro-Communist parties of today with the pre-war parties of Social Democracy. But what elements have changed since then?

It is true that the Euro-Communist parties are mass parties with a strong, militant membership but this was also the case with social democracy, for instance in Germany in 1918. Yet the leaders of such mass parties have presided over the reconstruction of the state and their base have been powerless to prevent them from within the party structures. The point is that it is not the mass base or lack of it which prevents a party from collaborating with the state. The base may provide some resistance to the government's policies but unless it forces its government to decisively break with the state and the bourgeoisie from the beginning, the path of Spain, Chile or Germany will be retraced. Is it really feasible that the base will be able to impose this on Berlinguer, Marchais or Mitterand?

Throughout Europe social democracy in power has moved rapidly to the right. In Britain, Germany and Portugal it is social democratic parties that are attacking the working class movement and stabilising the rule of capital. The PSI or PSF will attempt to do the same.

The role of the Communist parties will be similar. The programme of the PCI is explicitly a policy of capitalist recovery and rationalisation of the state. They reject in advance the need to break from the state or the bourgeoisie. In fact they want a governmental alliance with its political representatives.

Further, the leadership of the Communist parties is firmly entrenched within the parties as are their politics. *Il Manifesto's* strategy of gradually winning the party to the left, cannot take place without the splitting of the most militant sections of the party to a revolutionary pole.

Il Manifesto's strategy of entry into the left government as a left influence within it also has its historical precedents. The left government in Catalonia in 1936 also had a *revolutionary* pole within it – the POUM, which had a far greater base and spoke far more eloquently of the need to replace the bourgeois state by soviets than *il Manifesto* in Italy. But the POUM had to pay the price of its participation in such a government. Whenever there was a clash between the self-activity of its base and the need of the bourgeois state machine for *stability* in order *to get things done* the POUM accepted the need to discipline their own members and to destroy the autonomy of the workers' movement. Thus in November 1936 the leader of the POUM, Andrais Nin, had to persuade his members to dissolve the revolutionary committees that had displaced the state in Lerida. Six months later when the state machine had been rebuilt, it was to collaborate in the murder of Andrais Nin.

What applied to the anarchists and the POUM in the revolutionary ferment of Spain in 1936 will apply with equal force to the PCI and the leaders of *il Manifesto*. One cannot have one foot in the workers' movement and another in the camp of collaboration with the state. As the workers' movement grows, it will conflict with the bourgeois state. Revolutionaries must be based in the class in order to give it direction when that clash comes.

The proclaimed strategy of the left governments in Italy and France is bound to lead to that conflict. Their strategy is based on reforms in a time of capitalist crisis, and as such will be inherently unstable. Capitalism will demand the restoration of its privileges. The economy of the country will deteriorate as it is still locked into the world system which demands not reforms but increased sacrifices. As the bourgeoisie become increasingly worried with declining profit margins, economic sabotage will increase.

Mass right-wing movements can arise unless there exists a clear left wing alternative to the government, which mobilises workers against that government from an anti-capitalist position.

In summary, we can say that a left government has never broken decisively with the state machine and led the way to workers' power. In Germany in 1918, the government itself was the instrument of counter-revolution as it smashed the Spartacist revolt against the existing state. In Chile, the government's collaboration with the state meant that alternative organs of workers' power were suppressed or neutralised by the government and, as splits appeared in the base of the Popular Unity government, the armed state machine felt strong enough to destroy both government and movement.

In Italy and France, it is more likely that if and when the left comes to power, both Gaullists and Christian Democrats will use the opportunity to reorganise their forces as more efficient instruments of bourgeois rule. They will return reinvigorated as the working class become demoralised with the attempts of their parties to rationalise capitalism. Already Chirac in France is grooming himself as the leader of this reaction.

But there is a fourth possible outcome and that is the revolutionary overthrow of the government from the left and the creation of a workers' state. But this demands a clear understanding by revolutionaries of the necessary strategy to achieve this goal.

The position of the Third International

The debate in 1922 on the issue was the outcome of a struggle led by Lenin and Trotsky to force the ultra-left elements in the Comintern to accept the tactic of the united front as a way to break the hold of the social democrats on concrete questions. Why should this activity not culminate in a programme for a joint workers' government?

Unfortunately, it cannot be said that the discussion clarified the issue. The discussion was dominated by Zinoviev and Radek. Both argued strongly that the fight for a joint communist-socialist government was the logical outcome of agitation for a workers' united front. They implied that such a government would almost automatically lead to a deepened level of struggle and from there to the dictatorship of the proletariat.

Thus Radek's speech was extremely mechanistic:

> Where the Labour government comes into existence, it will merely be a stepping stone to the dictatorship of the proletariat, for the bourgeoisie will not tolerate a Labour government even though founded on democratic principles. The social democratic worker will find himself compelled to become a communist, in order to defend his rule.

But the *democratic principles* on which the government would be based are precisely those of working within the framework laid down by the state – structures designed to make impotent ministers with radical ideas. Further, the dominant forces in such a government are not social democratic workers who might change their ideas under the impact of events but the reformist bureaucrats who will do all in their power to deflate the struggle. Instead of this schema it is far more likely that the communist leaders would be sucked into the structures of government.

The actual motion passed was far more guarded than the speeches of Zinoviev and Radek. Strict conditions were laid down to ensure that the government "arose from the struggle of the masses". But it was still seen as inevitable that such a government would "meet immediately with the most stubborn resistance of the bourgeoisie". Thus "the most elementary tasks of a workers' government must consist in the arming of the proletariat".

There can be little doubt that the debate was confused. In part, this is to be expected; after all there was very little experience of governments being made up solely of workers' parties. Trotsky could write in 1923, for instance:

> [Once we] rally the majority of workers to this slogan [of a workers' government]...the stock of Renaudel, Blum and Jouhaux [the reformist leaders] will not be worth much, because these gentlemen are able to maintain themselves only through an alliance with the bourgeoisie.

Unfortunately, 55 years of bitter experience have shown that reformist governments without the participation of the bourgeoisie are quite possible without capitalism crumbling, and have often been used to strengthen its rule.

But this is not to say that under no circumstances can a *real* workers' government come into being before the dictatorship of the proletariat. In the past there have been workers' governments whose "most elementary task is the arming of the proletariat", though they were extreme exceptions. For instance in Hungary and Bavaria of 1919 bourgeois power virtually collapsed, and the government passed into the hands of people who based themselves on the slogans of soviet power. The workers' government came into being and afterwards had to create the structure of proletarian power – workers' militia, workers' councils and so forth.

The major component in these governments was openly revolutionary, and their key task was to create a new workers' state before the bourgeoisie could regroup. In Bavaria the Communist leader Leviné refused to join the first soviet government since it was made up of centrists and reformists who would not have been prepared to arm the workers and establish real workers' councils. Yet only such moves, he correctly insisted, could put the workers' government on a firm footing – by establishing the dictatorship of the proletariat. To establish a workers' government on any lesser basis would lead to counter-revolution.

Lenin's attitude was similar. In the weeks before October he insisted that the only way forward was for a government, *based on the soviets*, in which all the key positions were to be in the hands of the Bolsheviks. However, recognising that the Bolsheviks were still a minority in the working class, he stated that if the other socialist parties were to form such a government the Bolsheviks would act as a "loyal opposition'"which would continue to criticise its failings in front of the class. The Bolsheviks would take no responsibility for its policies and maintain their independence from it. The task was to win the masses from the reformist parties to Bolshevism, so as to be able to replace the government with the dictatorship of the proletariat in the future.

It is this legacy that must be adapted to today's world, rather than a wholesale adoption of the theses of the Comintern.

Revolutionary tactics for reformist governments

Although a left government cannot steer a path to socialism, revolutionaries are not indifferent as to whether such a government comes to power. Even though the bourgeoisie has only retreated from the frontline positions and still retains control of the economy and the state, immense possibilities can be opened up.

In both France and Italy the entry into government of both communists and socialists for the first time since the late 1940s would lead to increased confidence and perhaps, militancy of the workers' movement. To this extent the election of a left government provides the possibility of a major advance of the workers' movement, if the masses take advantage of the temporary confusion of the bourgeoisie. But the advance is not inevitable: the government will be attempting to stabilise the situation, and the bourgeoisie will be regrouping. If the workers fall into the delusion that they have taken power, rather than crossed the first barrier – if, in other words, they rely on the government rather than their own activity – then their *advance* will be limited to reforms which can be clawed back by a resurgent bourgeoisie. Hence the all-important paradox: the advent of a left government will only strengthen the workers' movement inasmuch as the class, or at least its vanguard, do not have illusions in this government. The more independent and strong the workers' movement is, the more reforms it will force from the government. The more it relies on its own forms of organisation, the more the way is open to a *fundamental* change in the balance of power between the workers and their allies and the bourgeoisie. But the more it is tied to the structures of state power, the greater is the possibility of bourgeois reaction.

This means that the role of revolutionaries is *not* to enter such a government "in order to accentuate the contradictions within it", for to do this is to precisely tie the workers to the bourgeoisie.

Rather the job of revolutionaries is to break the illusions that the workers have in a "left" government – and that means taking up all the partial limited struggles of workers, generalising them and leading them even if they conflict with the strategy of the government. In short, it is to organise a left opposition to the government, seeking to replace the reliance on the state with the self-organisation of workers.

Of course, tactically there are times when the revolutionary left defends the left government or perhaps particular measures; when it is open to attack from the right and the bourgeoisie trying to regain positions it has lost. But this should never obscure the fundamental positions that the revolutionary party has to adopt: the strategy of developing working class forms of power, which by definition will conflict with the bourgeois state power still in existence, in order to overthrow the government from the left and replace it with a workers' state.

Otherwise, revolutionaries can find themselves in the same situation the Chilean left found itself in occasionally – appearing to defend unpopular governmental decisions against movements of the workers and petty bourgeoisie, so allowing the forces of the right to manipulate those movements.

Breaking the links

The possibility of a government controlled by their own reformist parties, particularly after long years of rule by the parties of the bourgeoisie, can be of great attractiveness to many workers. It appears as a precondition for any fundamental change in society. Now revolutionaries must recognise firstly that this is a delusion. The workers cannot change society merely by their parties taking governmental power but leaving the state intact. Secondly we must also recognise that for many workers this delusion represents an increase in class consciousness; they are beginning to think in terms of their class controlling society rather than it being run to openly capitalist criteria.

Our job is to build on the increase in class consciousness but at the same time as breaking down the delusions in the role of a left government.

Effectively we have to say to non-revolutionary workers, "You believe that a left government can change society in the interests of the working class; we do not. But we will fight alongside you to put your views to the test. However, we repeat that you should rely on your own struggles, not put your faith in your political leaders."

The slogan of the left or workers' government is therefore not seen as a magic panacea; rather it is a tactical slogan that we support but subordinate to our general politics of developing the workers' struggle.

Our task is to raise slogans that mobilise workers in defence of their interests, to form unity in action with reformist workers and in the struggle to break down the illusions in the 'left government'. It is above all in action that consciousness changes.

That is why the Italian revolutionary left are so mistaken when they talk of "an alternative strategy to that of the PCI". They attempt to give solutions to a crisis of capitalism, without posing its overthrow. Thus they attempt to solve the balance of payments crisis of Italian capitalism by proposing rationing and import controls. But to solve any balance of payments crisis fundamentally you have to remove Italy from the capitalist system and that means the overthrow of the domestic bourgeoisie as a precondition. The left here adopt a basically nationalistic viewpoint which attempts to solve the Italian crisis at the expense of fellow workers in Britain or Japan or Germany. For import controls in one country means unemployment in another.

On a more general level, the revolutionary left cannot propose alternative strategies for the solution of the crisis of capitalism except by posing its overthrow. What it could propose however is a strategy for dealing with the effects of the crisis: a strategy against unemployment, against inflation, etc which workers can implement through their power in the workplaces and as a mass force. Such a fight would lead to the strengthening of workers' organisation and consciousness and point to the overthrow of capitalism. In such a movement unity would be formed between revolutionaries and the base of the mass reformist parties. It is this unity in action over partial objectives that can break workers from reformism as they see their leaders constantly vacillating between their base and the demands of capital.

The breaking of workers from reformism will not occur as the Italian left seems to think by proposing a radicalised version of the reformists' programme.

Faced with two reformist programmes (and that of AO/PdUP is to the *right* of the British Communist Party's) workers will choose that put forward by the reformists given it is the PCI and not the revolutionaries who will be the main force in a "left government" and thus capable of implementing the programme. Further, reformists and revolutionaries cannot unite in struggle around such a programme; they can only polemicise against each other.

The Italian left has fallen into precisely the trap that AO warned against only three years ago:

> Revolutionaries must not give advice to the PCI in its movement to government. That would be to tail the reformist strategy, to make the revolutionary process depend on their actions. It would mean not working to build an autonomous revolutionary strategy both on the level of self-organisation and in terms of politics. Finally this advice would be a source of confusion for the masses.

The sooner AO rediscovers its original strategy, the sooner will a start be made to clearing up the chaos in the Italian left.

By Chris Harman and Tim Potter. First published in the International Discussion Bulletin of the Socialist Workers Party in 1977

3: Russia and Eastern Europe

How the revolution was lost

The two revolutions

The period between the two revolutions of February and October 1917 was moulded by two concurrent processes. The first occurred in the towns, and was a very rapid growth of working class consciousness. By the July days, the industrial workers at least seem to have arrived at an understanding of the different interests of the classes in the revolution. In the countryside, a different form of class differentiation took place. This was not between a propertied class and a class that could not even aspire to individual ownership of property. Rather it was between two property-owning classes. On the one hand the landowners, on the other the peasants. The latter were not socialist in intention. Their aim was to seize the estates of the landowners, but to divide these upon an individualistic basis. In this movement even kulaks, wealthy farmers, could participate.

The revolution could not have taken place without the simultaneous occurrence of these two processes. What tied them together was not, however, an identity of ultimate aim. Rather it was the fact that for contingent historical reasons the industrial bourgeoisie could not break politically with the large landowners. Its inability to do this pushed the peasantry (which effectively included the army) and the workers into the same camp:

> In order to realise the soviet state, there was required the drawing together and mutual penetration of two factors belonging to completely different historic species: a peasant war – that is a movement characteristic of the dawn of bourgeois development – and a proletarian insurrection, the movement signalising its decline. [1]

The urban insurrection could not have succeeded but for the sympathy of the largely peasant army. Nor could the peasants have waged a successful struggle unless led and welded together by a centralised, external force. In Russia of 1917 the only possible such force was the organised working class. It was this possibility of drawing the peasantry behind it at the crucial moment that made it possible for the workers to hold power in the towns.

The bourgeoisie and its landowning allies were expropriated. But the classes which participated in this expropriation shared no simple long-term common interest. In the towns was a class whose very existence depended upon collective activity. In the countryside was a class whose members would only unite even amongst themselves momentarily to seize the land, but would then till it individually. Once the act of seizure and defence of that seizure was over, only external inducements could bind them to any state.

The revolution, then, was really a dictatorship of the workers over other classes in the towns – in the major towns the rule of the majority in soviets – and a dictatorship of the towns over the country. In the first period of the division of the estates this dictatorship could rely upon peasant support, indeed, was defended by peasant bayonets. But what was to happen afterwards?

This question had preoccupied the Russian socialists themselves long before the revolution. The realisation that a socialist revolution in Russia would be hopelessly lost in the peasant mass was one reason why all the Marxists in Russia (including Lenin, but excluding Trotsky and at first Parvus) had seen the forthcoming revolution as a bourgeois one. When Parvus and Trotsky first suggested that the revolution might produce a socialist government, Lenin wrote:

> This cannot be, because such a revolutionary dictatorship can only have stability...based on the great majority of the people. The Russian proletariat constitutes now a minority of the Russian population.

He maintained this view right up to 1917. When he did come to accept and fight for the possibility of a socialist outcome for the revolution, it was because he saw it as one stage in a worldwide revolution that would give the minority working class in Russia protection against foreign intervention and aid to reconcile the peasantry to its rule. Eight months before the October Revolution he wrote to Swiss workers that "the Russian proletariat cannot by its own forces victoriously complete the socialist revolution". Four months after the revolution (on 7 March

1918) he repeated, "The absolute truth is that without a revolution in Germany we shall perish."

The Civil War

The first years of soviet rule seemed to bear out the perspective of world revolution. The period 1918-19 was characterised by social upheavals unseen since 1948. In Germany and Austria military defeat was followed by the destruction of the monarchy. Everywhere there was talk of soviets. In Hungary and Bavaria soviet governments actually took power – although only briefly. In Italy the factories were occupied. Yet the heritage of 50 years of gradual development was not to be erased so rapidly. The old social democratic and trade union leaders moved into the gap left by the discredited bourgeois parties. The communist left on the other hand still lacked the organisation to respond to this. It acted when there was no mass support; when there was mass support it failed to act.

Even so the stabilisation of Europe after 1919 was at best precarious. In every European country the social structure received severe threats within the subsequent 15 years. And the experience of both the communist parties and the working class had put them into a far better position to understand what was happening.

The Russian Bolsheviks did not, however, intend to wait upon the revolution abroad. The defence of the soviet republic and incitement to revolution abroad seemed inseparable. For the time being anyway, the tasks at hand in Russia were determined, not by the Bolshevik leaders, but by the international imperialist powers. These had begun a "crusade" against the soviet republic. White and foreign armies had to be driven back before any other questions could be considered. In order to do this, every resource available had to be utilised.

By a mixture of popular support, revolutionary ardour and, at times, it seemed, pure will, the counter-revolutionary forces were driven out (although in the soviet Far East they continued to operate until 1924). But the price paid was enormous.

This cannot be counted in merely material terms. But in these alone it was great. What suffered above all was industrial and agricultural production. In 1920 the production of pig iron was only 3 percent of the pre-war figure; of hemp 10 percent; flax, 25 percent; cotton, 11 percent; beets, 15 percent. This implied privation, hardship, famine. But much more. The dislocation of industrial production was also the dislocation of the working class. It was reduced to 43 percent of its former numbers. The others were returned to their villages or dead on the battlefield. In purely quantitative terms, the class that had led the revolution, the class whose democratic processes had constituted the living core of soviet power, was halved in importance. In real terms the situation was even worse. What remained was not even half of that class, forced into collective action by the very nature of its life situation. Industrial output was only 18 percent of the pre-war figure, labour productivity was only one third of what it had been. To keep alive, workers could not rely on what their collective product would buy. Many resorted to direct barter of their products – or even parts of their machines – with peasants for food. Not only was the leading class of the revolution decimated, but the ties linking its members together were fast disintegrating. The very personnel in the factories were not those who had constituted the core of the revolutionary movement of 1917. The most militant workers had quite naturally fought most at the front, and suffered most casualties. Those that survived were needed not only in the factories, but as cadres in the army, or as commissars to keep the administrators operating the state machine. Raw peasants from the countryside, without socialist traditions or aspirations, took their place.

But what was to be the fate of the revolution if the class that made it ceased to exist in any meaningful sense? This was not a problem that the Bolshevik leaders could have foreseen. They had always said that isolation of the revolution would result in its destruction by foreign armies and domestic counter-revolution. What confronted them now was the success of counter-revolution from abroad in destroying the class that had led the revolution while leaving intact the state apparatus built up by it. The revolutionary power had survived, but radical changes were being produced in its internal composition.

Soviet power to Bolshevik dictatorship

The revolutionary institutions of 1917 – above all, the soviets – were organically connected with the class that had led the revolution. Between the aspirations and intentions of their members and those of the workers who elected them, there could be no gap. While the mass were Menshevik, the soviets were Menshevik; when the mass began to follow the Bolsheviks, so did the soviets. The Bolshevik Party was merely the body of coordinated class-conscious militants who could frame policies and suggest causes of action alongside other such bodies, in the soviets as in the factories themselves. Their coherent views and self-discipline meant that they could act to implement policies effectively – but only if the mass of workers would follow them.

Even consistent opponents of the Bolsheviks recognised this. Their leading Menshevik critic wrote:

> Understand please, that before us after all is a victorious uprising of the proletariat – almost the entire proletariat supports Lenin and expects its social liberation from the uprising[2]

Until the Civil War was well under way, this democratic dialectic of party and class could continue. The Bolsheviks held power as the majority party in the soviets. But other parties continued to exist there too. The Mensheviks continued to operate legally and compete with the Bolsheviks for support until June 1918.

The decimation of the working class changed all this. Of necessity the soviet institutions took on a life independently of the class they had arisen from. Those workers and peasants who fought the Civil War could not govern themselves collectively from their places in the factories. The socialist workers spread over the length and breadth of the war zones had to be organised and coordinated by a centralised governmental apparatus independent of their direct control – at least temporarily.

It seemed to the Bolsheviks that such a structure could not be held together unless it contained within it only those who wholeheartedly supported the revolution – that is, only the Bolsheviks. The Right Social Revolutionaries were instigators of the counter-revolution. The Left Social Revolutionaries were willing to resort to terror when they disagreed with government policy. As for the Mensheviks, their policy was one of support of the Bolsheviks against the counter-revolution, with the demand that the latter hand over power to the Constituent Assembly (one of the chief demands of the counter-revolution). In practice this meant that the party contained both supporters and opponents of the soviet power. Many of its members went over to the side of the Whites (e.g. Menshevik organisations in the Volga area were sympathetic to the counter-revolutionary Samara government, and one member of the Menshevik central committee, Ivan Maisky – later Stalin's ambassador – joined it).[3] The response of the Bolsheviks was to allow the party's members their freedom (at least, most of the time), but to prevent them acting as an effective political force – e.g. they were allowed no press after June 1918 except for three months in the following year.

In all this the Bolsheviks had no choice. They could not give up power just because the class they represented had dissolved itself while fighting to defend that power. Nor could they tolerate the propagation of ideas that undermined the basis of its power – precisely because the working class itself no longer existed as an agency collectively organised so as to be able to determine its own interests.

Of necessity the soviet state of 1917 had been replaced by the single-party state of 1920 onwards. The soviets that remained were increasingly just a front for Bolshevik power (although other parties, e.g. the Mensheviks, continued to operate in them as late as 1920). In 1919, for instance, there were no elections to the Moscow Soviet for over 18 months.[4]

Kronstadt and the NEP

Paradoxically, the end of the Civil War did not alleviate this situation, but in many ways aggravated it. For with the end of the immediate threat of counter-revolution, the cord that had bound together the two revolutionary processes – workers' power in the towns and peasant uprisings in the country – was cut. Having gained control over the land, the peasants lost interest in the collectivist revolutionary ideals of October. They were motivated by individual aspirations arising out of their individualistic form of work. Each sought to maximise his own standard of living through his activities on his own plot of land. Indeed, the only thing which could now unite peasants into a coherent group was opposition to the taxes and forcible collections of grain carried out in order to feed the urban populations.

The high point of this opposition came a week before the tenth party Congress. An uprising of sailors broke out in the Kronstadt fortress, which guarded the approaches to Petrograd. Many people since have treated what happened next as the first break between the Bolshevik regime and its socialist intentions. The fact that the Kronstadt sailors were one of the main drives of the 1917 Revolution has often been used as an argument for this. Yet at the time no one in the Bolshevik Party – not even the workers' opposition which claimed to represent the antipathy of many workers to the regime – had any doubts as to what it was necessary to do. The reason was simple. Kronstadt in 1920 was not Kronstadt of 1917. The class composition of its sailors had changed. The best socialist elements had long ago gone off to fight in the army in the front line. They were replaced in the main by peasants whose devotion to the revolution was that of their class. This was reflected in the demands of the uprising: soviets without Bolsheviks and a free market in agriculture. The Bolshevik leaders could not accede to such demands. It would have meant liquidation of the socialist aims of the revolution without struggle. For all its faults, it was precisely the Bolshevik Party that had alone wholeheartedly supported soviet power, while the other parties, even the socialist parties, had vacillated between it and the Whites. It was to the Bolsheviks that all the best militants had been attracted. Soviets without Bolsheviks could only mean soviets without the party which had consistently sought to express the socialist, collectivist aims of the working class in the revolution. What was expressed in Kronstadt was the fundamental divergence of interest, in the long run, between the two classes that had made the revolution. The suppression of the uprising should be seen not as an attack on the socialist content of the revolution, but as a desperate attempt, using force, to prevent the developing peasant opposition to its collectivist ends from destroying it.[5]

Yet the fact that Kronstadt could occur was an omen. For it questioned the whole leading role of the working class in the revolution. This was being maintained not by the superior economic mode that the working class represented, not by its higher labour productivity, but by physical force. And this force was not being wielded directly by the armed workers, but by a party tied to the working class only indirectly, by its ideas, not directly as in the days of 1917.

Such a policy was necessary. But there was little in it that socialists could have supported in any other situation. Instead of being "the self-conscious, independent movement of the immense majority in the interest of the immense majority", the revolution in Russia had reached the stage where it involved the exploitation of the country by the towns, maintained through naked physical force. It was clear to all groups in the Bolshevik Party that this meant the revolution must remain in danger of being overthrown by peasant insurrections.

There seemed to be only one course open. This was to accept many of the peasant demands, while maintaining a strong, centralised socialist state apparatus. This the New Economic Policy (NEP) attempted to do. Its aim was to reconcile peasants to the regime and to encourage economic development by giving a limited range of freedom to private commodity production. The state and the state-owned industries were to operate as just one element in an economy governed by the needs of peasant production and the play of market forces.

The party, the state and the working class 1921-28

In the period of the NEP the claim of Russia to be in any way "socialist" could no longer be justified either by the relationship of the working class to the state it had originally created or by the nature of internal economic relations. The workers did not exercise power and the economy was not planned. But the state, the "body of armed men" that controlled and policed society, was in the hands of a party that was motivated by socialist intentions. The direction of its policies, it seemed, would be socialist.

Yet the situation was more complex than this. First, the state institutions that dominated Russian society were far from identical with the militant socialist party of 1917. Those who had been in the Bolshevik Party at the time of the February Revolution were committed socialists who had taken enormous risks in resisting tsarist oppression to express their ideals. Even four years of civil war and isolation from the working masses could not easily destroy their socialist aspirations. But in 1919 these constituted only a tenth of the party, by 1922 a fortieth. In the revolution and Civil War, the party had undergone a continuous process of growth. In part this reflected the tendency of all militant workers and convinced socialists to join in. But it was also a result of other tendencies. Once the working class itself had been decimated, the party had had to take it upon itself to control all soviet-run areas. This it could only do by increasing its own size. Further, once it was clear who was winning the Civil War, many individuals with little or no socialist convictions attempted to enter the party. The party itself was thus far from being a homogeneous socialist force. At best, only its leading elements and most militant members could be said to be really part of the socialist tradition.

This internal dilution of the party was paralleled by a corresponding phenomenon in the state apparatus itself. In order to maintain control over Russian society, the Bolshevik Party had been forced to use thousands of members of the old tsarist bureaucracy in order to maintain a functioning governmental machine. In theory the Bolsheviks were to direct the work of these in a socialist direction. In practice, old habits and methods of work, pre-revolutionary attitudes towards the masses in particular, often prevailed. Lenin was acutely aware of the implications of this:

"What we lack is clear enough," he said at the March 1922 Party Congress. "The ruling stratum of the communists is lacking in culture. Let us look at

Moscow. This mass of bureaucrats – who is leading whom? The 4,700 responsible communists, the mass of bureacrats, or the other way round? I do not believe you can honestly say the communists are leading this mass. To put it honestly, they are not the leaders but the led."

At the end of 1922, he described the state apparatus as "borrowed from tsarism and hardly touched by the soviet world...a bourgeois and tsarist mechanism".[6] In the 1920 controversy over the role of the trade unions he argued:

Ours is not actually a workers' state, but a workers' and peasants' state... But that is not all. Our party programme shows that ours is a workers' state with bureaucratic distortions.[7]

The real situation was even worse than this. It was not just the case that the old Bolsheviks were in a situation where the combined strength of hostile class forces and bureaucratic inertness made their socialist aspirations difficult to realise. These aspirations themselves could not remain forever uncorrupted by the hostile environment. The exigencies of building a disciplined army out of an often indifferent peasant mass had inculcated into many of the best party members authoritarian habits. Under the NEP the situation was different, but still far from the democratic interaction of leaders and led that constitutes the essence of socialist democracy. Now many party members found themselves having to control society by coming to terms with the small trader, the petty capitalist, the kulak. They had to represent the interests of the workers' state as against these elements – but not as in the past through direct physical confrontation. There had to be limited cooperation with them. Many party members seemed more influenced by this immediate and very tangible relationship with petty-bourgeois elements than by their intangible ties with a weak and demoralised working class.

Above all the influence of the old bureaucracy in which its members were immersed penetrated the party. Its isolation from class forces outside itself that would sustain its rule meant that the party had to exert over itself an iron discipline. Thus at the tenth Party Congress, although it was presumed that discussion would continue within the party,[8] the establishment of formal factions was "temporarily" banned. But this demand for inner cohesion easily degenerated into an acceptance of bureaucratic modes of control within the party. There had been complaints about these by opposition elements in the party as early as April 1920. By 1922 even Lenin could write that "we have a bureaucracy not only in the soviet institutions, but in the institutions of the party".

The erosion of inner-party democracy is best shown by the fate of successive oppositions to the central leadership. In 1917 and 1918 free discussion within the party, with the right of different groups to organise around platforms, was taken for granted. Lenin himself was in a minority in the party on at least two occasions (at the time of his *April Theses* and nearly a year later during the Brest-Litovsk negotiations). In November 1917 it was possible for those Bolsheviks who disagreed with the party taking power alone, to resign from the government so as to force its hand without disciplinary action being taken against them. Divisions within the party over the question of the advance on Warsaw and over the role of the trade unions were discussed quite openly in the party press. As late as 1921 the Programme of the Workers' Opposition was printed in a quarter of a million copies by the party itself, and two members of the opposition elected to the Central Committee. In 1923 when the Left Opposition developed, it was still possible for it to express its views in *Pravda*, although there were ten articles defending the leadership to every one opposing it.

Yet throughout this period the possibilities of any opposition acting effectively were diminished. After the tenth Party Congress the Workers' Opposition was banned. By 1923 the opposition Platform of the 46 wrote that "the secretarial hierarchy of the party to an ever greater extent recruits the membership of conferences and congresses".[9] Even a supporter of the leadership and editor of *Pravda*, Bukharin, depicted the typical functioning of the party as completely undemocratic:

> The secretaries of the nuclei are usually appointed by the district committees, and note that the districts do not even try to have their candidates accepted by these nuclei, but content themselves with appointing these or those comrades. As a rule, putting the matter to a vote takes place according to a method that is taken for granted. The meeting is asked: "Who is against?" and in as much as one fears more or less to speak up against, the appointed candidate finds himself elected.[10]

The real extent of bureaucratisation was fully revealed when the "triumvirate" that had taken over the leadership of the party during the illness of Lenin split. Towards the end of 1925 Zinoviev, Kamenev and Krupskaya moved into opposition to the party centre, now controlled by Stalin. Zinoviev was head of the party in Leningrad. As such he controlled the administrative machine of the northern capital and several influential newspapers. At the 14th Party Congress every delegate from

Leningrad supported his opposition to the centre. Yet within weeks of the defeat of his opposition, all sections of the party in Leningrad, with the exception of a few hundred inveterate oppositionists, were voting resolutions supporting Stalin's policies. All that was required to accomplish this was the removal from office of the heads of the city party administration. Who controlled the bureaucracy controlled the party. When Zinoviev controlled it, it was oppositional. Now that Stalin had added the city to the nationwide apparatus he controlled, it became an adherent of his policies. With a change of leaders a Zinovievist monolith was transformed into a Stalinist monolith.

This rise of bureaucracy in the soviet apparatus and the party began as a result of the decimation of the working class in the Civil War. But it continued even when industry began to recover and the working class began to grow with the NEP. Economic recovery rather than raising the position of the working class within the "workers' state" depressed it.

In purely material terms the concessions made to the peasant in the NEP worsened the (relative) position of the worker.

> Everywhere acclaimed under war communism as the eponymous hero of the dictatorship of the proletariat, he was in danger of becoming the stepchild of the NEP. In the economic crisis of 1923 neither the defenders of the official policy nor those who contested it in the name of the development of industry found it necessary to treat the grievances or the interests of the industrial worker as a matter of major concern.[11]

But it was not only vis-a-vis the peasant that the status of the worker fell; it also fell compared with that of the directors and managers of industry. Whereas in 1922, 65 percent of managing personnel were officially classified as workers, and 35 percent as non-workers, a year later these figures were almost reversed, only 36 percent being workers and 64 percent non-workers.[12] The "red industrialists" began to emerge as a privileged group, with high salaries, and through "one-man management" in the factories, able to hire and fire at will. At the same time widespread unemployment became endemic to the soviet economy, rising to a level of one and a quarter million in 1923-24.

The divisions in the party 1921-29

Men make history, but in circumstances not of their own making. In the process they change both those circumstances and themselves. The

Bolshevik Party was no more immune to this reality than any other group in history has been. In attempting to hold together the fabric of Russian society in the chaos of civil war, counter-revolution and famine, their socialist intentions were a factor determining the course of history, but the social forces they had to work with to do this could not leave the party members themselves unchanged. Holding the Russia of the NEP together meant mediating between different social classes so as to prevent disruptive clashes. The revolution could only survive if the party and state satisfied the needs of different, often antagonistic, classes. Arrangements had to be made to satisfy the individualistic aspirations of the peasants, as well as the collectivist democratic aims of socialism. In the process, the party, which had been lifted above the different social classes, had to reflect within its own structure their differences. The pressures of the different classes on the party caused different sections of the party to define their socialist aspirations in terms of the interests of different classes. The one class with the capacity for exercising genuinely socialist pressures – the working class – was the weakest, the most disorganised, the least able to exert such pressures.

The Left Opposition

There can be no doubt that in terms of its ideas, the Left Opposition was the faction in the party that adhered most closely to the revolutionary socialist tradition of Bolshevism. It refused to redefine socialism to mean either a slowly developing peasant economy or accumulation for the sake of accumulation. It retained the view of workers' democracy as central to socialism. It refused to subordinate the world revolution to the demands of the chauvinistic and reactionary slogan of building "socialism in one country".

Yet the Left Opposition could not be said to be in any direct sense the "proletarian" faction within the party. For in the Russia of the twenties, the working class was the class that less than any other exerted pressure upon the party. After the Civil War, it was rebuilt in conditions which made its ability to fight for its own ends weak. Unemployment was high; the most militant workers had either died in the Civil War or been lifted into the bureaucracy; much of the class was composed of peasants fresh from the countryside. Its typical attitude was not one of support for the opposition, but rather apathy towards political discussions, which made it easily manipulable from above – at least most of the time. The Left

Opposition was in the situation, common to socialists, of having a socialist programme for working class action when the workers themselves were too tired and dispirited to fight.

But it was not only the apathy of the workers that created difficulties for the Opposition. It was also its own recognition of economic realities. Its argument emphasised that the objective lack of resources would make life hard whatever policies were followed. It stressed both the need to develop industry internally and the necessity for the revolution to spread as a means to doing this. But in the short term it could offer little to the workers, even if a correct socialist policy was followed. When Trotsky and Preobrazhensky began to demand increased planning, they emphasised that this could not be done without squeezing the peasants and without the workers making sacrifices. The unified opposition of "Trotskyists" and "Zinovievists" in 1926 demanded as first priority certain improvements for the workers. But it was also realistic enough to denounce as utopian promises made to the workers by Stalin that far exceeded its own demands.

There is no space here to discuss the various platforms produced by the Left Opposition. But in outline they had three interlinked central planks:

i. The revolution could only make progress in a socialist direction if the economic weight of the towns as against the country, of industry as against agriculture, was increased. This demanded planning of industry and a policy of deliberately discriminating against the wealthy peasant in taxation policy. If this did not happen the latter would accumulate sufficient economic power to subordinate the state to his interests, thus producing a Thermidor, internal counter-revolution.

ii. This industrial development had to be accompanied by increased workers' democracy, so as to end bureaucratic tendencies in the party and state.

iii. These first two policies could maintain Russia as a citadel of the revolution, but they could not produce that material and cultural level that is the prerequisite of socialism. This demanded the extension of the revolution abroad.

In purely economic terms, there was nothing impossible in this programme. Indeed its demand for planning of industrialisation and a squeezing of the peasant was eventually carried out – although in a manner which contradicted the intentions of the Opposition. But those who controlled the party from 1923 onwards did not see the wisdom of it. Only a severe economic crisis in 1928 forced them to plan and industrialise. For five years before this they persecuted the Left and expelled its leaders. The second plank in the programme they never implemented. As for the third plank, this had been Bolshevik orthodoxy in 1923,[13] only to be rejected by the party leaders for good in 1925.

It was not economics that prevented the party accepting this programme. It was rather the balance of social forces developing within the party itself. The programme demanded a break with a tempo of production determined by the economic pressure of the peasantry. Two sorts of social forces had developed within the party that opposed this.

The "Right" and the "Centre"

The first was the simplest. This was made up of those elements who did not see concessions to the peasant as being detrimental to socialist construction. They consciously wanted the party to adjust its programme to the needs of the peasant. But this was not just a theoretical platform. It expressed the interest of all those in the party and soviet institutions who found cooperation with the peasants, including the Kulaks and capitalist farmers, and NEPmen, congenial. They found their theoretical expression in Bukharin, with his injunction to the peasants to "enrich themselves".

The second drew its strength as much from social forces within the party as outside. Its ostensible concern was to maintain social cohesion. As such it resisted the social tensions likely to be engendered, were there to be conscious effort to subordinate the country to the town, but did not go as far in its pro-peasant pronouncements as the Right. In the main, it was constituted by elements within the party apparatus itself, whose whole orientation was to maintain party cohesion through bureaucratic means. Its leader was the chief of the party apparatus, Stalin.

To the Left Opposition at the time, the faction of Stalin seemed like a centrist group that oscillated between the traditions of the party (embodied in the Left programme) and the Right. In 1928, when Stalin suddenly adopted the first plank of the Opposition's own programme, turning on the Right as viciously as he had only months before attacked the Left, and beginning industrialisation and the complete expropriation of the peasantry (so-called "collectivisation"), this interpretation received a rude shock. Stalin clearly had a social basis of his own. He could survive when neither the proletariat nor the peasantry exercised power.

If the Left Opposition was the result of groups motivated by the socialist and working-class traditions of the party attempting to embody these in realistic policies, and the Right opposition a result of accommodation to peasant pressures on the party, the successful Stalinist faction was based upon the party bureaucracy itself. This had begun life as a subordinate element within the social structure created by the revolution. It merely fulfilled certain elementary functions for the workers' party. With the decimation of the working class in the Civil War, the party was left standing above the class. In this situation the role of maintaining the cohesion of the party and state became central. Increasingly in the state and then in the party, this was provided by bureaucratic methods of control – often exercised by ex-tsarist bureaucrats. The party apparatus increasingly exercised real power within the party – appointing functionaries at all levels, choosing delegates to conferences. But if it was the party and not the class that controlled the state and industry, then it was the party apparatus that increasingly inherited the gains the workers had made in the revolution.

The first result of this in terms of policies was a bureaucratic inertness. The bureaucrats of the apparatus offered a negative resistance to policies which might disturb their position. They began to act as a repressive force against any group that might challenge their position. Hence their opposition to the programmes of the Left and their refusal to permit any real discussion of them. While the bureaucracy reacted in this negative way to threats of social disturbance, it quite naturally allied itself with the Right and Bukharin. This concealed its increasing existence as a social entity in its own right, with its own relationship to the means of production. Its repression of opposition in the party seemed to be an attempt to impose a pro-peasant policy on the party from above, not to be a part of its own struggle to remove any opposition to its own power in state and industry. Even after its proclamation of socialism in one country, its failures abroad seemed to flow more from bureaucratic inertia and the pro-peasant policies at home than from a conscious counter-revolutionary role.

Yet throughout this period the bureaucracy was developing from being a class in itself to being a class for itself. At the time of the inauguration of the NEP, it was objectively the case that power in the party and state lay in the hands of a small group of functionaries. But these were by no means a cohesive ruling class. They were far from being aware of sharing a common intent. The policies they implemented were shaped by elements in the party still strongly influenced by the traditions of revolutionary socialism. If at home objective conditions made workers' democracy non-existent, at least there was the possibility of those motivated by the party's traditions bringing about its restoration given industrial recovery at home and revolution abroad. Certainly on a world scale the party continued to play its revolutionary role. In its advice to foreign parties it made mistakes – and no doubt some of these flowed from its own bureaucratisation – but it did not commit crimes by subordinating them to its own national interests. Underlying the factional struggles of the twenties is the process by which this social grouping shook off the heritage of the revolution to become a self-conscious class in its own right.

Counter-revolution

It is often said that the rise of Stalinism in Russia cannot be called "counter-revolution" because it was a gradual process (e.g. Trotsky said that such a view involved "winding back the film of reformism"). But this is to misconstrue the Marxist method. It is not the case that the transition from one sort of society to another always involves a single sudden change. This is the case for the transition from a capitalist state to a workers' state, because the working class cannot exercise its power except all at once, collectively, by a clash with the ruling class in which, as a culmination of long years of struggle, the latter's forces are defeated. But in the transition from feudalism to capitalism there are many cases in which there is not one sudden clash, but a whole series of different intensities and at different levels, as the decisive economic class (the bourgeoisie) forces political concessions in its favour. The counter-revolution in Russia proceeded along the second path rather than the first. The bureaucracy did not have to seize power from the workers all at once. The decimation of the working class left power in its hands at all levels of Russian society. Its members controlled industry and the police and the army. It did not even have to wrest control of the state apparatus to bring it into line with its economic power, as the bourgeoisie did quite successfully in several countries without a sudden confrontation. It merely had to bring a political and industrial structure that it already controlled into line with its own interests. This happened not "gradually", but by a succession of qualitative changes by which the mode of operation of the party was brought into line with the demands of the central bureaucracy. Each of these qualitative changes could only be brought about by a direct confrontation with those elements in the party which, for whatever reason, still adhered to the revolutionary socialist tradition.

The first (and most important) such confrontation was that with the Left Opposition in 1923. Although the Opposition was by no means decisively and unambiguously opposed to what was happening to the party (e.g. its leader, Trotsky, had made some of the most outrageously substitutionist statements during the trade union debate of 1920; its first public statement (the Platform of the 46) was accepted by its signatories only with numerous reservations and amendments), the bureaucracy reacted to it with unprecedented hostility. In order to protect its power the ruling group in the party resorted to methods of argument unheard of before in the Bolshevik Party. Systematic denigration of opponents replaced rational argument. The control of the secretariat of the party over appointments began to be used for the first time openly to remove sympathisers of the opposition from their posts (e.g. the majority of the Komsomol Central Committee were dismissed and sent to the provinces after some of them had replied to attacks on Trotsky). To justify such procedures the ruling faction invented two new ideological entities, which it counterposed to one another. On the one hand it inaugurated a cult of "Leninism" (despite the protests of Lenin's widow). It attempted to elevate Lenin to a semi-divine status by mummifying his dead body in the manner of the Egyptian pharaohs. On the other, it invented "Trotskyism" as a tendency opposed to Leninism, justifying this with odd quotations from Lenin of ten or even 20 years before, while ignoring Lenin's last statement (his "Testament") that referred to Trotsky as "the most able member of the Central Committee" and suggested the removal of Stalin. The leaders of the party perpetrated these distortions and falsifications consciously in order to fight off any threat to their control of the party (Zinoviev, at the time the leading member of the "triumvirate", later admitted this). In doing so, one section of the party was showing that it had come to see its own power as more important than the socialist tradition of free inner-party discussion. By reducing theory to a mere adjunct of its own ambitions, the party bureaucracy was beginning to assert its identity as against other social groups.

The second major confrontation began in a different way. It was not at first a clash between members of the party with socialist aspirations and the increasingly powerful bureaucracy itself. It began as a clash between the ostensible leader of the party (at the time, Zinoviev) and the party apparatus that really controlled. In Leningrad Zinoviev controlled a section of the bureaucracy to a considerable extent independently of the rest of the apparatus. Although its mode of operation was in no way different from that prevailing throughout the rest of the country, its very independence was an obstacle to the central bureaucracy. It represented a possible source of policies and activities that might disturb the overall rule of the bureaucracy. For this reason it had to be brought within the ambit of the central apparatus. In the process Zinoviev was forced from his leading position in the party. Having lost this, he began to turn once more to the historical traditions of Bolshevism and to the policies of the Left (although he never lost fully his desire to be part of the ruling bloc, continually wavering for the next ten years between the Left and the apparatus). With the fall of Zinoviev, power lay in the hands of Stalin, who with his unrestrained use of bureaucratic methods of control of the party, his disregard for theory, his hostility to the traditions of the revolution in which his own role had been a minor one, his willingness to resort to any means to dispose of those who had actually led the revolution, above all epitomised the growing self-consciousness of the apparatus. All these qualities he exhibited to their full extent in the struggle against the new opposition. Meetings were packed, speakers shouted down, prominent oppositionists likely to find themselves assigned to minor positions in remote areas, former tsarist officers utilised as *agents-provocateurs* to discredit oppositional groups. Eventually, in 1928, he began to imitate the tsars directly and deport revolutionaries to Siberia. In the long run, even this was not to be enough. He was to do what even the Romanovs had been unable to do: systematically murder those who had constituted the revolutionary Party of 1917.

By 1928 the Stalinist faction had completely consolidated its control in the party and state. When Bukharin and the Right wing split from it, horrified by what they had helped to create, they found themselves with even less strength than the Left Oppositions had. But the party was not in control of the whole of Russian society. The towns where real power lay were still surrounded by the sea of peasant production. The bureaucracy had usurped the gains of the working class in the revolution, but so far the peasantry remained unaffected. A mass refusal of the peasants to sell their grain in 1928 brought this home sharply to the bureaucracy.

What followed was the assertion of the power of the towns over the countryside that the Left Opposition had been demanding for years. This led certain oppositionists (Preobrazhensky, Radek) to make their peace with Stalin. Yet this policy was in its spirit the opposite of that of the Left. They had argued the need to subordinate peasant production to worker-owned industry in the towns. But industry in the towns was no longer worker-owned. It was under the control of the bureaucracy that held the state. Assertion of the domination of the town over the country was now the assertion not of the working class over the peasantry, but of the bureaucracy over the last part of society lying outside its control. It imposed this dominance with all the ferocity ruling classes have always used. Not only kulaks, but all grades of peasants, whole villages of peasants, suffered. The "left" turn of 1928 finally liquidated the revolution of 1917 in town and country.

There can be no doubt that by 1928 a new class had taken power in Russia. It did not have to engage in direct military conflict with the workers to gain power, because direct workers' power had not existed since 1918. But it did have to purge the party that was left in power of all those who retained links, however tenuous, with the socialist tradition. When a reinvigorated working class confronted it again, whether in Berlin or Budapest, or in Russia itself (e.g. Novo-Cherkassk in 1962), it used the tanks it had not needed in 1928.

The Left Opposition was far from clear about what it was fighting. Trotsky, to his dying day, believed that that state apparatus that was to hunt him down and murder him was the apparatus of a "degenerated workers' state". Yet it was that Opposition alone which fought day by day against the Stalinist apparatus's destruction of the revolution at home and prevention of revolution abroad.[14] For a whole historical period it alone resisted the distorting effects on the socialist movement of Stalinism and social democracy. Its own theories about Russia made this task more difficult, but it still carried it out. That is why today any genuinely revolutionary movement must place itself in that tradition.

First published in *International Socialism* 30 (first series), autumn 1967

Hungary 1956

In October 1956 in Hungary one of the great revolutions of modern times took place. A despotic regime was overthrown. In its place, briefly, ruled the direct democracy of the masses themselves.

Workers controlled production in the factories. Administration ceased to be the responsibility of a remote and specialised bureaucracy. The degree of government that existed was dependent for its power on its ability to conform to the wishes of direct workers' representatives.

The revolution began on 23 October in Budapest when a demonstration, mainly of students, had an attempt to broadcast their demands met by a shower of machine-gun bullets from the political police. But to understand its course one has to go back to 1944.

In that year Russian troops drove the Germans out of Hungary, overthrowing the fascist regime of Admiral Horthy that had run Hungary since 1919. In its place, a coalition regime was established of various bourgeois parties, the social democrats and the Communist Party. In 1945 elections were held and the Communist Party received 17 percent of the vote.

At the wartime conferences between the leaders of the Western capitalist powers and Stalin it had been decided that Hungary, together with most of Eastern Europe, was to lie within the Russian "sphere of influence" – regardless of what the Hungarians thought. Despite its low vote, the Communist Party was to have great influence in the government, provided it obeyed Russian dictates.

The Communists took control of the Ministry of the Interior and created within it a political apparatus for use against the other parties.

In the first five months of 1947 most of the leaders of the Smallholders, Party were arrested. The social democrats had to merge with the Communist Party. Most industry, however, remained privately owned.

The Western powers had agreed that Hungary should pay Russia enormous reparations for the war. All German-owned industries, although the result of the labour of Hungarian workers, were to be given to the Russians. In addition, specified amounts of various goods were to be handed over. In 1945 these accounted for 94 percent of the produce of the engineering and metal goods industries; in 1948, 25.4 percent of total government expenditure. Clearly one purpose of Communist control was to ensure that reparations were paid.

When party control of the country was complete, this form of economic subjugation to Russia was replaced by another. In March 1948 all industry was nationalised. But this was not intended to benefit the workers or to increase their control over production.

It took place on a public holiday. When the workers returned to work the next day, they merely found a new set of bosses in charge. It was not the workers who dealt with any of the old owners that protested, but the Russian army and the political police. In this way "socialism" was introduced into Hungary from above.

The purpose of this socialism in Hungary, as in the rest of Eastern Europe, soon became clear. In 1949 trade with Russia was three times the level of 1948. This enforced monopoly of trade enabled the controllers of Russia's economy to determine relative prices of Russian and Hungarian goods. At the same time Russia continued to directly control sectors of Hungarian industry – the uranium mines for example.

The period 1949-53 was in Hungary one of unimpeded one-party rule. Any opposition which objected to loss of economic independence was ruthlessly crushed. The subjection to the Russian economy meant an extremely fast rate of industrialisation. This was to be accomplished by forcing peasants off the land, so creating both a surplus of people to work in industry and a surplus of food to keep them. It was brought about by "collectivisation", whereby the regime took from the peasants the land it had distributed among them after the war.

But it encountered enormous resistance among the peasants. Although terror could overcome this to some extent it could not prevent the lack of cooperation of the peasants, causing cuts in production. This meant in turn shortages of food and discontent among urban workers.

In 1953, after the death of Stalin, the Russian leaders decided that the only way to overcome these problems was to reduce the rate of industrialisation in Hungary and to make concessions to the peasants. They ordered the party to elevate to the premiership one of the members who had been opposed to the existing policies for a long time – Imre Nagy. Unfortunately, the peasants accepted the talk about "concessions" too seriously and began taking their land back from the collectives and state farms. Only force prevented a general resurrection of private property in the countryside.

The established leaders of the Hungarian party, notably Rakosi, had objected to the loss of authority that Nagy's appointment involved. By 1955 they succeeded in removing him. But they could not restore the monolithic terror of the pre-1953 period.

Divisions within the party began to grow. Those who wanted to "liberalise" the regime – i.e. ensure its continued domination by making marginal concessions to the workers and peasants and reducing its subordination to Russia – were unable to win an outright victory. But the old guard, who still believed terror, both inside and outside the party, to be the best means of safeguarding their power, were unable to eliminate them.

Neither the political crisis nor the economic crisis underlying it seemed capable of any easy solution. At the same time the Russian leadership, which might have overcome the political crisis by direct intervention, was itself divided over similar issues.

In the spring and summer of 1956 the "liberalisers" in the party – many of whom were bitter about their imprisonment and even torture during the purges – began to organise openly against the established leadership. In particular, the intellectuals in their journals and the Young Communists at their meetings in the Petofi Circle began to castigate the regime in public.

Yet their criticisms of the regime did not seem fundamental to them. They wanted merely to reform the existing structure, not to replace it with anything else. They were loath to do anything which might threaten it altogether.

It was to Nagy – put into power in 1953 by the Russians – they wanted to return.

By the beginning of October 1956 not only party members but also large numbers of students were beginning to engage in political discussion. They expressed far more wide-ranging concerns than did the party members. They began in particular to question the domination by Russia.

But discussion was still restricted to relatively privileged sections of the population. It did not yet really touch upon the sources of frustration which impinged upon ordinary workers and peasants. For them, the discussion was still one between those who controlled their lives on how best to keep them in order.

Then suddenly on 23 October the long drawn-out disagreements within the regime erupted into open warfare.

A demonstration, consisting largely of students, demanded the right to broadcast their demands at the radio station. When they began to move in to implement their demand the political police, the AVO, fired on them.

Immediately, for large numbers of workers who had been watching, the issue was clear. What was involved was not now a private quarrel within the regime, but the question of the right of political discussion in general, of who was to control the institutions of society – the Communist Party apparatus and Russia, or the mass of people. Immediately workers from arms factories ran off to get weapons to fight back with. The revolution had begun.

Within hours workers in different factories, peasants in different cooperatives and students had begun to elect their own organs of direct power, their own committees of delegates subject to instant recall (what were called "soviets" in the Russian Revolution) and were producing their own manifestos, pamphlets and newspapers.

Fighting was to continue more or less continually for four days between Hungarian freedom fighters and Russian troops, although at least some Russian soldiers preferred to fraternise with the Hungarians and remain neutral.

The political situation was immediately transformed. The official government no longer had any support. The army and the ordinary police had either gone over to the uprising or at least taken a position of neutrality.

Only the Russian forces and AVO remained behind the government. In desperation, one demand of the insurgents was fulfilled. Nagy was made premier.

The first official act of the new government was to call upon Russian troops to restore order. This use of foreign troops was justified by reference to a non-existent clause in the Warsaw Pact.

After four days the Russian troops withdrew from Budapest. At first it seemed that against all the odds the revolution had been successful, as indeed it had in purely Hungarian terms. It transpired later that the withdrawal was only to wait for reinforcements with troops from across the Russian border.

In this period the full contours of the revolution began to reveal themselves. It was clearly not what it was to be labelled in Moscow – and by leaders of the Communist Party in this country – a "fascist" or even a "pro-capitalist" counter-revolution.

Although no doubt fascist and pro-Western individuals tried to utilise the reactions of the mass of people against the horrors of

Stalinism for their own ends, there is no evidence that they were at all successful. How could they be? For the forces involved in the revolution, in the cities at least, were those traditionally opposed to fascism and capitalism.

Until the Russian troops re-entered Budapest after four days on 4 November power was shared between the government and the workers. The government of Nagy had initially invited the Russians in, but was now identified with the revolution, or at least its version of it.

The workers now controlled the factories, not the party bureaucrats. The peasants had seized the land. In political life the government, in order to sustain any support among the masses, had been forced to take in representatives of the various political parties of 1945.

The dilemma of the party opposition was that while it had wanted a system in which the party members would be immune from terror, the revolution had destroyed the organs of terror completely. While the opposition had wanted concessions to the workers and peasants to keep them happy, the revolution had given the workers and peasants everything.

Faced with this outcome, the reaction of many members of the opposition was one of bemused horror.

The other power was composed of the workers' councils and, to a lesser extent, the students' councils. Although not centralised, or subject to overall strategy, the councils were increasingly to be the real focus of the revolution. They were responsible for what conscious planning there was behind the tactics of the revolution. It was in these by democratic discussion that the policies later accepted, albeit reluctantly, by the government were arrived at.

These two sources of power could not have remained in agreement indefinitely. One was tending to pull towards radical working class democracy in all spheres, the other towards restored power for the managers, the police, the party. But for a period there could be a limited harmony between them. In their immediate task of eliminating the remnants of the terror apparatus and of the Russian occupation there was substantial agreement.

The tension between these two social forces never had time to work itself out. On 4 November Russian tanks entered Budapest and began shelling.

Nagy fled to the Yugoslav embassy, from where he was later kidnapped and murdered. But another section of the party opposition, led by Kadar, decided the revolution had gone too far for its liking and formed a puppet government for the Russians.

Yet fighting continued for a week as Russian tanks physically destroyed one centre of resistance after another.

Increasingly, the working class basis of the revolution revealed itself. The worst damaged areas were the working class districts, the 8th, 9th, 20th and 21th, while the smart residential areas of the 12th district were hardly affected. Hospital statistics indicate that 80 to 90 percent of those injured were young workers, while students represented no more than 3 to 5 percent.

But by 10 or 12 November, it was clear that armed resistance was impossible. This did not mean that the Kadar government was in command of the city. The workers now held out against it with their last weapon – the general strike. Indeed, they were now organised on independent, class lines better than ever before. On 16 November a Central Workers' Council representing Budapest factories was formed.

Kadar tried everything in his power to get the workers back to work. He offered them economic concessions, he negotiated with the workers' councils, he threatened them. Even the presence in the factories of Russian soldiers ready to shoot could not raise output above 8 percent of its normal level.

For weeks the real power in the economic and administrative life of Budapest was the Central Workers' Council. Kadar did not even dare declare this dissolved until 12 December.

With the overwhelming military force behind it, Kadar's regime was bound to become consolidated eventually – but even then it was only able to achieve this by making numerous economic concessions to the workers. Between January 1956 and January 1957 average wages rose from 1,112 forints to 1,417, while the number of hours worked fell.

In other ways, too, the fear the government had of workers' self-activity led to improving conditions. Consumer goods were produced in increasing numbers and many of the puritanical features of pre-1956 society done away with.

There are many important lessons to be learnt from Hungary. The first is the need to drop old beliefs about Russia and the "socialist world". Both its treatment of Hungary and the other satellites after the war and its brutality in 1956 show that it is as willing to impose its great power interests on small nations as is any capitalist country. In both cases the motivation seems to be the same – desire to pump surplus value out of as many workers as possible. This must raise vital questions about the relation of the Russian leaders to their own workers.

Secondly, that despite talk both by professional pessimists and by apologists for the other side, the age of working class revolution is not yet dead. Although so suddenly cut off in mid-passage, the Hungarian Revolution exhibited all the features of the classic working class revolutions, the permanence of the revolution as its implications deepen and as new classes take it on where old ones leave it, the working class struggle finding its ultimate expression in democratic workers' councils – soviets.

Finally, it demonstrates how hollow is the worn-out distinction between the struggles for reforms and the revolutionary struggle. One is just the carrying of the other to its logical conclusion.

By their revolutionary courage and initiative, the Hungarian workers, even in defeat, obtained more from their oppressors than the cleverest reformist is ever likely to.

First published in *Labour Worker* 65, November 1966

Dubcek's downfall

With the removal of Dubcek, the imposition of virtually complete censorship and the carrying out of mass arrests, the Czech ruling group is attempting to resolve the crisis that has been developing since last summer.

When the Russians invaded Czechoslovakia, Dubcek remained in power because of two factors. The mass of Czech people were overwhelmingly behind him and he persuaded the Russians to trust him to dampen down the discussion over political and social issues threatening to go beyond the Czech borders.

For a period he was successful in both directions. Other politicians who had seemed more willing to cooperate with the Russians lost all prestige and were removed from positions of power.

At the same time, critical articles about the Russians stopped appearing in newspapers and periodicals, vigorous debate was no longer a feature of radio and TV.

Dubcek, balancing between the Russians and the mass of Czech people, seemed to be raised higher than either. Western journalists referred to an amazing triumph of "dignified non-violence".

In this period, too, those aspects of Dubcek's policy that might separate him off from the mass of Czech workers were cloaked by the Russian presence.

If he was basically a product of the Stalinist bureaucracy and had survived for many years within it without too many problems, and if his economic policies implied wage cuts, increased differentials and large-scale "redeployment", the Russian presence could divert attention from these.

But over the months it became clear that there were huge differences between the demands of the Russians and those of the mass of Czechs that even Dubcek could not resolve. The more that Dubcek and the section of the bureaucracy behind him were bound to try to implement policies demanded by the Russians, the more the Czechoslovak population began to organise to take action independently of the Communist Party.

When the students occupied the universities at the end of last year they found they had immense support from workers in the factories. The trade unions, in which government-appointed officials had been replaced by democratic elections, began to demand control over the factories by workers' councils elected from the shop floor.

Above all there was the growth of intense hostility to the Russian occupation at the base of society. This found its fullest and most clear-cut expression in the half a million strong demonstrations that followed the recent defeat of the Russians in an ice hockey match.

In every town people poured onto the streets. Every wall in Prague had the score scrawled onto it.

The Russians had invaded Czechoslovakia in order to curtail free debate. Yet that debate was now involving more people than ever before. One Russian newspaper complained that the situation was even worse than before the invasion.

As the two planks upon which it was resting moved further and further apart, the "progressive" section of the bureaucracy around Dubcek became more and more unsure of itself.

It had to "keep order" for the Russians, but the moment it tried to do this seriously it would lose its popularity with the Czechs. Meanwhile the forces of the state – particularly the army – were becoming more and more demoralised.

At the top, a few generals were threatening a coup against the government. At the bottom, the rank and file shared the sentiments of the masses. For instance, when the soldiers were sent out to patrol the streets with the police, few seemed to take the task seriously.

The very basis of the independent existence of the Czech bureaucracy was being undermined. In the factories the mass meetings of workers were a growing power.

The trade unions increasingly operated like an oppositional political party. Ministers and party officials began to speak about the dangers of anarchy. What they really feared was that their own power was being undermined.

And the economic situation of the country was growing worse. What caused the "progressives" around Dubcek to break with the old regime of Novotny was the growing difficulty the Czech bureaucracy was having in selling the goods produced by the industry it controlled on the world market.

But developments since the Russian invasion have made economic conditions still worse. The existence of independent trade unions has forced wages up. But the knowledge they still have that industry is controlled and operated in someone else's interests has prevented the mass of workers putting the initiative and effort into their labour that would raise the standard and level of production. The result has been rising inflation and continued difficulties in selling Czech goods abroad.

All this has forced the Czech ruling group to make a decisive break with the fundamental aspirations of the Czech people. In order to safeguard its integrity and control, the bureaucracy will increasingly side with the Russians and try to eliminate the areas of mass democracy.

The removal of Dubcek symbolises its determination to follow such a course – even though Dubcek himself did not seem unwilling to follow it.

This means that increasingly the lines of opposition will coincide with the class divisions in the country. The ruling class, the bureaucracy both "progressive" and "conservative" will be on one side, the workers' and students' organisations on the other.

Socialist Worker, 26 April 1969

The Eastern Bloc

The problem

In 1917 for the first time in history a workers' government took control of a major country. To millions throughout a world locked in a savage and futile war it offered new hope. In the years afterwards people everywhere turned from the grim alternatives of a declining capitalism – unemployment, poverty, fascist barbarity, the threat of new wars – to place their hopes for the future in the new society born of the revolution.

Yet today the USSR inspires support from few on the left. From the Moscow trials and the Stalin-Hitler Pact in the 1930s to the brutal and bloody suppression of the Hungarian Revolution in 1956 its actions turned thousands of militants against it. Even the official Communist Parties of the West protested, albeit in a half-hearted fashion, against the invasion and occupation of Czechoslovakia. Meanwhile the treatment of China – from withdrawing much-needed technical aid to threatening war over a few barren border areas – has disillusioned those who even today manage to praise Stalin.

For more than 40 years attempts to come to terms with what has happened in Russia, to understand why the hopes of 1917 were not realised, and to explain the dynamics of the society that took its place, have occupied a central place in all socialist discussions.

These problems have if anything increased since the years of the Second World War as a dozen or more countries have witnessed the establishment of societies more or less similar to that of Russia.

October

The revolution of October 1917 was clearly and unequivocally made by the industrial working class. Although it has often been argued since by the opponents of the Bolsheviks, whether from the anarchist left or from the social democrat or liberal right, that the working class played little or no role, and that Lenin seized power with an autocratically run party, without the workers or over their heads, facts just will not bear out such arguments. As one of the most prominent opponents of the Bolsheviks, Martov, wrote at the time. "Understand, please, what we have before us after all is a victorious uprising of the proletariat – almost the entire proletariat supports Lenin and expects its social liberation from the uprising".[1]

In fact, far from being small and operating in detachment from the mass workers, the Bolshevik Party was a mass organisation with 176,000 members in July 1917[2] and 260,000 members at the beginning of 1918.[3] Since there were a mere 2 million workers employed in factories undergoing inspection[4] something approaching 10 percent of the working class must have been members of the Bolskevik Party immediately after the "July days" - at a time when the party was virtually illegal and its leaders in hiding or in prison. Nor is there any truth in the claim that the party was "autocratically run" or even "totalitarian". Free debate, in which the whole party, and on occasion even workers outside the party, took part was an integral feature both in 1917 and afterwards right up to the tenth Party Congress of 1921.[5] Finally, the revolution itself was far from being a coup establishing a totalitarian or autocratic regime. Rather it replaced a provisional government, that was responsible to no one, by one freely chosen by the workers' and soldiers' delegates assembled at the second Congress of the Soviets – summoned there by an anti-Bolshevik executive.[6] In the months after October, different parties continued to debate freely in the soviets. Even at the height of Civil War in 1919 the Mensheviks, for instance, were still allowed to publish propaganda.

Ten years after

By 1927 little remained of the proletarian democracy of 1917. But this could hardly be blamed on those who took power in October. For during a long and bitter struggle against counter-revolution and foreign invasion the working class that had made the revolution was itself decimated. Cut off from its sources of raw materials, industry ground to a prolonged halt. By 1920 industrial production had fallen to about 18 percent of what it had been in 1916. The number of workers employed was about half of the 1916 figure. These could not keep alive on what their collective product would buy. Many had to resort to direct barter with peasants – exchanging their products, or even parts of their machines, for food. Large numbers of workers were at the front. Here, dispersed among a peasant army over a vast area, they could hardly exercise immediate and direct control over the soviet apparatus in the cities. The best and most militant of them were those likely to bear the burden of the fighting and to suffer the greatest casualties. Those who survived would return from the army not as workers but as commissars and administrators in the army and in the state machine. Their place in the factories would be taken by raw peasants from the countryside without socialist traditions or aspirations.

The Bolshevik Party had come to power as the most conscious section of a mass working class uprising; it was left holding power, although this class hardly existed by 1920. If the regime was still in some ways socialist, it was not because of its social base but because those who made decisions at the top still had socialist aspirations.

As Lenin wrote, "It must be recognised that the party's proletarian policy is determined at present not by its rank and file, but by the immense and undivided authority of the tiny sections that might be called the party's 'old guard'."[7]

In order to hold together the country after the decimation of the class that had made the revolution, the Bolshevik old guard were forced to employ various bureaucratic methods. They had no choice but to try to build a reliable state apparatus. To man this they were forced to utilise what in many cases were the only personnel at hand with the required skills, members of the old tsarist bureaucracy. But these shared none of the aspirations of 1917 and were accustomed to diametrically opposed methods in dealing with the mass of the people. Such methods and attitudes were bound to influence Bolshevik Party members working alongside them. Lenin was acutely aware of this:

> Let us look at Moscow. Who is leading whom? The 4,700 responsible communists, the mass of bureaucrats, or the other way round? I do not seriously think you can say the communists are leading the mass. To be honest they are not the leaders but the led.[8]

As Lenin was dying it became clear that even the top leadership of the party was not immune to the influences that were eating away at the rest of the party. Lenin's last political act was to argue for the removal of Stalin as party secretary because of crudely bureaucratic behaviour in relation to other party members. In the years that followed, the authoritarian methods that had entered the lower ranks of the party from its environment were used to eliminate from the leadership those who challenged the prevailing bureaucratic approach. First, Trotsky and the Left Opposition were subject to a torrent of systematic abuse of a kind that had never previously characterised discussion inside the Bolshevik Party. A year later the followers of Zinoviev and Kamenev were to receive the same treatment. Expulsion from the party and a police-enforced deportation to remote areas was to follow, finally imprisonment for those who did not recant. The same fate was to await the last source of disagreement – the "Right Opposition" of Bukharin and Tomsky.

The decimation of the working class in the Civil War had left power with the Bolshevik Party in absence of the class that party represented. In order to rule in such a situation, the party had no choice but to call into being a massive bureaucracy. It was the members of this that objectively controlled the state and the means of industrial production.

But the decisions taken and the policies implemented still flowed in part from the subjective intentions of those at the top of the party, who had spent their whole lives fighting for the working class. The factional struggles in the party in the 1920s were not so much struggles for different policies, as a struggle between those who ran the central bureaucratic apparatus and those who had led the party through the revolution. In this struggle those who ran the apparatus began to define their own interests in opposition to the revolutionary socialist tradition of October. In a series of key confrontations they broke decisively with that tradition, qualitatively changing the functioning of the party and state, physically forcing out of its ranks those who adhered, however inconsistently, to those traditions. Firstly there was the elimination of the elementary preconditions of scientific debate in the struggle against the Left Opposition, then the removal of any alternative sources of policy-making or propaganda in the struggle against the "Leningrad Opposition" of Zinoviev and the abandonment of all the traditions of socialist internationalism with the slogan of "socialism in one country", finally, with the use of force against dissidents, the end of any pretence of free discussion.

By 1929 those who had been part of the party that made the revolution had, with only one or two exceptions, been removed from effective influence over events. They were replaced by men whose role in the revolution had been insignificant – the second-order functionaries that had manned the apparatus of the Bolshevik Party, those who had passed over to Bolshevism from Menshevism after the revolution, the new breed of bureaucrats that had multiplied in the 1920s. These new rulers finally celebrated their victory in the Moscow trials when they physically liquidated the party of 1917 – not just the followers of Trotsky, Zinoviev and Bukharin, but also those who had collaborated with Stalin and the apparatus on their road to power.[9]

Since it was the old guard, not a confident, self-active working class, that safeguarded the traditions of the revolution and ensured their transformation into socialist policies, the defeat of the old guard was a defeat of the revolution itself.

The controllers of the apparatus already controlled industry and the forces of the state by 1923. Certainly there was not a working class controlling these in the ways Lenin had outlined in *The State and Revolution*. But the bureaucrats did not yet rule in a conscious manner, aware of interests of their own. In Marx's terms they were a "class in themselves", a collection of individuals occupying a similar relationship to the means of production, not yet a "class for itself", a group aware of its common interests and acting together as an independent historical force to achieve these.

Between 1923 and 1929 this ruling group became aware of their separate interests, opposed to those of the working class embodied in the traditions of 1917 and personified by the old guard, in the main in a negative sense. They feared and fought against any perspective that might disturb their positions of bureaucratic privilege and make life harder for themselves. Their chief characteristic was inertia and complacency. At home it meant acquiescing to pressures from the peasantry; abroad subordinating foreign Communist Parties to the need to ensure international security for the Soviet Union. Both policies were justified by the slogan of "socialism in one country", with its quietist implication that there would be "growing into" socialism without convulsion or much conscious effort by apparatus.

In this period, although the Russian state was no longer anything like "the state which is not a state", the "commune state", the "workers' state" of Lenin's *State and Revolution*, neither did it aim at goals diametrically opposed to those of the mass of workers. Policy was directed less and less by the revolutionary programme of Bolshevism, but not yet by some clearly articulated alternative. The men of the apparatus were extending their control over all potential sources of power and were more and more becoming aware of their own distinct interests, but they had not yet fully defined these. As a result policies seemed to drift in this direction or that, depending upon various pressures exerted: the acquiescence to the peasants in the countryside, the pressures from the trade union apparatus, the need to outflank a particular demand of the opposition, the need to prove the opposition wrong, the interests of this or that particular section of the apparatus.

There was still a sense in which the state could be called a "workers' state", although a "degenerate" one, as Trotsky did. For the interests of the workers still influenced the formation of policy.[10] In the factories the *troika* still functioned to some extent, with managerial directives being influenced by the trade union committees and the Communist workers.

Workers still had the right to strike and exercised this (although to a diminishing extent). A third of strikes were settled in their interests. Trade union functionaries showed some concern for the needs of their members and engaged in collective bargaining with the employers.[11] Real wages showed a long-term tendency to rise in this period to at least pre-war levels.[12] Although the bureaucrats were tightening their grip on the last sources of power and eliminating any opposition, their policies still reflected some of the interests of the workers (just as the most bureaucratic independent trade union in the capitalist countries does). One index of this was that until 1929 the wage of a party member, whatever his employment, was restricted to that of the skilled worker.

1929

At the end of 1928 the policies of the Russian leadership suddenly underwent a dramatic reversal. For five years Stalin with Bukharin and Tomsky had been arguing against the criticisms of the Left Opposition, who held that the rate of industrial growth was too slow and that the policy towards the countryside was strengthening the kulaks who would eventually use their strength to attack the regime.[13] In 1928 these predictions were validated when there was a massive spontaneous refusal of the peasants to sell their grain to the state. Stalin and his supporters then turned on Bukharin and Tomsky and began to implement policies apparently similar to ones previously opposed.

In fact Stalin began "attacking the kulaks" and carrying through industrialisation on a scale never dreamt of by the Left Opposition. Armed detachments were sent into the countryside to procure quantities of grain needed to feed the growing population of the towns. The same forces "encouraged" the peasants to pool their land in "collectives". This occurred at a speed that Stalin could not have predicted. The First Five Year Plan of the end of 1928 only estimated 20 percent collectivisation in five years – the actual rate was to be at least 60 percent. In order to achieve this, a veritable civil war had to be fought in the countryside, in which millions of peasants – and not all of them kulaks – died.

The purpose of the collectivisation was to both destroy the economic power of the peasantry and to pump foodstuffs and raw materials from the countryside to the towns where they could feed a growing industrial workforce, without having to give the peasants manufactured goods in return. Even though collectivisation did not lead to an increase in total agricultural production (in the early 1950s this was hardly higher than before the First World War) and led to a catastrophic decline in the production of many foodstuffs, it enabled the bureaucracy to get more grain off the peasants by reducing the level of consumption.

The industrialisation plans of the Left Opposition which had been severely criticised by Stalin had called for a rate of industrial growth of less than 20 percent per year. By 1930 Stalin was talking about a rate of growth of 40 percent.

In this reversal of party policy, not only did the peasants lose what they had gained from the revolution – ownership of the land – but the conditions of the workers rapidly deteriorated. In September 1929 regulations were introduced radically reducing the powers of the *troika* in the factories. "The adoption of the plan ended the period during which the trade unions had, with increasing difficulty, enjoyed a certain independence within the Soviet economy".[14] In accordance with the new policy, strikes were no longer permitted or even reported in the press. Nor, from the end of 1930 on, were workers allowed to change jobs without permission.[15] The average wages of workers and employees were cut over the seven-year period from 1929 on by anything up to 50 percent.[16] At the same time wage differentials were sharply increased, and the rule restricting the earnings of party members to that of skilled workers modified. Meanwhile the system of forced labour was introduced for the first time. The number of those in penal camps jumped from 30,000 in 1928 to 662,257 in 1930. In the next five years this figure was to rise to somewhere in the region of 5 million or more.[17]

Until 1928 the state and industrial apparatus pursued policies that expressed a combination of the interests of its bureaucratic controllers, and the pressures of workers and peasants on it. From 1929 it began to act in a clear and determined manner to pursue policies that undermined the conditions of life of both workers and peasants. Economic policy no longer drifted this way and that because of various forces at work which articulated arguments for their point of view. It moved decisively in one direction, with a seeming dynamic of its own. Yet this hardly seems to have been one consciously arrived at. "Down to that time [the spring of 1929] debates were conducted in the leading party organs on major issues of policy...though the free expression of opinions hostile to the party was increasingly restricted. This – almost suddenly – ceases to be true after the spring of 1929".[18] That is to say, the goals of policy were no longer a matter for conscious debate and choice. They were now taken for granted without argument, as if they were imposed from outside by some unchangeable alien force. This continues to be the case today – and not just for Russia, but also for the other Communist states.

The task that any theory that attempts to interpret Stalinism must set itself is to locate this dynamic.

The Soviet Union and the world economy

In the early years of the revolution it had been an almost self-evident truth to all the Bolshevik leaders that the relatively small working class in Russia would not be able to hold power for long, let alone develop the advanced forces of production needed to overcome scarcity and build socialism, without assistance from successful revolutions in the advanced capitalist countries. In 1924 Stalin and Bukharin revised this doctrine to suit the new mood of the apparatus. They argued that socialism could be built in backward Russia at "snail's pace" through a policy of making concessions to the peasantry. To this end there should be a slow but steady increase in production of consumer goods from light industry, which would then encourage the peasant to produce more grain and send it to the town. This policy of "socialism in one country" corresponded to the interests of a whole stratum of bureaucrats who feared the risks to their own position that any struggle against the peasants at home or any international revolutionary events abroad might entail. It meant subordinating everything to their personal inertia.

The Left Opposition argued that such a policy could only lead to the defeat of the revolution in the long term, for in reality there were superior productive forces at the disposal of the capitalist powers that could lead to the downfall of the revolution, through either direct military action, or through subversion of the revolution as the prospect of cheap foreign goods appealed to bourgeois elements, peasants and sections of the party. As one of the leaders of the Opposition, Smilga, put it in 1926, "We must orient ourselves on our own resources; we must act like a country that does not wish to turn into a colony, we must force the industrialisation of the economy".[19] The conclusion, the need for industrialisation, however, was not regarded as making possible the building of socialism but merely the defence of the revolution until it should spread abroad.

The Opposition was concerned that industrialisation should proceed so as to safeguard and extend the gains of the revolution. That is why they linked it to the demands for improved conditions for the workers, to an extension of workers' democracy and a struggle against bureaucracy, and to a consistent revolutionary international orientation. Until 1928 the major task for the bureaucracy was to combat such dangerous challenges to its own position. But once its own control over the state and industry was assured against any disturbance from the Left, the arguments for industrialisation began to appeal to at least a section of the apparatus.

Industrialisation would mean both increasing its power vis-à-vis other classes in Russian society – particularly the peasants – and protecting its control over Russian industry from foreign threats.

The defence of Russia, however, particularly if there was no belief in the possibility or necessity of revolution abroad, meant shifting the emphasis in industrial development from light industry that could produce goods for which peasants would voluntarily exchange their food products, to heavy industry. A shift in this direction began to take place from the middle of 1927. Following a heightening of international tension those factions of the party around Stalin began to declare that "we must tie in plans for industrial development more closely with the defence capacity of our country".[20] In the months that followed there was an increased emphasis on the development of industry. This shift began to create further interests in the apparatus concerned with industrialisation. "The drive for further expansion came as much from officials and managers – many of them now party members – as from party leaders".[21]

This development of heavy industry was not yet at anything like the rate it was to reach from 1929 on. But it did signify the opening up of divisions within the bureaucracy, between those for whom what mattered was an easy life through acquiescence to peasant and worker pressures and those who saw their own long-term interests as being more important, identifying these with the development of heavy industry, regardless of the consequences. The refusal of the peasants to supply grain to the towns in 1928-29 put the whole plan for industrialisation in danger. The only way of placating them would have been to accept the arguments of Bukharin and Tomsky and subordinate the development of heavy industry, and therefore of modern weaponry, to the demand of the peasants for consumer goods. This difference of interests within the bureaucracy became a complete split, with the majority then turning on both the peasants and workers and developing heavy industry at their expense.

In order to achieve this development, the consumer goods industries were hardly developed at all. While in 1927-28 only 32.8 percent of industrial investment took the form of means of production (as against 55.7 percent means of consumption), by 1932 this had grown to 53.3 percent, from which level it was to rise continuously until it reached 68.8 percent in 1950. In other words, everything – above all, the living standards of workers and collective farmers – was subordinated to the production of means of production used to produce other means of production. Industry grew, but living standards deteriorated.[22]

Stalin himself made clear the motive behind these policies:

> To slacken the pace [of industrialisation] would mean to lag behind; and those who lag behind are beaten. We do not want to be beaten. No we don't want to. The history of old Russia...she was ceaselessly beaten for her backwardness...by the Monghol Khans...by Turkish Beys...by Polish-Lithuanian Panz...by Anglo-French capitalists...by Japanese barons, she was beaten by all – for her backwardness, for military backwardness, for cultural backwardness, for political backwardness, for industrial backwardness, for agricultural backwardness... We are 50 or 100 years behind the advanced countries. We must make good this lag in ten years. Either we do it or they crush us.[23]

Or again:

> The environment in which we are placed...at home and abroad...compels us to adopt a rapid rate of growth of our industry.[24]

For the section of the bureaucracy around Stalin the collectivisation and industrialisation, the subordination of consumption to an accumulation of means of production, no longer seemed like a question upon which an arbitrary choice could be made. It had become a question of life or death to them. Either there was accumulation or the "environment" abroad would crush them. Accumulation had to take place so that Russia, their Russia, the Russia that they owned through their control over the state and industrial apparatus, a Russia readily identifiable with the Russia of the tsars in speeches such as Stalin's quoted above, could be defended against attack. If accumulation did not produce consumer goods for the working population of Russia, it did produce the weapons to ensure that the bureaucracy would not lose the means of production it controlled to international imperialism.

In fact, the Stalinist bureaucracy was responding to the same choice that every non-capitalist ruling class throughout the world faced from the second quarter of the 19th century onwards. As industrial capitalism developed in Western Europe and North America, extending its tentacles so as to drain resources from the remotest areas of the globe, it threatened the position of all existing ruling classes. Everywhere it tried to replace their rule by its rule, or at least to reduce them to the level of being its continually humiliated agents. And given the unprecedented growth of the means of production under capitalism, together with the concentration of the major part of the Earth's resources in the hands of the rulers of metropolitan capitalism, the means – military and economic – were available to bring this about.

The only way that existing ruling classes could resist this subjection was to change radically their own mode of exploitation of the local population. All pre-capitalist societies are characterised by one feature: however great the extent of exploitation of the mass of the population, it is determined by the consumption needs of the ruling class. The main function of exploitation is to allow the ruling class and its hangers-on to live in luxury. The actual extent and efficiency of exploitation is therefore to a certain extent accidental, depending upon the desires of the ruler, as well as the extent of the resistance of the oppressed. As Marx put it, "the walls of the lord's stomach determine the limits of the exploitation of the serf". Any improvement in the general level of culture or any advance in the forces of production is an accidental by-product of the consumption of the ruling class. Thus, for instance, in imperial China the peasants were as exploited as much as possible, but the result was merely to enable a massive bureaucracy to live in luxury, not to develop the means of production, except intermittently and accidentally.

Under capitalism, on the other hand, however high the luxury consumption of the ruling class, this is not the motive force of the system. In order to safeguard his own position, each entrepreneur has to continually invest a large amount of his profits in new means of production. Only in this way can he reduce his costs of production and prevent any rival from undercutting him on the market. At the same time and for the same reason, he has continually to keep close watch on the actual process of exploitation so as to ensure that his wage costs are at a minimum. In order to survive, the capitalist has continually to expand production at the expense of consumption. Production in the interests of further production, accumulation in the interests of further accumulation, are the motive forces of capitalism, not as with pre-capitalist societies (and also, incidentally, socialist society) production and accumulation in the interests of consumption.

> Except as personified capital, the capitalist has no historical value, and no right to that historical existence... But so far as he is personified in capital, it is not values in use and the enjoyment of them that spurs him to action, but exchange value and its augmentation that spur him into action. Fanatically bent on making value expand itself, he ruthlessly forces the human race to produce for production's sake...so far, therefore, as his actions are a mere function of capital his own private consumption is a robbery perpetrated on accumulation. Therefore, save, save, i.e. reconvert the greatest possible portion of surplus value or surplus product into capital! Accumulation for accumulation's sake, production for production's sake.[25]

This continual accumulation provides capitalism with the means to guarantee success in its attempt to subdue other societies. Unless, that is, the ruling classes of these societies can change the basis on which they themselves rule. They can only protect themselves if they can develop the forces of production at a comparable rate to that of the established capitalisms (or, actually, since they start in the race later, at a faster rate). In other words, if they too can change their mode of exploitation so as to subordinate everything else to the accumulation of means of production in order to accumulate other means of production, they can protect themselves from an expanding capitalism – if they can transform themselves so as to successfully imitate the absurd rationality of that capitalism.

In the 19th century various ruling classes attempted to protect themselves in this way. Thus there was an early but unsuccessful attempt to transform an oriental despotic Egypt in this manner. In tsarist Russia the regime encouraged the development of industry. In Japan alone, however, was the attempt fully successful. For hundreds of years the Japanese ruling class had tried artificially to cut the country off from foreign penetration (a policy of "feudalism in one country"). In the 1860s the arrival of an American gunboat proved the futility of such a policy unless there were the productive forces to manufacture armaments to back it up. At this point a section of that ruling class carried through the Meiji Restoration, by which it took control of the state and used this control to subordinate the whole of Japanese society to the development of industry on a capitalist basis.

In 1929 the Stalinist ruling stratum in Russia faced exactly the same dilemma: follow the logic of capitalism and accumulate in order to further accumulate or face subjection to international capitalism. The only other alternative, that of the Left Opposition, of undermining the basis of this dilemma by subordinating internal developments in Russia to the needs of spreading the revolution abroad (and given the social convulsions that did take place in the 1930s – in Germany, in France, in Spain, this was not an absurd perspective. Certainly if the policies of the International Left Opposition had been followed by the Communist Parties of these countries, there would have been a strong possibility of success) was one which the bureaucratic stratum ruling Russia could not accept because it would have undermined its own privileged position.

Forced industrialisation and the collectivisation of the peasantry were the only ways the bureaucratic ruling stratum knew of defending itself. But in order to carry these through, it had to turn upon every other class in Russian society, to subordinate them to its needs of accumulation. That is why the year of inauguration of the five year "plans' was the year of the abolition of independent trade unions, of the abolition of the right to strike, the year when for the first time wages were forced downwards by the bureaucracy. It also meant that the bureaucracy itself had to be transformed from a coalition of different privileged interests into a homogeneous class, dedicated to the single goal of accumulation, in which no degree of free discussion over objectives remained.

Russia – state capitalist

There is a tendency for people to identify capitalism with one or other of its superficial characteristics – the stock exchange,[26] periodic economic crises, unemployment, "thirst for profits"[27] or the "final money form of capital".[28] They quite naturally conclude that because such characteristics do not exist in Russia then that country cannot be a variant of capitalism. Marx, on the other hand, was concerned not with these external aspects, but with the underlying dynamic of capitalism that produced these. This he located in two basic features:

i. That each individual act of labour is related to each other, not by conscious planning, but by an unplanned and anarchic comparison of the products of that labour. In this way each commodity has its price determined by the proportion of the total labour of society needed to produce it. "The different kinds of private labour, which are being carried on independently of each other...are continually being reduced to the quantitative proportions in which society requires them".[29] The "relation of producers to the sum total of their labour is presented to them as a social relation, existing not between themselves, but between the products of their labour".[30] Thus, the labour of individuals is related in a quantitative fashion to the labour of all other individuals in society by the relations that come to exist between the products of their labour. This in turn means that each production process is determined by factors outside itself, that is, by the relation of its costs to those of production taking place elsewhere. There is "regulation of mutual production by the costs of production...the product is related to itself as a realisation of determined quantity of general labour, of social labour time".[31] The methods of production of each producer have continually to be changed as there are unplanned and anarchic changes in the methods of all other producers.

ii. There is a separation of producers from the means of production. Workers can then only survive by selling their own ability to work (their "labour power") to those who own the means of production. The price they receive (i.e. their wages) will be continually reduced by their mutual interaction to the cost of production of this labour power, that is, to the historically and culturally determined level of subsistence for themselves and their families.

These two factors together produce a situation in which rival owners of means of production are producing goods in competition with one another. Each can use the surplus obtained through exploitation to develop the means of production, so increasing production and lowering costs, thereby forcing out of business rivals unless they do likewise. Each, therefore, has to try to resist the inroads of the other by expanding the means of production controlled.

> That which in the miser is a mere idiosyncrasy, is in the capitalist the effect of the social mechanism of which he is but one of the cogs. Moreover, the development of capitalist production makes it constantly necessary to keep increasing the amount of capital laid out in a given industrial undertaking, and competition makes the immanent laws of capitalist production to be felt by each individual capitalist as external coercive laws. It compels him to keep constantly expanding his capital in order to preserve it, but extend it he cannot except by means of accumulation.[32]

This relationship between different accumulations of alienated labour (the means of production) defines each as *capital* for Marx and their owners as *capitalists*. It also determines the interactions of capitalists with one another and with their workers, so as continually to reproduce the competition.

Now when Marx describes the mechanisms whereby different accumulations of alienated labour are compared with each other, he talks in terms of the mechanisms of the market. But in principle there is no reason why other mechanisms which relate independent acts of production to one another in an unplanned manner should not play the same role. Any process by which the organisation of production is continually being transformed through comparison with production taking place elsewhere in an unplanned fashion will have the same results.

In fact, as capitalism develops, the direct role of the market in relating different processes of production tend to diminish. As Hilferding wrote 60 years ago, "The realisation of the Marxian theory of concentration – the monopoly merger – seems to lead to the invalidation of the Marxian law of value".[33]

Within the giant firm deliberate, planned decisions of the management, not the direct impact of the market, seem to determine the allocation of resources, the wages of workers, the speed of the production process at each individual point. These decisions are not taken in a vacuum, however. Even the largest of the giant firms has to worry about competition on an *international* scale. It can survive only so long as it can expand at the expense of its rivals. Although the conditions under which each separate item is produced need not necessarily be competitive, overall production has to be. The anarchy of the international market still determines the tyranny of the firm.

With the development of a war economy or a permanent arms economy, the direct role of the market diminishes still more. The typical situation for a large proportion of the economy is of the monopoly firm producing for a single buyer – the government – at a price determined by the decisions of the latter.

> When capitalists work for defence, i.e. for the government treasury, it is obviously no more "pure" capitalism, but a special form of national economy. Pure capitalism means commodity production. Commodity production means working for an unknown and free market. But the capitalist "working" for defence does not "work" for the market at all.[34]

But the Marxian law of value does still operate – in so far as the government, responding to various pressures upon itself, consciously attempts to relate the price it pays for arms to the costs of producing goods elsewhere. The government consciously decides on prices; to this extent the market plays no role. But the government makes its decisions in accordance with the level of costs of production in society as a whole so that every change in costs elsewhere in the economy will eventually have its effect on the process of arms production. In other words the government forces the arms-producing firm to behave as if it did confront the market. The government imposes the law of value on the firm. Should it fail to do so the consequences are clear. Either a greater proportion of national resources are devoted to arms production than is the case with foreign rivals, therefore (through taxes, inflation of raw material costs, etc) making non-arms-producing firms uncompetitive in international markets; or there is insufficient development of military potential, so that the national ruling class loses out in physical confrontations with its competitors. Again the international market imposes discipline in the long run.

Since 1929 the Russian economy has been subordinated to needs arising out of its interaction with the capitalist West. This has not in the main taken the form of direct market competition.[35] But there has been a mediating mechanism between the Russian economy and the economies of the capitalist West that has played a similar role to that of direct market competition: competition through arms production. As we have shown above, what motivated the Stalinist bureaucracy when it first began systematically to build up heavy industry at the expense of light industry and the living standards of workers and peasants was its fear of losing out in military competition with Western rulers. The ability of the Western rulers to threaten Russia was based on a development of industry through the continued extraction of surplus value. Stalin, in order to be able to produce armaments of a similar level, was forced to try to develop a similar level of heavy industry. This he could only do, given the low level of industrialisation of Russia, by actually pumping a surplus out of the Russian population at a greater rate than that extracted in the West. Competition between capitalists in the West forces each to reduce the level of consumption of their workers to a historically and culturally determined minimum and to accumulate capital. Competition with the West forces the Russian bureaucracy to reduce wage levels inside Russia to a historically and culturally determined minimum in a similar way.

Many Western socialists have tried to ignore such realities. The bureaucratic rulers of Russia, however, do have some idea of the forces impelling them to act in a certain way; for instance, *Pravda* recently (24 April 1970) reported a speech in which:

> Comrade Brezhnev dwelt on the question of the economic competition between the two world systems. "This competition takes different forms," he said. "In many cases we are coping successfully with the task of overtaking and outdistancing the capitalist countries in the production of certain types of output...but the fundamental question is not only how much you produce but also at what cost, with what outlays of labour... It is in this field that the centre of gravity between the two systems lies in our time."

This is not a once and for all process. The very success of the Russian bureaucracy in developing heavy industry and arms production becomes a force compelling accumulation in the West, which in turn compels further accumulation inside Russia. In other words, a total system of "reified" relations is set up in which the anarchic and unplanned interaction of the products of labour determines the labour process.

> The object which labour produces confronts it as something alien, as a power independent of the producer... The worker is related to the product of his labour as to an alien object... The more the worker spends

himself, the more powerful the alien world becomes which he creates over against himself... The worker puts his life into the object; but now his life no longer belongs to himself but to his object.[36]

Marx's classic description of alienation applies as much to Russia as to the capitalist West. And so does the feature which above all makes capitalism a distinct mode of production for the mature Marx: that whereas under pre-capitalist societies production is determined by the desires of the ruling class and under socialism by the desires of the mass of the population, under capitalism the nature and dynamic of production results from the compulsion on those who control production to extract a surplus in order to accumulate means of production in competition with one another. The particular way in which the ruling class owns industry in Russia, through its control of the state, does not affect this essential point. That is why the only meaningful designation in Marxist terms for the society that has existed in Russia for the last 40 years is "state capitalism".

The Stalin period

Not only the mass of workers, peasants and slave labourers suffered as everything inside Russia was subordinated to the building up of heavy industry. Within the bureaucracy itself a reign of terror operated. Those who had any scruples about the exploitation of the rest of the population were imprisoned, exiled, tortured and finally executed during the great purges. The last furtive remnants of Bolshevism in the state and party apparatus were eradicated.[37] Anyone who might conceivably act to impede the extraction of a surplus and its transformation into means of production was eliminated. Fear of what would happen should there be a failure to meet demands from above had to be great enough to counteract pressures from workers and peasants below. This had its corollary in the enforcement of a monolithic political line: any discussion within the bureaucracy might easily come to reflect the repressed aspirations of the exploited masses outside. Hence the continual and seemingly absurd exactions of the police apparatus.

Yet it was not just fear that made for stability during the Stalin period. For however much the individual suffered from the terror, however great the continual paranoia and insecurity, the bureaucracy as a whole benefited from Stalin's rule. Above all, industry, over which it ruled, grew in size. Its power increased and its position internationally was protected. So although everywhere Stalin was hated, no one could seriously suggest an alternative. Given the goals that the social position of the bureaucracy forced it to accept – building up Russian industry in competition with the West – Stalin's policies and methods seemed inevitable.

While industry continued to expand at an unprecedented rate, many individuals outside the bureaucracy could also benefit. The majority of workers suffered a lowering of living standards, but tens of thousands rose to positions of privilege in the expanding apparatus of control and supervision. At the same time millions moved from the primitive harshness of peasant life to the towns where, if conditions were still miserable, opportunities were greater, horizons wider.

Despite the prophecies of early doom by many of its opponents[38] the Stalin regime displayed considerable resilience and survived even the crushing military setbacks of the earlier part of the Second World War. Indeed, after the defeat of Germany it extended its area of direct control considerably. At the same time it was able to establish regimes in Eastern Europe[39] in many ways identical to the Russian one and subordinate to it.

Imperialism and counter-revolution

Stalin's foreign policy flowed from the same motives as his home policy. In the 1930s this implied opposition to revolutionary developments abroad. In the 1940s, 1950s and 1960s there continued to be this hostility; Stalin's lack of support for Mao in China and Tito in Yugoslavia[40] is well documented. Similarly it was pressure from Stalin that made the Italian Communists support the reactionary Badoglio government in Italy at a time when the Socialist and Action Parties both opposed it from the left, and it was Stalin's pressure that made French Communists enter De Gaulle's government in 1944.

But this did not mean, as many of Stalin's leftist opponents believed,[41] that the Russian rulers would not extend their own rule when they got the chance. At the same time as opposing all and every attempt by revolutionaries in the West to topple capitalism, Stalin set about establishing regimes in the areas of Eastern Europe under the direct or indirect control of the Red Army identical to that existing inside Russia. Here Russian influence was used to ensure that Communists obedient to Moscow would be able to use control over the state apparatus – obtained through participation in coalition governments with the bourgeois and social democratic parties – to eliminate all other political and social forces, to carry through a "revolution from above" and to dominate society through a Stalinist apparatus.

In fact there was no contradiction in Stalin's attitude. He was only prepared to support the establishment of Communist regimes where he was convinced that he would be able to control them and where he would not encounter too much hostility in so doing. Such was the case with most of Eastern Europe (and North Korea). A division of the world into Anglo-American and Russian spheres of influence had been decided at the Potsdam and Yalta conferences between Churchill, Roosevelt and Stalin. Although there was jostling at the boundaries (Berlin, Korea) both sides kept to this bargain throughout the post-war period. Stalin did nothing while British and American troops reimposed a reactionary monarchy in Greece by force. The Americans did nothing but make easy propaganda when workers of Berlin and Budapest rose up.

An examination of the economic relations between Russia and the satellites soon reveals the major motivation underlying Russian policy. Control over the states of Eastern Europe was used to subordinate them to the accumulation goals of the Russian bureaucracy. This initially took the form of a more or less crude extraction of booty from these countries. In the case of the countries that had been allied to Germany in the war there were huge "reparations" (by which those who had first suffered from the policies of reactionary rulers – the ordinary workers and peasants of these countries – were expected to pay for the crimes abroad of their former oppressors). In fact the policy followed was no different to that followed elsewhere, as, for instance, in Manchuria, where the Russian army announced it was seizing industrial equipment as "war booty".

The long-term economic development of these countries was subordinated to the demands of Moscow. At the same time the population of these countries was exploited through trade. After 1948 all of them redirected their trade from the West towards Russia. The Russians used a monopoly position to pay less than world market prices for imports from the satellites and to charge more than world prices for their exports to them.[42] One of the major accusations made by the Yugoslavs when they split with the Cominform in 1948 was that Russia's "revolutionary phraseology conceals counter-revolutionary attempts to prevent industrialisation of our country".[43] The same desire not to be reduced to a mere supplier of cheap raw materials for the rest of Eastern Europe underlay Romania's breach with Russia in the 1960s. Again, one of the complaints made by the Chinese has been that "the prices of many goods we imported from the Soviet Union were much higher than those on the world market".[44]

In order to ensure compliance in such policies there was continual purging of the local Communist bureaucracies of Eastern Europe in the early years. Particularly after Tito's break with Stalin, every individual in the leadership of these parties who might conceivably question Russian hegemony was liquidated. In Czechoslovakia the secretary of the Communist Party and ten government ministers were hanged; in Hungary Rajk was executed, Kardar imprisoned and tortured; in Bulgaria Kostov was executed; in Poland Gomulka imprisoned. At the same time thousands of subordinate functionaries and hundreds of thousands of workers also suffered as Russian imperialism tightened its grip.

The failure of monolithism

The Russian and Eastern European regimes have been among the most repressive and totalitarian societies in history. Although there were many examples in the pre-capitalist era of societies in which a bureaucracy ruled as a class through its collective control over the state and the major means of production, operating in a coherent fashion to prevent the organisation of any other social force, the utilisation of modern techniques permits systematic repression on an unprecedented scale.

At the same time, however, unlike previous bureaucratic societies, the state capitalist regimes are forced to continually transform the economic basis of their own rule. Their motive force is the continual expansion of the means of production. Inevitably this comes into conflict with the rigid, monolithic and lifeless political structure.

This is most apparent in the international relations of the different Eastern states. As the economies over which they rule change, so the different rulers make differing demands on each other. Each is motivated by the need to build up industry at the fastest possible pace. They will cooperate with the other states only insofar as doing so helps them to achieve that goal. But the moment this is no longer so, cooperation is replaced by violent polemic, mutual condemnation, physical threat and even military conflict. Just as competition between private capitalist states reached its high point in war, so does competition between so-called "socialist" state capitalist ones. Thus, once Stalinist regimes independent of Russia were established the disintegration of the international Communist monolith was inevitable. This in turn made it possible for former Russian satellites like Romania or North Korea to assert a degree of independence.

But internally as well tensions arise that can tear society apart. For although the state capitalist form of organisation can develop industry at an unprecedented rate under certain conditions, it is not universally successful at doing this.

Oppressive, bureaucratic organisation of production can only succeed in forcing an ever expanding surplus out of the working population when a more or less complete external control over the actual process of work is possible. But there are production processes that by their very nature are dependent upon the initiative and involvement of the worker. These cannot be completely controlled from above, if only because no external supervisor can follow every elaborate detail of work.

This has in fact been an element distorting the overall development of the Russian economy from the beginning of the Stalinist era. In agriculture, above all in animal husbandry, the initiative and commitment of the individual worker is central. Bureaucratic methods, far from increasing agricultural production, could actually lead to a decline.

What is true for agriculture is also true for many essential sectors of advanced industrial production. Here too bureaucratic forms of control mean a low level of productivity and poor quality production. This can only be overcome by permitting a devolution of initiative from the central bureaucrats to both local bureaucrats and workers. But these will only respond by improving their output if they feel sufficiently committed to the system to work well without external constraints. So improved productivity demands a raising of living standards and improved working conditions. Failure to provide these can only mean a long-term fall in the rate of accumulation and a weakening of the ability of the bureaucracy to compete internationally.

These problems are aggravated as industrialisation proceeds because previously unemployed resources are used up. In Stalin's time an abundance of resources permitted industrial growth to take place even though these were not efficiently used and labour productivity might be very low. This was no longer possible by the 1950s and 1960s. The result has been a decline in growth rates in all the industrial Stalinist states.

In order to stop this fall in growth rates the bureaucrats have to reorganise their own forms of control over the rest of the population. At the same time they have to transfer resources to sections of the economy producing goods that can raise the living standards of the masses, i.e. to the previously stagnating agricultural and consumer-goods sections.

Compound annual growth rates of national income			
	1950-55	1955-60	1960-65
East Germany	11.4	7.0	3.5
Czechoslovakia	8.0	7.1	1.8
USSR	11.3	9.2	6.3
Hungary	6.3	6.5	4.7
Poland	8.6	6.6	5.9
Bulgaria	12.2	9.7	6.5

Two unavoidable problems beset the bureaucracy when it tries to do this:

i. Continued short-term competition with the West (and increasingly with other state capitalist countries) produces strong pressures for a continued high level of investment in heavy industry and arms production. Thus "owing to the international situation it has not been possible to allocate as many resources as intended to agricultural investment and whilst the 1969 figure exceeds that for 1968 it is below that envisaged in the Directives for 1966-70".[45] This undercuts the possibility of any long-term improvement in productivity.

ii. Any change in the organisation of industry also involves a change in the internal power structure of the bureaucracy itself. Some sections lose out in the process. Among these are the ones most strongly placed to resist such changes: those in charge of the organs of repression, higher managers in heavy industry, etc. Those who exercised power in the past in order to implement the goals of the whole bureaucracy continue to have this power and can now use it to sabotage changes needed to realise production goals under new conditions. They find large numbers of supporters at every level of the state and industrial apparatus. Furthermore, the monolithic organisation of society makes discussion about changes, even within the bureaucracy, difficult. Those who demand changes may well find themselves subject to repression, intimidation, arrest and so on.

So reforms needed to maintain the rate of accumulation cannot be carried through unless there is conscious organisation within the monolithic apparatus to bring them about. Those sections of the apparatus that see the need for reforms have to take countermeasures to protect themselves against powerfully placed conservative bureaucrats.

The classical form under which these processes work themselves out was shown in Hungary and Poland in 1956 and in Czechoslovakia in 1968. In all three cases, those who identified the long-term needs of the bureaucracy as implying reform were unable to overcome conservative resistance by persuasion. Even where formal approval was obtained, reforms were sabotaged in practice. Pressed on by the increasingly urgent economic situation and by fear of what would happen to themselves personally if they lost out, the reformers began to look for allies that would help paralyse their opponents while they themselves took over complete control. At a certain point this meant looking beyond the boundaries of the ruling bureaucracy itself to intermediate groups like students and intellectuals, and even elements among the workers. But in order to gain such support the reforming bureaucrats had to raise slogans expressing the general hostility of society to the police apparatus and Stalinism.

In Poland Gomulka carried this whole manoeuvre through successfully. Once he had taken over the apparatus, he then proceeded to re-establish total bureaucratic control, complete with Stalinist repression.[46]

In Hungary and Czechoslovakia, on the other hand, the attempts by the reformers temporarily to paralyse the repressive apparatus led, although at very different tempos, to the involvement of the mass of the population in the political debate. This in turn led a large section of the reformers, fearing complete popular destruction of their class rule, to change sides at a certain point (in Hungary Kadar, in Czechoslovakia Cernik, Svoboda, etc). It also produced Russian intervention as the only means capable of ensuring continued bureaucratic control.

At the high points in the bureaucratic in-fighting the "reformers" in all three cases made seemingly radical, democratic and socialist speeches. Much of the Western press took them at their face value. In fact, however, those who put such slogans forward often came from Stalinist backgrounds, and did not intend in any way to undermine the overall rule of the bureaucracy. They merely wanted to change its particular form. The real significance of what happened in Hungary and Czechoslovakia was not the speeches of Nagy or Dubcek but the fact that the revolution became permanent, moving from bureaucratic to intermediate strata and from these to workers in the factories and streets, culminating in the organisation of workers' councils.

In Russia the chronic crisis of the 1950s and 1960s never became as acute as it did in parts of Eastern Europe. There were bitter power struggles at the top. There were also campaigns aimed at transforming the mode of operation of the whole apparatus (as in the anti-Stalin campaigns of 1956 and 1961-62). But these did not reach the point of completely paralysing the apparatus or of mobilising extra-bureaucratic groups. That was why the Russian state apparatus was able to step into Eastern Europe to redress the balance. At the same time, however, the relative cohesion of the apparatus meant that the fundamental issues at stake in Russia were never confronted. Reforms attempted under Khrushchev were only partially carried through, and in many cases later abandoned.[47]

The experiences of Hungary and Czechoslovakia have demonstrated to the bureaucracy the dangers of division within itself. This, together with the continued immediate pressure of arms competition with the West, strengthens the position of elements opposing wholesale reform. Over the last couple of years there has been a reversion to a crudely repressive approach to problems. Instead of attempting to come to terms with changes in social forces so as to guarantee its long-term strength, the apparatus tries to freeze them. Reforms are put into effect only half-heartedly and on a tentative basis. Instead there is a crude display of force externally in relation to Czechoslovakia and china, internally in relation to dissident intellectuals.

But the apparatus as a whole cannot ignore forever its long-term economic problems. The need to come to terms with these continually clashes with the need to reassert cohesion vis-à-vis the rest of society. Instead of having a clear idea of what it is doing and where it is going, the bureaucracy increasingly tries merely to muddle through. Unable to display a clear and determined line of action to the rest of society, its reversion to crude repression will not be enough to frighten dissidents. Despite threats of arrest, imprisonment, loss of livelihood, these continue to make their voices heard in a way impossible under Stalin. No one expects the poets and intellectuals put on trial today to plead guilty and make confessions. At the Moscow trials of the 1930s, despite years of experience in opposing oppressive governments, all the defendants[48] confessed.

The difference arises because today the bureaucracy is unable to impress even itself that it really knows what it is up to. While increasing the degree of repression, it also behaves in such a way as to increase opposition to repression – so as to necessitate more repression. This in turn makes more difficult the implementation of reforms needed to solve its problems. It is trapped in a vicious circle from which there is no way out. The only alternatives are: relative economic stagnation, and therefore increased discontent both within the bureaucracy itself and more importantly, throughout the population, leading eventually to an elemental explosion of popular forces; or a clear split within the bureaucracy, again leading to the self-mobilisation of popular forces. When this occurred in 1956 and 1968 the forces of the state were as affected as the rest of the masses. Only foreign intervention could restore bureaucratic rule. When the eruption hits Moscow and Leningrad, such foreign forces will no longer be available. As the imprisoned Polish revolutionaries Kuron and Modzelewski have written, "Revolution is a necessity for development... Revolution is inevitable".[49]

Other interpretations of Russian development

So far we have attempted to account for the degeneration of the Russian Revolution and to interpret what has taken place since. It is worth referring briefly here to other interpretations of Russian developments and what follows from them.

Adherents of the most important interpretations still consider Russia to be some form of socialist or workers' state. In so far as these try to account for the reality of Russian society, they do so by seeing the oppressive features of state policy as flowing from deformations in a basically sound structure. Such interpretations have become increasingly prevalent among leftist and revolutionary circles in the West in recent years. Since the invasion of Czechoslovakia they have even been popular among various leaders of Western Communist Parties. But the earliest and most far-reaching attempt to carry through such an analysis was that made by Trotsky in the 1930s.[50]

Trotsky argued that the bureaucracy was a foreign body that had grown up in Russia because of the "contradiction between city and village; between the peasantry and the proletariat; between the national republics and the districts; between the different groups of peasantry; between the different layers of the working class; between the different groups of consumers; and finally between the Soviet state as a whole and its capitalist environment... Raising itself above the toiling masses the bureaucracy regulates these contradictions".[51] In this way it was able to develop as a "parasitic caste". But it was unable to alter the fundamental nature of Russia as a workers' state. "The bureaucracy lacks all these social traits [of a class]. It has no independent position in the process of production and distribution".[52] Rather it had arisen merely to "regulate inequalities within the sphere of consumption", to act as a "gendarme" in the sphere of distribution.

This meant that the dynamic of development of Russian society could only be seen as resulting from forces other than the bureaucracy. Because it could only survive by balancing between these forces, Stalinism's life span was bound to be very short. "Bonapartism, by its very essence, cannot long maintain itself: a sphere balanced on the point of a pyramid must invariably roll down on one side or the other".[53] So the alternatives before the USSR were clear: "Either the bureaucracy, becoming more and more the organ of the world bourgeoisie within the workers' state, will overthrow the new forms of property and plunge the country back into capitalism or the working class will crush the bureaucracy and open the way to socialism".[54] And these alternatives would be posed "within just a few years or even a few months".

So despite the relative autonomy of its political decision-making, for Trotsky the bureaucracy could only register the balance between other forces. It had no independent historical role of its own to play. "A tumour can grow to a tremendous size and even strangle the living organism, but a tumour can never become a living organism".[55]

The bureaucracy, however, does display a living dynamic of its own. This was clear even in Trotsky's time. In 1929 the bureaucracy did not just preserve the nationalisation resulting from 1917 – it actually nationalised more property through its "collectivisation" than the revolution had. Nor was this done, as Trotsky depicted it, because the "centrists [i.e. Stalinists] found their support among the workers".[56] In fact, as we have shown above, the bureaucracy, after years of playing off other social forces one against the other, finally struck out on its own in 1929, hitting at workers and peasants simultaneously. From that time onwards, attacks on the peasantry did not necessitate concessions to the workers. Nor did attacks on the workers or the few remaining Bolshevik elements in the party necessitate concessions to the peasantry. Failure to see this led to another mistake in Trotsky's analysis – a tendency continually to overestimate the "strength of bourgeois tendencies within the 'socialist' sector itself",[57] for instance, the "rich collective farmers".

Trotsky himself was honest enough to recognise the inadequacies of his own previous analyses as developments incompatible with them took place. But this meant that he was continually being forced to revise both fundamental definitions and conclusions drawn from them.

Thus in 1931 he writes:

> The recognition of the present Soviet state as a workers' state not only signifies that the bourgeoisie can conquer power in no other way than by an armed uprising, but also that the proletariat of the USSR has not yet forfeited the possibility of submitting the bureaucracy to it, or of reviving the party again and of mending the regime of the dictatorship – *without a new revolution, with the methods and the road of reform.*[58]

Thus the state is a form of workers' state because the workers can take control of it peacefully.

But by 1935 the reality of conditions in the USSR and of the international policies of the Comintern forced Trotsky to see that only a workers' revolution could re-establish a healthy workers' state. According to his 1931 definition he should have admitted that Russia was no longer any sort of workers' state. Rather than do this he thought it better to change his definition of what was a "workers' state" – and incidentally the definition of Marx, Engels and Lenin – to one in which what mattered was not actual (or even potential) workers' control over the state, but the fact that property was nationalised. He justified this by arguing that such nationalisation was only possible on the basis of the October Revolution. The bureaucracy "is compelled to defend state property as the source of its power and its income. In this aspect of its activity it still remains a weapon of the proletarian dictatorship".[59]

When he wrote these words a decisive argument against the Russian bureaucracy being a new class seemed to Trotsky to be that the "bureaucracy has not yet created social supports for domination in the form of special types of property".[60] Yet he was to abandon even this argument, when in one of his last articles[61] he admitted the hypothetical possibility of a ruling class based upon nationalised property.

After the Second World War (and after the murder of Trotsky) developments took place that could not be explained at all within the compass of Trotsky's theory. Firstly, the Russian bureaucracy survived a major historical crisis (the defeats of the Russian armies in the early stages of the war) and emerged, despite all of Trotsky's prophecies, actually strengthened. It extended the physical area of its rule enormously, apparently confounding Trotsky's clear-cut characterisation of its role as "counter-revolutionary". Secondly, regimes with characteristics more or less identical to those of Russia were established in several countries without a workers' revolution, without a conscious socialist leadership, and, in several cases, without even the intervention of the Russian "degenerated workers' state".

Those who continued to adhere to the same interpretation of Russia as Trotsky were then, and have been since, completely at a loss to understand these events. Some have arbitrarily differentiated between different states, calling some "deformed" or "degenerated workers' states", but not the rest. Others have accepted all states with nationalised property as workers' states. In either case, however, what is important is that the line of demarcation is arbitrary. It is not based upon Trotsky's theory but on ad hoc assumptions added in a quite pragmatic and empiricist manner after the event. Above all, in order to avoid an arbitrary distinction between clearly identical regimes in Russia and in the other Eastern states, they are forced to revise a basic element in Marxism: that the establishment of workers' states must be the result of working class revolution led by a party of conscious militants. In order to defend the form of Trotsky's theory they have to abandon the whole of the Marxist conception to which Trotsky adhered.

The basic fault with all such theories is that they cannot and do not locate the motive forces behind Stalinist policies. They see the body as having a basically socialist metabolism impeded in its operation by warts on it that need erasing, or even by cancers that have to be surgically removed. They do not understand that the very nature of the metabolism has changed. They do not explain what has happened since 1929. They merely record changes afterwards as deviations from a norm. Above all, this inability expresses itself in a failure to understand the international behaviour of the different bureaucratic regimes, the nature of their conflicts with Western imperialism, and the forces that lead them inevitably to conflict and even war with one another.

What is true of Trotsky's theory is true of all other similar theories. By describing Russia and the other bureaucratic states as "bureaucratised", "degenerated" or "deformed" "socialist" or "workers' states", they nowhere locate the forces that determine their development.

What is involved is not just as matter of mistaken definition. Something much more fundamental is at stake. The strength of Marxism as a view of the world lies in the fact that it sees socialism as being possible for the first time in history, so enabling the alienation and exploitation, inhumanity and misery, violence and war that characterise class society to be overcome. The establishment of workers' states is to be the first stage in this process forward. Yet the development of the Eastern states in no way signifies a movement away from alienation, exploitation, misery and war. Experience shows that their policies lead as inevitably to all of these as do those of the ordinary capitalist states. To call such regimes "socialist" or "workers' states" is to empty Marxism of its fundamental meaning.

Conclusion

In the past the revolutionary left in the West has continually suffered through its failure to understand that the revolution of 1917 was wiped out by Stalinism 40 years ago. Instead it has shown a false solidarity, has defended the indefensible, has tried to hide from itself realities it could not hide from others. Inevitably this has lowered its ideological credibility, led to disillusion of tens of thousands of its supporters, paralysed it when action was most imperative.

A clear analysis of these regimes is a necessary precondition for renewed growth of the left in the West. Only a theory which centres on the basic problem for the rulers of these countries – that of accumulating capital – and sees this as forcing them into collision with each other and with the working class can comprehend the forms their rule takes and the policies they pursue at each historical point.

This of necessity means recognising the existence of a world system which dominates the ruling classes, both bourgeois and bureaucratic, that sustain it. None of these can behave other than it does without denying the basis for its very existence. None can control the processes that their mutual competition inevitably set into motion. All contribute without hesitation to sustaining forces that in turn compel each to build up industry without reference to human need and to develop monstrous weapons that might destroy human need forever. To believe that any one of the ruling classes that participates in this system will be able to end it is absurd. The left hand of Frankenstein's monster can never devour the rest of the body. What is necessary is to organise the real oppositional forces that the system itself breeds. These do exist, on a world scale, as much in the streets of Berlin, Poznan, Budapest or Prague, the factories of Moscow and Leningrad, the prisons of Siberia, as in the paddy fields of Vietnam or the ghettos of the American cities.

First pubished in *World Crisis: Essays in Revolutionary Socialism*, edited by Nigel Harris and John Palmer (Hutchinson, 1971)

State capitalism:
the theory that fuels the practice

With the fall of the Berlin Wall, many on the left concluded that socialism had failed. Others of us saw these countries as state capitalist and an integral part of the world system. This theory has renewed relevance today.

When I joined the Socialist Review Group, the precursor of the Socialist Workers Party, back in 1961, our opponents on the left called us the "state caps" – short for "state capitalists". This was not because we were in favour of state capitalism (although rumour had it that one of our members had joined for that reason). It was because we rejected the notion that the USSR, China and the Eastern European states were in some way socialist or workers' states.

If the workers could not even discuss government policies without fear of incarceration, we argued, how could anyone possibly believe they controlled the state and were freely building socialism?

This was very much a minority position on the far left at the time, both in Britain and internationally. Even people who were critical of some aspects of Russia or China would feel that these must be more progressive than Western capitalism.

But there was more to our theory than just that. For our use of the term "state capitalism" made us a minority within the minority. Most of those who agreed with us that the USSR was not socialist came to the conclusion that it was a radically different sort of society from Western capitalism – that it was a class society, but with a ruling class and an economic mechanism completely different to capitalism. This was the view given theoretical form by a supporter of Trotsky from the 1930s, the American socialist Max Shachtman. It was also the view encapsulated in George Orwell's *Nineteen Eighty-Four*.

That view could have very dangerous practical conclusions. It could lead you to believe that the USSR was not only just as bad as Western capitalism, but qualitatively worse. If that was so, there was a logic in supporting Western capitalism against the USSR – and against those on the left who identified with it. This logic led Orwell to pass on the names of Communist sympathisers to the authorities, and Shachtman to support the attempted US invasion of Cuba in 1961.

The "state capitalist" theory led to a very different conclusion. It was based on recognition that the parameters within which the rulers of the Eastern Bloc states operated were determined by competition. This was not internal competition, but external competition with the West European states. An increasing amount of this competition was for markets, but most was military. This might seem different from what happened with competition between firms in a Western economy, but it had the same effect in terms of the economic dynamic of the system.

The various Eastern rulers could only survive this competition if they exploited workers to the maximum, using the surplus they obtained to build up industry. This was exactly the same picture as that presented by Karl Marx in *Capital*, where he showed that the competition between capitalists to sell commodities led to each undertaking "accumulation for the sake of accumulation".

Competitive accumulation had a double consequence. On the one hand it would lead to a new period of massive economic crises. On the other hand it was building up a working class that had the potential to overthrow the ruling class. No state mechanism, however repressive or totalitarian, could indefinitely subdue that working class.

The originator of the theory, Tony Cliff, had set this out in general terms in a book he had written in 1947. We spelt it out more concretely in our perspectives for the next decade in 1970. The USSR would eventually crack apart as a result of an economic crisis with roots similar to those of the crises of Western capitalism.

To most on the left it still seemed the deepest sort of pessimism to write off the states that ruled a third of the world. But with the fall of the Berlin Wall in 1989, when the truth could no longer be avoided, they often concluded that socialism as such had failed.

For us, by contrast, 1989 showed that capitalism in any form is vulnerable to mass resistance from those it exploits.

One additional point followed from the theory. If the crisis in the Eastern states was a result of competitive accumulation within a world system, then simply moving to the Western model of capitalism would not bring it to an end. How right we were was shown by the way economic crises that had begun under Brezhnev and Gorbachev deepened in the early 1990s – and have now returned with a vengeance during the present world crisis.

Some people will ask, is any of this relevant today? It is, in two ways. First, state capitalism as a theory never simply applied to the Eastern states. It also had relevance in the West, since at least a third of every Western economy is in the state sector. While otherwise excellent Marxists like David Harvey continue to see this sector as somehow standing outside capitalism, we see it as an integral part of the system.

And that leads to a very practical conclusion. When I joined the Socialist Review Group, our statement of aims started, "War is the inevitable result of the division of society into classes." War is still with us, precisely because the state is part of the capitalist system and one of the forms that the competitive struggle between states takes is the accumulation of armed strength.

There can be no revolutionary practice, Lenin once wrote, without revolutionary theory. He was exaggerating a little. But there is no doubt that the left as a whole would have been stronger if more people had accepted our arguments about state capitalism.

First published in *Socialist Review* 341, November 2009

4: Economics

The crisis of bourgeois economics

An enormous change has taken place in the tone of mainstream economics over the last 30 years. In the 1960s anyone coming across the subject was confronted with a single confident set of ideas, set down in textbooks claiming to dish out the unquestionable truth in much the same way as primers in A-level physics or chemistry, complete with tick-in multiple choice questionnaires at the end of each section to make sure you learned the correct answers by rote.[1] Economists believed their "understanding of the economy was nearly complete".[2] Typically, Paul Samuelson, adviser to the Kennedy government and author of a bestselling textbook, claimed that this understanding meant economic crises were a thing of the past. "The National Bureau of Economic Research", he told a conference of economists in 1970, "has worked itself out of one of its first jobs, namely business cycles".

Today the textbooks can be just as bland, repeating the same formulae as 30 years ago, and politicians continue to insist we have to obey "the economic laws" contained in them. But such bravado cannot conceal a deeper unease. Thirty-five years of economic boom have given way to 25 years of repeated crises. Unemployment, which averaged 1.7 percent in Britain in the years 1948-70, has since doubled and more than doubled again. Across the advanced world figures of 8 percent, 12 percent or even more than 20 percent (Spain, Ireland, Finland) are common. And there seems to be no end to the destruction of jobs and job security through "downsizing".

But it is not only workers who have felt the effects of the changed economic environment, even if they have suffered on a scale beyond the ken of those who employ them. Giant corporations have been knocked off balance by the wild ups and downs of the system, with a level of bankruptcies in the early 1990s recession (Pan-Am, BCCI, Maxwell Communications Corporation, etc) inconceivable in the mid-1960s. As a result, top businessmen who are only too happy to repeat old adages when it comes to explaining the need for sackings and wage cuts can be scathing when speaking to each other about the economists who proclaim those adages. They complain that most of the economics profession is devoted to producing mathematical models with no relevance to reality and which provide economic "forecasts" that cannot predict major events like the recession that hit the US and Britain in 1990, the longest economic downturn Japan has known in half a century or renewed recession on the European mainland as I write.

Some of them even sponsor conferences which challenge the economics taught in the textbooks, as with a conference on "Complexity and Strategy – the Intelligent Organisation" held in London in May 1995, backed by the banking group Citicorp and charging firms £2,500 a head booking fee.

Meanwhile, that section of the economics profession not devoted either to the exam-passing textbook orthodoxy or working out irrelevant mathematical formulae has split into rival schools – the "new classicists", the "supply siders", the "monetarists", the "new Keynesians", the "Austrians", the "neo-Ricardians", the "chaos and complexity theorists". Each promotes its ideas and denigrates its rivals through its own journals, conferences and books. Yet none of them can explain the central issue that has destroyed the old certainties – the intractability of the crises which afflict the advanced industrial heart of the capitalist world.

Lost illusions

The economic consensus of 30 years ago claimed it had solved the problem of crises for once and for all. The answers, it claimed, had been provided by a "revolution" in economics which occurred with the publication, in January 1936, of John Maynard Keynes's *General Theory of Employment, Interest and Money*. Before that, it was admitted, economics had had a great yawning hole in the middle of it. Its "microeconomic" descriptions of how the market "worked" as people bought and sold could provide no explanation of slumps.

Keynes had filled this hole, it was said, by providing a "macroeconomic" account of how the economy as a whole worked and how government intervention in the market could avoid slumps.

Such was the orthodoxy in government circles, the media and the educational system. It was also the orthodoxy for Labour politicians. Marx was out of date, argued Anthony Crosland and John Strachey in two very influential books that appeared in 1956, since he had seriously underestimated the possibilities of stabilising the capitalist system.[3] The application of Keynes's teaching could ensure that there would never be slumps again and that poverty would be completely eradicated within a few years.

Then, suddenly, in the mid-1970s this "Keynesian" orthodoxy fell apart. The advanced Western economies were all afflicted by recessions – and far from providing governments with a means to avoid them, the methods preached by Keynes seemed only to produce inflation alongside unemployment. Keynesianism suddenly ceased to be fashionable, and was replaced by "new classical" economic theories based on the previously fringe ideas of Milton Friedman and Friedrich von Hayek.

They preached a return to versions of the old ideas that had preceded Keynes. Government intervention, they insisted, worsened rather than improved the performance of an economy. The only "legitimate" economic role any of them accepted for government was the "monetarist" one of controlling the money supply and preventing "unnatural monopolies" interfering with markets, especially the labour market. If left to itself, the market would then always find its own feet, without either deflationary recessions or inflationary booms getting out of hand.

Yet the policies of Friedman and Hayek have been no more capable of stabilising the capitalist system than have those of Keynes. Governments that took them to heart, like the Thatcher governments in Britain, were unable to prevent either inflation or further recessions. As a result, the Hayekian and monetarist economists quarrel openly among themselves. Yet the social democratic parties which used to insist it was so easy to reform the system using "Keynesian methods" have no alternative to the Hayekian and monetarist prescriptions. They declare "Keynesian" reform to be impossible because of "globalisation" and embrace the "infallibility of the market" just as, in theory and in practice, the failures of the market are to be seen more clearly than ever.

There is a crisis in bourgeois economics in the sense that it cannot begin to explain what has gone wrong with the system in the last quarter century or how to put it back on the right track. It is caught between, on the one hand, providing bland apologies for the market of the sort which are to be found in the textbooks or the reports of the IMF and the World Bank or, on the other hand, of pointing to faults in the system to which it freely admits it has no answers.

Bourgeois economics before Keynes

The pre-Keynesian economic orthodoxy was what is normally called the "neo-classical" or "marginalist" school (although, confusingly, Keynes in his own writings usually referred to it as "the classical school"). This arose in the 1870s and 1880s out of attempts by the Austrians Menger and Böhm-Bawerk, the Englishmen Jevons and Marshall, the Frenchman Walras, the Italian Pareto, and the American Clark to resolve problems which had beset mainstream economists over the previous half-century.[4]

Until then economists had relied on the ideas of the Scottish economist of the mid-18th century, Adam Smith, and the English economist of the early 19th century, David Ricardo. Smith and Ricardo had written at a time when modern capitalism was still fighting for supremacy with old landed and mercantile interests. Their main concerns had been with what encouraged the wealth of society to grow and what determined its distribution between the different classes in society – especially between the rising capitalist class and the old landowners. They saw an objective measure of value as a precondition for coming to terms with these issues. Smith suggested it was to be found in labour, although he failed to develop the idea consistently. Ricardo went further, and built his whole system around the notion.

But Ricardo left succeeding bourgeois economists with two major problems. One was theoretical: to explain how profits could be averaged out between industries which employed the same amount of capital but different amounts of labour.[5] The other was ideological: how to provide some account, other than the robbery of one class by another, to justify the existence of profit at all. Otherwise, they would not be able to prevent radical critics of existing society from turning Ricardo's system into an attack not just on landowners but on capitalism as a whole.

For half a century bourgeois economists floundered as they tried to deal with both problems. As Marx pointed out, they alternated between a scholasticism which consisted in merely repeating abstract expressions from Ricardo, without showing how they related to concrete reality, and abandoning Ricardo's insights so as to apologise for profit. In either case, they abandoned the scientific approach to be found in Smith and Ricardo, which at least attempted to cut through superficial appearances to find underlying causes, in favour of a shallow "vulgar economics".

The marginalists took this process a stage further. They proclaimed they could cut through all the problems in Ricardo's system by dropping the very idea of an objective measure of value as mistaken.

But they did not reject everything said by Smith and Ricardo. They enthusiastically embraced those of their contentions which seemed to justify the untrammelled play of market forces – for instance Adam Smith's "hidden hand" view that the best way to serve the general good was to allow free competition between producers whose only concern was with their individual interests, and Ricardo's "theory of comparative advantage" defence of free trade. At the same time, they put at the centre of their system a "law" promulgated by the French economist Jean-Baptiste Say and accepted by Ricardo. This held that generalised crises of overproduction were impossible because "supply created its own demand". The extra value of the goods produced by any firm over and above material costs, Say said, was equal to the wages paid to its workers plus the profit paid to the capitalist. So for the economy as a whole, the total amount in people's pockets from wages and profits must be exactly the same as the amount needed to buy all goods that had been produced.

Slumps, then, were logically impossible unless for some reason a group of people were refusing to sell the goods at their disposal or to spend the money in their pockets. John Stuart Mill had expressed the prevailing view some 20 years before the marginalists developed their own ideas:

> Each person's means for paying for the production of other people consists in those commodities that he himself possesses. All sellers are inevitably by the meaning of the word buyers... A general over-supply...of all commodities above the demand is...an impossibility... People must spend their...savings...productively; that is, in employing labour.[6]

The marginalists were only too happy to incorporate this view as a central feature of their own system. Where they broke with the Smith-Ricardo tradition was over what the main concern of economics should be. What mattered to them was not the creation of wealth and its distribution between classes, but rather showing that the fixing of prices through the market, without conscious human intervention, automatically led to the most efficient way of running an economy. And so they abandoned the old view of value, with its concentration on the objective necessity of labour for production.

Value became for them not an objective measure at all, but rather a subjective estimation by individuals of the "utility" they got from every extra amount ("marginal increment") of any commodity. Curves could be drawn showing how people compared the "marginal utility" of one commodity with another, and these would indicate the relative amounts they would be prepared to pay for each commodity if they were allowed a free choice in an unfettered market.

Curves could also be drawn showing the cost of producing goods. The marginalist economists measured this in two different ways. Some, like Jevons and Marshall, started from the assumption that production involved people in various sorts of hardship, of negative utility or "disutility". Workers had to toil, whereas most would have been happier doing nothing. And investors had to "sacrifice" present consumption of some wealth so that it could be used to produce more wealth in future. Wages and profits "rewarded" the "disutility" each had incurred, and, of course, were equally justified.[7] Other marginalists like Böhm-Bawerk, recognising the difficulty of crudely equating the hardship of labour with the "sacrifice" of saving, adopted a different approach. They claimed the costs of production depended on the "utility" of the various goods used in production (the consumption goods of the workers plus the materials, machines, etc) with an addition to take account of the increase in output which occurred when goods were used as means of production over time and not consumed immediately. This extra element provided the basis for payment of interest on capital.[8]

All the marginalists insisted that labour and capital were alike "factors of production" and that each received a "reward" (wages or profits) for increasing total "utility". The costs of supplying extra amounts ("marginal increments") of each good could be plotted on a "demand curve". And the point where such a demand curve crossed a supply curve was the point at which the "marginal cost" of producing a good corresponded with the 'marginal utility' it gave to someone who bought it. At that point, the price for the goods would ensure that the needs of the consumer were being satisfied in the most efficient way by the producer.

There was only one "equilibrium" point, all the marginalists insisted, at which this could happen. This was because, they argued, demand and supply curves would always slope in different directions and cross each other only once. On the demand side, people's desires for any particular good tended to get the less the more of it they had, and so the "demand" for it would decline the more there was available. On the supply side, by contrast, they claimed, applying to industry a "law of diminishing returns" established by Ricardo for agriculture, the cost of producing goods increased the more that were turned out.[9] The one million and first widget or screw or motor car or hamburger would always cost more to produce than the one millionth. Because of this supply costs would always rise with output, while the price people were prepared to pay for something would fall the more of it was available.

What is more, they claimed, supply and demand curves existed not just for each good, but for the whole pool of goods produced in any economy. Provided they were free to spend their money as they liked, buying whatever they wanted within their means, consumers would choose the range that gave them the greatest utility at a particular set of prices. And providing they were free to produce whatever they wanted and to charge whatever price they could get for it, producers would adapt their output to satisfy these utilities at cost to themselves – that is, with the most economical combinations of land, labour and capital.

The whole economy, according to this picture, is like a street market where the buyer of fruit and vegetables calculates what combination of apples, tomatoes, potatoes, etc gives them the best value for the money they have got in their pockets, while the stallholders calculate the best price they can get for each of their goods. As each adjusts their calculations to the others', the whole product gets sold. And since the seller is, in turn, the buyer from the wholesale market, and the wholesalers in turn are the buyers from the growers, in this way a whole network of prices is set up which ensures that what is produced is exactly what people want.

So if you lumped together all the supply and all the demand curves for society as a whole, you could show that the range and number of goods produced in the whole economy had to coincide with what people were prepared to buy. This the French economist Walras claimed to do, with hundreds of pages of equations and graphs.[10]

Problems could only arise if some people insisted on trying to get more for their goods than other people were prepared to pay – that is, than the "marginal utility" of those goods. Then the equations would not balance, markets would not "clear" and there would be stocks of unsold goods. This, however, was the fault of the sellers of the goods for trying to evade charging the "natural" price, and they would soon be brought to their senses by the pressures of the market providing there was no impediment to its free operations – that is, providing sellers were free to compete with each other and buyers free to shop where they wanted.

Labour, from this standpoint, was no different to any other good. If workers demanded wages greater than the extra utility created by their labour, then no one would employ them and unemployment would exist. But if they were prepared to lower the wages for which they would work, then supply and demand would once more coincide and full employment would return. All that was necessary for Say's law to operate was that there should be no "artificial" inducement against them accepting lower wages (pressure from the unions, or state benefits enabling workers to survive without work). The argument still underlies the contention that the introduction of a minimum wage would destroy jobs.

Marginal problems

The development of these "neo-classical" ideas took place over 40 or 50 years, and there were differences of interpretation between the various marginalist economists. So, for instance, many gave in to the obvious criticism that there is no way of comparing the amount of "utility" one person gets from one good as against the "utility" another person gets from another good and that, therefore, the whole idea of "utility curves" for society as a whole is nonsense. They responded by replacing the term "utility" by "ophelimity" or even by dropping any notion of value altogether – although "marginal utility" continues to be taught in school and college textbooks to this day as the "modern" answer to the labour theory of value.

The most prestigious of the English marginalists, Marshall, accepted in his major work, *The Principles of Economics*, that in the real world the economy could deviate in many of these ways from the marginalist model. He admitted that the notion that a multi-millionaire living in luxury received profits as payment for "abstemiousness" was rather far-fetched, and preferred to refer to "waiting" rather than "abstemiousness". He devoted several passages and appendices to what happened if there were not diminishing returns. Consequently supply and demand curves intersected differently than expected or even crossed each other at more than one point – something which threatened to undermine the whole notion of a single stable equilibrium point. Elsewhere he suggested there might occasionally be merit in using a labour theory of value: "the real value of money is better measured for some purposes in labour rather than in commodities", although he hastened to add, "This difficulty will not affect our work in the present volume".[11]

Marshall admitted, in passing, to an enormous gap in his theory – that it had nothing to say about what happened to an economy as it changed through time. The marginalist account of prices was in terms of what happened when a given level of demand, based upon a certain set of consumer choices, encountered a given pattern of supply, based on an existing set of techniques and existing land, labour and capital resources. It paid no heed to the reality that capital was continually accumulating and the techniques of production were continually developing, so transforming both the pattern of supply and the pattern of demand for those products that served as inputs to production. "Time", Marshall wrote, is "the source of many of the greatest difficulties in economics",[12] and went on to admit that the process of accumulation caused enormous problems for the marginalists:

> Changes in the volume of production, in its methods, and its costs are ever mutually modifying one another... In this world, therefore, every plain and simple doctrine as to the link between cost of production, demand and value is necessarily false... A man is likely to be a better economist if he trusts his common sense and practical instincts rather than if he professes and studies the theory of value and is resolved to find it easy.[13]

Walras too recognised momentarily that "production requires a certain lapse of time." But he simply shrugged the problem off. "We shall solve the...difficulty purely and simply by ignoring the time element at this point".[14]

He went on to argue that prices would remain unchanged through time, as if the transformation of the whole productive apparatus brought about by accumulation would not also mean a transformation of the structure of supply and demand:

> There may be a small element of uncertainty which is due solely to the difficulty of foreseeing possible changes in the data of the problem. If, however, we suppose these data constant for a given period of time and if we suppose the prices of goods and services and also the dates of their purchase and sale to be known for the whole period, there will be no occasion for uncertainty.[15]

In other words, his whole analysis of the capitalist economy was posited on the assumption that those most characteristic features of that economy – accumulation, technical change and a consequent reduction of production costs – do not occur!

Finally, the marginalists had to accept that in practice the economy experienced a "trade cycle" or "business cycle" of booms and recessions, in which for some reason supply and demand did not always balance as their theory claimed. Their reaction was to blame these things on external factors that somehow led to temporary distortions in a fundamentally healthy system. So Jevons wrote that the business cycle was a result of sun spots which, he claimed, speeded up and slowed down the trade winds, while Walras saw crises as disturbances caused by the failure of prices to respond to supply and demand, comparable in effect to passing storms on a shallow lake.[16] They did not allow what they saw as short-term aberrations to undermine their faith in an unchallengeable system of laws which laid down how any efficient economy must operate.

The logic of marginalism was that the existing economic system was the best in the best of all possible worlds, providing the "optimal"[17] conditions for production and laying down rules for any situation in which "scarce resources" had to be allocated between "competing ends".[18] It was, for people like the English establishment economist Robbins, or the Austrian von Mises, nothing less than an expression in economic terms of democracy: by freely spending their money as they wanted, consumers were "voting" through the price mechanisms for those items they wanted to be produced. This could even justify existing inequalities in wealth and incomes:

> That the consumption of the rich weighs more heavily in the balance than the consumption of the poor is in itself an "election result", since in a capitalist society wealth can be acquired and maintained only by a response corresponding to the consumers' requirements. Thus the wealth of successful businessmen is always the result of a consumers' plebiscite.[19]

Not all the marginalists were as reactionary as this. Bernard Shaw tried to base arguments for Fabian socialism on Jevons's version of marginalism. And some academic marginalists claimed there had to be a socialist redistribution of wealth and income for the neo-classical model to find full expression in reality.

But the left wing marginalists believed as much as the right wing ones that their economic theory had proved the efficacy of the market.

They all held that they had developed an unchallengeable system of economic laws and had proved that any interference with the workings of the market would do more harm than good. Even if state intervention was regarded as necessary, it had to be in accordance with these "laws", rather than aimed at overriding them.

Keynes and Say's law

Keynes's *General Theory* contains many attacks on certain of the contentions of neo-classical economists. But it was far from being an attack on the whole theory. Keynes had studied under Marshall and believed for many years that the "free" market would work well were it not for the blundering of politicians. In the mid-1920s he provided his Cambridge students with "rosy prophecies of continually increasing capitalist prosperity,"[20] even if he was strongly critical of particular government policies. He assured people, "There will be no further crash in our lifetime".[21] Even after the experience of the great slump at the beginning of the 1930s he continued to take the main marginalist concepts for granted.

But he did now challenge two of the economic orthodoxy's central contentions – Say's law and the idea that wage cutting was the way to restore full employment.

His attack on Say's law was simple and direct. The law, as we saw above, states that the wages and profits paid out during the production of goods are equal to the total sum required to buy them, and that therefore they can always be sold.

The argument, Keynes points out, depends on supposing that, whenever someone saves, the labour and commodities they would otherwise have consumed are "automatically invested in the production of capital wealth". This might be true in "some kind of non-exchange Robinson Crusoe economy", where the individuals produce everything they want themselves and where "saving can only occur if they devote some of the products of their present activity to the purpose of future production".[22] But it is certainly not the case in a money economy, where saving can mean simply hoarding money without using it to buy things.

If such saving can occur, then some of the money paid out in wages and profits is not spent on goods, and all the goods produced need not be bought. An overproduction of goods in relation to the market for them can then arise.

Not to see this, Keynes argued, was to be "deceived by an optical illusion which makes two essentially different activities appear to be the same". It was to assume that, because investment cannot take place unless some labour and goods are saved rather than immediately consumed, then saving and investment were the same thing. But they were not. They were different activities, often undertaken by different people for different reasons. This could lead people to want to undertake saving on a higher level than they chose to invest.

People save, Keynes argued, for a variety of motives – because they want to buy things later rather than immediately, because they know they will incur certain costs at some point in the future, because they want to guard themselves against unexpected events, and for speculative reasons. The combination of all these factors determines their "propensity to save".

By contrast, he insisted, the level of investment depends on the profits businessmen believe they will make in future (what he refers to as "the marginal efficiency of capital"). If these expected future profits are low – and he expected them to decline as capitalism got older – then investment will not take place on any scale, regardless of how high savings are. And if this happens, the total output of the economy cannot be sold. "Overproduction", the thing ruled impossible by Say's law, will occur.

An initial excess of supply over demand would leave firms with goods they could not sell. They would react by reducing output (or going bust) and paying out less in wages and profits. Only when this process had reduced saving until it was at the same level as investment would an "equilibrium" be reached at which the total expenditure would provide a market for all the goods produced.

Keynes, in effect, turned the old orthodoxy about supply and demand on its head. It had been assumed that, if saving increased, investment would increase to create full employment and full capacity operation of industry. He insisted that, if investment was not as high as saving, the economy would contract until saving fell to the same low level:

> Thus given the propensity to consume and the rate of new investment, there will be only one level of employment consistent with equilibrium... But there is no reason in general for expecting it to equal full employment.[23]

Indeed, as he wrote shortly before the appearance of *The General Theory*, "unemployment is increased by whatever figure is necessary to impoverish the community so as to reduce the amount people desire to save to equality with the amount they are willing to invest".[24]

What is more, a vicious circle can arise. If businessmen do not believe the economy is going to grow, then they will expect profits to be low and will reduce their investments accordingly, so bringing about the lack of growth they fear. The level of economic output then depends on guesses by investors as to what other investors are going to do. And that level certainly does not have to be one at which supply and demand ensure full employment of labour and resources, as the old orthodoxy claimed.

"We have reached the third degree," Keynes observed, "where we devote our intelligence to anticipating what average opinion expects average opinion to be".[25] But this meant investment depended on speculation, rather than "genuine long-term expectation", and, "when the capital development of a country becomes a by-product of the activities of a casino, the job is likely to be ill done".[26]

The great failure of the orthodoxy – which Keynes rather unfairly blamed on the influence of Ricardo – had been its inability to see any of this, despite the all too palpable reality of mass unemployment and repeated crises of "overproduction". The hold of orthodoxy was, Keynes argued, "a curiosity and a mystery", explicable only for ideological reasons, because of its "complex suitabilities...to the environment into which it was projected":

> That it reached conclusions quite different from what the ordinary uninstructed person would expect added, I suppose, to its intellectual prestige... That its teaching, translated into practice, was austere and often unpalatable, lent it virtue. That it could explain much social injustice and apparent cruelty as an inevitable incident in the scheme of progress... commended it to authority. That it afforded a measure of justification to the free activities of the individual capitalist, attracted to it the support of the dominant social force behind authority.[27]

Keynes and wage cutting

Just as stringent as Keynes's attack on Say's law was his criticism of the idea that cutting wages would cause a rise in employment. The existing economic orthodoxy could not simply ignore the very high level of unemployment experienced in Britain from 1921 onwards, and especially in the early 1930s. But it could attempt to explain it away, using the arguments of Pigou, Marshall's successor as professor of economics at Cambridge. He had claimed unemployment was high, not because of the untrammelled market system, but because of an imperfection in the labour market.

Workers, Pigou argued, were more interested in money wages than real wages. This led them to resist cuts in money wages even when prices were falling (as they were from 1920 onwards) and the real value of their wages was rising. In this way, they were pricing themselves out of work without realising it. Keynes himself had for a long time accepted this argument. But the sheer scale of the slump of the early 1930s led him to challenge it. He pointed to two central flaws in Pigou's argument.

First, it assumed that reductions in money wages right across the economy would increase the demand for goods. But although reducing the pay bill might help one firm sell more goods at the expense of its competitors, it could not have this effect throughout the economy as a whole. Indeed, it would merely decrease the demand for consumer goods, without automatically increasing investment sufficiently to compensate for this.[28] By redistributing income from workers to entrepreneurs and shareholders, groups who tend to spend a smaller portion of their income on consumption than do workers, the effect could be to reduce effective demand and to increase unemployment:[29]

> There is, therefore, no ground for the belief that a flexible wage policy is capable of maintaining a state of continuous full employment... The economic system cannot be made self-adjusting along these lines.[30]

There would be a vicious circle, by which cuts in wages led to cuts in employment, and cuts in employment led to further cuts in wages: "If real wages were to fall without limit whenever there was a tendency for less than full employment...there would be no resting place...until either the rate of interest was incapable of falling further or wages were zero".[31]

Second, he argued, there was in fact no way an individual worker or group of workers could cause their real wages to fall, even if they wanted to: "The classical i.e. neo-classical theory assumes that it is always open to labour to reduce its real wage by accepting a reduction in its money wage...that labour itself is in a position to decide the real wage for which it works."

But all versions of neo-classical theory also assumed that prices depended, at least in part, on wages. If all workers accepted a cut in wages, then all prices would fall – and there would be no reduction in the buying power of wages:

> Thus if money wages change, one would have expected the...school to argue that prices would change in almost the same proportion, leaving the real wage and the level of unemployment practically the same as before... There may exist no expedient by which labour as a whole can reduce its real wage to a given figure by making revised wage bargains with entrepreneurs.[32]

Although these are Keynes's two central arguments about wages and jobs, he throws in a third, for polemical purposes, which is not nearly as strong: that in practice workers are concerned with comparing their money wage to that of other groups of workers, and not with their real wage.[33] This "monetary illusion" argument has often been presented as Keynes's central argument, although (or perhaps because) it is not nearly as radical as the other two arguments – and, in fact, reopens the door to Pigou's arguments to the effect that it is the obsession with money wages which causes unemployment.

As Axel Leijonhufvud has pointed out, many "Keynesians have, in fact, reverted to explaining unemployment in a manner Keynes was quite critical of, namely by "blaming" depressions on monopolies, labour unions, minimum wage laws, and the like". This leads to the conclusion that "if competition could only be restored, 'automatic forces' would take care of the employment problem".[34] Paul Mattick in his *Marx and Keynes* bases part of his criticism of Keynes on the same misunderstanding:

> Keynes did not question the assertion that under certain conditions unemployment indicated the existence of real wages that are incompatible with economic equilibrium, and that lowering them would increase employment by raising the profitability of capital and thus the rate of investment. But he found that wages were less flexible than had been generally assumed.[35]

In fact, Keynes looks at the argument that cutting wages will create employment by increasing profits and investment and argues that generally this will not be the case.[36] As one of Keynes's collaborators at Cambridge, Joan Robinson, noted:

> The Keynesian revolution began by refuting the then orthodox theory that cutting wages is the best way to reduce unemployment. Keynes argued that a general cut in wages would reduce the price level more or less proportionally, and so raise the burden of debt, discourage investment and increase unemployment.[37]

She also noted that Michal Kalecki, who had independently developed a theory similar to Keynes's, had added that the argument was just as strong even without the neo-classical view that prices depend on wages: "If prices do not fall, it is still worse, for then real wages are reduced and unemployment is increased directly by the fall in the purchase of consumption goods".[38]

Radical words and conservative policies

Keynes was a trenchant critic of the notion now popular in ruling circles once more, that the "free market" system could automatically solve all of humanity's problems. He insisted again and again that the answer to unemployment was not to cut wages, or to provide the rich with "incentives" for saving. And on occasions his talk of the evils of the "free market" could sound very radical indeed. So, for instance, in a lecture in Dublin in 1933 he lambasted the orthodox economic view:

> We have to remain poor because it does not "pay" to be rich. We have to live in hovels, not because we cannot build palaces, but because we "cannot afford" them ... With what we have spent on the dole in England since the war we could have made our cities the greatest works of man in the world... Our economic system is not enabling us to exploit to the utmost the possibilities for economic wealth afforded by the progress of our technique.[39]

In *The General Theory* he is scathing about the idea that interest is a reward for the abstinence of the saver, insisting that "interest today rewards no genuine sacrifice, any more than does the rent of land", and goes on to urge the gradual "euthanasia" of the "*rentier*" who lives off dividends.[40]

Yet he did not regard any of this as implying, in any sense, a revolutionary challenge to the existing economic system. "In some respects," he argued, his theory was "moderately conservative in its implications".[41] All that was needed for the existing system to work was for the existing state to disregard the old orthodoxy and to intervene in economic life to raise the level of spending on investment and consumption. Two sorts of measures were necessary.

First, he argued, governments could intervene in money markets to drive down the rate of interest. This would both encourage better off people to spend rather than save their incomes, so providing a market for the output of others and encourage firms to invest – although, Keynes noted, he was "somewhat sceptical of the success of a merely monetary policy directed towards influencing the rate of interest".[42]

Second, governments could undertake direct expenditures of their own, to be financed by borrowing. Such "deficit financing" would increase the demand for goods and so the level of employment. It would also pay for itself eventually through a "multiplier effect" (discovered by Keynes's Cambridge colleague Kahn). The extra workers who got jobs because of government expenditures would spend their wages, so providing a market for the output of other workers, who in turn would spend their wages and provide still bigger markets. And as the economy expanded closer to its full employment level, the government's revenue from taxes on incomes and spending would rise, until it was enough to pay for the previous increase in expenditure.

These two measures were soon seen as the archetypical "Keynesian" tools for getting full employment. It was these that both conservative and social democratic politicians took for granted as the key to economic management in the 1940s, 1950s, 1960s and early 1970s.

At some points in *The General Theory* Keynes seemed to look to more radical forms of state intervention. The state, he argued, was "in a position to calculate" the long-term results of investment, and so could take "an ever greater responsibility for directly organising investment".[43] "I conceive" he argued, "that a somewhat comprehensive socialisation of investment will prove the only means of securing an approximation to full employment".[44] But even this did not depend on "state socialism", since "it is not the ownership of the instruments of production which it is important for the state to assume".

If the state simply determined "the aggregate resources" to be devoted to new investments, "it will have accomplished all that is necessary".[45] So there was the possibility of "all manner of compromises and devices by which the public authority will cooperate with private initiative", bringing about the necessary changes "gradually and without a break in the general traditions of society".

The "socialisation of investment" would follow inevitably as low interest rates weakened the position of bondholders, while industrialists, dependent on government stimulation of the economy, allowed it to play an increasingly central role. There would be no need for any sort of radical break with the past.

So unrevolutionary did Keynes conceive such change to be that he argued that once it was in place, the existing economic orthodoxy would then be applicable:

> If our central controls succeed in establishing...full employment...the classical theory comes into its own again...Then there is no objection... against the classical analysis of the manner in which private interest will determine what in particular is produced, in what proportions the factors of production will be combined to produce it, and how the value of the final product will be divided between them.[46]

Reform versus revolution

Keynes believed his approach was the only one which could save capitalism from itself and win young people from the lure of Marxism. A friend of Keynes at Cambridge, Julian Bell, described in 1933 how the student body was pulled sharply to the left under the impact of the world economic crisis and the rise of fascism in Europe:

> In the Cambridge that I first knew in 1929 and 1930...as far as I can remember we hardly ever talked or thought about politics. By the end of 1933 we have arrived at a situation in which the only subject of discussion is contemporary politics, and which a very large majority of the more intelligent undergraduates are Communists or almost Communists.[47]

This state of affairs horrified Keynes, "who was scathing in his attacks on Marxism". He told Bell that Communism was a "religion", and that "Marxism was the worst of all, and founded on a mistake of old Mr Ricardo's".[48] He claimed in a letter to Bernard Shaw at the beginning of 1935 that his new theory would "knock away...the Ricardian foundations of Marxism".[49] Later in the year he told students, "Marxism...was complicated hocus pocus, the only value of which was its muddleheadedness."

He put his argument rather more logically during a series of lectures outlining his new theory in 1934. Marxism, he argued, was wrong because it accepted, as much as the neo-classical orthodoxy, that state intervention could not improve the operations of capitalism:

> The Marxists have become the ultra-orthodox economists. They take the Ricardian argument to show that nothing can be gained from interference. Hence, since things are bad and mending is impossible, the only solution is

to abolish capitalism and have quite a new system. Communism is the logical outcome of the classical theory.[50]

He believed his "general theory" showed how capitalism could be saved by relatively simple reforms, and that therefore the Marxists were fundamentally mistaken. It was an argument some at least of the 1930s left wing intellectuals accepted, especially as they became disillusioned with Stalinism after the Stalin-Hitler Pact in 1939. And it was a view which spread when the boom of the post-war failed to give way to the imminent slump many predicted.

In Britain, John Strachey had been by far the best known Marxist writer on economics in the 1930s. His *The Nature of the Capitalist Crisis*, *The Coming Struggle for Power* and *The Theory and Practice of Socialism* had taught Marxist economics to a whole generation of worker activists and young intellectuals. Yet by 1956 he was arguing, in his *Contemporary Capitalism*, that Keynes had been right and Marx wrong on the crucial question of whether the capitalist crisis could be reformed away: "There are no specifically economic fallacies in the Keynesian case...If the Keynesian remedies can be applied they will have broadly the predicted effects".[51]

Keynes's only mistake, Strachey held, was that he thought the capitalists or their political parties would introduce such remedies of their own volition. In fact it required pressure from below, from the workers' parties and unions. "The Keynesian remedies...will be opposed by the capitalists certainly: but experience shows they can be imposed by the electorate".[52] Keynes helped "the democratic and democratic socialist forces to find a way of continuously modifying the system, in spite of the opposition of the capitalist interests...And in doing so he helped show the peoples of the West a way forward which did not lead across the bourne of total class war".[53]

Strachey was articulating what became the conventional social democratic argument throughout the 1950s and 1960s. Capitalism had experienced a deep slump in the inter-war years and governments had been unable to cope. But this was not because of the intrinsic faults of capitalism as a system. It was because governments had adopted the wrong policies, imprisoned by a hidebound doctrine that led them to cut public expenditure and wages, pushing down consumption when really the need was to do the opposite. They need never make the mistake again, now that Keynes's theory had provided them with a new intellectual tool for understanding what was happening. Indeed, it was said, British governments need not have made the mistake in the inter-war years themselves since, even before he published *The General Theory*, Keynes had advised them against going on the Gold Standard in 1926 and cutting public expenditure to balance the budget in 1931.

It is an argument which people like *The Observer* editor Will Hutton try to revive today when they argue that, if only governments would abandon "dogma" and follow in Keynes's footsteps, there would be an alternative to economic crisis and social deterioration. But there is one glaring fault with this argument. It does not take into account what really happened, either in the inter-war years or during the long post-war boom.

Keynes: the failure of practice

A brief look at the record shows that Keynes did not pose consistent alternatives to the decisions taken by British governments during the inter-war years.

Take, for instance, the return to the Gold Standard in 1925, which led directly to the lockout of the miners and the general strike in 1926. Part of Keynes's reputation as providing an alternative to the misery of the inter-war years rests on the pamphlet he wrote soon afterwards – *The Economic Consequences of Mr Churchill*. This criticised the decision to return to the Gold Standard for increasing the cost of exports and depressing the economy. Keynes's most recent biographer, Robert Skidelsky, tells us that Keynes blamed Europe's rulers for disrupting the "harmonious" pre-1914 economy through war and now expecting "workers to bear the cost of trying to restore it". But in the key months before the decision to return to the Gold Standard, "for tactical reasons he abandoned outright opposition to the return and pushed the case for delay... In the final stages of the debate he oscillated between pointing out the practical difficulty of deflating money wages to the amount required to restore equilibrium at the pre-war parity and urging the authorities to attend to this before deciding to go back".[54] Keynes's testimony to the government Chamberlain Committee considering the matter "helped to crystallise the view that the pre-war parity could be regained and maintained without detrimental effect on the real economy".[55] Keynes behaved in this way because "he had his reputation to consider; he could not appear to be in favour of a policy which smacked of inflation".[56]

In 1931 there was again a sharp contrast between his analysis of the disastrous direction government policy was going in and the timid corrections he suggested making to it. When the government-appointed May Committee recommended enormous cuts in public expenditure, Keynes wrote an article for the *New Statesman* denouncing the idea: "The reduction in purchasing power which would follow the recommended economies would add 250,000-400,000 to the unemployed... At the present time," Keynes wrote, "all governments have budget deficits. They are nature's remedy, so to speak, for preventing business losses from being...so great as to bring production altogether to a standstill".[57] Yet Keynes went on to welcome the May Committee report, because "it invites us to decide whether to make the deflation effective by transmitting the reduction of international prices to British salaries and wages".[58] And in a letter to the prime minister, MacDonald, he hedged his bets even more, saying he himself "would support for the time being whatever policy was made, provided the decision was accompanied by action sufficiently drastic to make it effective".[59] His "hesitations", according to Skidelsky, "were seen by MacDonald as reinforcing the Bankof England's advice to carry out the May Report's recommendations... Once more, at the critical moment...Keynes's...counsel was clouded".[60] This did not stop Keynes from denouncing the course taken by MacDonald and his chancellor, Snowden, as "replete with folly and injustice" in the *New Statesman*, but only after the event.

The same vacillation between radical talk and cautious policy occurs again and again before, during and after the writing of *The General Theory*. So in 1929 he had backed Lloyd George's call for public works to deal with unemployment. But in 1933 his advice to a Stockholm banker was to go slow on public works "if this would help as a transitional method towards much lower interest rates".[61] Later in 1933 he wrote "an open letter" to President Roosevelt for the *New York Times*. The future of "rational change" throughout the world depended on Roosevelt, he wrote. But, for this very reason, there had to be care about pushing "business and social reforms which are long overdue" in case they "complicate recovery" through an "upset" to "the confidence of the business world".

Every proposal Keynes made, notes Skidelsky, was tailored, "taking into account the psychology of the business community. In practice he was very cautious indeed".[62] Thus a series of articles Keynes wrote for *The Times* in 1937 suggested that Britain was approaching boom conditions, even though unemployment remained at 12 percent. He claimed that "with unemployment now largely confined to the 'distressed areas', the risk was that further expansion in demand would cause inflation to take off. This justified the Treasury in making cuts elsewhere to compensate for the cost of special assistance to these".[63] Keynes's timidity was not an accident. His account of how investment took place was in terms of the "expectations" of businessmen. But he was only too aware that they would shy away from any policy which seemed likely to damage profits in the short term. And so, in practice, he avoided recommendations which might frighten them.

The wrong remedies

But it was not only big business suspicions that limited the effectiveness of Keynes's remedies. There is strong evidence that they could not have worked unless accompanied by moves much more radical than any he contemplated.

Estimates suggest that the Lloyd George public works programme supported by Keynes could not have shaved more than 11 percent off the unemployment figure between 1930 and 1933 – at a time when the figure grew 100 percent.[64] Another estimate calculates that to provide the 3 million jobs needed to restore full employment at the deepest point of the 1930s slump there would have to have been an increase in government spending of some 56 percent.[65] Such an increase was not possible using the "gradualist" methods acceptable to Keynes, since it would have led directly to a flight of capital abroad, a rise in imports, a balance of payments deficit and a steep rise in interest rates.[66] Carrying it through would have required "the transformation of the British economy into a largely state-controlled, if not planned, economic system".[67]

Such radical intervention did not, in fact, occur in any of the advanced Western states until the establishment of full-blooded war economies, first in Nazi Germany from 1935 onwards, and then in Britain between 1939 and 1940, and in the US in 1941. Prior to that, economic "recovery" was only cyclical, with output rising from 1933 to 1936 and then dipping very sharply, with the US experiencing "the steepest economic decline in the history of the US" in the autumn of 1937 – despite the use of government deficit financing on a substantial scale in the years 1933-36.[68] And with the war economies, what was established was not a "gradual" increase in the power of the state, but a takeover by the state of all major decision making about investment: by 1943 the American state was responsible for no less than 90 percent of total investment.[69] If this was "Keynesianism", it was of a much more radical form than that suggested by Keynes himself during the Depression years, when he argued that governments should not "muddle up spending with planning, recovery with social reform".[70] Keynes certainly showed in the 1930s that the free market economy had no answer to slump. But his call for limited state intervention in the economy provided no better answer.

Keynesianism and the post-war boom

Economists and social democrats of the Strachey sort based their support for Keynesian remedies on the post-war experience. The long boom, they argued, had come about because governments now accepted Keynes's doctrines in a way in which they had not before. So pervasive was this view that it was hardly questioned over more than two decades, and was even accepted by some Marxist critics of Keynesianism. Thus Paul Mattick ascribed the boom to government efforts to bring together "labour and idle capital for the production of non-market goods" through "deficit spending and government-induced production".[71]

But this view did not fit the facts any more than the previous claim that Keynesian policies would have stopped the 1930s slump. British governments, for example, did not use budget deficits Keynesian-style. Matthews pointed out, at the height of the boom:

> Throughout the post-war period, the government, far from injecting demand into the system, has persistently had a large surplus. This surplus...has been much larger than at any time in the 20th century.[72]

When governments did intervene, it was "a question of reducing the size of the deficit", not of "turning a surplus into a deficit". The "overall effect" was "one of restraint".[73] Nor could government socialisation of investment have lain behind the boom. "Investment in the public sector has been on average a smaller proportion of total investment in the post-war period than it was in the inter-war years".[74] And the public sector borrowing requirement actually fell in the 1950s and 1960s.[75] In fact, the main form government intervention took until the 1970s was of "credit squeezes" to slow down the economy, rather than deliberate increases in spending to speed it up.

It was only when the long boom came to an end and the economies of the advanced countries went into recession in 1974-76 that governments turned to Keynesian policies of deliberately expanding demand. And it was when they found these policies did not work, fuelling inflation but not increasing production substantially, that they abandoned them, throwing Keynesian economists into complete confusion. Not that government deficits themselves disappeared. In the 1990s all major Western governments have had budget deficits, ranging from about 1.5 percent of gross domestic product (GDP) in the case of the US to about 7 percent in the cases of Italy and Japan, without bringing their economies to the level of full employment taken for granted in the non-deficit 1950s.[76]

The evidence suggests, then, that the long boom could not have been a result of Keynesian "deficit financing". Something else had happened during the years of the long boom which had enabled the economy to expand continually, without being punctuated by deep recessions. This in turn had then provided a situation in which capitalists could have "expectations" of future profits and invest accordingly, so providing the sort of stable environment which enabled other capitalists to be optimistic about their investments.

What was this "something" which underlay the long boom, but which clearly had not been present in the inter-war years and was to be absent again from the mid-1970s onwards? During the long boom itself two of Keynes's former collaborators, Michal Kalecki and Joan Robinson, had suggested that its roots did not lie in government expenditure as such, but in a special form of that expenditure, spending on armaments.[77] Arms production, they argued, was a form of government-organised investment which was acceptable to private capital and which could explain the operation of a capitalist economy at near full employment for a long period of time. It could provide private capital with an expectation of ready markets and high profits, so encouraging private investment. This dependence of the capitalist economy on armaments was, for Kalecki, one reason to object to it: "He thought the post-war American experience illustrated the role of armaments expenditure as wasteful and dangerous, and saw the apparent need to resort to this form of expenditure to maintain high levels of demand as a major shortcoming of capitalism".[78] Yet even Kalecki assumed there had to be permanent budget deficits in the US.[79]

If economies seemed to have escaped from mass unemployment in the aftermath of the "Keynesian revolution" it was for reasons which were difficult to explain on the basis of Keynes's own arguments. It is hardly surprising, therefore, that when the economy entered a new period of crisis from the mid-1970s onwards, the Keynesians were at a loss to say why.

The failure of eclecticism

"He who only half makes a revolution digs his own grave", said the French Jacobin leader Saint-Just. But the Keynesian revolution was not, in theoretical terms, even half a revolution. Keynes challenged the idea that if the "free enterprise" system was left to itself the law of neo-classical economics would ensure full employment and a maximum use of resources. But he tried to do so while leaving most of the theoretical structure of the neo-classical edifice intact. And when he found this insufficient for his needs, he simply glued onto it new bits of theory of his own in an ad hoc fashion, however ill they fitted with the rest.

Most of the way through *The General Theory* Keynes uses the concepts of marginalism. For him, as much as for his "orthodox" opponents, firms will expand their output until marginal output costs equal the price people are prepared to pay for goods. He accepted the argument that a rise in real wages above this level will prevent goods from being sold. And so he also accepted that any rise in output would have to be accompanied by falling real wages. His disagreement with the orthodoxy was not over the principle, but over its application. He denied the practical possibility of bringing about the cuts in real wages needed to sell more goods. This was why governments had to stimulate the economy. Once this had happened, the economy could then work along lines put forward by the neo-classical orthodoxy.

So much did Keynes accept the neo-classical framework that he rejected damning criticisms of it from economists who were close to him personally. As we have seen, Marshall had already been forced to question in part the assumption of diminishing returns. Keynes's friend and Cambridge colleague Piero Sraffa went further in a keynote article in 1926 and argued that not diminishing but increasing returns were the norm. This threw into question the whole edifice of neo-classical theory, as he tried to explain to Keynes: "If a firm's costs of production fall as its output rises, there is no stable equilibrium between supply and demand, and nothing to stop its size expanding indefinitely. The problem then is how equilibrium is reached".[80]

The point was devastating. As the influential economist J.H. Hicks admitted 13 years later, unless "marginal costs...rise as the firm expands" there is nothing to stop a firm growing into a monopoly which has "some influence over the prices at which it sells". But "a universal adoption of the assumption of monopoly must have very destructive consequences for economic theory... The basis on which economic laws can be constructed is shorn away" and there is "wreckage of the greater part of economic theory".[81]

The only way to save existing economic theory, Hicks wrote, was to take the "dangerous step" of assuming that most markets are "competitive markets". In fact, the great mass of economic teachers and economic textbooks have taken this step with hardly a thought. And so did Keynes. For him there could be no talk of a root and branch abandonment of the neo-classical framework. He still insisted, more than a dozen years after Sraffa first put his arguments, "I have always regarded decreasing physical returns in the short period as one of the very few incontrovertible propositions in our miserable subject".[82] As Skidelsky notes, "Keynes did not consider the theoretical problems for value theory raised by Sraffa to be of serious practical importance".[83]

Theoretical issues which people banish through the front door have a habit of reappearing through the back. This was certainly true with value theory for Keynes. At one point in *The General Theory* he had to deal with the question of how to measure increases in economic output. He recognised that you cannot simply add together different sets of physical commodities at one point in time and compare them with a different set at a later point.[84] To make such comparisons involves "covertly introducing changes in value".[85] To deal with this problem, he drops the usual assumptions of neo-classical theory and makes half a turn to a labour theory of value,[86] to "the general assumption that the amount of employment associated with a given capital equipment will be a satisfactory index of the amount of resultant output".[87] He explains later, "I sympathise with the pre-classical [*sic*] doctrine that everything is produced by labour, aided by what used to be called art and is now called technique, by natural resources...and by the results of past labour, embodied in assets".[88]

But the half-turn away from neo-classical theory is never carried through to its logical conclusion. It is introduced into the work to deal with one problem, in a quite eclectic manner, and then forgotten. The main body of the work remains wholly within the neo-classical framework. This had a number of important implications.

Keynes could not fully avoid having to say something about what would happen if workers did not simply put up with falling living standards that would, according neo-classical theory, have to accompany rising output. This led him at points to fall back on the need for unemployment to discipline workers:

> Our methods of control are unlikely to be sufficiently delicate or sufficiently powerful to maintain continuous full employment...and in practice I should probably relax my expansionist measures a little before technical full employment had actually been achieved.[89]

The General Theory begins with a diatribe against the idea that wage cutting can end a slump. But here Keynes himself is close to saying that wages are a problem and that there is a necessary level of unemployment to hold them down – what right wing economists came to call "the natural level of unemployment" in the 1970s and 1980s.

The eclecticism is strongest – and most damaging – when it comes to his discussion of why investment is below the full employment level. Although this question is absolutely central to his whole theory, he does not provide a clear account, but refers to four different possible reasons.

First, there is the level of interest rates. The importance of these is often downplayed in discussion of Keynes's work. Yet an awful lot of *The General Theory* is devoted to them – its full title is, after all, *The General Theory of Employment, Interest and Money*.

Part of Keynes's critique of the old orthodoxy was that it tended to equate the rate of profit and the rate of interest, seeing both as determined by the amount of saving on the one hand and the amount of investment on the other. It held that if saving rose above investment, interest rates would fall, making investment cheaper and encouraging it to rise to the level of saving. This was the rationale behind its contention that the key to economic growth was saving. It has also served to justify both profit and interest: they were the "reward" to saving for the extra economic output obtained with increased use of capital. Indeed, the rate of interest was equal to the marginal output per extra unit of investment.

Keynes challenged this view strongly. He insisted the rate of interest was different to the rate of profit, being determined not by the productivity of capital but by the willingness of people to hold their savings in the form of ready cash or as loans to entrepreneurs, bankers or the state (their "liquidity preference"). The greater their desire for ready cash, the higher the rate of interest – and the greater the cost to entrepreneurs of borrowing. Far from the level of borrowing determining the rate of interest, the rate of interest determined the level of investing. But the government could influence the desire of people to hold on to cash, and the rate of interest, by its own operations in the money markets. And if it did so in such a way as to hold interest rates down, it would stimulate investment.

Keynes was doubtful whether low interest rates alone would be sufficient to end a deep slump like that of the 1930s. But he believed they had an important role to play – a view that could easily be interpreted as meaning all governments had to do to keep the economy expanding was to tinker with interest rates through the money markets.

The second factor he saw as causing investment was, as we have already seen, the expectation of entrepreneurs about future prospects. But "the outstanding fact is the extreme precariousness of the basis of our knowledge on which the estimates of prospective yield have to be made".[90] Since the success of any one entrepreneur's investment depended on the willingness of other entrepreneurs to provide a market for goods by investing themselves, what came to determine overall investment was not its real efficiency, but the crowd psychology, "the average preferences of the competitors as a whole". "Investment based on genuine long-term expectation is so difficult today as to be scarcely practicable".[91] Here again, however, Keynes implied government could quite easily come to the rescue, since "then the state...is in a position to calculate the marginal efficiency of capital goods on the long view and on the basis of general social advantage, taking an ever greater responsibility for directly organising investment".[92]

But there was an important proviso here, for Keynes's "expectations" were determined not just by what the government did, but by the way businessmen viewed what it did.

If the fear of a Labour government or a New Deal depresses enterprise, this need not be the result either of reasonable calculation or of a plot with political intent; it is the mere consequence of upsetting the delicate balance of spontaneous optimism. In estimating the prospects for investment, we must have regard, therefore, to the nerves and hysteria and even the digestions and reactions of the wealthier of those upon whose spontaneous activity it largely depends.[93]

In other words, at one point state intervention is easy, but at another it is very difficult.

Thirdly, Keynes connected the willingness to risk investment not merely with how investors thought other investors were going to behave, but also with individual psychology – what he referred to as the "animal spirits" of entrepreneurs:

> Most, probably, of our decisions to do something positive, the full consequences of which will be drawn out over many days to come, can only be the result of animal spirits – of a spontaneous urge to action rather than inaction... Thus if the animal spirits are dimmed and the spontaneous optimism falters...enterprise will fade and die.[94]

The implication of this notion is that deep slumps like that of the inter-war years are a result not of economic causes at all, but of changes in psychology.

But Keynes also suggested there was an objective economic reason for the level of investment by individual firms and individuals to decline over time. He argued that the very process of expanding capital investment led to a decline in the return on it – "the marginal efficiency of investment". Such a decline increased the risks of further investment, and so increased the likelihood that the "animal spirits" would not be strong enough for capitalists to take the risk of investing and undermined any expectation that economic growth would justify any particular investment.

He believed the declining "marginal efficiency of capital" to be an empirical fact which could be found, for instance, in the inter-war "experience of Great Britain and the United States".[95] The result was that the return on capital was not sufficiently above the cost to the entrepreneurs of borrowing as to encourage new investment, so tending "to interfere, in conditions mainly of laissez-faire, with a reasonable level of employment and with the standard of life which the technical conditions of production are capable of furnishing".[96]

Keynes's explanation of this decline was grounded in his overall "marginalist" approach, with its acceptance that value depended on supply and demand. As the supply of capital increased it would grow less scarce. As a result the value to the user of each extra unit would fall until, eventually, it reached zero – something that could happen in "a properly run community equipped with modern technical resources...within a generation".[97]

This theoretical reasoning seems to have been too obscure for most of Keynes's followers. The "declining marginal efficiency of capital" hardly appears in most accounts of Keynes's ideas. Yet it is the most radical single notion in his writings. It implies that the obstacles to full employment lie with an inbuilt tendency of the existing system and not just with the psychology behind "propensities to save", "liquidity preferences", "expectations" and "animal spirits". If that is so, there would seem to be no point in governments simply seeking to "restore confidence": there is nothing to restore confidence in! As such the notion has obvious parallels with Marx's theory of "the tendency of the rate of profit to decline" – although Marx based his theory on an objective labour theory of value, while Keynes rested his on his own peculiar interpretation of marginalism. Both had implied that capitalism as we know it is no longer an advancing system with a great future.

Marx, of course, drew revolutionary conclusions from this – that workers had to seize control of the means of production so as to transform the whole basis of decision making on investment. Keynes, as a liberal committed to capitalism, could not draw such conclusions. At some points he shies away from any stress on the objective character of "marginal efficiency", emphasising instead its "dependence" on "expectations". At others he claims the decline will make capitalists accept the gradual reform of their own system, with "a gradual disappearance of the rate of return on accumulated wealth" providing "a sensible way of gradually getting rid of many of the objectionable features of capitalism".[98] Yet, whatever Keynes himself might have thought, the implication remained that the very development of capitalism itself implied deepening crisis. No doubt this, as well as the obscurity of the theoretical argument, led to the notion disappearing from view after the publication of *The General Theory*.

But dropping the "decline in the marginal efficiency of capital" from Keynes's overall theory leaves an enormous hole in it – however ill worked out the notion is and however unpalatable to defenders of the existing system. For it is the only attempt in *The General Theory* to consider what happens when capital accumulation occurs. Omitting it leaves *The General Theory* as an account of the capitalist economy in which a central characteristic of that economy is missing. As Joan Robinson, one of those Keynesians who dropped "the declining efficiency of capital", says:

> The main topic of *The General Theory* was the consequence of a change in the level effective demand within a short period situation with given plant and available labour. The consequences of changing the stock of plant as investment matures hardly come into the story... Keynes himself had almost nothing to say about growth.[99]

In showing this general lack of concern with accumulation, Keynes was, as in so many other respects, keeping within the neo-classical tradition. To jettison the notion of the declining "marginal efficiency of capital", as most followers of Keynes did, was to jettison his most important, if flawed, attempt to go beyond neo-classicalism.

The post-war synthesis

The version of Keynesianism – sometimes called "orthodox Keynesianism" or the "post-war synthesis" – which hegemonised mainstream economics for the 30 years after the Second World War involved precisely such a purging from Keynes's theory of its non-neo-classical elements. The theory was then reduced to a set of equations showing the alleged interaction between income, interest rates, investment, saving, and the supply of and demand for money – the so called "IS/LM diagram", first drawn up by J H Hicks in 1937.

It turned "Keynes's logical chain of reasoning designed to expose the causes which drive the economy towards a low employment trap into a generalised system of simultaneous equations, devoid of causal significance".[100] This "model" of the total economy could then be treated as a simple addition to the old neo-marginalist account of how prices led to individual commodities being produced in the right quantities to satisfy consumer "demand". And it seemed to lay down golden rules for governments to smooth out the slump-boom cycle and maintain full employment. It thus served "to reconcile revolution and orthodoxy in a double sense: in terms of the discipline of economics, and in terms of the continuity of political and social institutions".[101]

Every element in Keynes's work which might have been construed as a radical critique of free market capitalism was removed. What remained was an account of how easy it was for governments to intervene so as to restore "the best of all possible worlds" – and to do so without upsetting the owners of capitalism. In this way Keynesianism became, in the economics textbooks of the 1950s and 1960s, an apology for capitalism and its main line of defence against the challenge from Marxism.

Joan Robinson, who resented this deradicalisation of Keynes and claimed it was a "bastard Keynesianism" (although she had to admit Keynes himself prepared the ground for it), pointed out that in a certain sense it even restored Say's law. For it portrayed the system as self-equilibrating, provided governments intervened in accordance with its "economic laws":

> The old orthodoxy against which the Keynesian revolution was raised was based on Say's law – there cannot be a deficiency of demand. Spending creates demand for consumption goods, while saving creates demand for investment goods such as machinery and stocks.
>
> Keynes pointed out the obvious fact that investment is governed by decisions of business corporations and public institutions, not by the desire of the community to save.
>
> An increase in household saving means a reduction in consumption; it does not increase investment but reduces employment.
>
> According to the bastard Keynesian doctrine it is possible to calculate the rate of saving that households collectively desire to achieve, and then governments by fiscal and monetary policy can organise the investment of this amount of saving. Thus Say's law is artificially restored, and under its shelter all the old doctrines creep back again.[102]

Among these "old doctrines" was the one Keynes wrote *The General Theory* to refute – the doctrine that unemployment can be cured by cutting wages. For the new orthodoxy's set of equations indicated that if governments intervened according to the rules full employment could be achieved. They purported to show "that any amount of capital will provide employment for any amount of labour at the appropriate equilibrium real wage rate".[103] If unemployment persisted then, it could only be "because wages are being held above the equilibrium level".[104]

Leijonhufvud pointed out nearly 30 years ago that the mainstream "Keynesians" had come to accept the main tenets of "neo-classical resurgence", employing the same basic model and seeing Keynes's theory as a 'special case' of the neo-classical theory.[105] "The Keynesians have, in fact, reverted to explaining unemployment in a manner Keynes was quite critical of, namely by 'blaming' depressions on monopolies, labour unions, minimum wage laws, and the like".

Their conclusion was that "if 'competition' could only be restored, 'automatic forces' would take care of the employment problem. Thus the modern appraisal is that Keynesianism in effect involves the tacit acceptance of the traditional theory of markets with the proviso that today's economy corresponds to a 'special case' of the theory, namely the case that assumes rigid wages".[106]

In fact, the Keynesians came to assume the "rigidity" of wages meant there was an inflationary price to be paid if unemployment was to be cut below a certain point – a notion embodied in a diagram, the "Phillips curve", which purported to show there was a "trade off" between unemployment and inflation. It was only a small step from this to accepting that there was a "natural rate of unemployment" – and that if the average level of unemployment rose over time, it was not because of the irrationalities in the system mentioned by Keynes himself, but because "rigidities in the labour market" were forcing the "natural rate" up.

The differences between "orthodox" Keynesians and monetarist adherents of the old pre-Keynesian orthodoxy became technical differences about how to use a model they shared, not differences of fundamental analysis. Even Milton Friedman, the high priest of monetarism, could call Keynes "one of the great economists of all time", differing with the Keynesian orthodoxy not so much on the overall model of the economy as on important details within it (the importance of controlling the money supply by open market operations).[107]

The disintegration of consensus

The fact that they shared the same basic model of the economy as the monetarists made it easy for lifelong "orthodox" Keynesians to abandon key aspects of their master's teaching when the long boom gave way to a new period of crises in the mid-1970s. All they had to do was to switch from one technical interpretation of the model to another and to argue that little could be done about soaring unemployment except perhaps to clamp down on wages and welfare benefits. Joan Robinson acerbically described the change in their shared message:

> The spokesmen of capitalism were saying: Sorry chaps, we made a mistake, we were not offering full employment, but the natural level of unemployment. Of course, they suggested that a little unemployment would be enough to keep prices stable. But now we know that even a lot will not do so.[108]

Labour's prime minister James Callaghan virtually admitted this when he told his party's conference in September 1976:

> We used to think you could just spend your way out of recession by cutting taxes and boosting government borrowing. I tell you in all

candour that that option no longer exists; and insofar as it ever did exist, it worked by injecting inflation into the economy. And each time that has happened, the average level of unemployment has risen.

The point was repeated by Labour's current economic spokesman, Gordon Brown, at a conference on "global economic options" in September 1994:

> Countries which attempt to run national go it alone macroeconomic policies based on tax, spend, borrow policies to boost demand, without looking to the ability of the supply side of the economy, are bound these days to be punished by the markets in the form of stiflingly high interest rates and collapsing currencies.[109]

The politicians and academics who were brought up on Keynesianism have come to accept the same parameters for deciding economic policy as their old opponents. And like these opponents, they have come to accept that there is no alternative to high levels of unemployment, welfare cuts, "flexibility" to make workers "more competitive" and laws to restrain "trade union power". This is the message to be found today in the speeches of politicians of all mainstream parties, in media commentaries on the economy and in IMF/World Bank reports on particular countries.

Yet the message is not nearly as powerful for defenders of existing society as the Keynesian orthodoxy of 30 years ago, despite the volume at which it is broadcast. It is not as ideologically reassuring to tell people their lives are insecure and going to get worse as to tell them they've "never had it so good", as a Tory prime minister famously did in 1959. And as crises can cause enormous headaches, even to capitalist giants like General Motors and IBM, there is bound to be increasing dissent even at the highest levels of the system at the inability of the dominant economic ideas to provide any explanation of crises and why they tend to get worse.

The result in recent years has been a flourishing of dissident economic schools.

Kalecki and the radical Keynesians

There was an alternative interpretation of Keynes's ideas to that of "orthodox Keynesianism" from the moment *The General Theory* hit the bookshops. Certain of Keynes's closest disciples at Cambridge, such as Richard Kahn, Joan Robinson and Nicholas Kaldor, took up some of those elements in *The General Theory* which questioned the ability of capitalism to attain a full employment equilibrium without "socialisation" of investment.

This "radical" Keynesianism became much more critical of many neo-classical assumptions than Keynes ever was, subjecting them to destructive criticism. But it remained as ambivalent as Keynes himself was as to what to do when faced with the crises of the system. It was stranded, like Keynes, between radical talk on the one hand and recognition of the limits of what is acceptable to those who run the system on the other.

Two economists influenced by Marxism had an impact on the thinking of the radical Keynesians – the Pole Michal Kalecki and the Italian Piero Sraffa.

Kalecki had actually foreshadowed some of the key notions of Keynes's in papers published in Polish (and so unknown to anyone in Britain or the US) in the three years before *The General Theory* appeared.[110] He was much more left wing in his attitudes than Keynes, coming from a family which was hit by unemployment after the First World War, and supported the left wing of the Polish Socialist Party during the 1930s. He was forced to return to Poland in the 1950s by McCarthyism in the US, but then fell out with the Stalinist government because he would not accept that planning should subordinate consumption to accumulation.

Kalecki got from Marx and the Polish-German revolutionary Rosa Luxemburg something not to be found in mainstream economics before Keynes – the view of the economy as a totality, with the level of effective demand dependent upon prior decisions about investment.[111] Kalecki's own experience as a business statistician also convinced him that the central neo-classical assumption of diminishing returns was wrong. Diminishing returns, he argued, occurred only in the production of raw materials, but not in manufacturing, where increasing returns were the rule.

However, Kalecki disregarded key elements in Marx's own theory: the labour theory of value, the tracing of profit back to surplus value acquired by exploitation in the production process, and the tendency of the rate of profit to fall. He showed no interest in value theory and saw profit as dependent on the degree of monopoly control a firm exercised over the market. This in turn meant that "from Kalecki's approach there is no clear prediction on the course of the rate of profit".[112]

Instead he saw a tendency to "a slowing down in the growth of capitalist economies in the late stages of development", resulting "in part from the decline in the intensity of innovations" connected with "the declining importance of the discovery of new sources of raw materials, of new lands to be developed, etc." and with "the increasing monopolistic character of capitalism" which "would hamper the application of new inventions".[113]

He expected there to be a rising trend in the level of unemployment after the war that only deficit government budgeting would be able to counter. When, instead, the system experienced the longest sustained boom in its history, the great majority of economists showed no interest in "the problems raised by Kalecki" such as "the question of whether the stimulation of private investment can be adequate for long-term full employment, and, if not, how a policy involving a permanent deficit" is possible.[114]

Once the boom was under way, Kalecki and the "radical Keynesians" he influenced tended to see the problem of maintaining "effective demand" and full employment not as an economic problem, intrinsic to the dynamics of the system, but as a political problem – that of persuading big business to go against its own instincts and accept government intervention in investment decisions. The arms economy was important for him, because it involved a form of spending easily accepted by big business, not because of its influence on some aspect of the fundamental dynamics of the system.

Sraffa and the onslaught on marginalism

Sraffa too came from a left socialist background and was influenced by Marxism: he had written for Gramsci's paper *Ordine Nuovo* in the early 1920s, maintained a correspondence with him in prison for the ten years before his death in 1937 and acted as his main connection to the outside world. He was also friendly with Keynes, owing to him a position at Cambridge and a job editing Ricardo's collected works. But his approach to economics was very different to that either of Kalecki or Keynes. His concern was not with either effective demand or the cause of unemployment, but to destroy the theoretical basis of neo-classical theory and to reinstate the approach to be found in Ricardo and Marx. This he attempted to do in *The Production of Commodities by Means of Commodities*, published in 1960.

The work is a highly formalistic model of an economy, showing how it is possible to derive the set of physical quantities of different commodities and the prices at which they exchange by starting from the assumptions made by Ricardo and abandoned by marginalism. Far from supply and demand playing the central role ascribed to them by mainstream economics for the last century, each is shown to be a mere by-product of the existing technical organisation of production and the distribution of output between investment, capitalists' consumption and workers' consumption.

As Joan Robinson summarises the work's conclusions, "There is no room for demand equations in the determination of equilibrium prices." "The marginal productivity theory of distribution" – which is used by mainstream economists to justify profit and oppose minimum wage laws – "is all bosh...Sraffa...demonstrates conclusively that there is no such thing as a 'quantity of capital' which exists independently of the rate of profit".[115]

The radical Keynesians at Cambridge took up Sraffa's point, insisting that the neo-classical economists' elaborate algebraic calculations and geometrical curves rested on a tautology as meaningless as that which says, "An egg is an egg." The neo-classicists said profits and interest were "rewards" for "abstention", "waiting" or "production time", and were equal to the increase in value ("marginal product") produced by extra capital. So the rate of profit was marginal product divided by the value of the total capital. But how was the value of that capital to be measured? It could not be arrived at by adding together the different physical measurements of goods that made up the means and materials of production (tons of iron, gallons of oil, kilowatts of electricity, etc.). In fact, it depended, according to marginalist theory, on the value of the marginal product – the same thing that the measurement of profit depended on. In that case, there was no way of arriving at a figure for the ratio of the profit to the capital, that is, at the rate of profit. Or, to put it another way, the rate of profit and interest depended on the amount of capital, and the amount of capital depended on the rate of profit and interest.[116]

Neo-classical economics became a set of equations referring to nothing real. As Joan Robinson put it:

> Quantitative utility has long since evaporated, but it is still common to set up models in which quantities of "capital" appear, without any indication of what it is supposed to be a quantity of. Just as the problem of giving an operational meaning to utility used to be avoided by putting it into a

diagram, so the problem of giving a meaning to the quantity of "capital" is evaded by putting it into algebra.[117]

The analysis of marginalist "capital theory" led to another, related conclusion which destroyed the old argument that workers would always be able to get jobs if only they accepted lower wages. The marginalist argument rested on the assumption that as wages fell it would always be profitable for capitalists to switch from "capital-intensive" to "labour-intensive" techniques of production, so absorbing unemployed workers. Kaldor and Robinson showed that, in fact, a growth of profits at the expense of wages could so alter prices as to cause a process they called "reswitching" – a change making it more profitable for the capitalist to cut the workforce by using capital-intensive rather than labour-intensive methods.[118] Garegnani has gone further and suggested that if neo-classical theory were to take account of this phenomenon of "reswitching" it would have to paint a picture not of an economy in a state of equilibrium, but of one much more unstable than "has ever been observed in reality". This, he has argued, reflects "the absence of a factual base" for neo-classical theory.[119]

In these ways Sraffa's work laid the basis for tearing apart the logical foundations of marginalism, while proving that a theory of value based on the tradition of Ricardo and Marx could work. To this extent, it threw into question the great body of textbook economics. As Joan Robinson put it, "This knocked the bottom out of the logical structure of orthodox theory, but mainstream teaching goes on just the same".[120]

Sraffa's writings did not, however, replace marginalism with any positive analysis of economic issues. They could not, because they were simply a formal proof that a model based on Ricardo's arguments would work, and did not attempt to provide real-life examples of what was involved. Robinson admits, "Sraffa's model is too pure to make a direct contribution to formulating answerable questions about reality, but it makes a very great contribution to saving us from formulating unanswerable questions".[121]

In fact, Sraffa himself did not claim it could do more than this. It was, the subtitle of the work proclaimed, a "prelude to" – a clearing of the ground for – "a critique of political economy". But this of necessity meant it could not begin to measure up to the writings of Ricardo, let alone Marx, when it came to saying anything about the dynamics of the system.

Sraffa himself told people that "he would not have been able to write the *Production of Commodities by Means of Commodities* if Marx had not written *Capital*... He had been strongly influenced by the work of Marx, and he felt more sympathy with him than with those he called the 'whitewashers' of capitalist reality".[122] Joan Robinson reports, "Piero always stuck close to pure unadulterated Marx".[123]

Yet some radical Keynesians claimed that Sraffa provided an alternative "neo-Ricardian" method to that of Marx which showed the irrelevance of the labour theory of value and, with it, the falsity of his theory of the declining rate of profit.[124] These "neo-Ricardians" drew the conclusion that in the real capitalist world the only thing that could produce a fall in the rate of profit was a rise in the share of output going to wages – or, as Marx would have put it, "a fall in the rate of exploitation".

Their conclusion was that the crisis of capitalism was a result of low levels of investment because of the sharpness of the class struggle – an argument presented in the early 1970s, for instance, by two left wing economists, Glyn and Sutcliffe, in a popular paperback, *British Capitalism, Workers and the Profits Squeeze*.[125] Glyn and Sutcliffe themselves put a left slant on this, arguing that it showed the wages struggle had to be political and challenge the system as a whole if it was not to lead to unemployment. But the argument easily led back to the old orthodoxy that wages were to blame for unemployment and that, therefore, the way out of the crisis lay through wage cuts – whether these were pushed through in the "pre-Keynesian" way by the individual employer or in a "Keynesian" way using incomes policy.

Sraffa's writings may have torn the pretensions of neo-classicalism apart, but the "neo-Ricardian" system built on them acted as a bridge between radical Keynesians and their "orthodox Keynesian" colleagues, just as these were reaching a degree of consensus with the old pre-Keynesian orthodoxy.

Other criticisms of neo-classicalism

The arguments of Kalecki and Sraffa were not the only ones the radical Keynesians could use against the neo-classical assumptions of the "orthodox" Keynesians. A whole range of other anti-marginalist arguments emerged in the 1940s and 1950s. It was pointed out, for instance, that the neo-classical assumption of rapid and automatic adjustment of supply and demand through the price mechanism was impossible in reality.

Walras had written as if there were some "auctioneer" acting for the economy as a whole to bid prices up and down. But in reality any adjustment only takes place on an ad hoc basis, commodity by commodity, over time. Even before supply and demand have come into line for one commodity, the conditions of production for other, related commodities can have changed, so altering the conditions of supply and demand for the first commodity. For instance, by the time the price of grain has moved in such a way as to balance supply and demand, the price of fertilisers used to produce the grain can have further changed, so altering the costs of supplying the grain – and preventing the price from maintaining the balance with demand.

As the economist Schumpeter – a non-Marxist and non-Keynesian whose own ideas grew out of Böhm-Bawerk's version of marginalism – summarised the argument in the early 1940s:

> Once equilibrium has been destroyed by some disturbance, the process of establishing a new one is not so sure and prompt and economical as the old theory of perfect competition made it out to be... The very struggle for adjustment might lead such a system farther away from instead of nearer to a new equilibrium.[126]

Again Schumpeter could point out that the neo-classical assumption of perfect competition was incompatible with firms making any long-term investment in innovation. For perfect competition should mean that the moment a firm started reaping rewards from its investment, other firms would be able to muscle in on its markets, taking advantage of innovations it had initiated. "The introduction of new methods of production and new commodities is hardly compatible with perfect and perfectly prompt competition from the start... As a matter of fact, perfect competition has always been temporarily stemmed whenever anything new is being introduced".[127]

He saw the "dynamism" of capitalism as resting on the "creative destruction" wrought by the struggle of competing near monopolies, not on the neo-classical picture of perfect competition and flexibility of prices. Schumpeter held that far from tending "to maximise production" these features of the pure neo-classical model "might in depression further unstabilise the system".[128]

The neo-classicalists could not reply to these arguments. But there was a sense in which they did not need to. While the long boom lasted there did seem, to those who could not be bothered to look beneath the surface of economic events, to be some correspondence between the orthodox Keynesian neo-classical "synthesis" model and the reality of continually growing, more or less full-employment economies. Even economists like Schumpeter and Galbraith who saw the logical flaws in neo-classicalism argued that the capitalist economy could grow rapidly and improve people's living standards despite – or even because of – them.[129] There was little obstacle to the neo-classicalists continuing as if their arguments had never been questioned. As Joan Robinson writes:

> Orthodox theory reacted to this challenge, in true theological style, by inventing fanciful worlds in which the difference between the past and the future does not arise and devising intricate mathematical theorems about how an economy would operate if everyone in it had correct insight about how everyone else was going to behave.[130]

"New classical" and "supply side" counter-revolution

Even the ending of the long boom in the mid-1970s did not destroy the confidence of the neo-classical economists. Indeed, at first it reinforced it. What had failed, they claimed, was not the "free market" but attempts to "interfere" with its free operation. All that was necessary to return to the best of all possible worlds, argued "new classical economists", was to end that interference. As two of their critics write:

> The Keynesian consensus faltered in the 1970s. The new classical economists argued persuasively that Keynesian economics was theoretically inadequate, that macroeconomics must be built on firm microeconomic foundations. They also argued that Keynesian economics should be replaced with macroeconomic theories based on the assumptions that markets always clear and the economic actors always optimise... They imply that the invisible hand always guides the economy to the efficient allocation of resources.[131]

The extreme logic of this position was to argue against any government intervention in the economy: "The central lesson of economic theory is the proposition that a competitive economy if left to its own devices will do a good job at allocating resources".[132] Recessions would cure themselves:

> Recession in a laissez-faire society is a period of readjustment...a manifestation of individuals exercising legitimate property rights. Entrepreneurial alertness and freedom to profit from it promote the most rapid discovery of exchange possibilities that end recession and reduce unemployment.[133]

Because of this, they insisted, von Mises had been quite right to conclude, "Unemployment in an unhampered market is always voluntary".[134] Or, as the new classicalist Edward Prescott, put it, "rhythmic fluctuations" in unemployment are really "counter-cyclical movements in the demand for leisure".[135]

The job of governments was not to try to speed up or slow down the total "macroeconomic" functioning of the economy. Instead, their job was to pull back from intervention as much as possible, in particular by cutting taxes on incomes, so increasing the "supply side" incentives to entrepreneurial initiative. So effective would cuts in tax rates be, argued the most politically influential of the "new classical economists" in the Reagan years – the so-called "supply siders" – that total government revenue was bound to rise, balancing the budget automatically as the free market caused the economy to return to its natural boom condition.

Even the failure of Friedman's monetarism to control the money supply, inflation and the cyclical movement of the economy in the 1980s (for instance, under Thatcher in Britain) did not dent the enthusiasm of the most thoroughgoing of the new classicalists for their reborn dogma. For, they argued, Friedman fell into the same trap as Keynes by urging government intervention to shift the money supply: he was, in a certain sense, "a Keynesian".[136] Such moves could not alter business behaviour in the hoped-for way, since the "rational expectations" of entrepreneurs would always lead them to discount government intervention in advance. Fiddling with the money supply, like government deficit spending, stopped supply and demand reacting to each other properly. "Booms and slumps", it was claimed, "are the outcome of fraudulent Central Reserve banking".[137]

It is an amazing commentary on the remoteness of most academic economics from any contact with reality that the "new classicals" could maintain intellectual credibility when they denied the instability and irrationality of the laissez-faire economy in a period which saw three major international recessions. But they had one very important asset on their side: their ideas were very comforting to the ruling class and its placemen and women holding positions of influence in the media and the universities. On this Joan Robinson was quite right:

> The radicals have the easier case to make. They have only to point to the discrepancies between the operation of the modern economy and the ideas by which it is supposed to be judged, while the conservatives have the well nigh impossible task of demonstrating that this is the best of all possible worlds. For the same reason, however, the conservatives are compensated by occupying positions of power, which they can use to keep criticism in check... The conservatives do not feel obliged to answer radical criticisms on their merits and the argument is never fairly joined.[138]

The high point of these sort of ideas was in the mid to late 1980s. The short-lived boom in the advanced Western countries seemed to vindicate their optimism about the benefits to economic growth of deregulation, privatisation and dropping all restraints on the greed of the rich. At the same time the crisis and then collapse of the old "Communist" bloc seemed to prove that attempts at national planning were doomed to failure. Its ex-planners were suddenly lauding the virtues of the Western market and lapping up the pre-Keynesian pure market message preached by Milton Friedman and Friedrich von Hayek. In the third world, "dependency economists", who had looked to the national state as the only way to break the stranglehold of the first world over economic advance, now embraced the free market balanced-budget "structural adjustment" programmes of the IMF and the World Bank. In the West many prominent left wing intellectuals concluded that capitalism had proved its economic superiority to "socialism": the editor of *New Left Review* in Britain could write a long article suggesting that the critique of "socialist planning" by von Mises and Hayek was vindicated by the Russian experience.[139]

The breakdown in orthodoxy: the "Austrian school"

Just as the boom of the late 1980s gave a boost to "free market" and "new classical" views, the recession of the early 1990s inevitably caused a reaction against these. It produced a sense of panic which the bland reassurances of the "new classicals" did little to calm down. In this climate there was a new hearing, even in respectable bourgeois circles, for ideas which questioned some of the tenets of neo-classical equilibrium theory.

Three main sets of "heterodox" views have gained prominence as a result, known respectively as the "Austrian school", the "New Keynesians", and the "complexity" or "chaos" theorists.

The first school is as committed to unfettered free markets as the "new classicals" and has its origins in the marginalist theories of Menger and Böhm-Bawerk as developed in varying ways by von Mises, Hayek and Schumpeter. Hayek was an early critic of Keynes in the 1930s. But it was in the 1980s that he achieved real prominence. He was Margaret Thatcher's favourite economist because he had argued for years that, if only regulation was abandoned and unions were weakened, then the economy would automatically be restored to its optimal condition. "The regular cause of extensive unemployment is real wages that are too high," he had insisted in one of his more popular writings in 1970. The responsibility for unemployment then lies with trade unions which use their power "in a manner which makes the market ineffective". Union power had to be curbed "at its source".[140]

This version of Hayek's argument hardly differed from that of the "new classical" economists, and gained him popularity in right wing circles for similar reasons. But it was possible to put a gloss on his more academic writings which seemed to protect them from the accusation of simply ignoring the reality of crises. For in the course of the 1930s Hayek had in part broken away from his previous view that slumps were simply a result of mistaken government monetary policies. His works at points came close to accepting that there was something intrinsic to capitalist production that led to investment growing too rapidly in boom periods, with slumps as an inevitable counter-reaction.[141] He could talk about "the limits of traditional neo-classical theory" and accept that "economic agents...different expectations about the world might lead to divergence rather than convergence of behaviour".[142] He referred to the term "equilibrium" which "economists usually use to the describe the competition process' as 'unfortunate",[143] noting that the "fundamental problem" about "the relevance of the concept of equilibrium" is "the explanation of a process taking place in time",[144] and preferring, himself, to use the term "order". He could even, in one passage, admit that Marx was responsible for introducing, in Germany at least, ideas that could explain the trade cycle, while "the only satisfactory theory of capital we yet possess, that of Böhm-Bawerk", had "not helped us much further with the problems of the trade cycle".[145]

"Competition is valuable", he wrote later, "only insofar as its results are unpredictable and on the whole differ from those which anyone has, or could have, deliberately aimed at".[146] "Spontaneous order produced by the market does not ensure that what general opinion regards as more important needs are always met before the less important ones".[147]

These writings mean that, while the likes of Margaret Thatcher acclaim Hayek for showing the wonders of the unrestrained market, some economists now claim that he produced a non-apologetic version of market economics which broke away from the crudities of the neo-classical school. This seems, for instance, to be the attitude of Paul Ormerod, who writes of "the much misunderstood Hayek".[148] The implication is that a non-apologetic economics, which drops neo-classical equilibrium theory but retains marginalism, can be built on a Hayekian basis.

But there is no such possibility. Hayek may have been forced at points in the 1930s to concede the inadequacy of the neo-classical notion of equilibrium. But he could never fully drop such a key assumption of the marginalist theories on which he based himself. In both his academic and his popular writings he again and again reverted to it, taking it for granted that the market left to itself will tend to produce the best possible organisation of production. Thus he wrote of "the price mechanism" as a "self-equilibrating system" in one of the very works which attempted to describe the pressures driving to boom and slump;[149] the only problem, as he saw it, was that "money by its very nature constitutes a kind of loose joint" in this apparatus – as if the apparatus could exist without money! He might claim to reject "equilibrium theory", but he was capable in the same passage of arguing that it is possible to avoid a "disequilibrating effect", and "to rescue as much as possible this slack in the self correcting forces of the price mechanism".[150]

So one minute he rejected the notion of equilibrium and the next he embraced it. It is this which enabled him to suggest elsewhere that if only "conditions in general are conducive to easy and rapid movements of labour" then this will "create stable conditions of high employment".[151]

He wanted to have his cake and eat it – to attack the notion of equilibrium when it clearly clashed with the harsh empirical reality of mass unemployment and the slump-boom cycle, but to return to it when he was intent on polemicising against trade unions and in defence of free markets.

He believed the unrestrained market led to the best of all possible worlds, since it encouraged entrepreneurs to undertake new and more efficient methods of production in a dynamic way. But at the same time he could not avoid recognising that it produced enormous and repeated disruption of people's lives: "In a continuously changing world, even mere maintenance of a given level of wealth requires incessant changes in the direction of greater effort of some, which will be brought about only if the remuneration of some activities is increased and that of others is decreased".[152]

Hayek would insist that competition would only "work" by rejecting any attempt to ease the burden of change on the mass of people. In one rare passage he even expressed the fear that "the communist countries" had the advantage over "the capitalist countries" of being "freer from the incubus of 'social justice' and more willing to let those bear the burden against whom development turns".[153]

The ambiguities built into Hayek's writings has led, in recent years, to a growing division among Hayekians over how to interpret the master's ideas. "This problem has, in recent years, split the Austrians into two camps" – between those who believe the market leads to a coordination of supply and demand, and those who "question whether markets coordinate".[154]

This second group tends to be influenced not only by Hayek's writings, but also by Schumpeter, who, as we have seen, could be as critical of neo-classical notions of "perfect competition" and "perfect knowledge" as any radical Keynesian, and whose own account of the overall functioning of the system is, at points, closer to Marx's than to that of the neo-classical orthodoxy. But Schumpeter insisted he differed fundamentally with Marx – and, for that matter, Keynes – in his view of the future of the system. Neither Marx's "rate of profit" nor Keynes's "marginal efficiency of investment" was going to decline, and there would be no tendency for crises to worsen. Precisely because the system was based on monopoly and imperfect competition, innovation would lead to economic growth on a scale which, he predicted in 1950, would within "half a century" "do away with anything that according to present standards could be called poverty".[155]

This version of the "Austrian" model, with its picture of a system driven to create unimaginable levels of output, but only on the basis of "creative destruction" and the boom-slump cycle, has had a certain appeal in recent years to politicians running capitalism and wanting some excuse for their inability to avoid slumps. So it is that Nigel Lawson, who as Tory chancellor of the exchequer claimed he was presiding over an "economic miracle" during the late 1980s boom, now says he is not responsible for the slump which followed because the "business cycle" is inevitable. But it is a picture that can hardly appeal to those whose lives are torn apart by the "creative destruction" of the slump and whose support capitalist politicians seek in the run-up to an election. A stress on the inevitability of further slumps is not likely to win many votes. Whatever they may think in private, most current politicians are likely to repeat in public the reassuring nostrums of the "new classicals" and claim that if only the "supply side" is efficient then maximum employment will follow.

The "New Keynesians" and the complexity theorists

Alongside the revival of interest in the ideas of Hayek and Schumpeter there has also been the emergence, especially in certain US academic circles, of the sort of criticisms of neo-classicalism and "free market" capitalism made by the followers of Keynes half a century ago. "ew Keynesians" like Mankiw and Romer[156] have returned to the old arguments about monopoly, imperfect competition and the failure of supply and demand to adjust to each other. Joseph Stiglitz has emphasised the failure of market prices to transmit information in the way the neo-classical economists claim and the incompatibility of "perfect competition" with innovation; neo-classical theory is "simply not robust at all", he concludes.[157] Card and Kreuger have shown that the contention that minimum wage laws cost jobs is empirically wrong.[158]

Will Hutton has transmitted popularised versions of these ideas to a quite wide audience in Britain through his regular columns in *The Guardian* and *The Observer* and in his bestselling attack on British economic policy, *The State We're In*. He claims:

> Over the last decade a new generation of Keynesians, American almost to a man and woman, have been mounting a vigorous fightback, resurrecting and updating Keynes's ideas – and devastating the free market position as much as Keynes ever did. They show how the neo-classical idea that the world of money somehow stands apart from the real world of production and exchange is unsustainable; they demonstrate that markets necessarily have profoundly disruptive imperfections.[159]

The "new Keynesian" assault on free market orthodoxy has been joined from a rather different direction by a group of theorists which grew out of seminars on "chaos" and "complexity" run by mathematicians and physicists at Stanford University, California. They applied their mathematical methods to the economy and found that, far from a system based on the adjustment of supply and demand through the movement of prices arriving at an equilibrium state, it behaves according to chaos theory, possessing "an extremely high number of natural ground states, or equilibria".[160] As Medio puts it, "when the stability hypothesis" was put to the test using systems of equations, "no compelling reason could be found for the equilibrium system to be stable". What is more, the conditions which would have produced stability "were found to correspond to...economically arbitrary constraints".[161] Or, as Peter Smith of Manchester University has put it, "chaos theory suggests that even without external disturbances, permanent, large, patternless oscillations can occur". It "radically challenges" the "received wisdom" that competitive markets are "inherently stable" and that "they provide a benign system of informative price signals".[162] In other words, there was no reason to expect an economy built on neo-classical principles to settle down to a condition of full employment.

So convincing have such arguments been that they have won over Kenneth Arrow, who was joint author with Debreu of a very influential updated exposition of the neo-classical "general equilibrium system". Now he admits that this "Walrasian system" only works "if you assume no technological progress, no growth in population and lots of other things". Otherwise:

> We can have perfectly good examples where everybody perfectly foresees the future and seeks to equilibrate supply and demand on all markets present and future simultaneously and where the economy simply whirls round; it does not converge to a steady state... With different kinds of goods, it is possible to produce examples where the economy can produce almost any kind of behaviour.[163]

Not surprisingly, Arrow is scathing about attempts to explain away unemployment and crises using the old orthodoxy: "The new classical theorists tell various stories that I do not find convincing... The new classical economics is built on market clearing. And I do not believe markets clear".[164]

Paul Ormerod has provided a popular exposition of some of these "new Keynesian" and "chaos theory" attacks on the neo-classical orthodoxy in his book *The Dead of Economics*, where he compares its "understanding of the world" to "that of the physical sciences in the middle ages"[165] (although, interestingly, he does not go so far as to repeat the far more thoroughgoing criticisms of marginalism to be found in the "Cambridge school" writings of Sraffa and Robinson, neither of whom he even mentions).

Yet if the criticisms of the orthodoxy made by both groups of theorists are devastating and expose the hollowness of what passed for "the laws of economics" among not just right wing, but also Labour and social democratic politicians and opinion makers, their conclusions are not necessarily at all radical.

They may be more trenchant in their critique of neo-classical assumptions than were the "orthodox" post-war Keynesians, but they do not go any further than them in their criticism of the system which neo-classical economics attempts to sanctify. Again and again their practical conclusion is to suggest a reliance on the same failed techniques of limited government intervention, through taxation, borrowing and monetary policies, as the old "orthodox Keynesians". Indeed, it is often the case that a more radical criticism is combined with even less reliance on government action.

Some of the American "new Keynesians" are not even clear whether it is the neo-classical model of the economy which will not function, or whether instead – as in Pigou's pre-Keynesian explanation of unemployment – the problem is that the real economy suffers from "monopolistic" practices and "sticky" prices and wages not to be found in the model.[166] This can easily be interpreted by politicians as meaning all that is required to deal with recession is to wage a war on monopolistic practices, including union practices, as the free market economists urge.

For Will Hutton's *The State We're In* the problem is not capitalism, but the British model of capitalism, which, he claims, is dominated not by the long-term drive of industry for competitive investment, but short-term profit taking by financial institutions. He suggests that, if only a "German", a "Japanese", or even an "American" model of capitalism was adopted, everything would be all right. Yet, as even he sometimes admits, these countries too have all been hit by the recession of the first half of the 1990s, with the most intractable problems seeming to be in his most favoured model, Japan.

For Stiglitz, the conclusions to be drawn are not dissimilar to those of Hayek. The neo-classical model is wrong, and the system does not come to any easy equilibrium. The result is that people suffer, in a way that the neo-classical economists refuse to admit. But at the end of the day, there is no alternative to this messy state of affairs and we have to accept recessions and a certain level of waste, if not as the best of all possible worlds, then as the least bad.[167]

Ormerod manages to go in a complete circle. He begins his book *The Death of Economics* with a devastating attack on existing economic orthodoxy – and ends up with diagrams suggesting the very conventional conclusion that if only people would accept lower living standards, high employment would result: "The solution to mass unemployment would require many people in employment to surrender income in exchange for leisure".[168]

More recently, in a letter to *The Guardian* defending the policies of Blair and Brown, he argues that Hayek pointed to "theoretical reasons", which are backed up by chaos theory's "recognition of the limits of knowledge in non-linear systems", for the failure of "social reform programmes" to promote "equality of opportunity".[169] In other words, because the economy operates in a chaotic manner, all we can do is hope for the best. The message is that we live in an irrational world and we have to grin and bear it. The critic of the neo-classical orthodoxy ends up with the same attitude of resignation in face of the disorder and inhumanity of the economic system as a whole (the "macro-economy") as do the "new classical" apologists for the system.

Conclusion

In 1936 Keynes suggested there was a fundamental feature of the system which led crises inevitably to grow deeper in a free market system – the "declining efficiency of investment". He also suggested this could not be countered except by the state going beyond trying to influence the parameters within which businessmen took decisions; there needed to be a "socialisation" of investment. The "orthodox" post-war Keynesians retreated from these radical positions – and so have the "new Keynesians".

The radical Keynesians did attempt to hold to the notion of the "socialisation" of investment. But they did so within a framework which took for granted certain features of capitalism – the relation of wage labour and capital, the inevitable subordination of living labour to dead labour, the need for "economies" to be competitive with each other. This was what was involved in the rejection of

Marx's theory of value, with its depiction of the whole accumulation process as alienated labour taking on a life of its own. The result was, on the one hand, an underestimation of the contradictions of capitalism, abandoning Keynes's notion of "declining marginal efficiency of capital" without embracing Marx's insight into the tendency of the rate of profit to fall. On the other hand, it was to see the future as lying with the "planned" state capitalisms of the Eastern Bloc and parts of the third world. When these entered into crisis, the radicals were left with little to say.

The limited revival of Keynesian ideas today in the writings of Will Hutton and others is a testimony to the depths of the crisis of the system. But the modern Keynesians are even less willing than Keynes was to talk of radical solutions – hence their complete silence over his call for "socialisation of investment". If he was not willing, in practice, to fight for the implementation of such talk but instead bowed down before the need to maintain the "confidence" of industrialists and financiers, they are certainly not going to fight for more far-reaching action. So they vacillate between criticising parties like Labour or the Democrats in the US, who have accepted the revived laissez-faire orthodoxy, and endorsing their latest proposals.

This reinforces a simple truth. The questions the Keynesians, old and new, have raised about how to deal with the inbuilt tendency of capitalism to economic crisis are not ones that can be solved in Keynesian terms. For a time capitalism did seem to have an answer to the problem. But it was not the liberal or social democratic answer suggested by the Keynesians. Rather it involved the most barbaric of measures – the militarisation of the economy, the waging of all-out war and the stockpiling of weapons of mass destruction. And today, even such barbarism is no longer enough to prevent repeated crises.

Keynes was right to suggest that the secret of overcoming the tendency to crisis lies in the socialisation of production. Only that can allow people's expectations when they undertake production to correspond to any great degree to the circumstances that exist when production comes on stream. And only this can ensure that investment continues as profit rates tend to decline below levels that would motivate private capital. But Keynes was quite wrong to suggest that such socialisation of investment could come about gradually, with the acquiescence of private capital, even in his own day. It is certainly not going to happen today, with giant firms increasingly organised on a multinational basis and able to move funds from country to country to wreck the plans of any government that challenges their investment decisions while leaving untouched their control of the means of production.

Labour and social democratic politicians and economists say that "globalisation" prevents any state challenging the multinationals. They are wrong. The multinationals can be challenged, but only by action much more radical than that of which Keynesians, old or new, have ever dreamt. As Rosa Luxemburg once wrote, "Where the chains of capital are forged, there they have to be smashed." There has to be a battle in every workplace to seize control of the means of production from capital as part of the battle to create a new sort of state, based on direct workers' representatives, if there is to be the real planning of investment which Keynes, in his more radical moments, saw as necessary. Keynes, as we have seen, hated the very idea of such a revolution. The fate of the post-war orthodoxy built around his ideas shows that without such a revolution his dream of resolving the crisis of the system cannot be fulfilled.

Appendix: Sraffa and the neo-Ricardian criticism of Marx

The 'Neo-Ricardian' argument against Marxism by Steedman and others rests on the claim that Sraffa showed it was possible to build a model of a functioning capitalist economy using a standard basket of goods ('the standard commodity') as the basis for measuring value, without any need to refer to labour.

The claim is misplaced. Not only did Sraffa himself not make such a claim, but the 'standard basket of goods' approach only works if you ignore the changes in production that take place with accumulation – that is all the time in any real capitalist economy. For such changes involve continual changes in the proportions of different goods produced through the economy, so that a 'standard basket of goods' which might serve as a measure of output at one time cannot serve as such a measure at some other time. If you want a measure of value which is not subject to such a change, you have to find something which remains fixed as output changes – that is, you have to look to labour as the measure of value.

The confusion arises because Sraffa's own model is not really a model of capitalist accumulation at all. It assumes that each round of production produces the same goods in the same proportions as each previous round of production – or, to use Marx's language, it is a model of 'simple reproduction', not expanded reproduction.[1]

Like the neo-classical theory it attacks, it is a model of the economy that exists outside time. That is why it can serve as a 'prelude to a critique of political economy', but nothing more. It certainly does not begin to deal with questions that are central to Marx – the dynamic of competitive accumulation, the drive for 'dead labour' to grow more rapidly than living labour, the consequent increase in the productivity of labour and the loss in value of already produced goods, the effect of these changes on the ratio of profit to investment (the rate of profit) and thus on the ability for accumulation to proceed at the necessary pace to provide a market for all the goods that are being turned out. Marx's work begins with the analysis of the commodity and the location of value in labour, but goes on to point to the endemic contradictions of the system, the way these lead to periodic crises of 'overproduction', and the long term trends in the system that tend to make these get worse over time.

By contrast, Sraffa does not even approach the question of short term, cyclical crises of overproduction. As Robinson points out while praising Sraffa: 'There is no discussion of the realisation of surplus as profit. It is merely taken for granted that whatever is produced is disposed of at such prices as to result in a uniform rate of profit in all lines of production.'[2] 'Consequently, there is no causality in Sraffa's system. The capitalists do not decide what labour to employ, what prices to set and what investment plans to draw up. All they do is meekly to fulfil the equations that the observing economist has written down'.[3]

Indeed, in this respect, Sraffa's work is a step backwards from Ricardo. He did begin to touch on such questions in the chapter *On Machinery* added to the third edition of his *Principles of Political Economy*. Here he accepted that the mechanisation of production can be detrimental to the interests of the worker.

The neo-Ricardian school that claimed to base itself on Sraffa's work, therefore, was moving backwards, not forwards, when it counterposed itself to Marxism. What is more, the 'neo-Ricardians' have proven completely incapable of explaining the increased incidence of crisis over the last quarter century.

The key issue here became that of profitability. Sraffa's timeless model takes the technical conditions of production as fixed and then makes the rate of profit depend solely on the division of the product between wages, profits and rents. There can then be no fall in the rate of profit without an increase in the workers' share of output. But the 'workers' share' has fallen virtually everywhere in the 1980s and 1990s, without restoring the old rates of profit and growth of the system.[4]

By abandoning Marx, the neo-Ricardians have left themselves as incapable of explaining what has gone wrong with the system as the outright apologists for it. The disproof of the neo-Ricardian pudding is in the eating.

First published in *International Socialism* 71, summer 1996

The rate of profit and the world today

The "tendency of the rate of profit to fall" is one of the most contentious elements in Karl Marx's intellectual legacy.[1] He regarded it as one of his most important contributions to the analysis of the capitalist system, calling it, in his first notebooks for *Capital* (now published as the *Grundrisse*), "in every respect the most important law of modern political economy".[2] But it has been subjected to criticism ever since his argument first appeared in print with the publication of volume three of *Capital* in 1894.

The first criticisms in the 1890s came from opponents of Marxism, such as the liberal Italian philosopher Benedetto Croce and the German neo-classical economist Eugen von Böhm-Bawerk. But they have been accepted since by many Marxists – from Paul Sweezy in the 1940s to people such as Gérard Duménil and Robert Brenner today.

The argument was and is important. For Marx's theory leads to the conclusion that the there is a fundamental, unreformable flaw in capitalism. The rate of profit is the key to capitalists being able to achieve their goal of accumulation. But the more accumulation takes place, the more difficult it is for them make sufficient profit to sustain it: "The rate of self-expansion of capitalism, or the rate of profit, being the goal of capitalist production, its fall... appears as a threat to the capitalist production process".[3]

This "testifies to the merely historical, transitory character of the capitalist mode of production" and to the way that "at a certain stage it conflicts with its own further development".[4] It showed that "the real barrier of capitalist production was capital itself".[5]

Marx and his critics

Marx's basic line of argument was simple enough. Each individual capitalist can increase his (or occasionally her) own competitiveness through increasing the productivity of his workers. The way to do this is by using a greater quantity of the "means of production" – tools, machinery and so on – for each worker. There is a growth in the ratio of the physical extent of the means of production to the amount of labour power employed, a ratio that Marx called the "technical composition of capital".

But a growth in the physical extent of the means of production will also be a growth in the investment needed to buy them. So this too will grow faster than the investment in the workforce. To use Marx's terminology, "constant capital" grows faster than "variable capital". The growth of this ratio, which he calls the "organic composition of capital",[6] is a logical corollary of capital accumulation.

Yet the only source of value for the system as a whole is labour. If investment grows more rapidly than the labour force, it must also grow more rapidly than the value created by the workers, which is where profit comes from. In short, capital investment grows more rapidly than the source of profit. As a consequence, there will be a downward pressure on the ratio of profit to investment – the rate of profit.

Each capitalist has to push for greater productivity in order to stay ahead of competitors. But what seems beneficial to the individual capitalist is disastrous for the capitalist class as a whole. Each time productivity rises there is a fall in the average amount of labour in the economy as a whole needed to produce a commodity (what Marx called "socially necessary labour"), and it is this which determines what other people will eventually be prepared to pay for that commodity. So today we can see a continual fall in the price of goods such as computers or DVD players produced in industries where new technologies are causing productivity to rise fastest.

The arguments against Marx

Three arguments have been raised time and again against Marx.

The first is that there need not be any reason for new investment to take a "capital-intensive" rather than a "labour-intensive" form. If there is unused labour available in the system, there seems no reason why capitalists should invest in machines rather than labour. There is a theoretical reply to this argument. Capitalists are driven to seek innovations in technologies that keep them ahead of their rivals. Some such innovations may be available using techniques that are not capital-intensive. But there will be others that require more means of production – and the successful capitalist will be the one whose investments provide access to both sorts of innovation.

There is also an empirical reply. Investment in material terms has in fact grown faster than the workforce. So, for instance, the net stock of capital per person employed in the US grew at 2 to 3 percent a year from 1948 to 1973.[7] In China today much of the investment is "capital-intensive", with the employed workforce only growing at about 1 percent a year, despite the vast pools of rural labour.

The second objection to Marx's argument is that increased productivity reduces the cost of providing workers with their existing living standards ("the value of their labour power"). The capitalists can therefore maintain their rate of profit by taking a bigger share of the value created.

This objection is easy to deal with. Marx himself recognised that rises in productivity that reduce the proportion of the working day needed for workers to cover the cost of their own living standards could form a "countervailing influence" to his law. The capitalists could then grab a greater share of their workers' labour as profits (an increased "rate of exploitation") without necessarily cutting real wages. But there was a limit to how far this counter-influence could operate. If workers laboured for four hours a day to cover the costs of keeping themselves alive, that could be cut by an hour to three hours a day. But it could not be cut by five hours to minus one hour a day. By contrast, there was no limit to the transformation of workers' past labour into ever greater accumulations of the means of production. Increased exploitation, by increasing the profit flowing to capital, increased the potential for future accumulation. Another way to put the argument is to see what happens with a hypothetical "maximum rate of exploitation", when the workers labour for nothing. It can be shown that eventually even this is not enough to stop a fall in the ratio of profit to investment.

The final objection is "Okishio's theorem". Changes in technique alone, it is claimed, cannot produce a fall in the rate of profit, since capitalists will only introduce a new technique if it raises their profits. But a rise in the profit rate of one capitalist must raise the average profit of the whole capitalist class. Or as Ian Steedman put it, "The forces of competition will lead to that selection of production methods industry by industry which generates the highest possible uniform rate of profit through the economy".[8] The conclusion drawn from this is that the only things that can reduce profit rates are increased real wages or intensified international competition.

Missing out from many presentations of this argument is the recognition that the first capitalist to adopt a technique gets a competitive advantage over his fellow capitalists, which enables him to gain extra profits, but that this extra profit disappears once the technique is generalised. What the capitalist gets in money terms when he sells his goods depends upon the average amount of socially necessary labour contained in them. If he introduces a new, more productive technique, but no other capitalists do, he is producing goods worth the same amount of socially necessary labour as before, but with less expenditure on real, concrete labour power. His profits rise.[9] But once all capitalists producing these goods have introduced these techniques, the value of the goods falls until it corresponds to the average amount of labour needed to produce them using the new techniques.[10]

Okishio and his followers use the counter-argument that any rise in productivity as a result of using more means of production will cause a fall in the price of its output, so reducing prices throughout the economy – and thereby the cost of paying for the means of production. This cheapening of investment will, they claim, raise the rate of profit.

At first glance the argument looks convincing – and the simultaneous equations used in the mathematical presentation of the theorem have convinced many Marxist economists. It is, however, false. It rests upon a sequence of logical steps which you cannot take in the real world. Investment in a process of production takes place at one point in time. The cheapening of further investment as a result of improved production techniques occurs at a later point in time. The two things are not simultaneous.[11] It is a silly mistake to apply simultaneous equations to processes taking place through time.

There is an old saying: "You cannot build the house of today with the bricks of tomorrow." The fact that the increase in productivity will reduce the cost of getting a machine in a year's time does not reduce the amount the capitalist has to spend on getting it today.

Capitalist investment involves using the same fixed constant capital (machinery and buildings) for several cycles of production. The fact that undertaking investment would cost less after the second, third or fourth round of production does not alter the cost of undertaking it before the first round. The decline in the value of their already invested capital certainly does not make life any easier for the capitalists. To survive in business they have to recoup, with a profit, the full cost of their past investments, and if technological advance meant these investments are now worth, say, half as much as they were previously, they have to pay out of their gross profits to write off that sum. What they have gained on the swings they have lost on the roundabouts, with "depreciation" of capital due to obsolescence causing them as big a headache as a straightforward fall in the rate of profit.

The implications of Marx's argument are far reaching. The very success of capitalism at accumulating leads to problems for further accumulation. Crisis is the inevitable outcome, as capitalists in key sections of the economy no longer have a rate of profit sufficient to cover their investments. And the greater the scale of past accumulation, the deeper the crises will be.

The crisis and the rate of profit

The crisis, however, is not the end of the system. Paradoxically it can open up new prospects for it. By driving some capitalists out of business it can permit a recovery of the profits of others. Means of production can be bought at bargain basement prices, raw material prices slump and unemployment forces workers to accept low wages. Production once again becomes profitable and accumulation can restart. There has long been a dispute among economists who accept Marx's law about the implications of this. Some have argued that the rate of profit will tend to decline in the long-term, decade after decade. Not only will there be ups and downs with each boom-slump cycle, there will also be a long term downward trend, making each boom shorter than the one before and each slump deeper. Others Marxists, by contrast, have argued that restructuring can restore the rate of profit to its earlier level until rising investment lowers it again. According to this view, there is a cyclical motion of the rate of profit, punctuated by intense crises of restructuring, not an inevitable long-term decline. So Marx's law should be called "the law of the tendency of the rate of profit to fall and its countervailing tendencies".[12]

There have been periods in the history of the system in which crises got rid of unprofitable capital on a sufficient scale to stop a long-term decline in profit rates. There was, for instance, a decline in profit rates in the early stages of the industrial revolution, from very high rates for the pioneers in the cotton industry in the 1770s and 1780s to much lower rates by the first decade of the 19th century.[13] This led Adam Smith and David Ricardo to see falling profit rates as inevitable (with Smith blaming them on competition and Ricardo on the diminishing returns of physical output in agriculture). But profit rates then seem to have recovered substantially. Robert C Allen claims they were twice as high in 1840 as in 1800.[14] His figures (if accurate) are compatible with the "restructuring restoring the rate of profit" argument, since there were three economic crises between 1810 and 1840, with 3,300 firms going bust in 1826 alone.[15]

If crises can always counteract the fall in the rate of profit in this way Marx was wrong to see his law as spelling the death knell of capitalism, since the system has survived recurrent crises over the past 180 years.

But those who rely on this argument assume restructuring can always take place in such a way as to harm some capitals but not others. Michael Kidron presented a very important challenge to this contention in the 1970s. It was based on understanding that the development of capitalism is not simply cyclical, but also involves transformation through time – it ages.[16]

The concentration and centralisation of capital

The process by which some capitals grow at the expense of others – what Marx calls the "concentration and centralisation" of capital – eventually leads to a few very large capitals playing a predominant role in particular parts of the system. Their operation becomes intertwined with those of the other capitals, big and small, around them. If the very large capitals go bust, it disrupts the operation of the others – destroying their markets, and cutting off their sources of raw materials and components. This can drag previously profitable firms into bankruptcy alongside the unprofitable in a cumulative collapse that risks creating economic "black holes" in the heart of the system.

This began to happen in the great crisis of the inter-war years. Far from bankruptcies of some firms bringing the crisis to end after a couple of years they deepened its impact. As a consequence, capitals everywhere turned to states to protect them. Despite their political differences, this was what was common to the New Deal in the US, the Nazi period in Germany, the emerging populist regimes in Latin America or the final acceptance of Keynesian state intervention as the economic orthodoxy in wartime Britain. Such interdependence of states and big capitals was the norm right across the system in the first three decades following the Second World War, an arrangement that has variously been called "state capitalism" (my preferred term), "organised capitalism" or "Fordism".[17]

The intervention of the state always had double-edged repercussions. It prevented the first symptoms of crisis developing into out-and-out collapse. But it also obstructed the capacity of some capitals to restore their profit rates at the expense of others.

This was not a great problem in the first decades after 1945, since the combined impact of the inter-war slump and the Second World War had already caused a massive destruction of old capital (according to some estimates a third of the total). Accumulation was able to restart with higher profit rates than in the pre-war period, and rates hardly declined, or did so slowly.[18] Capitalism could enjoy what is often now called its "golden age".[19]

But when profit rates did begin to fall from the 1960s onwards the system found itself caught between the danger of "black holes" and of failing to restructure sufficiently to restore those rates. The system could not afford to risk restructuring by letting crises rip through it. States intervened to ward off the threat of big bankruptcies. But in doing so they prevented the system restructuring sufficiently to overcome the pressures that had caused the threat of bankruptcy. The system, as Kidron put it in an editorial for this journal, was "sclerotic".[20]

As I wrote in this journal in 1982:

> State intervention to mitigate the crisis can only prolong it indefinitely. This does not mean the world economy is doomed simply to decline. An overall tendency to stagnation can still be accompanied by boomlets, with small but temporary increases in employment. Each boomlet, however, only aggravates the problems of the system as a whole and results in further general stagnation, and extreme devastation for particular parts of the system.

I argued that "two or three advanced countries" going bankrupt might "provide the system with the opportunity for a new round of accumulation", but that those running the other parts of the system would do their best to avoid such bankruptcy, lest it pulled down other economies and the banks, leading to "the progressive collapse of other capitals". My conclusion was that "the present phase of crisis is likely to go on and on – until it is resolved either by plunging much of the world into barbarism or by a succession of workers' revolutions".[21]

The empirical picture

How does the empirical record of profit rates over the past 30 years measure up to these various arguments? And what are the implications for today?

There have been a number of attempts to calculate long-term trends in profit rates. The results are not always fully compatible with each other, since there are different ways of measuring investment in fixed capital, and the information on profits provided by companies and governments are subject to enormous distortions (companies will often do their best to understate the profits to governments, for tax reasons, and to workers, in order to justify low wages; they also often overstate their profits to shareholders, in order to boost their stock exchange ratings and their capacity to borrow). Nevertheless, Fred Moseley, Thomas Michl, Anwar Shaikh and Ertugrul Ahmet Tonak, Gérard Duménil and Dominique Lévy, Ufuk Tutan and Al Campbell, Robert Brenner, Edwin N Wolff, and Piruz Alemi and Duncan K Foley[22] have all followed in the footsteps of Joseph Gillman and Shane Mage who carried through empirical studies of profit rate trends in the 1960s.

A certain pattern emerges, which is shown in graphs given by Duménil and Lévy (figure 1) for the whole business sector in the US and by Brenner (figure 2) for manufacturing in the US, Germany and Japan.

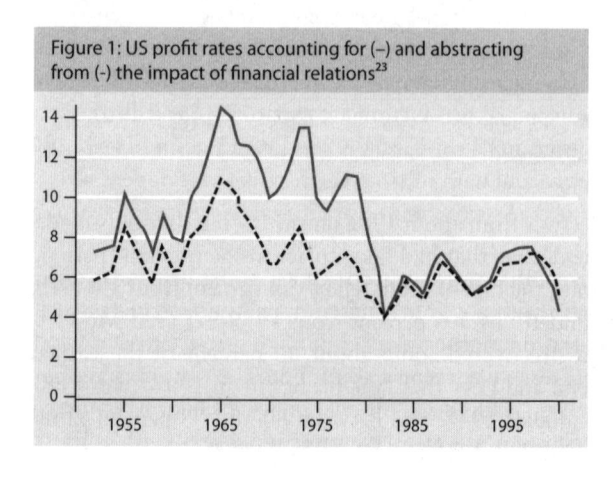

Figure 1: US profit rates accounting for (–) and abstracting from (-) the impact of financial relations[23]

There is general agreement that profit rates fell from the late 1960s until the early 1980s. There is also agreement that profit rates partially recovered after the early 1980s, but with interruptions at the end of the 1980s and the end of the 1990s. There is also an important area of agreement that the fall from the mid-1970s to the early 1980s was not a result of rising wages, since this was the period in which US real wages began a decline which was not partially reversed until the late 1990s. Michl,[24] Moseley, Shaikh and Tonak, and Wolff[25] all conclude that the rising ratio of capital to labour was an element in reducing profit rates. This conclusion is an empirical refutation of the Okishio position. "Capital- intensive" investments by capitalists aimed at raising their individual competitiveness and profitability have had the effect of causing profitability throughout the economy to fall. Marx's basic theory is validated.

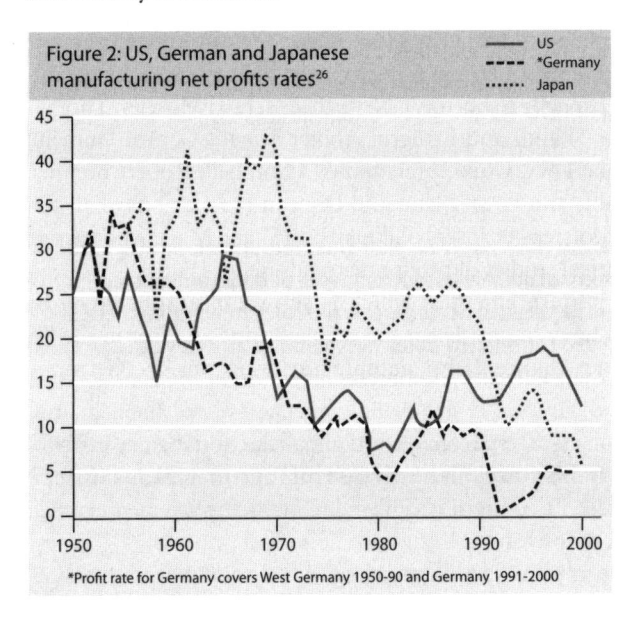

Figure 2: US, German and Japanese manufacturing net profits rates[26]

*Profit rate for Germany covers West Germany 1950-90 and Germany 1991-2000

Profit rates did recover from about 1982 onwards – but they only made up about half the decline that had taken place in the previous period. According to Wolff, the rate of profit fell by 5.4 percent from 1966-79 and then "rebounded" by 3.6 percent from 1979-97; Fred Moseley calculates that it "recovered...only about 40 percent of the earlier decline";[27] Duménil and Lévy that "the profit rate in 1997" was "still only half of its value of 1948, and between 60 and 75 percent of its average value for the decade 1956-65".[28]

Explanations

Why did profit rates recover? One important factor was an increase in the rate of exploitation throughout the economy, as shown by the rising share going to "capital" and opposed to "labour" in national output: Moseley showed a rise in the "rate of surplus value from 1.71 in 1975 to 2.22 in 1987".[29]

There was, however, also a slowdown in the growth of the ratio of investment to workers (the "organic composition of capital"), at least until the mid-1990s. An important change took place in the system from around 1980 onwards – crises begin to involve large-scale bankruptcies for the first time since the inter-war years:

> During the period from World War II through the 1970s, bankruptcy was not a major topic in the news. With the exception of railroads, there were not many notable business failures in the US. During the 1970s, there were only two corporate bankruptcies of prominence, Penn Central Transportation Corporation in 1970 and W T Grant Company in 1975.

But:

> During the 1980s and early 1990s record numbers of bankruptcies, of all types, were filed. Many well known companies filed for bankruptcy... Included were LTV, Eastern Airlines, Texaco, Continental Airlines, Allied Stores, Federated Department Stores, Greyhound, R.H. Macy and Pan Am... Maxwell Communication and Olympia & York.[30]

The same story was repeated on a bigger scale during the crisis of 2001-02. For instance, the collapse of Enron was, as Joseph Stiglitz writes, "the biggest corporate bankruptcy ever – until WorldCom came along".[31]

This was not just a US phenomenon. It was a characteristic of Britain in the early 1990s as bankruptcies like those of the Maxwell empire and Olympia & York showed, and, although Britain avoided a full recession in 2001-02, two once dominant companies, Marconi/GEC and Rover, went down, as well as scores of recently established dotcom and hi-tech companies. The same phenomenon was beginning to be visible in continental Europe, with an added twist in Germany that most of the big enterprises of the former East Germany went bust or were sold off at bargain basement prices to West German firms,[32] and then in Asia with the crisis of 1997-98. On top of this there was the bankruptcy of whole states – notably the USSR, with a GDP that was at one stage a third or even half that of the US. Most of the left held a confused belief that these were "socialist" states. This prevented many commentators from understanding that these states collapsed because the rate of profit was no longer high enough to cover their cost of equipping themselves for international competition.[33] It also prevented them from analysing the impact that writing off these vast amounts of capital had on the world system.[34]

What occurred through these decades was a process of recurrent "restructuring through crisis" on an international scale. However, it was only a limited return of the old mechanism for clearing out unprofitable capitals to the benefit of the survivors. There were still many cases in which the state intervened to prop up very big firms or to pressurise the banking system to do so. This happened in the US with the near bankruptcy of Chrysler in 1979-80,[35] with the crisis of the S&Ls (effectively US building societies) in the late 1980s and the collapse of the giant derivatives gambler Long Term Capital Management in 1998. On each occasion fear of economic, social and political instability prevented the crisis clearing unprofitable capitals from the system. Orlando Capita Leiva tells how in the United States "the state supported...restructuring. In 1970 public investment was only 10 percent of private investment. It increased to 24 percent in 1990 and from then on maintained levels almost double those of 1970".[36]

Official use of the rhetoric of neoliberalism does not preclude a continuing strong element of state capitalism in actual government policy. This is true not just of the US. Governments as varied as those of the Scandinavian countries and Japan have rushed to prop up banks whose collapse might damage the rest of the national financial system – even if, as a last resort, this involves nationalisation.[37] The government of Germany poured billions into the eastern part of the recently unified country after companies found their newly acquired subsidiaries could not be profitable otherwise. And the world financial institutions have reacted to successive debt crises with schemes that protect big Western banks from going under, despite occasional complaints from, for instance, the *The Economist* to the effect that this prevents the system from taking the only medicine that will restore its full vigour.

Unproductive labour and waste

Moseley, Shaikh and Tonak, and Simon Mohun have all noted another feature of capitalism's most recent development – one highlighted by Kidron back in the 1970s. This is the growing "non-productive" portion of the economy.

Mainstream neo-classical economics regards all economic activities involving buying and selling as "productive". This follows from its limited focus on the way transactions take place in markets. Marx, like Adam Smith and David Ricardo before him, had a deeper concern – to discover the dynamics of capitalist growth. He therefore further developed a distinction to be found in Smith between "productive" and "unproductive" labour. For Marx, productive labour was that which created surplus value through expanding production. Unproductive labour was that which, rather than expanding production, was simply distributing, protecting or wasting what was already produced – for instance, the labour of personal servants, policemen, soldiers or sales personnel.

Marx's distinction was not between material production and "services". Some things categorised as "services" add to the real wealth of the world. Moving things from where they are made to where they can be consumed, as is done by some transport workers, is therefore productive. Acting in a film is likewise productive insofar as it yields a profit for a capitalist by giving people enjoyment and so improving their living standard. By contrast, acting in an advert whose only function is to sell something already produced is not productive.

Marx's categorisation has to be refined to come to terms with present-day capitalism, in which things like education and health services are much more important than when he was writing. Most present-day Marxists would accept that those elements of teaching that increase the capacity of people to produce things (as opposed to merely disciplining children) are at least indirectly productive. Kidron went further and argued that what was productive was that which served the further accumulation of capital. The production of means of production did this, and so did the production of goods that kept workers and their families fit and healthy enough to be exploitable (i.e. good that replenished their "labour power"). But production that merely provided luxuries for the capitalist class and their hangers-on should not be regarded as productive, nor should that which went into arms.[38]

Unproductive labour is of central importance to present-day capitalism, regardless of the exact definition given to it. Fred Moseley estimates the numbers in commerce in the US grew from 8.9 million to 21 million between 1950 and 1980, and the number in finance from 1.9 million to 5.2 million, while the productive workforce only grew from 28 million to 40.3 million.[39] Shaikh and Tonak calculate that the share of productive out of total labour in the US fell from 57 percent to 36 percent between 1948 and 1989.[40] Simon Mohun has calculated that the share of "unproductive" wages and salaries in "material value added" in the US grew from 35 percent in 1964 to over 50 percent in 2000.[41] Kidron calculated that, using his wide definition, "three fifths of the work actually undertaken in the US in 1970s was wasted from capital's own point of view".[42]

Moseley, Shaikh and Tonak, and Kidron in his later writings[43] had no doubt. The burden of providing for unproductive labour serves as a drain on surplus value and the rate of profit.[44] Moseley, and Shaikh and Tonak, calculated the rate of profit in "productive" sectors (the "Marxian rate of profit"), and then compared their results with those provided for the economy as a whole by corporations and the US government's National Institute of Pension Administrators (NIPA).[45] Shaikh and Tonak calculate that from 1948 to 1989 "the Marxian rate of profit falls by almost a third... The NIPA-based average rates even faster, by over 48 percent, and the corporate the fastest of all by over 57 percent. These more rapid declines can be explained by the relative rise in the proportion of unproductive to productive activities".[46] Moseley concludes that "in the post-war US economy through the late 1970s the conventional rate of profit declined even more than the Marxian rate" – by 40 percent as opposed to 15-20 percent. He has argued that in the 1990s it was mainly the rise in the level of unproductive labour that stopped the rate of profit fully recovering.

Why have unproductive expenditures grown like this, even to the extent of choking off what might otherwise be healthier profit rates? Different factors are involved, but each is itself a reaction to low profit rates (and attempts by firms and governments to keep crisis at bay):

i. Capitals pour greater resources into attempts to defend and expand markets in unproductive ways.
ii. Wave upon wave of speculative investment occurs as capitalists seek easy profits through gambling in money markets, financial adventures, hedge funds and so forth.

iii. Managerial hierarchies grow in an effort to exert increased pressure on those at the bottom – a typical feature of both the public and private sectors today.
iv. The costs to the system of trying to maintain social peace increase through both "security" expenditures and minimal benefits for those it cannot productively employ.
v. States resort to military adventures as a way to offload the problems faced by capitals within them.

Contradictory effects

There is a vicious circle. Reactions by individual firms and states to the falling rate of profit have the effect of further reducing the resources available for productive accumulation.[47]

But the effect of unproductive expenditures is not only to lower the rate of profit. It can also reduce upward pressure on the organic composition of capital. This was an insight used by Michael Kidron to explain the "positive" impact of massive arms spending on the system in the post-war decades. He saw it, like luxury consumption by the ruling class and its hangers-on, as having a beneficial side effect for those running the system – at least for a time.

Labour which is "wasted", he argued, cannot add to the pressure for accumulation to be ever more capital intensive. Value which would otherwise go into raising the ratio of means of production to workers is siphoned out of the system. Accumulation is slower, but it continues at a steady pace, like the tortoise racing the hare in Aesop's fable. Profit rates are weighed down by the waste, but do not face a sudden thrust into the depths from a rapid acceleration of the capital-labour ratio.

This account seems to fit the early post-war period. Arms spending at around 13 percent of US national output (and with indirect expenditures, perhaps 15 percent) was a major diversion of surplus value away from further accumulation. It was also an expenditure that the US ruling class expected to gain from, in that it helped their global hegemony (both in confronting the USSR and binding the European capitalist classes to the US) and guaranteed a market to some important productive sectors of the US economy. In this sense, the capitalists could regard arms, like their own luxury consumption, as something to their advantage – very different in this sense to "unproductive" expenditures on improving the conditions of the poor. And if it reduced the rate of accumulation, this was not catastrophic since the restructuring of capital through slump and war had already boosted accumulation to higher trajectory than that known in the 1930s. Domestically, all firms suffered the same handicap, and so none lost out to others in competition for markets. And internationally, in the early post-war years, other countries involved in significant economic competition with the US (such as the old imperial powers of Britain and France) were handicapped by relatively high arms spending of their own.

Today things are very different. Since the early 1960s the re-emergence of major foreign economic competitors has created a powerful pressure for the US to reduce the share of national output going towards arms. Boosting arms spending in the mid-1960s during the Vietnam War and in the 1980s during the "second Cold War" gave only a short-term fillip to the US economy before revealing immense problems. George Bush's rise in arms spending from 3.9 percent to 4.7 percent of GNP (equal to about a third of net business investment) has exacerbated the US's burgeoning budget and foreign trade deficits.

The effect of all of these forms of "waste" is much less beneficial to the system as a whole than half a century ago. They may still reduce the downward pressures on the rate of profit from the organic composition of capital – it certainly does not rise as rapidly as it would if all surplus value went into accumulation. But the price the advanced capitalist countries pay for this is slow productive accumulation and slow long-term rates of growth. Hence the repeated "neoliberal" attempts by capitals and states to raise profit rates by cutting back on what they pay employed workers, the old, the unemployed and the long-term sick; the resort to market mechanisms to try to reduce costs in education and health; the insistence that third world countries pay their pound of flesh on their loans; and the US adventure of trying to seize control of the second-biggest source of the world's most important raw material.

It is wrong to describe the situation as one of permanent crisis[48] – rather it is one of recurrent economic crises. The economic recoveries of the 1980s (especially in Japan) and 1990s (in the US) were more than "boomlets". Low levels of past profitability do not stop capitalists imagining that there are miraculous profits to be made in future and sucking in surplus value from all over the world to be ploughed into projects aimed at obtaining them. Many of these are purely speculative gambles in unproductive spheres, as with bubbles in real estate, commodity markets, share prices and so on. But capitalists can also fantasise about profits to be made by pouring resources into potentially productive sectors, and so create rapid booms lasting several years. Investment in the US doubled between 1991 and 1999.[49] When the bubble burst it was discovered that an immense investment in real things such as fibre optic telecommunication networks had been undertaken that would never be profitable, with the *Financial Times* writing of a "$1,000 billion bonfire of wealth".[50]

That was a period in which there was some real recovery of the rate of profit. But that did not do away with the "irrational exuberance" of expecting speculative profits where they did not exist. Virtually every major company deliberately inflated its profits so as to take make speculative gains, with proclaimed profits around 50 percent higher than real profits.[51]

There are many signs that in the US (and probably Britain) we may be approaching a similar phase now. Investment in the US, after declining in the last recession, is now back to the levels of the late 1990s.[52] But the US recovery has been based upon massive government deficits, on balance of payments deficits covered by inflows of lending from abroad, and on consumers borrowing to cover their living costs as the share of "employee incomes in US GDP has fallen form 49 percent to 46 percent".[53] This is the background to the upsurge of speculative ventures such as hedge funds, derivatives markets, the housing bubble and, now, massive borrowing for private equity takeovers of very big corporations (very reminiscent of the "barbarians at the gate" issue of junk bonds in the giant takeovers of the late 1980s). Against such a background, corporate profits will be being puffed up until they lose touch with reality, and things will seem to be going very well until overnight it is discovered they are going badly. And, as they say, when the US gets a cold, the UK can easily catch influenza.

For the moment profit rates in Britain appear to be high. According to one calculation they reached 15.5 percent for all non-financial private corporations in the fourth quarter of 2006 – the highest figure since 1969. Under New Labour the share of profits in GDP has reached a record of nearly 27 percent.[54] But the figures for average profits rates will have been boosted by the current high levels of profit on North Sea oil and gas. And calculations of profits made by British firms are not the same as profits made in Britain, given the very high dependence of big firms on their overseas activities (more so than in any other large advanced capitalist country). "Service sector" profitability is high. However, profitability in the much diminished but still important industrial sector has fallen from about 15 percent in 1998 to about 10 percent now. As in the US there are currently many enthusiasts for capitalism who fear the good times are about to end as they eventually did in the 1970s, the 1980s and the 1990s.

There are even doubts about the one part of the world system where immense productive investments are taking place – China. Some commentators see this country as the salvation of the system as a whole. Chinese capital has been able plough much more surplus value back into investment – more than 40 percent of national output – than in the US, Europe or even Japan. It has been able to exploit its workers more, and it has not so far been held back by the levels of unproductive expenditure that characterise advanced capitalist countries (although the present real estate boom is characterised by a proliferation of office sky scrapers, hotels and shopping malls). All this has enabled it to emerge as a major competitor with the advanced capitalist countries in export markets for many products. But its very high levels of investment are already having an impact on profitability. One recent attempt to apply Marxist categories to the Chinese economy calculates that its profit rates fell from 40 percent in 1984 to 32 percent in 2002, while the organic composition of capital increased by 50 percent.[55] There are some Western observers who are convinced that the profitability of some big Chinese corporations is very low, but that this is concealed by the pressure on the big state-run banks to keep them expanding.[56]

Speculation about what will happen next is easy, but pointless. The general contours of the system are decipherable, but the myriad individual factors that determine how these translate into reality in the course of a few months or even years are not. What matters is to recognise that the system has only been able to survive – and even, spasmodically, grow quite fast for the past three decades – because of its recurrent crises, the increased pressure on workers' conditions and the vast amounts of potentially investable value that are diverted into waste. It has not been able to return to the "golden age" and it will not be able to do so in future. It may not be in permanent crisis, but it is in a phase of repeated crises from which it cannot escape, and these will necessarily be political and social as well as economic.

First published in *International Socialism* 115 (2nd series), summer 2007

5: The state we're in

The new "new left" – a critique

Socialist thought has suffered from stultification for a long time. Marxism, while, as a method, remaining virtually unassailable, has rarely been fruitfully applied in the last three decades. The New Left compilation *Towards Socialism* contains the latest batch of essays on faulty application.

I do not intend here to go into factual criticism of the essays by Tom Nairn and Perry Anderson that constitute the core of the book. A discussion on these factual premises has been begun (and probably ended) by Edward Thompson in the *Socialist Register*, 1965. Instead I intend to concentrate on the methodological and practical origin of the tendency to distort reality which Thompson exposes.

The centre of the Anderson-Nairn writings is the argument that because the English bourgeoisie never made its own revolution it never became a truly "hegemonic" class, but rather remained ideologically and politically subservient to a conservative aristocracy. "The aristocracy became and remained the vanguard of the bourgeoisie." The bourgeoisie instead of articulating a coherent political ideology of its own is seen as never moving beyond the banalities of utilitarianism. This is seen as infecting the British labour movement. "In England a supine bourgeoisie produced a supine proletariat." The latter also has never produced a hegemonic ideology of its own: it has remained narrowly "corporative".

The trouble with this analysis is that while it attempts to say everything, when put under scrutiny, it says nothing. For its fundamental terms "hegemonic" and "corporative" are at best purely descriptive, and at worst deliberately ambiguous. 'Hegemonic' seems to mean what socialists have traditionally referred to as "revolutionary"; and "corporative" to what Lenin called "trade union" or "economistic" consciousness. The Anderson-Nairn categorisation neglects a whole tradition in the British labour movement that is not easily schematised as economist or corporative, which has been fighting against reformism inside the labour movement. It also neglects the periods – in particular 1910-14 and 1918-21 – when, in the movement as a whole, the predominance of reformism and the piecemeal approach has been in question. Finally it neglects the concrete texture even of official Labour thought: the admixture of demands that implied a radically different kind of society, with an acceptance of the institutional framework of present society and its ideological backing.

If shallow as description, the Anderson-Nairn typology is certainly not explanation. To understand why the labour movement is as it is, one would have to carry out a discussion of the concrete problems facing working people in Britain over the last 150 years, how they have responded to these in terms of action and ideas, how this response has both challenged capitalism and been contained by it. Briefly, what is needed is an understanding of how the working class has created itself as a class (that is as an independently acting component of history) in response to the day-to-day exigencies of existence.

But this is precisely what Anderson and Nairn refuse to do. The real problems and situations of the class – slump, boom, changing industrial structures, war and permanent war economy – hardly appear in their writings. Workers' actual responses to these – wildcat strike or general strike, electoral protest or near insurrection – appear almost as infrequently, and only to be subsumed under the most abstract and barely descriptive of categories.

The result is a description of the labour movement in which the agent producing it (labour) is not present. Instead it exists as a mere mass to be moulded by an elite of intellectuals. In the last analysis, it seems, if there is an explanation for the failure to move beyond corporatism, it lies with these. Although described as a "second, conjunctural determinant" "the failure of any significant body of intellectuals to join the proletariat until the end of the 19th century", seems at points to be the only determinant. Despite the historical evidence that the Fabians had little direct effect on the early labour movement, it is they who are seen as producing the intellectual stupor of Labourism. That this stupor might have arisen out of, rather than caused the form of response made by workers- to capitalism, and is intimately related to the growth of a labour bureaucracy oriented solely towards insertion in the bourgeois political process, is not discussed. That despite an articulate and able body of Marxist theoreticians in Germany (Luxemburg and Mehring in particular) a similar phenomenon occurred there with the "revisionist" controversy, is never mentioned.

This refusal to discuss the concrete meaning of their categories, what they mean in terms of individual human action in particular historically produced circumstances, is not just a product at a certain stage in the Anderson-Nairn analysis. It also underlies their whole methodological approach. And necessarily so. For Marxism is about human action in the world. Its categories are only real insofar as they express what underlies this action. For instance "class" as a concept only adds something to our description of reality when it expresses an independent component of the activity of the individuals subsumed under it. The failure of Anderson and Nairn to utilise their concepts in this way does not only mean that their work is bad analysis – it is also in a very real sense non-Marxist, with categories that do not express the "interior" of the social world, i.e. the concrete human actions that have produced it, but have only an external relation to it. Hence a false dialectic of abstract terms with an ambiguous and indefinite content is imposed upon reality. Despite much admirable talk about the need to take account of the "mediations" of reality, terms are merely counterposed without such mediations. Again, despite a somewhat more questionable tendency to borrow terminology from Sartre and from French translations of Hegel, the writing is essentially pre-dialectical. Categories are used which do not express reality, but there is no feeling of this. An awareness of what Hegel called the "infinitude" of being – a constant flux that makes any set of fixed, abstract categories automatically produce self-contradiction – is completely absent from these writings. Categories are held to, not as a guide to understanding and action, but as a priori truths. Anderson admits as much in his rejoinder to Thompson in the current *New Left Review*, when he argues that the bourgeoisie could not originate in agricultural capitalism because the word "bourgeois" means to do with the town.

The result of this imposition of categories upon reality is a treatment which oscillates between imperfect description and distortion. Reality is seen as moving in mechanical fashion in response to the movement of the categories. All the Hegelian terminology in the world cannot obscure this. This is brought out most fully in Anderson's piece "Problems of Socialist Strategy". Distortion occurs, as in his other pieces, in the treatment of history. For instance, Leninism, it is claimed, industrialised the Soviet Union, and conquered Eastern Europe. That both these accomplishments were in clear contradiction to the explicit democratic conception of Lenin's major theoretical work *The State and Revolution*, that the group carrying them through was completely different in every way (social composition, relationship to other social groupings and ideology) to the Bolshevik Party of 1917, and that this group came to power by a struggle against the party of 1917 (the left and right oppositions, the destruction of the old Bolsheviks, etc) although formally within its confines, does not matter. Collectivism, purges, deportations etc, are described as contingent political choices. Therefore, for Anderson, they must be accepted as "socialist crimes"; it does not matter for him that they were choices made on the basis of the destruction both of any direct expression of working class power and of the core of the party that had originally led the revolution. For him the relation of history to human agency is only a contingent one. Socialism is no longer human liberation. It means only having "socially not privately appropriated economies and a socialist ideology". That the "social" appropriation is still an appropriation for a minority and that the "socialist ideology" is of the "all men are equal, but some more so than others" sort, is for him a minor irrelevancy. To draw attention to this as obviating the whole categorisation of them as "socialist", as somehow related to the emancipation of the working class by the working class itself, is to him "pedantic and parochial."

This leads us to a second distortion: the presentation of the history of socialism as a straight choice between Stalinism (what he calls Leninism) and social democracy. He ignores a whole dimension of the international working class movement. The really revolutionary tendencies and leaders have always had a profoundly democratic vision, both of socialism and of the institutions which can bring it about. One only has to think of Marx and Engels themselves, or of Luxemburg and Lenin. Anderson, to whom human action is not important, is completely unable to comprehend that socialists have ever conceived it differently.

Given this complete inability to understand the real divisions over strategy that have historically existed inside the socialist movement, Anderson's own ideas on the subject are inevitably neither original nor practicable. If he sees the past in terms of Stalinist elitism and social democratic "democratism", he sees the future in terms of an amalgam of the two.

Anderson argues for a "hegemonic party". This, it seems, is a party which has a vision of socialist culture and institutions replacing capitalism. A great idea. This is something socialists have always desired, although often using less grandiloquent descriptions for it. But the difficulty is to obtain it, for it cannot be magicked out of thin air. It can only be built out of the struggles of those – the workers – who are thrown into conflict with capitalism. But there is no room in the Anderson schemas for the workers as active agents. All that is needed is to take the working class institutions that exist, and impose a socialist "ideology" upon them. (That the leaders of these institutions do not want such an "ideology" is an unfortunate fact that he ignores.) This, it seems, is to be a job for the "intellectuals" (by this he seems to mean himself and his friends). The Labour Party has to be transformed into a "hegemonic party" and the first step is to...make election day a national holiday!

There is no doubt that the existing institutions and ideas of the working classes are inadequate for any transition to socialism – and probably even for the present problems posed by capitalism. But these ideas and institutions will not be changed by adding "hegemony" to the existing Labourite mixture. They will change when workers feel the need for a new comprehension of reality, that is, when their present ideas are already seen by them to impede their practical struggles. They will welcome the help both of intellectuals and Marxist ideas in this task of reconstructing their view of the world. But they will not require the self-contained intellectualism of Anderson-Nairn, with its disdain for reality. The British labour movement does suffer from an appendix of old ideas and inadequate concepts, but a violent attack of Perritonitis will not cure it of these.

In the abstractness of the categories, its disdain for the real situation of men, its falsification of reality, the Anderson-Nairn ideology has more in common with, say, the writings of Talcott Parsons than with a genuine Marxist conception of a theory which both explains reality and corresponds to the needs of workers to change it.

From *The Agitator*, magazine of the LSE Socialist Society, early 1966. The book referred to is P Anderson & R Blackburn (eds), *Towards Socialism* (Collins, 1965)

The summer of 1981:
a post-riot analysis

The most violent and extensive disturbances on Britain's streets since the war. That was the press's verdict on the week of 3-11 July. And for once the press was right. The barricade, the overturned police van, the milk floats driven at police lines, the burnt out cars and pubs and the looted hi-fi shops – all were something new on the streets of Britain. Above all, the novelty was symbolised in the cascades of petrol bombs. The weapon of Budapest '56 and Watts '65, of Paris '68 and Derry '69 was now the weapon of Brixton and Southall, of Toxteth and Moss Side.

The sequence of riots began before 3 July – 14 months earlier, to be precise, in the St Paul area of Bristol. Police raided a black cafe and attempted to make an arrest. A crowd gathered and soon the police were retreating from the area under a hail of broken bricks. For several hours they did not dare return: shops were looted at will and buildings were burnt down.

Bristol was the shape of things to come. Nevertheless, 12 months elapsed before the next great riot, in Brixton, on 10-12 April. The scale of the disturbances was even greater than in Bristol. Petrol bombs were used on a wide scale, a bus was hijacked and driven at the police, dozens of cars were burnt out and a number of pubs burnt down, scores of shops were looted. It required thousands of police to "restore order".

In the wake of Brixton there were a number of minor disturbances, especially with crowds of youths attending fun fairs in the London area (Finsbury Park, Wanstead, Ealing, Peckham), fighting the police and in Sheffield a demonstration of skinheads against police violence ending with a rampage through the streets to chants of "Brixton,

Brixton". But it was only on 3-4 July that anything on the scale of Bristol or Brixton took place.

On that Friday a group of Nazi-inspired skinheads got off a coach in Southall to go to a gig at a pub called the Hambrough. On the way they stormed into an Asian shop and beat up a woman. Crowds of Asians soon began to gather to take over the street in the area of the pub. Police arrived to protect the skinheads, and later the Asians barricaded the road, and threw bricks and petrol bombs at the police. The battle raged for a couple of hours, with the police eventually evacuating the pub. But they were not able to prevent the Asian youth breaking through their lines and burning it to the ground. A week of rioting had begun which was to involve full-blooded riots in a number of major inner-city areas, to less serious disturbances in dozens of places and to panic boarding up of shops in wide areas of many cities.

The biggest confrontation was in Toxteth, Liverpool. It began with a relatively small disturbance the same night as Southall (3 July): the police tried to arrest a black youth who, they claimed (wrongly) had stolen the motorbike he was riding; a crowd rescued him, but another black, whose family had been subject to a campaign of police harassment, was seized. The next evening rioting erupted on a huge scale. Barricades were built with overturned cars and a builders' compressor; scores of petrol bombs were thrown at the police; rioters donned Ulster-style masks to avoid identification.

The police could not cope. The press reported, "the police produced a show of force sufficient to enrage the black population, but not enough to quell the riots." The streets were barricaded again the next night. "By then as many whites as blacks had joined the rioting".[1]

The rioters seized a fleet of milk floats and a concrete mixer to drive at the police lines, forcing the 800-strong force to retreat. Several buildings were burnt down, including the National Westminster Bank and the businessmen's club, the Racquets. With the area clear of police, "there was an assumption that anyone who was not police would help themselves" in the wholesale looting of shops.[2] Reports told of middle-aged women, white and black, queuing with shopping trolleys to loot supermarkets. Of the rioters, "fewer than 40 percent were black".[3] The deputy chief constable, Peter Wright, made it clear that "at the savage climax of the trouble, the rioters were mostly white". There were smaller, "imitation" disturbances in white areas like Kirkby, Scotland Road, Walton, Woodchurch and Birkenhead.

The rioting began to die down the next night. By calling in the police from as far afield as Manchester, the authorities were able to regain control of the Toxteth area. That night the rioting tended to be in the white areas on the edge of Liverpool 8, away from the storm centre of the Saturday and Sunday night.[4]

No doubt the police chiefs heaved a sigh of relief on Tuesday evening. Their immediate troubles seemed to be over. But not for long. About 3am on Wednesday a brick was thrown through the window of a clothes shop in Moss Side, Manchester. Apparently some police had shouted insults at a group of youth, mainly black, who were leaving a club.[5] The youths responded by breaking windows and setting fire to shops, while holding the police at bay with petrol bombs. There were about seven arrests that night.

As in Toxteth this initial disturbance was quite minor. But again as in Toxteth, the arrest fuelled further unrest. Throughout that Wednesday groups began to gather on street corners, wondering what was going to happen. The groups coalesced into a 1,500-strong crowd of black and white youths who attacked the police station that evening, shattering its windows and trying to break in. Failing to do so, they turned their attention to burning out and looting shops.[6] Hundreds of black and white youths were involved in building barricades and throwing petrol bombs. Yet in the lulls between fighting, there was a carnival atmosphere. There were only 47 arrests during the savage rioting of Wednesday.

Thursday night the police took their revenge. "Police swamped the Moss Side area. Vans swept about carrying teams of the Tactical Action Group (Manchester SPG)...police swooped on any potential gathering of people, white or black – and made any necessary arrests".[7] There were three times as many arrests on this night of very low-level rioting as on the previous two nights combined. Virtually anyone who was foolish enough to be seen on the streets of the area could be picked up. The savagery of the police provoked bitter complaints from all sections of the local population. But it also succeeded in stopping the disturbances.

After Moss Side came what the press referred to disparagingly as "copycat riots". This was meant to downgrade what was happening. But several of these disturbances were on a sizeable scale. In Handsworth (Birmingham) "black and white youth, mostly Asian" stoned the police, and when they had been driven from the area looted and attacked the police station and the British Legion club.[8] There were 329 arrests. In a "repeat" riot in Southall, people expected a return of the Nazi skinheads after police had told shopkeepers in nearby Hounslow to board up the windows and 600 youths – "60 percent Asian, but some whites and West Indians" – marched up the road, confronted a police cordon and then broke windows, threw petrol bombs, set fire to parked cars, built two barricades and looted Woolworths; "the riot was as militant as the first riot, but less angry".[9] In Chapeltown (Leeds) "the police weren't strong enough to cope" after "all types of youth, black and white", responded to racist attacks and a police raid on a black club by "stoning, throwing petrol bombs, burning cars, setting fire to police vans".[10] In Bolton, "300-400 Asians and anti-racists hijacked a milk float and attacked police with bricks, bottles, stones, driving the police 200 yards back... The police got a hammering..."[11] In Luton, "Black and white youth began by attacking racists, and then moved on to attack the police and the Tory Party HQ," throwing stones and petrol bombs, breaking windows and looting shops; there were 102 arrests.[12]

In Leicester, even though police from four counties had assembled close to the Highfields area during the Saturday that evening "300 to 500 people in their early twenties, West Indian and white mixed, with a few Asians, kept them out of the area using petrol bombs and burning barricades"; the fighting continued for two more evenings, with "people in the flats joining the rioting, leaving their doors open so that people could escape from the police".[13] In Nottingham rioting developed on both the Friday, in response to a huge build-up of police presence, and on the Saturday night after racists from outside the town had attacked blacks under the cover of the riots; the fighting began as a confrontation with the police using stones and petrol bombs, with shop windows only being broken "accidentally" – but looting developed later; the rioters were "always of mixed races, ages, employed and unemployed".[14] In Brixton, the arrest of a well-known figure in the black community led to a night of fighting, but the police were prepared for it and it was not on the same scale as the first riot in April.

The other "copycat" riots were generally at a much lower level. For instance, they did not generally involve the use of petrol bombs (although there are reports from Hackney in East London of "failed petrol bombs",[15] from Hull of petrol bombs "being made, but not used,"[16] from High Wycombe of a petrol bomb "landing on a police car but failing to go off", and even from the Cotswolds town of Cirencester of "young kids" throwing two petrol bombs[17]). But they were much more than normal Friday night punch-ups. So there were incidents of fights with the police and looting in Wood Green (London), Southampton, Halifax, Bedford, Gloucester, Hull (where a Friday night battle between skins and bikers turned into a united 150-strong battle against the police),[18] Walthamstow (where the banning of a funeral demonstration for victims of a racist murder led to hundreds of youth, "mainly Asian, but black and white as well"[19] attacking racists, the police and property, but not looting), Sheffield, Coventry, Portsmouth, Bristol, Edinburgh and dozens of other places.

The next wave of "copycat" riots swept the country on the weekend of 10-12 July. Yet by the 14th the riots everywhere were over. Now all that were to take place were a scattering of one-night disturbances – after police harassment in Brixton and Toxteth (where a police van killed a white youth), in Edinburgh, in Sheffield, in Reading.

The incidents which ignited the disturbances varied enormously from place to place. In Toxteth and the second Brixton riot, the key flashpoint came with police harassment. In some cases – Southall, Luton, Leeds, Bolton, Reading – the catalyst was racial attacks, although usually involving no more than a handful of racists (there is no evidence that the Nazis were able to mobilise any numbers of white youths once the rioting had started). In some cases the eruptions were "spontaneous" – youth on the streets just started looting and that was it.

Finally, there were a whole series of disturbances provoked by rumours that something was going to happen, rumours often encouraged by the police themselves. This seems to have been what happened in Woolwich, Southeast London, on the Thursday (9 July) when police went round telling shopkeepers to board up their shop windows because of skinheads who were supposed to be about to attack an Anti Nazi League (ANL) meeting in the Sikh temple that evening: the result was a concentration of 250 blacks and 50 white youth on the streets, prepared to take on the skinheads, and when they did not materialise, breaking windows and looting.[20]

The pattern was repeated in one form or another the next day, Friday 10 July. In Handsworth the police told shops to board up and the schools to go home early; when the "community police" went to reassure groups of black and white kids who were gathering that no skinheads were expected, the youth turned on them and started stoning them.[21] In Southall the second riot followed rumours of a renewed skinhead invasion.[22] In dozens of other areas, the rumour was simply that something was going to happen, and people gathered in expectation.

The rumours that swept the cities on that weekend were slightly reminiscent of the "great fear" in rural France at the beginning of the revolution in 1789: those with property believed that marauding mobs were about to descend on them, signalled their fear by taking precautions (boarding up shops, closing school, concentrating police on the streets), and in so doing created an atmosphere in which youth congregated on the streets, ready to join in any bother.

The police in many areas seem to have positively encouraged and welcomed this panic, to the point in some cases of provoking riots where they would not otherwise have occurred. In Dalston, East London, for example, a heavy concentration of police on street corners was bound to provoke trouble, and the police must have known it. Their reasoning seems to have been that trouble was possible anyway, and the best thing was to provoke it prematurely so as to nip it in the bud. The result was that the overwhelming majority of arrests took place that weekend, and took place generally in areas where the disturbances were less extensive. Looking at these figures, *Socialist Worker* showed that the greater the number of police injuries, the fewer were the arrests.[23]

Comparisons: the British experience

Riots may have been scarce in post-war Britain, but they are by no means something completely new. Crowds clashing on the streets with the forces of law, arming themselves in some way or other, smashing windows, looting shops, burning down buildings, besieging police stations – these are all very old features of urban life. They were among the forms of popular protest that pre-dated industrial capitalism proper. With the development of forms of struggle based on the strength workers can exercise at the point of production – with strikes and unions – the role of the riot tends to diminish. But it can re-emerge in two instances – when strike action alone no longer seems enough to win workers' demands, or when sections of workers lose their faith in the ability of the organisations based upon industrial action to achieve their goals.

An example of the first was what happened in Britain in the years 1910-12. Union organisation outside a few areas of skilled work was weak or non-existent; real wages were declining and working conditions were deteriorating. A series of great strikes broke out, often unofficially, and usually in circumstances where it was clear that the employers would be able to hold out against merely peaceful forms of action. So, for instance, violent scenes marked the South Wales coal strike of 1910. At Tonypandy in November, "strikers, beaten back from the colliery by the police, expressed their bitterness and frustration by looting shops in the main square of the village. Further clashes with the police took place such that by the early hours of the following morning, one striker was dead and many strikers and policemen injured".[24]

A few months later, it was the turn of the railway and the transport strikers in Liverpool to take to the streets: "The Liverpool strike reached its climax in the week or so following 13 August".[25] The police and the military violently dispersed a demonstration of workers, leading to "injuries among the demonstrators and many arrests".[26] "Street fighting was particularly intense as the working class communities of the North End of Liverpool fought to prevent an encroachment of civil and military into their territory in pursuit of demonstrators". The *Liverpool Daily Post and Mercury* reported that "residents in many instances took sides with the rioters against the police, throwing bottles, bricks and stones from houses and from roofs. The whole area was for a time in a state of siege. We hear of bedding being set alight to make the road impassable to mounted police".[27] What *The Times* called "guerrilla warfare" continued for days, with crowds erecting "barbed wire entanglements" and barricades. It reached a climax on 15 August when two strikers were shot dead by troops during an attack on a prison van carrying rioters to Walton jail.[28]

However, the most interesting comparisons from our point of view are with two different periods of riot, in both of which workers were faced with high levels of unemployment without industrial-based organisation being able to offer them any way forward. These were during the long-drawn-out economic slump of the 1880s – known to economists of the time as "the Great Depression" – and during the great slump of the early 1930s. In the first case, the unions were by and large confined to a small skilled minority of the class and were, in any case, too weak to deal with the effects of the slump. In the second, the defeat of 1926 had left the majority of the workers without any faith in the efficacy of militant union action (union membership fell 50 percent in the years after the general strike and almost all unions swung sharply to the right).

Let us look at each experience in turn:

> The economic depression which began in 1875 reached its lowest depth in 1886. The number of unemployed had greatly increased; discontent spread in an ever-deepening circle... In addition, the disruption of the Liberal Party consequent upon Mr Gladstone's Home Rule Bill (promising limited self-

rule to the whole of Ireland) deepened the general unrest. It was therefore a very easy matter to arrange large demonstrations in London. In the provinces also, in Manchester, Birmingham, Leicester and elsewhere unemployed processions were organised.[29]

Socialist organisations had only been in existence in Britain for a couple of years, and the two groups – the Social Democratic Federation (SDF) and the Socialist League – were both fairly small. Yet the socialists were able to organise unemployment agitation with apparent ease. At first they faced competition from a Tory outfit campaigning for protectionism (the Fair Trade League – at that time no avowed socialist dreamt of demanding import controls!) But when on 8 February the League called a demonstration of the unemployed in Trafalgar Square, the SDF was able to put up rival speakers and pull most of the crowd around it. Led by a red flag the socialists began a march towards Hyde Park followed by unemployed dock and building workers. As the unemployed went past the rich men's clubs in Pall Mall and were taunted by their clients, their anger broke loose:

> The march turned into a riot, all forms of property were assailed, all signs of wealth and privilege were attacked. In St James' Street all the club windows down one side of the street were broken and in Piccadilly looting began... In Hyde Park...the crowd...overturned carriages and divested their wealthy occupants of their money and jewellery. They then moved on to South Audley Street, looting every shop along their route... The progress of the crowd had been virtually unhampered since a misheard order had dispatched the police to guard Buckingham Palace and the Mall.[30]

There is some contention to how serious the riot really was. Both Friedrich Engels and Eleanor Marx thought it was rather a minor event.[31] But it caused immediate panic in the propertied classes. The next day police went round warning shopkeepers to expect another attack. On 10 February, London was hit by the same "great fear" it was to witness again in July 1981. "The rumour spread that 10,000 men were on the march from Deptford to London, destroying as they came the property of small traders." All over South London "the shops closed and people stood at their doors straining their eyes through the fog for the sound of the 10,000 men". By mid-afternoon 'the terror was so general that board schools were literally besieged by anxious parents eager to take their children home under their protection'. In Whitehall a mob was said to be marching down the

Commercial Road; at Bethnal Green the mob was said to be in Green Street; in Camden Town there was a rumour that the mob would go from Kentish Town to the West. In the City and the West End all approaches were guarded. Banks and private firms closed down. Shops were shuttered and fortified.

> But just as those with property were prepared to defend it, so those without prepared to join the revolutionary hoard. A crowd began to assemble at the Elephant and Castle in expectation of joining the mob from Deptford. By 4.30pm. the crowd had grown to 5,000 and was beginning to make assaults on local shops... Again, a crowd of around 2,000 assembled in Deptford High Street to await the arrival of the mob.[32]

The scare came to nothing. But the response of the unemployed to it, showed how easily they could be drawn into riots. There were riots in Leicester from 11 to 16 February and in London. Unemployed demonstrations in Trafalgar Square – often leading to clashes with the police – continued to be a regular event. In the late summer of the next year, the fears of the middle classes were again aroused. The unemployed took to sleeping out in Trafalgar Square and St James' Park, and the SDF again began organising the unemployed in the square under the slogan "Not charity but work". The police began clearing the square using force, so that minor clashes between the police and the unemployed became a daily event. Finally, all meetings in it were banned.

A large protest movement developed, involving not only the small socialist organisations, but the working class radical clubs of London that were aligned with the Liberal Party and the Irish nationalist organisations protesting at the imprisonment of an MP. They came together to defy the ban on demonstrations in the square on 13 November 1887 – a day that has become known as "Bloody Sunday".

Contingents of the unemployed, the socialists, the radicals and the Irish formed in different parts of London to march to the centre; four thousand police were assembled in the Charing Cross Road, Strand and Parliament Square areas to bar their path, while 650 troops with fixed bayonets defended Trafalgar Square itself.

Fighting broke out as the different columns came up against the police lines. Thus "columns from Peckham, Battersea and Deptford, some 8,000 in all, met and crossed Westminster Bridge, the foremost linking arms, they rushed Parliament Square, using pokers, lengths of gas pipe, iron bars and oyster knives to defend themselves against the horse and foot police who laid about them with staves and truncheons".[33]

A week later, when a much smaller group of the unemployed once again defied the ban on assembling in Trafalgar Square, a spectator, Alfred Linnel, was run down by a police horse and killed. His funeral was the occasion for a huge 120,000-strong procession.

But this was the final throw of the street agitation of these years. "Trade improved, the opportunities for work were plentiful, and the unemployed agitation lost its hold on the masses".[34] A new stage of capitalist expansion – what Marxists were later to call "imperialism" – provided a way out of the Great Depression and for more than two decades the conditions of 1886-87 were forgotten.

Chronic depression returned, however, in the inter-war years, and with it continuous high levels of unemployment. The jobless total never fell below 10 percent between 1920 and 1939. And in the winter of 1931-32, just after the National Government had cut the dole by 10 percent and imposed a harsh means test that deprived many families even of this, one person in five was unemployed. In the so-called "depressed areas" the figure was much higher – in Eastern South Wales it was 44.5 percent, in Bishop Auckland 50.4 percent, in Jarrow 56.8 percent.

Unemployed demonstrations gave rise to clashes with the police in one part of the country after another. Thus in October 1931, 50,000 Glasgow unemployed defied a police ban on their demonstration and tore up iron railings to use as weapons in their self-defence: "The battle extended throughout the centre of the city. For hours it raged, shop windows were broken and extensive damage was done".[35] There was fighting between unemployed and the police in the same week in London and Manchester, and the week after in Port Glasgow, Blackburn, Cardiff, and again in London, where "fighting spread from Westminster into Lambeth and Southwark districts and continued to past midnight with many casualties on either side".[36] In November, to stop the repeated clashes between the unemployed and the police outside London labour exchanges, Lord Trenchard, the Commissioner of the Metropolitan Police, banned unemployed meetings in the vicinity of the exchanges. But further clashes took place in December in London, Wallsend, Liverpool, Leeds, Glasgow and Kirkaldy. However the largest riots were not until September 1932. They broke on Merseyside where 34 percent of adult men were unemployed.

"In the last two weeks of September 1932, Birkenhead and Liverpool were in a state of near insurrection. Demonstrations, battles with the police and looting of shops went on in Birkenhead for four days from 15 September." A 5,000 strong demonstration "fought police with stones and spikes from iron railings were thrown at the police's legs"; the police station was besieged; trip wires were stretched across the street and the covers removed so that the police would fall down manholes. Eventually the police pushed the crowd back into a tenement building. According to one participant, "The police came in and went berserk. They battered down doors. People got dragged out of their beds, women and children, and got beaten up. The inhabitants responded by throwing furniture down the stairs at the cops, who finally got their revenge when truncheon blows made one demonstrator fall from a window sill to his death".[37]

A week later there were similar riots in Liverpool.[38]

Against such a background the entry of a National Unemployed Workers' Movement hunger march into London on 27 October was almost bound to produce violent confrontations: "The workers kept the police back at the meetings (in Hyde Park); several times mounted police charged forward, only to be repulsed by thousands of workers who tore up railings and used them as weapons and barricades for the protection of their meetings. Many mounted policemen were dragged from their horses".[39]

There are obvious analogies between what happened in the worst years of the last two great periods of crisis, in 1886-87 and 1931-32, and what has been happening this time round as unemployment has surged to the highest level for more than 40 years. On both previous occasions, as the economic crisis drove people to desperation and peaceful "trade union methods" seemed useless those who had been previously "law abiding" hit out at the symbols of their oppression. This time round the trade union movement is immensely stronger than it was on those two occasions, but it has failed utterly to deal with the impact of the recession and the level of industrial struggle has fallen to its lowest since 1942. The biggest strikes have ended in defeats or near defeats, and 99 percent of closures have gone through with no resistance. The inability of workplace organisation to cope has led sections of the class to revert, as in 1886-87 and 1931-32, to forms of street confrontation that are more normally to be found before trade unionism developed, in the early period of industrial capitalism.

Yet there are also clear differences with the two previous periods. Those were struggles which, despite a powerful spontaneous element, were focused around political demands (for relief measures in the 1880s, against the means test in 1931-32) and inside them political organisations (the SDF, the Communist Party) played a key agitational role. In 1981 there have been no simple political goals, and political agitation within the riots has been more or less non-existent.

At the same time, the major riots have been confined to one kind of working class area only – the so-called inner-city areas – and an important factor in igniting the riots has been the response of young black people to police harassment and/or racial attacks.

These factors suggest a different analogy to that of 1886-87 or 1931-32 – the ghetto uprisings of the US in the mid-sixties.

Comparisons: the US experience

Between 1964 and 1968 literally hundreds of riots shook the US cities. They originated from a variety of triggering factors and they varied enormously in intensity, from small-scale fights between groups of youths and the police to the armed defence of areas which could only be ended by the deployment of the national guard or (in the case of the Detroit riot of 1967) the federal armed forces complete with tanks. Yet they did all have one thing in common: they were all revolts of the black population of the inner-city areas, involving what the official government-sponsored report of the 1967 riots described as the "symbols of white American society authority and property in the Negro neighbourhoods".[40] And, although only a minority of the ghetto population were actively involved in the fighting, they enjoyed passive support from very large numbers of people: in Watts (1965) 22,000 people, or 15 percent of the population were "actively" involved in the riots and another 51,000 or 35-40 percent were "active spectators";[41] in Detroit (1967) 11 percent of people admitted to active participation and 20-25 percent classified themselves as "bystanders";[42] in the Newark riots of the same year, 45 percent of blacks aged 15-35 living in the riot areas described themselves as "rioters".[43]

Typically, the riots began with incidents of police harassment: the shooting of a 15 year old boy in Harlem 1964, a rumour that police had beaten up a black cab driver in Newark 1967; a police raid on a drinking club in Detroit 1967. But the fighting with the police was soon accompanied by the breaking of windows, mass looting and the firebombing of buildings.

The pattern had already shown itself many years before in the riots which shook Harlem in 1935 and 1943: "Blind fury swept the community... The available symbols of the oppressor were the shining plate glass windows of the stores... At the beginning there was no looting. Later from the more poverty struck areas of Harlem poured those who entered the stores and began looting".[44]

In the 1960s riots, the looting was rarely random. In Watts, "Wherever a store keeper identified himself as a 'poor working Negro trying to make a business' or a 'blood brother', the mob passed the store by. It even spared a few white businesses that allowed credit... and made a point of looting and destroying stores that were notorious for their high prices and hostile manner".[45]

And above all, "For the rioters, the riots were fun... There was a carnival in the middle of the carnage. Rioters laughed, danced, clapped their hands, many got drunk. Children stayed out all night ... contrary to the usual pattern of riots, there was hardly any sexual delinquency".[46]

The feeling that the riots had been worthwhile persisted after the riots – even though the casualty rate was always at least four rioters dead or injured to each cop who suffered.

In all the riots (except for Detroit where *Newsweek* reported "white terrorists" among the snipers and three whites were shot by police as suspected rioters[47]) the rioters were 100 percent black. Yet these were not *race* riots; as the Kerner report noted, they did not involve blacks acting "against white persons". In this respect, the riots were quite different from what had happened in Springfield and Atlanta in 1906-08, in St Louis in 1917, in Chicago in 1919, in Tulsa, Oklahoma in 1935, in Detroit and Los Angeles in 1943. In each of these cases mobs of whites gave vent to their frustrations by roaming the streets beating up and shooting any blacks they came across and burning out black houses.

The ghetto uprising did not involve one ethnic group turning its aggression against random members of another ethnic group. On the contrary, the black participants in the risings turned against the symbols of authority and property – and in doing so began to create the conditions where some whites at least could sympathise with their goals. So a survey after Watts showed that 33 percent of Los Angeles whites "showed sympathy with the riots"[48] even if none were involved in the rioting. And in the biggest of the uprisings, Detroit, there were reports of a very few white rioters and of "some...integrated gangs of looters".[49]

The more or less all-black character of the US riots followed from what had happened to the black population over the decades. Until the First World War the overwhelming majority of them were still where they had been put by slavery, in the Southeastern states, working as sharecroppers, denied any normal citizenship rights (excluded from the vote, discriminated against in the courts, subject to attacks by white racist lynch mobs if they stepped out of place). Even in the 1930s, half the black population still lived in the "black belt" of the South. But as European immigration to the US was reduced by legal controls, black people from the South travelled north to fill the gap this created in the labour market and to take the place of successive generations of migrants in the inner areas of the cities.

By the 1960s, just as the governments of Kennedy and Johnson were responding to the civil rights movement in the South by updating the form of capitalist rule there to provide for formal equality for blacks, three quarters of the blacks were now in the North, living in inner-city areas which were by now 90 percent black, employed in the worst paid jobs (with average wages only 54 percent of the white average)[50] and with a steadily rising level of unemployment so that by 1962 it was, at 11 percent, twice the white level (as compared to only 112 percent of the white level in 1940)[51] and one teenage boy in four was jobless. Something more than *talk* of "equality" and "integration" was needed. The slogan "black power" and the action of the rioters were responses to this need.

As the Kerner report admitted, the riots were "generated out of an increasingly disturbed social atmosphere, in which typically a series of tension-heightening incidents over a period of weeks or months became linked in the mind of many of the Negro community with a reservoir of underlying grievances". These grievances found sharpest expression in the attitude to the police: the all-black ghettos were policed by all-white police forces which treated the blacks in ways remarkably similar to those of the Southern white segregationists. Indeed, "The police were not merely a 'spark' factor. To some Negroes, police have come to symbolise white power, white racism and white repression."[52]

The rioters came from a complete cross-section of the younger population in the ghettos. They were not, by and large, the "marginal" types – those who dropped permanently out of the job market and were attracted to hustling and petty thieving. In the case of Watts "the great majority" of rioters were "currently employed"[53] – despite the fact that 25 percent of high school graduates in Watts could not get jobs. In Detroit, the typical rioter was a teenager or young adult, somewhat better educated than his non-rioting Negro neighbour and usually underemployed or employed in a menial job".[54]

How does the experience of Britain in 1981 compare with the American uprisings? The similarities are obvious: the role of police harassment and racial attacks in igniting many of the riots; the concentration of the disturbances in inner-city areas with a relatively high black population; the high level of support in some at least of the localities for the rioters, even if active participants were a quite small minority. But there is one important – very important – difference, which if not taken account of completely distorts one's appreciation of the British events: in *virtually all* the British riots there has been significant white involvement alongside blacks, and the involvement has not just been of white leftists, but of white working class youth.

Thus, for instance, the first Brixton riot broke when "the police attempted to arrest a black guy... Black and white people went over to help... Before the van took off, it had three windows smashed".[55] "The riot was mostly youth. It was a fair cross-section of younger people, black and white".[56]

Again in Bristol last year, the crowd which drove back the police in the first confrontation was "almost a third white" and "if there was limited participation of whites in the fighting, white people were heavily involved in the looting".[57] In the case of the first Southall riot this year, very few whites were involved in the fighting. But *The Guardian* could write of the onlookers that "one remarkable thing about the riot was the complete absence of racial tension among the white and Asian residents who mingled together".[58] And in the second riot, a week later, "60 percent of the rioters were Asian, the rest were West Indian and white".[59]

In the case of Toxteth, the first rioting was mostly black. But some white youths seem to have been involved from the beginning and by the end of the main night of rioting, the rioters were at least 50-50 black and white.[60]

In Moss Side, of the 106 arrests for public order offences, according to the police "78 were white, 11 non-white and 12 black".[61] In Wood Green in London, there were 'large numbers of Cypriot kids and West Indians and a slightly smaller number of whites".[62] In Handsworth, the riots were "black and white, but mostly Asian youths".[63] In Woolwich there were "250 blacks and 50 whites".[64] In Leeds, "there was no evidence among the rioters of racial differences. All types of youth were involved".[65] In Bolton, there were "Asians and anti-racists", including "some skins and punks".[66] In Halifax there was "a right good mix of skinheads and Asian youth".[67]

The considerable involvement of whites in the riots mean they cannot crudely be fitted into schema from the American uprisings, any more than into the schema of Britain in 1886-87 or 1931-32.

To understand them you have to combine elements from both sets of experiences, to see that as in the 1880s and early 1930s the development of the crisis and the sharp rise in unemployment has created conditions in which sections of the working class break with old forms of respect for authority and property, but that this change is particularly concentrated among certain sections of the class who are much more affected by the crisis than the average – those who are young, those who are in the inner-cities, those who are black.

The crisis and unemployment: The immediate background to the riots lies, as in 1886-87 and 1931-32, in a huge increase in unemployment. In the 12 months to July 1981, the official figures show a rise of 955,000. The real rise will be greater, since these figures ignore a growing number of men who are retiring early as they find they cannot get jobs, a growing number of married women who do not bother to register since they are not eligible for benefit (either because they have been unemployed more than 12 months or because they have been out of employment in the last couple of years bringing up children), and a large number of school leavers who were deprived of benefit over the summer months under a new government regulation.

The rise in unemployment has, however, tended to hit different sections of the working class in a different way than on the two previous occasions. In 1886-87, the most dramatic impact was in London, where manufacturing industry had been in decline for more than half a century even though every year tens of thousands of migrants from the British and Irish countryside were entering the city (half the population was made up of such immigrants). Most of the working class was unskilled and depended upon employment in casual trades like the docks and small-scale sweat shops much affected by seasonal trades. The crisis savaged employment in these areas, forcing a large section of the working population into extreme poverty, especially when cold winters hit riverside and building employment. The age group most affected tended to be those past their mid-twenties, since there was still a high demand for youth in dead-end jobs such as messengers and cartboys.[68]

In the early 1930s, the hardest hit places were the "depressed areas", the traditional centres of large-scale manufacturing (shipbuilding, iron and steel, heavy engineering, textiles) and mining – Scotland, South

Wales, the North East, parts of the North West. These had known high levels of unemployment since the end of the post First World War boom in 1921, were driven into complete misery by the crisis of 1929-33, and did not enjoy real recovery until 1940 (while in the South East and the Midlands, recovery began with the growth of new light engineering and automobile employment from 1933 onwards).

Today's pattern shows features of both the 1880s situation and that of the 1930s. Certain traditional centres of heavy industry have been hit. Hence the devastation of Merseyside, Clydeside and parts of the North East. But the industries which grew up in London and the West Midlands in the 1930s have also been deeply affected. And these trends have come on top of a long-term tendency to industrialisation in the old areas of working class habitation immediately around the centres of the major cities (the inner-city areas). Between 1971 and 1976 manufacturing employment fell 20 percent in the inner area of Manchester/Salford, 21 percent in the Liverpool inner area, 23 percent in the Birmingham inner area, 30 percent in inner London.[69]

In July 1980 (when national unemployment was a million less than it is now), the average level of unemployment for males[70] in London as a whole was 3.9 percent, but in inner London it was already 7.5 percent and in inner North East London 8.6 percent.[71] And that was when the effects of the decline in manufacturing jobs was still partly compensated for by a rise in service jobs. Now, with the service sector also declining, the picture will be worse.

What is bad in London is catastrophic in Merseyside. In June 1980 the Liverpool City Planning Office was already calculating that the real level of unemployment in the inner city area was 22 percent.[72] Since then the Department of Employment figure for the city as a whole has risen by 50 percent, and a survey by Liverpool University suggests that the real level of unemployment in the Toxteth area has risen to around 45 percent.[73]

Youth and unemployment: Not all age groups have been hit equally by unemployment. Those already having jobs have been at least partly able to protect themselves against the impact of the crisis. Where union organisations have been strong, they have been able to negotiate redundancies in many cases, so that much of the shrinkage of the workforce has been through "natural wastage" and no recruitment. The brunt of the crisis has therefore hit particularly hard those *without* jobs – particularly young people entering the labour market for the first time. The result has been an average level of unemployment of those aged 16-24 *twice* the average figure – even before taking into account the way 250,000 youngsters who are really unemployed are removed from the register by YOPS and similar schemes. At the same time, unemployment can mean much greater than average hardship for the young. Someone who has worked 10 or 15 years in a factory or office at present gets a considerable lump sum on redundancy, is paid wage-related dole for the first six months of his or her unemployment and is also quite likely to be in receipt of a considerable sum in tax rebates. The result is that in the first six months of unemployment you can be virtually as well off as when you were working; among adults it is the 40 percent of the officially registered who have been unemployed for six months or more who really suffer.[74] But school leavers and many young workers do not get redundancy pay and are not eligible for wage-related benefits. And so their unemployment begins with them down on the poverty line.

Even for those with jobs, the hardship created by mass unemployment does not disappear. Usually those starting work for the first time switch jobs two or three times before settling down to one that is just about tolerable to them. With present levels of unemployment that option disappears. You stick to a job if you can get it, no matter how unbearable it is. The present crisis is making life into a soulless prison for the young employed and unemployed alike – which is why it is so much nonsense for Tory ministers to claim that the riots have nothing to do with unemployment because employed youth have been among those arrested.

Black people and unemployment: When the bulk of black immigrants came to Britain in the 1950s and 1960s, unemployment was not a problem for most of them. They came precisely because there were jobs here for them – even if the jobs tended on average to be slightly worse paid than the white workers' jobs and in industries with conditions (such as shift work) that many white workers would not tolerate while there were jobs elsewhere.[75] And so, although in February 1963 "minority groups" were four times as likely to be unemployed as the average population, by 1970 "unemployment was at roughly the same level among minority groups as the general population".[76]

But the rise in unemployment in the 1970s has hit black workers disproportionately hard. "As total unemployment rises, so the minorities tend to make up a greater proportion of the total".[77] Between November 1974 and February 1980 total unemployment doubled, whereas the number of black people on the register quadrupled.[78]

Since then the number of unemployed from "minority groups" has all but doubled again – while average unemployment has grown somewhat less, by about 50 percent. Black unemployment is rising at twice the speed of white unemployment.[79] A number of reasons have been suggested for this:[80]

i. Racism meant that even before the recent rise in unemployment "a black person had to make twice as many applications as a white person before finding a job."[81] Even in areas of high black unemployment, one firm in five employs *no* black workers.[82]
ii. Discrimination particularly affects white collar employment which so far has been hit much less by the slump than manual employment: only 8 percent of West Indian males have white collar jobs, as opposed to 40 percent of white males.
iii. The last-in, first-out procedure often adopted in cases of redundancy can hit recent immigrants most.
iv. Some of the fastest-growing levels of unemployment are in areas where black people are concentrated – particularly the inner-city areas of the West Midlands.

Finally, the higher level of youth unemployment hits the black population disproportionately because there is a much greater proportion of young people in the black population than there is on average.

The effect of racism on top of this is to make life particularly bleak for black youth in the inner-city areas. There are few enough jobs to go round for youth anyway, and those that are available are now more likely to go to whites. So in Lewisham in 1978, "unemployment among black school leavers was three times as high as among white school leavers, despite the fact that they tried just as hard to get jobs".[83] A House of Commons subcommittee was told earlier this year that in Toxteth, "60 percent of the black population were unemployed".[84] No wonder a survey of a small sample of black youth in Handsworth in November 1977 showed that although most had jobs, they saw unemployment as the main problem facing them (just ahead of racial discrimination by whites).[85]

In looking at black unemployment, it is quite important not to make a simple logical mistake. The fact that black youth are more likely to be unemployed than white youth does not mean that they are the majority of the unemployed or even the youth unemployed

– that would hardly be possible given that black people only make up 3.4 percent of the total population, while the official level of unemployment is now 11.8 percent.

Even in Handsworth, Birmingham, where 31 percent of the population is black, 60 percent of the unemployed in November 1977 were white. Nor is it the case that these figures mean that most black youth are unemployed. At least until the most recent upward surge of unemployment, the overwhelming majority of blacks between 16 and 25 have been in employment.[86]

On the basis of the figures, if there were an exact repeat of the events of 1886-87 or 1931-32, you would expect them to take place in the inner-city areas and for a quarter or more of the rioters to be black. But the riots of 1981 were not a simple repeat of these two previous occasions. The direct motivation was not agitation over unemployment, but usually a response to police harassment or racial attacks.

Racialism, inner city areas, unemployment and the police

For many people – including many people on the left – racialist attitudes are something unchanging, inbuilt, part of the character, which can only be prevented from having effect by moral persuasion.

But the view human beings have of other human beings – the stereotypes they fit them into – are not in reality unchanging. Received notions have continually to make sense of changing experiences. When they fail to do so, people find themselves holding contradictory notions – those they have held in the past and those arising out of their new experiences. New forms of activity challenge old ideas. If racist notions persist in the majority of the British working class today (as they do) it is no good explaining this in terms of natural nastiness, some "instinctive fear" or the conditioning by the ideology that was fed to people during the days of the British Empire. Instead, it is necessary to see how racism in the past has interacted with economic development to confine black people to certain sorts of jobs and certain sorts of living conditions, so creating a specific pattern of their interaction with white people. Racism then determines not merely the stereotypes white workers have of blacks, but also, to some extent, the objective experience of life alongside them.

Concretely, when Afro-Caribbeans and Asians came to Britain they found that the only jobs they could get were ones (for instance, foundry work, night shifts in textiles, welding) which most white workers were unwilling to take, the only housing available was in dilapidated, inner-city areas which many whites were already preferring to move away from, their children were forced by language problems and teacher racism into the lower streams. The already worse areas of the cities tended to become "the black areas", the worst jobs became "jobs for blacks", the lower streams in the schools tended to become "the black classes". As the racist stereotypes moulded into the white population in the past delimited what black people could do and where they could live, the stereotypes were reproduced and reinforced. Those who suffered the worst conditions became blamed for those conditions. Successive governments have played their role in this by responding to every wave of racist agitation with tighter immigration controls directed against black people.

The economic crisis has tended to reinforce racist attitudes still more. Once one section of the working class tends to believe that another section is responsible for the bad condition in which it lives, then it tends also to blame it for the general run-down of the inner-city areas consequent upon the crisis and to see the jobs blacks have as jobs which could go to whites.

Among the majority of white workers, however, this stereotyping is always to some extent counteracted by something else. Capitalism always has to unite the working class as well as divide it. Even while its politicians and ideologues try to set white against black, in the factories and the offices it has to integrate them into common production processes; to make them work together to some extent, so that it can effectively exploit them both. And in so doing it forces them to try to create 100 percent strong organisation to reduce the scale of such exploitation. Under such circumstances, even the most racist of workers can dimly perceive that his or her racial stereotypes are a hindrance to stopping an increase in the tempo of work or to struggling for a pay rise. Hence the widespread experience that white workers who will make the most vicious racist comments while at home or in the pub with their friends, at least put on an act of being friendly with black people at work. Among employed workers, therefore, the stereotypes are continually being undermined, blunted by some experiences even while they may also be being reinforced by other experiences.

But there are two groups within the working class who do not experience these counter-tendencies. The first are the unemployed in white neighbourhoods, who unless they are organised into activity against the system, find themselves stuck at home or on the street corners, with no direct experience of black people to break down the racial stereotypes. That is why the unemployed have always been and will always be much more open to influence by fascist groups than employed workers.

The other group is the police. The nature of their work necessarily pushes them to a much greater than average acceptance of racist stereotypes. The main task of the police is to protect property against those who would infringe upon it and to suppress those by-products of alienation (personal violence, drug taking, excessive drunkenness) that impede the process of "peaceful" exploitation and accumulation.

An economic crisis creates more infringements upon private property and more of the symptoms of alienation – and it produces them in a concentrated form among those groups who live in the most oppressive conditions, have the worst jobs and the highest levels of unemployment. There are growing levels of certain sorts of "crime" – especially among those most affected by the crisis – the employed who live in the inner cities. A *minority* of these are pushed into certain sorts of petty thieving.[87] (One sign of the way in which they are forced down by the crisis is that they often do not even think of the opportunities available for serious crime.)

Hence the growth in the number of robberies against the person in the 1970s. A thousand percent increase in the level of youth unemployment between 1973 and 1976 was accompanied by an 800 percent increase in the number of robberies from the person – just as in the only year that youth unemployment fell, 1973, there was a fall in the number of these robberies.

Given the way in which black youth suffer much more than the average from unemployment and are much more likely to live in the inner cities, it is not surprising that they are likely to be involved more than the average in petty crime[88] – although the great majority of such crimes are still the work of white people.

Under such circumstances, those who would blame the victims of the crisis for its consequences can easily get to work. Just as they blame those who live in the worst housing for the conditions they have to suffer, they blame the petty crime that results from unemployment on the unemployed, and on the black unemployed in particular. This was the significance of the invention by the press and the police of the term "mugging" in the mid-1970s, with its connotation that anyone who walked through a London street was in grave danger from "dark forces"[89] (even though the average Londoner still has to live in the city 2,000 years before having an even chance of being mugged and even then the odds are three to one against a weapon being used)[90] or of the great press publicity given to a sociologist who claimed that in Handsworth "200 youths of West Indian origin have drifted into a life of idleness and crime" [91] – despite the fact that there were only 215 cases of theft from the person in the area in 1977 and these were nearly all of small amounts. [92] In fact, it is clear that only a small minority of black unemployed youth can be involved in these crimes.

However, for the policeman who is charged with suppressing the crime, the racist stereotype seems to fit. If robberies occur more from the unemployed than the average, then if you harass the unemployed you are more likely to catch robbers. If youth are more likely to commit petty crimes than the average, then devote your attention to the youth. If the inner cities are the places where there are a higher than average number of thefts from the person and of cases of drugs and drunkenness then have your patrol cars prowling round inner-city streets and not the suburbs. If blacks are more likely to be unemployed and to live in the inner city than average, then make it part of your routine to stop them in the streets and search them.

Above all, if you want a good record of arrests, then treat every young, unemployed black you see on an inner-city street as if he is a criminal. Assert yourself against him, don't put up with any cheek, let him know who's boss – and if you can't find any evidence of crime, plant it so that he doesn't get away scot free. Or as the Metropolitan Police have said in writing, "Our experience has taught us the fallibility of the assertion that crime rates among those of West Indian origin are no higher than those of the population at large". [93]

It is not a long way from this assertion to the organisation of "nigger hunts" by keen young officers out for arrests and promotion. They follow logically from the task set the police of protecting property and "law and order" in a society in a deep crisis which hits black people disproportionately hard. Racial harassment is not something that can be understood apart from the aggravation of the economic crisis, but has to be seen as one of its by-products. It cannot be fought merely by outraged liberal protests over police behaviour or racism in general. It has to be tackled at the root.

Once you grasp this, you can also see why it is not only black people who suffer from "hard" policing. Such harassment is a feature of all areas of high unemployment. Hence the fate of a Liddle Towers or a Jimmy Kelly. Hence the way in which a survey of attitudes to the police in the North West in April 1980 found that although most people had confidence in the police, there was marked hostility in two areas of high unemployment – Huyton, Merseyside, which is almost entirely white, and Moss Side, Manchester, which is mixed black and white.[94]

As the crisis deepens, growing sections of white youth are also going to be on the receiving end of police harassment. After all, they too are more likely than not unemployed, they too hang about the streets, they too disturb "law-abiding property owners", they too are potential, if not actual criminals. Hence a recent speech by the chief constable of South Yorkshire who used phrases about white youth that you normally expect to hear about blacks: "44 percent of all robberies in South Yorkshire last year were carried out by so-called skinheads...the skinheads were also responsible for 50 percent of all assaults".[95]

As Pete Barry of the Liverpool 8 defence committee has pointed out, police harassment now is against both black and white. To the police, "down here if you're black you're a nigger, and if you're white you're a nigger-lover. That's the racial abuse white people have to suffer".[96]

It is important in this connection not to overlook an important difference between the typical inner-city area in Britain and in the US. In the US the tendency has been for virtually all white people to move to the suburbs in the last 30 years, leaving the inner-city areas as overwhelmingly black. In Britain, with its much smaller black population, this has not happened.

As one sociologist has noted of St Paul's in Bristol, "Above all it must be emphasised that the St Paul-Montpelier area was in no sense a 'ghetto'... In the US it is the Negro population that tends to live in the most ethnically segregated neighbourhoods of the large cities, where 90 percent or more of the population may be black. The spatial separation of Negroes and whites gave rise to a characteristic Negro subculture and segregated institutions, including churches, stores, banks, insurance companies, politics and styles of recreation... The Bristol area differed from either a Jewish or a Negro ghetto in a number of important respects. Racially and ethnically the population was extremely heterogeneous... There was no distinctive subculture pervading the area as a whole".[97]

Another sociological study, of Handsworth, Birmingham, shows that 69 percent of its population are white (even if half these are over the age of 60) and concludes, "Clearly the term 'ghetto' is inappropriate".[98]

This does not mean there is no racialism in the inner-city areas – far from it. Nor does it mean that there is no tendency for large numbers of people to mix almost entirely with members of their own ethnic group. In St Paul's for instance, "Although coloured immigrants lived in close physical proximity to other residents and there was a good deal of face to face interaction in the street and at work, primary group relations within the area were almost entirely confined to others of the same racial, national or religious grouping".[99]

The fact that the areas are *not* ghettos has important effects. It means there is not the de facto segregation of the educational system that exists in some US cities, so that there is a certain tendency for mixed gangs of youth to grow up. It means that the very high levels of inner-city unemployment affect whites as well as blacks (so that in Handsworth in 1977 19 percent of Asians and West Indians were unemployed but also 13.3 percent of white, with long-term unemployment tending to be about the same level for whites and West Indians;[100] while in Toxteth earlier this year, 47 percent of blacks were jobless but also 43 percent of whites[101]). It means that police harassment is something witnessed, and to some extent suffered, by whites. Thus in Moss Side, after the riots "ordinary law-abiding folk and supporters of the established order...were shocked to see the police in a new light during the riots. They are coming to believe that longstanding complaints from the black community about police harassment and racism may have some substance".[102]

Capitalism divides and rules. It separates off the problems of one group of workers from those of another – young from old, unemployed from employed, the inner-city dweller from those in the suburbs, black from white. In certain historically conditioned circumstances, the divisions become virtually complete – the young unemployed black inner-city dweller suffers conditions, especially police harassment, that just cannot be comprehended by the older, white, employed suburban worker. Rebellion then is isolated rebellion, which at best gets passive sympathy from a minority of workers elsewhere. This was the experience in the US in the 1960s. This too was the pattern of most of the clashes between young blacks and the police in Britain in the early and mid-1970s – from the "battle of Atlantic Road" in 1969, through the Brockwell Park disturbances of June 1973, the Carib Club raid of 1974, and the Chapeltown bonfire clashes of 1975, to the defence of the Notting Hill Carnival against the police in 1976.

But the divisions are by no means watertight. That is why since the anti-Nazi confrontations at Wood Green and Lewisham in 1977 there has been a tendency for white youth to join the struggles of blacks on the streets. That is why the explosions at Bristol, Brixton, Toxteth, Moss Side and Handsworth were *black-led but multi-racial*. And that is why they could produce "copycat" riots, often almost entirely white, in scores of other places.

Reformism is always taken by surprise by any great upsurge of popular rebellion. It is thrown off balance and at first does not know how to respond. But it is rarely long before it tries to regain control, by blunting the edge of popular militancy so as fit it back into its schemes for patching up the system.

In the case of the riots, this has meant separating out the issues that produced the riots, picking on this or that aspect of the situation and treating it as something that can be dealt with in isolation from the general crisis of society. The reformist politicians or social workers can then present themselves as the essential mediators between those who rioted and the system, alone able to defuse tension and prevent new riots.

Different groups of reformists pick upon different issues to separate out and present as the key to future social peace. But the method is the same in all cases. There have been four main sorts of reformist response:

i. *Youth employment reformism.* The "wets" in the government and the Labour front bench alike combine strong support for the police ("We have to put the police in a position to deal with serious violence immediately" – Michael Foot, 15 July; the opposition "accept that the police should be properly protected" – Eric Heffer, 15 July) with pleas for Thatcher to take measures to reduce the immediate level of youth unemployment. They demand the extention of YOPS and other youth training schemes so as at least to reduce the number of school leavers on the register and they suggest schemes for public sector capital investment – as, for instance, the TUC's plan for £5 billion a year capital spending to create an extra half a million jobs. The weakness of all these schemes is self-evident: they remove the school leaver from the dole queue for a short time only, they give them a "wage" which is hardly more than the dole, and they would still, even if successful, leave the permanent level of unemployment at 2.5 million.

ii. *Inner-city reformism.* The idea that the crisis of the inner cities can be solved without fundamental alteration in the system goes back at least to 1968, when the then Labour government introduced a £15 million a year "urban aid programme". The 1970-73 Tory environment minister, Peter Walker, (one of today's "wets") followed this through with a wide-ranging review of the problems of the inner-city areas; the 1974 Labour government finally brought in "partnership schemes" for these areas which involved spending £113 million last year. Today the riots have led to the digging up of all the surveys and suggestions from the Peter Walker era and to still more talk of reform. Yet all these schemes have been completely ineffective. They have not been able to stop the deindustrialisation, the run-down in services caused by the wider spending cuts (the £133 million of partnership money last year contrasts with the £200 million the inner-city areas lost through the cuts in the rate support grant), the persistence of unemployment totals double regional averages, the growth of despair, vandalism, petty crime and, of course, police harassment.

"Inner-city reformism" has been inspired by the plethora of schemes introduced in the US after the ghetto uprisings of the 1960s. But the "success" of these schemes was not in producing any permanent reduction in unemployment or any permanent improvement in the conditions of the inner-city areas. They defused the tensions that produced the "uprisings" – but only because they led to a massive expansion in the layer of black middle class mediators between the ghetto and the outside world (businessmen, social workers, community organisers, Democratic Party politicians). The worsening of the economic crisis in the last ten years has meant a deterioration of the conditions of the majority of the ghetto populations, leading to widespread predictions now of a new wave of ghetto revolts.[103] If such were the meagre results of "inner-city reformism" in the still powerful American economy of the late 1960s, much, much less can be expected in the feeble, crisis-ridden Britain of the 1980s.

iii. *Race relations reformism.* The American black uprisings had another by-product in Britain – the growth of a flourishing race relations industry, based upon a network of full-time workers for the Commission for Racial Equality (CRE) nationally and the different Community Relations Councils (CRCs) locally. So in a typically inner-city area you will find at least half a dozen CRC staff plus a host of other social and community workers employed by local councils or funded by charitable trusts, all aiming to tie the day-to-day grievances of black people into the structures of the local and national state.

Those involved in this type of reformism see their job as being to push certain demands of black people in such a way as to get them settled without the need for any great change in the structures of society. They react against any attempt to see the riots as an outcome of the wide social crisis with its affects on unemployment and housing conditions as well as racialist and police harassment. They see any talk of these issues as diverting attention from the particular problems of the group they mediate for – black people. And so discussion on the riots gets reduced to discussion on particular discriminatory practices in employment and how to weed out individual racialists from the police force.[104]

iv. *Community policing reformism.* The final palliative offered is a change of police methods. There is a weak and a strong version of this. The weaker version is pushed by some in the police hierarchy itself and by Liberal and Labour politicians: it is the call for the return of the local bobby who walks round the neighbourhood getting to know local people and ingratiate himself with them.

This method of policing has actually been introduced in Handsworth in Birmingham. In the first days after Toxteth, it was praised as the way to avoid inflaming riots. For example, John Brown of Cranfield Institute of Technology told The *Guardian* on 1 July that the Handsworth scheme was a great success: "It is succeeding and is therefore much more of a threat to political extremists than repressive policing. The police have the backing of the Asian community and many rastafarians in Birmingham".

Three days later Handsworth exploded and as local youth turned on the "community police"; the "friendly bobbies" took their revenge with 329 arrests.

The stronger version of "community policing" involves a change in the structures of *control* over the police, so as to subordinate them to elected local bodies. This is what is demanded by Labour councillors like Ted Knight of Lambeth, Ken Livingstone of the GLC and Lady Simey of Toxteth.

Unlike the softer version, this does at least focus on police violence, police harassment and police racism. But it suffers the great weakness of assuming that these aspects of police behaviour can be detached from the role the police play in a crisis-ridden society as a whole. Police violence is seen as the product of an autonomous self-sustaining development within the police hierarchy, of a move to a "strong state" produced by the momentum of the state structures themselves. It fails to see the most elementary things: the police exist to keep present-day society in order; this order consists in protecting the propertied from the propertyless; such protection is going to require ever higher levels of repression as the material condition of the propertyless gets more and more desperate. Those who do not see these links end up in the contradictory position of exaggerating the power of police repression, and yet suggesting it can be ended by the exercise of a little political pressure through parliamentary channels.

To see what is wrong with the idea of community control over the police, you simply have to question: how would a police force controlled by the Knights, the Livingstones and the Simeys react if the unemployed took it into their heads to engage in a bit of looting for basic goods they could never afford to buy? One suspects that Labour councillors would soon see the need to reassure local property owners by sending in the police to restore order, and that the police would do so by using violence to restrain the looters. But if the police force is going to be given carte blanche to use violence against looting, it is going to use it to stop petty thefts, to stop handbag snatchings, to stop gangs of youth hanging about the street ready, it seems to the police, to engage in such crimes the moment their backs are turned.

The reformists conceal from themselves this reality of the state as a product of capitalist society. Instead, they reify it, see it as a thing existing outside of a society based upon the dynamics of capital accumulation, refer to it in an almost anarchist way as *the* enemy. But because this enemy exists for them in a vacuum it can be reformed out of existence without any great struggle. The struggle becomes not a struggle against the system, but to build pressure groups to get rid of individual, particularly nasty, police officers.

Each sort of reformism focuses on one, important, factor in producing the riots. But by taking that factor in isolation from the total situation, each ends up trying to channel the anger that exploded onto the streets into channels that are safe for the system.

Of course, revolutionaries do not abstain from the campaigns the reformists launch – whether over youth unemployment, against racial discrimination, for more funds for the inner cities or to curtail the repressive actions of the police. But we seek to build out of these campaigns wider political generalisation, while the reformists seek to substitute narrow, one-issue pressure group politics for the generalised anger shown in the riots.

Black separatism and the riots

Among Britain's black population the reformist ideas we have outlined above are not the only ones that are prevalent. Of considerable significance among the more radical layers of black youth, especially Afro-Caribbean youth, are versions of black separatism – the idea that black people can only win by organising and fighting autonomously from white people of all sorts.

Like all political ideologies, black separatism exists at two levels – on the one hand as widespread, often not fully articulated currents of popular attitudes; on the other as more or less coherent analyses of the world and programmes of action propounded by formal political organisations.

In the "popular" form what this amounts to is a tendency for many West Indian youth to identify with symbols of black assertiveness – in the late 1960s with the black power slogans from the US, today with some of the imagery of Rastafarianism and with reggae music.

The number of committed, believing members of the Rastafarian cult is very small. But the number of youth who vaguely identify with its symbolism is much higher. A survey of a group of black youth in Handsworth showed that half thought Rastafarianism "significant".[105]

A sociologist who studied an inner-city area in a Midlands town [106] has described 'a recently formed youth subculture, based around distinctive speech patterns, appearance, fashion and music forms... within one distinguished a small, strictly religious group, a wider "political" grouping which has "assimilated various Rasta conventions – speech, fashion and appearance: the locks, patois, ganja smoking and hatred of Babylon". [107] Finally, there is a much wider youth culture based upon reggae.

A study of St Pauls, Bristol, by a West Indian sociologist concludes, "In Bristol (and elsewhere), reggae took hold and helped to inject a much needed sense of identity and cultural solidarity into the lifestyle and thinking" of a typical younger West Indian, "not only because it was an easy kind of dance music, but also because its self-conscious critical messages on society were relevant to his needs and desires. The eruption of music in the late 60s coincided with the worsening of race relations in Britain". [108]

Both Rastafarianism and reggae were initially a reaction among lower classes in Jamaica to a society where the heritage of slavery still meant that the darker your skin was, the lower was your social status, and where to be black was almost certainly to be poor. The West Indian immigrants who came to Britain in the 1950s and 1960s expected things to be different here. They found in practice that they were discriminated against for being black when it came to housing, jobs and treatment at the hands of the police. They were prepared, by and large, to put up with this because they still felt as "foreigners" in Britain. The second generation find they suffer all the same problems as their parents, plus the frequent indignity of being out into the "inferior" streams at school. But they are not nearly so prepared to simply tolerate these conditions. They want to put up some resistance.

But forms of successful physical resistance are difficult to arrive at, particularly since they find racist attitudes among the white people who live and work alongside them. As one black youth in Leeds summed up a very widespread feeling, "I'm an apprentice precision engineer. Out of 300 workers, I'm the only black one there. I think all white men are two-faced, and you never know what they are thinking". [109] Of the black youth interviewed in Handsworth, only a "minority" said they "got on well with whites". [110]

For such youth, a diluted version of Rastafarianism could become a means of maintaining their own feelings of identity in the face of a hostile white society, of defending their self-respect in the face of racialism from police, from landlords, from employers – and, all too often, from fellow workers.

But as a form of resistance to the racialism from which black youth have suffered it has had one great defect. It has been a form of cultural resistance, of reaction to the ideology of a society that downgrades you because you are black. But it has left untouched the material features of that society. It has been a defensive reaction to that society, not a perspective for organising a successful fightback against it.

This is shown even more clearly when you look at what has happened to the small political groupings that have attempted to build some sort of continuing organisation out of this much wider "popular" separatist sentiment.

There were a plethora of such groups in the late 1960s, mainly basing themselves on the experience of the American black power movement. But many withered in the early 1970s and no *national* black consciousness or black nationalist movement developed. In most localities all that exist are small black bookshops or centres, run by half a dozen activists, the political groups that could provide some national structure for these being very small.

Of these probably the most influential (although not necessarily the biggest) is the *Race Today* collective, who have produced a monthly magazine for the last seven years and who have played a role in leading struggles such as that of the East End Bengali community in 1976, the Carnival Development Committee Campaign in 1977, the George Lindo Campaign in Bradford in 1979, the New Cross Massacre Action Committee in 1981. An examination of *Race Today*'s analyses and demands shows in a clear form the limitations involved in any attempt at separatist black "revolutionary" politics in Britain today.

Race Today's political message goes something like this: The black population in Britain finds itself in a colonial situation vis-à-vis the British state. Its ultimate liberation will be through revolution. But this can only be achieved if each oppressed group develops its own struggle, without influence from outside. Whenever we struggle against the system, the magazine's editor, Darcus Howe, told a meeting in Bradford in 1978, "there is one distinctive position we had to maintain...that we had to come through on our own as blacks, independently... The main vehicle of that must be our willingness...to develop independent movement... The black working class will be in charge... The black struggle has an independent validity and vitality of its own".[111]

This perspective means that any attempt to involve black workers in joint organisation with white workers is seen as dangerous. So the conclusion in November 1977 was that "the Grunwick strike demonstrates that a victory is only possible if an autonomous leadership emerges which is capable of an international appeal and free from the traps inherent in (trade) unionism". The mistake of the strike committee was to "believe that involving white workers had to be their primary purpose". The mistake flowed from assuming that the traditions of "the Tolpuddle Martyrs and the matchgirls" were the traditions of black workers, whereas, *Race Today* argued, black workers had quite different traditions: "Our history as black workers...has forced us to create our own methods of struggle." The strike committee failed to raise this, and so failed "to tap the powerful national and international linkage of black struggle" which could have brought victory.[112]

At the time of the one-day Asian stoppage in the Spitalfields area against racist attacks in 1978, the conclusion was that "the Bengalis will create their own organisational vehicle to carry their struggle forward, come what may", but that it would have to avoid attempt to lead it astray by "the CRE, the ANL and the labour movement".[113]

In November 1979 the future lay with "a radical and insurrectionary movement of Asian youth", with the way forward being shown by the various Asian youth movements provided again that they could avoid "the influence of the white left groups".

For *Race Today* the "autonomous" black movement is always threatened from two sides – from the black middle class certainly, but also from revolutionary left.

How exactly will the black community organise itself? In the mid-1970s a lot of attention was paid to the predominantly Asian workforces that struck at Mansfield Hosiery, Imperial Typewriters and so on. But in recent years the focus has moved away from the factories to the streets, with hardly a mention of black strikers in recent issues of the magazine. What instead has tended to develop is an analysis of "youth" as the vanguard. So Darcus Howe describes the conflicts of black youth with the police: "A section of the British working class, distinguishable by the colour of our skins, had declared open rebellion against the British state".[114]

The rebellion does not, however, involve simply fighting the police. It also involves opting *for* unemployment as preferable to the "slavery" of work: "And how they rebelled. *En masse* young blacks refused to follow their parents into the (unskilled, deadly, boring and repetitive) jobs".[115]

Yet whichever emphasis *Race Today* has followed, the record of attempts to organise blacks on a separatist basis has not been a great success – despite the clear rhetorical appeal of parts of the separatist message. As Darcus Howe has admitted, "We are weak on organisation".[116] *Race Today*'s attempt to generate mass self-defence of the Bengali community through the setting up of a "command council" led nowhere: "the euphoria of the self-defence movement has produced neither the disciplined paramilitary organisation that can undertake systematic self-defence, nor has it produced the organisation that can undertake campaigns over material rights".[117]

Race Today was able to organise a very large demonstration over the Deptford firebombings – but not to build any lasting organisation. In the wake of this summer's riots, separatist groups in several areas (Brixton, Leeds, Woolwich) have argued for *all-black* defence committees – despite the fact that about half those arrested have usually been white. The main result has usually been to stop any effective defence campaign at all getting off the ground. These failures are not an accident. They follow necessarily from the whole separatist approach.

Separatist agitation can only make sense for black people when they find themselves already separated from whites, so that self-organisation is the only way to get protection against the racism that exists around them. Such a situation can exist on the streets, where youth can congregate together, virtually ignoring whites except when it is a question of fighting back against the police or racists. It can exist in small factories, where whole departments, whole shifts or even the whole workforce can be black. But it cannot exist in the large factories where, after all, most black people work – and work alongside whites.

Even on the streets and in the small factories separatist agitation faces problems. *Confrontation* with the police on the streets – as opposed to merely receiving punishment from them – is actually only an occasional occurrence. And the confrontations rarely last very long – even the biggest riots this year started fading after two nights. The great majority of the time, black youth on the street are not acting together in any collective struggle, but are hanging about passing the time, generally being passive. The subculture that develops in these circumstances is not going to be a *revolutionary* subculture, concerned with fighting back. Instead, it is going to be one that stresses a protective *withdrawal* from existing society. That is perhaps why a vague Rastafarianism, which if taken seriously means worrying about Africa, not Britain, has taken over from the more confident black power talk of the late 1960s.

On the streets or in the black clubs, those who set the style are likely to be those who find themselves with most time on their hands, those who don't work – whether this means the unemployed, the hustlers or the petty racketeers. Hence the way in which those who seek to organise black youth on the street all too often come back with the story that they are not interested in "the right to work" – or even "work" – although the vast majority of black youth have always worked (at least until this year's catastrophic youth unemployment figures).

The whole experience of the revolutionary movement is that very little in the way of permanent organisation can be built from those who drop out of the capitalist employment market. In America too, one reason the Black Panthers eventually collapsed was that, "The party's orientation towards 'street youth' resulted in a very unstable base and as a result Panther membership was frequently like a revolving door. Furthermore the party's orientation to this sector resulted in a rank and file which was difficult to control and would not act in a disciplined fashion. The leadership did not intend the emphasis on armed self-defence and the exaggerated significance of guns to mean immediate armed conflict with the police. But the membership did not always accept such an interpretation, and there was a continual tension between the leadership and the rank and file over questions of adventurism".[118]

There is a very good reason why Marxists have always put enormous emphasis on the need for *employed* workers to lead other oppressed groups. It is not because they necessarily *suffer* most under capitalism, but because the capitalist economy itself, in its drive to expand the output of value and surplus value, binds workers together into coherent groupings that can fight back against it in a disciplined, conscious manner.

Even before capitalism, you would get occasional, very violent disturbances from the urban poor. But it is only with the creation of an industrial working class that you get long drawn-out, organised struggles under the control of the workers themselves, that can lay the basis for the exploited to emancipate themselves.

What this means in practice is that those who orient on "street youth" as the vanguard alternate between extravagant predictions of armed insurrection when rebellion flares up, and then lapsing into low-level, defensive activities of the most unrevolutionary sort when the police and the courts get their revenge.[119] In this way the separatists merely participate in a division of labour with the race relations industry, for all their revolutionary rhetoric.

When it comes to black workers, the problems for separatist agitation is even greater. For the only *all-black* workplaces are small and in non-struggle parts of the economy. It is in hosiery and clothing industries, textiles, certain small plastic and light engineering factories that you find workforces, or at least night shifts, that are all black – it is not in motors, the docks, the mines, the power stations, the railways, even though some of these industries have many black workers working alongside whites. In general, workers in small, non-strategic workplaces are only able to enter into struggle with confidence when the big battalions have already broken through. Hence, there was a wave of "black" strikes in the years 1972-75 *after* the struggles of UCS. The miners and the dockers had shown the way forward and dented the confidence of the ruling class. But with the decline in the level of successful industrial struggle by the big battalions from 1975 onwards, you find an even bigger decline in the number of *all-black* strikes.

This did not mean that no black workers were involved in struggle: many were – in the Ford strike of 1978, the "low paid" strikes of hospital and local authority workers in early 1979, and the one and two-day engineering strikes later in that year. But these were not *all-black* workforces and therefore were of no interest to the separatists for there was no way they could relate to black workers who worked, as a minority, alongside whites on the basis of telling them just to organise themselves and to stop worrying about whites. And so the black separatist papers hardly mention such struggles. *Race Today*, for instance, has only ever had one article on Fords Dagenham and that was back in 1976, even though 13,000 or 14,000 black workers are employed there.

Even in the case of a majority black strike *Race Today* did deal with, Grunwick's, it had nothing real to say in terms of strategy. As we have seen, its only positive suggestion was for the strike committee to rely upon "the national and international linkage of black struggle". It is not clear how that would have stopped the scabbing which finally broke the strike, especially as one of the strike leaders, Mrs Desai, actually told *Race Today*, support from the black communities for the strike was limited: "We are beginning to see some support from our community, but it is only verbal support".[120]

Despite its appeal to sections of black youth, separatism fails completely as a strategy for black people to fight back against their oppression. It is bound to. In Zimbabwe, where blacks are 97 percent of the population, a black-only struggle could defeat white racism. Again in the US where blacks are 12 percent of the population and the clear majority in the inner areas of many of the cities, they have the ability to force certain limited concessions if they fight alone. In Britain where they are only 3.5 percent of the population, and even in the inner-city areas a minority of 15 to 20 percent, a long-term strategy on fighting alone is a strategy of inevitable defeat. Separatism is, at best, a defensive reaction against the racism of British society by black youth – but it is not a defensive reaction that can lead anywhere.

Socialists defend the *right* of black people to turn away from British society and its racism by adopting a defensive, separatist cultural stance. But at the same time, we cannot keep quiet about the fact that such a defensive cultural stance cannot *defeat* the forces that oppress black people. Unless they can move forward from it, to participation in a wider movement that does not need to be purely defensive, then in the long run they will be defeated.

For black youth to accept the slogans of black power and black consciousness, for them to don Rastafarian colours, for them to insist on speaking the West Indian dialect that their teachers regard as "bad English", can be a step forward in the building of self-confidence. But it is a limited step forward if it still leaves them believing that they cannot change society and instead have to dream of opting out. Much more far-reaching is the transformation of consciousness that can take place as black workers and youth gain self-confidence from *leading* other white workers and youth in struggle.

As Mort Mascarenhas has written:

> Black consciousness is...a counter to white chauvinistic interpretations of history and culture. Since the first days of imperialism and slavery the oppressor forces, in order to justify their actions and maintain power, have deliberately denigrated black people, our culture, intelligence and traditions. This rewriting of history has been extremely successful and explains the "slave" mentality of many black people. Black Consciousness, through emphasising the dignity and equality of being black (hence the black is beautiful campaign) is a very progressive and necessary force. People must feel they have a right to freedom, equality and justice before they will fight for such demands.

> However Black Consciousness, while being progressive, cannot in itself

provide solutions or a programme of action through which oppressed people can gain liberation. It is simply a counter to psychological oppression while oppression has very glaring *physical* manifestations. As such it can go two ways, it can slide towards the dead end of Black Nationalism or it can develop into a Marxist understanding.[121]

The demand for physical forms of black self-defence is certainly quite correct if a black locality is under attack from the Nazis or the police. But to be effective, black self-defence has rapidly to pass over into defence involving anti-racist white workers and youth as well, to encompass industrial action from the *mixed* workforces of the large factories as well as just fighting on the streets. To refuse to encourage this because of a commitment to "black autonomy" is to endanger black lives.

First published in *International Socialism* 14, autumn 1981

The urgent challenge of fascism

The outburst of racialist sentiment and activity since Enoch Powell's Birmingham speech marks the beginning of a new phase in British politics. A section of the ruling class (although not yet by any means the dominant section) is resorting to the crudest forms of prejudice in order to confuse, divide and divert workers from the real struggle. It does so in a situation where British capitalism is forced to cut real living standards, keep unemployment at a relatively high level, and raise rents and prices, while fearing that its rule is no longer guaranteed by the mass complacency of 1950s and early 1960s. Powell thinks he can overcome these problems by developing a mass following on a racist programme. The ready response to his speech has revealed the prevalence of racialist ideas among workers, which had been inculcated by centuries of capitalism and imperialism. Paradoxically it also indicates the extent to which people are fed up with existing society. They are disillusioned with established politics and have lost their faith in the succession of leaders who have betrayed their trust. But instead of blaming actual enemies and looking for the real source of their frustrations, they blame the immigrants.

The traditional organisations of the left have totally failed either to offer real, socialist alternatives to capitalism or to combat the racist upsurge. The Labour left has completely lost touch with the mass of workers. The Communist Party, despite its many individual militants, responded to the racism too little and too late. Internationalist propaganda did not immediately appear. Counter-demonstrations were not organised. As for the bulk of trade union officials, with a few honourable exceptions, their chief concern seems to have been to avoid any responsibility, hoping that the upsurge would die of its own accord.

The events of the last few weeks have exposed the extreme isolation and fragmentation of genuinely anti-racialist forces. Many a militant in industry found himself quite alone when confronted with the racist tide, despite his success in leading purely economic struggles in the past.

An urgent reorganisation of these socialist forces is necessary if the onward march of racialism is to be checked and any long-term fascist development fought against. (Previous differences have to be subordinated to the struggle against the common threat.) Socialist alternatives to frustrations and anxieties created by capitalism must be presented and linked to systematic anti-racist propaganda on a massive scale.

A SINGLE ORGANISATION OF REVOLUTIONARY SOCIALISTS IS NEEDED TO FIGHT THESE NEW AND URGENT BATTLES.

We invite all those who agree with the following programme to come together in trying to build this:

1. Opposition to imperialism; for the victory of all genuine national liberation movements.
2. Opposition to racism in all its forms and to controls on immigration.
3. Opposition to state control of trade unions; support for all progressive strikes.
4. Workers' control of society and industry as the only alternatives to fascism.

If you are interested in discussing possible sorts of action, contact International Socialism at the address overleaf.

International Socialists leaflet, 1968

Climate change and class conflict

In the past two years the question of climate change has moved from the margins of mainstream political debate to the centre. Hardly a week goes by without some international meeting discussing it. Politicians and corporations of all hues now declare their commitment to do something; even George Bush admits that there is a problem.

There is a mixture of motives here. Tory leader David Cameron's installation (and subsequent removal) of a rooftop micro wind generator involves pure publicity seeking. But some of those who run world capitalism understand that the environment on which their system depends is in danger of disintegrating within a generation or two.

There is no longer much dispute about what is happening. A build-up of certain gases in the atmosphere is causing the average temperature across the world to rise with potentially catastrophic consequences. New weather patterns will affect the crops we rely on for food. The likelihood of storms and droughts will increase. Ice caps will melt. Rising sea levels threaten to flood low-lying regions such as the Nile Delta, Bangladesh and parts of Florida (and eventually central London and Manhattan).

Most of the gases responsible are produced by burning carbon (in the form of coal) and hydrocarbons (in the form of petroleum products). This is the source of nearly all the energy on which present-day society depends.

There are various difficult calculations showing what may happen if the build-up of these gases continues, but there is now widespread agreement on a range within which global temperatures will increase and on the likely effects. Estimates are provided, for instance, by the Intergovernmental Panel on Climate Change (IPCC) and were contained in the British government's Stern Review last October, although some scientific research suggests these understate the problem.

The Stern Review and the European Union argue that temperatures have to be prevented from rising by any more than two degrees Celsius. A two-degree increase would cause immense problems for people in the poorest parts of the world and anything higher would be devastating for them. But present policies will not hold temperature rises below even this limit. The concentration of gases causing global warming can be measured in parts per million (ppm) of "carbon dioxide equivalents". At present this is 459 ppm. The IPCC estimates that if the level reaches 510 ppm there is a one in three chance of the temperature rise exceeding two degrees; if the level reaches 590 ppm there is a nine out of ten chance.

Yet the emissions target of the Stern Review is 550 ppm. That of the British government is 666 ppm (if all greenhouse gases and not just carbon dioxide are included). This, according to author and activist George Monbiot, gives a 60 to 95 percent chance of a three degrees Celsius increase in warming and a likelihood of very dangerous climate change.

Last month's G8 meeting in Rostock did not even accept these targets. After declaring there was a major problem, the world's leaders postponed even beginning to do anything about it for two years. Even then all they will consider will be an attempt to halve emissions of the gases leading to climate change by 2050, whereas an 80 percent cut in emissions would be required to have a chance of keeping global warming below two degrees.

The roots of the problem

Governments and businesses have a genuine interest in stopping climate change, just as their predecessors a century and a half ago had a genuine interest in dealing with typhoid and cholera in slum working class districts in order to stop the diseases affecting upper class districts as well.

What is at stake for them now is greater. Not just their lives are threatened, but the stability of global capitalism. But they cannot achieve their goal without trying to dampen down the momentum of competitive capital accumulation, the very basis of their system.

Environmental degradation has always been a consequence of

capitalism. Karl Marx showed this in the chapter on machinery in *Capital*, "Moreover, all progress in capitalistic agriculture is a progress in the art, not only of robbing the labourer, but of robbing the soil; all progress in increasing the fertility of the soil for a given time is a progress towards ruining the lasting sources of that fertility. The more a country starts its development on the foundation of modern industry, like the United States, for example, the more rapid is this process of destruction."

In early 19th century Britain the damage to the health and fitness of the working class caused by the drive for profit posed more of a danger to the capitalists than the infectious diseases themselves. It threatened eventually to create a shortage of workers fit enough to be exploited. The interests of the capitalist class as a whole lay in legislation and state inspection to prevent the debilitation of the workforce. But individual capitalist interests fought tooth and nail against such measures. Most of them only understood that a healthy working class was more exploitable than an unhealthy one after the state imposed controls.

Capitalism has now reached out to envelop the whole world and it damages not only localities but the global environment on which it depends. The factory fumes causing bronchitis in working class tenements have now become greenhouse gases threatening to devastate the whole of humanity.

It is precisely because this is a global problem that those who support the system find it difficult to deal with. The drastic measures needed to reduce emissions will present opportunities for other firms and states to intrude on markets. Capitalism is in the situation of destroying the very ground on which it stands. Our futures – or at least our children's or grandchildren's futures – are also at stake.

How should we respond?

There are those who say that the only possible response is to see climate change as the issue that overshadows all others. Everything else has to be subordinated to building a campaign such as has never been seen before in an effort to force governments and firms to take the necessary action.

But campaigns focused purely on climate change will not be the answer to the problem. They can raise awareness of what is happening, but this is not the same as providing an organised force capable of imposing solutions. The most successful single-issue campaigns, such as the anti-war movement, mobilise tens, sometimes hundreds, of thousands of people. In this way they can exert pressure sometimes sufficient to force governments to retreat from unpopular measures, or even, on occasions, to force the adoption of beneficial measures.

This is shown by the way the anti-war movement has increased the difficulties the US and British governments face waging war on Iraq. But for deep-seated change more is needed – there must be a power capable of imposing its will on strong capitalist interests. The people who have twice bombed Baghdad to defend their domination of the world's oil supplies will not be beaten simply by public opinion.

This is especially the case with climate change. The carbon economy is intertwined with every aspect of the system's functioning, including the lives of those of us living within it. Recognition of this leads many environmental activists to the conclusion that the only solution is for people to change their individual lifestyles. Since we all depend on carbon-based energy, we all seem to be part of the problem.

But solutions based on this way of thinking cannot work. It is not just a question of people individually being selfish. For the great mass of people there are no other ways to fulfil our basic needs at present. You can think (as I do) that it is irrational that individuals go to work encased in a tonne of metal propelled by pumping out carbon dioxide. But there is little choice but the private car for workers without access to proper public transport.

There are brilliant designs for carbon neutral homes, but hundreds of millions across the world do not live in such homes and cannot afford to buy new ones. In practice the easiest means for individuals to avoid using carbon-derived energy – low-energy light bulbs or remembering to turn the computer off – have almost as much effect on combating climate change as spitting on the soil in dealing with the effect of a drought.

Recognition of such realities leads people who once looked upon individual actions as the solution to look to the state for action. This is what George Monbiot does in his generally excellent book *Heat*. He shows that only the world's states can bring about the reduction in greenhouse gas emissions necessary to end climate change without a fall in people's living standards. What he does not show is how to create the agency, the active mass force, that can compel the governments of the world's most polluting states to implement such measures. He puts forward a generally excellent political programme for a political force that does not exist.

Can such a force be created through the usual forms of electoral politics? The effort to create it comes up against the same powerful obstacle that makes individual solutions impossible. Environmental activists can end up tailoring their demands to what they think can be achieved without too great a disturbance to the present system. So they lobby for countries to sign up to the Kyoto agreement on the grounds that "at least it is a beginning", even though it has not stopped greenhouse gas emissions soaring. Or they join governments that have no intention of taking serious measures against climate change, as the Irish Green Party has just done.

What are governments up to?

The G8 meeting showed different governments taking apparently very different approaches. Even some of the most committed neoliberals such as Angela Merkel, Nicolas Sarkozy and Tony Blair claimed to want the controls which George Bush vetoed.

This reflected the fact that some capitalist economies are marginally less dependent on carbon energy than others. The western European states, for instance, are less profligate in carbon use than the US because historically they have not had oil supplies of their own and have sought to keep consumption low. France has massive nuclear energy facilities. Britain's greenhouse gas emissions were declining because of the halving of manufacturing industry. So European states can press for limited controls knowing it will hit their global competitors —the gas-guzzling US or the rapidly expanding Chinese economy – harder than themselves. But they still shy away from the far-reaching controls necessary to prevent climate change. Instead they favour "emissions trading" and "carbon offset" schemes which allow the big polluters to continue as before, providing they encourage some emission-reducing scheme somewhere else in the world.

Planting trees as supposed "carbon sinks" which absorb carbon dioxide is a favourite – even though trees die and decompose, releasing carbon gases. The market in this case, as in so many others, is not an effective mechanism. Firms that are expert at fiddling their books to avoid paying taxes can easily find ways to fiddle their emissions.

Particular governments promote the alternatives that are most advantageous to their own specific capitalist interests. One reason for Bush's sudden conversion to biofuels is that they open up the prospect of immensely enhanced profits for US agribusiness. Millions of acres which were making only average profits by producing food now stand to make superprofits by turning out an alternative to petrol. Multinational corporations that control vast swathes of land in tropical third world countries are looking forward to producing diesel from oil seed plants.

This is already having an important impact. It is raising food prices worldwide at the fastest rate since the 1970s, according to the *Financial Times*, even though biofuel use is only equivalent to 1 percent of petroleum use. In the medium term it can do much worse than this. It can lead to a depletion of the world's grain and oil seed reserves just as changing weather patterns due to climate change increase the likelihood of harvest failures in some of the major food-producing regions. The result would not only be price rises but famine, affecting hundreds of millions of people.

Class conflict

There is an important general conclusion to be drawn from the biofuel example. By damaging the very environment on which the capitalist system depends for its continued expansion and accumulation, climate change is going to open enormous fissures within the system.

Sudden changes in climate impinge on people's lives on a massive scale and create immense social and political tensions. All the class and racial contradictions in US society came to the fore with the destruction of New Orleans by Hurricane Katrina. In Darfur the combination of drought and imperialist meddling caused agriculturalists and herders who had coexisted peacefully for generations to turn on each other in civil war.

Climate scientists rightly warn that we cannot say with certainty that a single weather event like Katrina or the Darfur drought is a result of global warming. But what we can say with certainty is that climate change will produce many, many cases like those.

Earlier this year Mexico City saw an enormous protest – the "tortilla march" – over the cost of the country's staple foodstuff. Its price was soaring as the maize from which it is made is increasingly turned into biofuel. Filling SUV fuel tanks in California was causing hunger in Mexico. We can expect many similar protests in the years ahead – battles pitting class against class and also, it is to be feared, state against state and ethnic or religious groups against one another.

There have been previous instances of civilisations collapsing due to ecological devastation as did the Maya civilisation that flourished in southern Mexico around 1,200 years ago. Over-farming of the land led to a decline in fertility until starvation threatened the mass of people. But the upper classes did not suffer in the same way, and bitter class struggles erupted which tore society apart as people were forced to abandon their old way of life.

It will not be any different as climate change takes effect. There is unlikely to be one great movement, but there will be 1,001 struggles as different classes respond to the impact. The real issues in these struggles may often seem complex. Capitalists and states will react to the need to do something about greenhouse gases by price and tax measures that inevitably hit the living standards of the poor (just as Ken Livingstone's congestion charge allows the rich to drive more easily through central London).

So there will be protests, strikes and uprisings whose immediate goal will be to reverse such price rises. The underlying motivation could be a strong sense of class grievance, yet these movements can also be manipulated by sections of the ruling class to advance the capitalists' interests in producing greater emissions. And there will be many, many cases when states and capitalists take measures to hurt the living standards of the mass of people, but disguise them as methods of addressing climate change.

Faced with these struggles, there will be a particular onus on those who see climate change as resulting from the blind advance of capitalist accumulation to understand their class dynamic. That means trying to give struggles a direction that protects people's living standards and conditions while at the same time presenting real alternatives to pouring greenhouse gases into the atmosphere.

The only sure protection against climate change is the replacement of a society based on accumulation for profit with one based on production for need. But that will not come about if we wait for it. The impact of climate change will cause an intensification of all the struggles bred by capitalism, just as it will cause spasmodic protests over particular climate change issues. There is only one way to build the forces needed to put an end to the system that creates climate change. That is through participation in all these struggles, pulling them together into a force that can challenge capitalism as a whole.

First published in *Socialist Review*, July/August 2007

6: Imperialism and resistance

Ho: he gave the Third World a heart

Revolutionaries throughout the world are mourning the passing of Ho Chi Minh. In recent years this frail old man seemed to many to personally embody the determination and courage of the Vietnamese people in forcing back the US war machine.

And the struggle of the Vietnamese came to be the focal point for the hopes of millions throughout the third world who would no longer tolerate the poverty, exploitation and misery resulting from imperialism. In the Middle East, in southern Africa, in Latin America those fighting take heart from the Vietnamese revolution and name sections of their organisations after its leader.

We have to give the fullest possible support to such struggles. The same big business concerns that daily exploit the workers of the advanced capitalist countries have throughout the underdeveloped countries wreaked havoc in their search for easy profits, destroying old established societies, pillaging their resources, forcing semi-starvation upon their populations, using napalm and fragmentation bombs against them should they resist.

The national liberation movements arise as the populations of these countries fight back. But if the leaders of these movements fight the same enemies as revolutionary socialists, they do not always fight for the same goals.

For instance, in Vietnam the many movements that fought and were bloodily suppressed by the French invaders from the 1860s until 1916 were led by members of the old Vietnamese ruling class, the Mandarinate. The next movement to develop, the VNQDD (similar to the Kuomintang in China) was led by sections of the middle class.

In both cases the leaders hated French imperialism and often gave their lives fighting it. But in neither case because they were socialists. The Mandarinate wanted a return to the pre-capitalist class society that had existed before the invasion, the VNQDD wanted the development of native Vietnamese capitalism.

It was not only the workers and peasants directly exploited by the French who suffered under colonialism. So did thousands whose class background made them look forward to a privileged position that was denied them by the French presence.

The movement that Ho Chi Minh built was in many ways different from these earlier movements. It learned from the failures of previous movements and from the successes of the Russian Revolution that the only way to defeat imperialism was to get mass popular support.

This was not possible without overcoming the traditional prejudices of the middle classes and without bringing the peasants to see their immediate economic interests as being served by the revolution (for example, through protection against tax collectors, usurers and in some cases through land reform).

It also learned that only through state ownership of industry and agriculture was it possible for there to be any new independent economic development in a world already overcrowded by rival imperialisms.

But at the same time it would be wrong to forget, as so many people do, that those who constituted the leadership of Ho's movement were not the workers and peasants. Instead they were overwhelmingly from a middle class that saw little future for itself while imperialism cramped indigenous economic development.

Even today in the Vietnamese Communist Party "the worker content is only 18.5 percent and the higher the echelon the lower the worker stock". (Le Duc Tho, quoted in the Sunday Times, 7 September). It has always sought to appeal to sections of the exploiting class, as, for instance, in the programme of the Vietminh, which addressed itself to "rich people, soldiers, workers, peasants, intellectuals, employees, traders, youth, women..."

It was from Stalin and Mao, not from the Russian Revolution, that Ho learned that fragments of the old middle class could be welded together in a party controlled from the top down, with no internal democracy, so as to form the basis of a new state capitalist ruling class. This would fight against imperialism and to that extent work in the interests of workers and peasants, only to exploit them in its own interests later, after victory.

When forced to fight, Ho and his followers did so courageously. Ho himself was for many years exiled or in prison. To get support in these periods they stood up for the peasants. But when in 1945-46 and in 1954 there seemed to be a chance for an indigenous state capitalist development through a compromise with imperialism, they refused to continue to fight for a victory that was within sight.

In 1945 this not only meant accepting continued French dominance over the southern province of Cochin China and allowing French troops to peacefully reoccupy key strategic points in Hanoi, it also meant the Vietminh itself murdering those, particularly the still influential Trotskyists around Ta Thu Thau in the south, who agitated for the continuation of both the class and the national struggle.

Again in 1954 at Geneva, when the French were only too eager to withdraw from Vietnam, Ho and his party accepted the artificial division of their country so as to build "socialism" in half a country. In the south the resistance was left to fend for itself against the more or less fascist regime of Diem.

From Hanoi all it received was discouragement until well into 1959.

In the North this was the period in which land previously given to the peasants in land reforms was taken away from them through "collectivisation". This resulted in an insurrectionary class struggle against the new regime by the peasants of Nghe An in 1956 that had to be put down by the army.

After both 1946 and 1959 the realities of imperialist oppression smashed Ho's illusions (fostered in the latter case by China as well as Russia) that a compromise would permit any sort of independent national development. In both cases the fight was taken up again courageously.

This deserves our admiration. But it should not prevent us from recognising mistakes and their origins in Stalinist theory and state capitalist practice. Nor should it lead us to forget what happened to those other courageous Vietnamese revolutionaries.

This does not mean in any way diluting our support for the Vietnamese struggle against the US. But the way to give this support is not to delude ourselves into thinking that North Vietnam and its leaders are other than what they are.

Let us be clear. North Vietnam is a one-party regime of the Stalinist sort. In this respect it is like, say, Poland or Romania. It has nothing in common with socialism.

Ho was not a genial uncle. But he was forced to fight Western imperialism.

A victory in this struggle will be an asset, not just for the class Ho represented, but for the workers and peasants of Vietnam, even though later they will have to take up the fight against Ho's successors. It will also be an inspiration for all those fighting imperialism.

And it will be for this that Ho will be remembered.

Socialist Worker, 11 September 1969

Defend Arab revolution

Jordan has seen one of the great national uprisings of modern times in the last week. The overwhelming majority of the population, led by the guerrilla organisations and the units of the popular militia, have fought to overthrow Hussein's reactionary government.

Even Western journalists report that the king's soldiers are complaining: "The people helped the guerrillas when we came in." The Royal Army has started to crush the popular movement in the only way it knows.

For the last week the full firing power of the artillery and tanks has been directed at the densely packed, poorer sections of Amman where the guerrillas have the bulk of their support.

The shells have been tearing apart the corrugated iron huts, tents and crude concrete dwellings where the refugees somehow eke out an existence. Whole blocks of flats have been blown apart in order to "flush out" a single sniper.

Estimates of those killed already approach 15,000 and the king's army has no scruples about firing upon the Palestinian hospitals where some of the wounded could be tended.

Yet even in Amman, where Hussein's forces have been concentrated, the resistance seems far from crushed.

The Palestinians go on fighting because they feel they have little choice. For 20 years they have been herded into refugee camps, kept alive by a 7d a day handout from the United Nations and told to be quiet.

Now they see the chance to exercise control over their own future. They are not going to let that chance slip and rifle and submachine gunfire still blaze back in deadly defiance from the slums.

The British press has attempted to paint Hussein as a modern hero, surrounded on all sides, standing alone against all the odds.

This is only natural. It was a British government that carved an artificial kingdom on the east bank of the Jordan for Hussein's grandfather, Abdullah, 45 years ago. And it was British troops that propped up Hussein's throne in 1958.

When Western commentators fear that Hussein will fall they are really afraid that British and American big business interests will be weakened – particularly the oil monopolies who control most of the wealth of the Arab lands.

But it is not just Western governments that are backing Hussein. The Russians see in the revolutionary fervour of the Palestinians a threat to their own great power interests, such as the early reopening of the Suez Canal. This explains Russian pressure on the Syrians to stay out of Jordan.

Meanwhile Nasser, for long the self-proclaimed "leader of the Arab revolution", stands on the sidelines, hoping that the king will win.

With the successes of the Palestinian forces in the north of Jordan, the Western press has raised the cry of "foreign invasion", apparently from Syria. A "crime" has been committed of sending tanks to

---

THE GUERRILLAS

El Fatah or **Palestine Liberation Movement**. Leader Yasser Arafat. Main guerrilla organisation. Fights for the right of Palestinians to return to democratic, non-racialist, non-sectarian Palestine but holds that the struggle for this goal is a separate 'stage' to the socialist revolution in the Middle East. Financed by Arab governments.

Popular Front for the Liberation of Palestine. Leader George Habbash. One of the two left wing guerrilla groups. Concentrates on spectacular 'direct action' such as recent hijackings. Differs from Fatah on this point and openly claims to be a Marxist-Leninist organisation fighting for socialist Middle East.

Popular Democratic Front. Leader Naif Hawatmeh. Broke from the PFLP since, it claimed, PFLP's socialist commitment was mostly verbal. Involves itself in workers' and peasants' struggle and depends on them for money instead of Arab governments.

Palestine Liberation Organisation. Broad umbrella organisation of guerrilla groups. Dominated by Fatah but includes PDF and PFLP.

Palestine Liberation Army. Regular military units as opposed to guerrilla forces, organised by PLO and attached to Arab armies. PLO claims the tanks entering Jordan from Syria were PLA units.

> **WILL BRITISH TROOPS GO IN?**
>
> Information received by *Socialist Worker* this week indicates that the British Army reserve has been put on stand-by duty.
>
> Reservists have received documents telling them to prepare for call-out in the event of national broadcast. They will travel to army camps usually reserved for transporting troops overseas.
>
> This information indicates that the government, in collusion with the United States, must be seriously contemplating action in the Middle East.
>
> As with Suez in 1956, such action could be under the guise of 'peace maker'. Or the flimsy excuse of rescuing British citizens in Jordan could be given.
>
> But the labour and trade union movement should be in no doubt that British intervention will be on the side of Hussein and the oil monopolies and against the Arab masses.

resist the tanks, guns and jets supplied by the West which Hussein has used to pummel the local population.

Stories of Syrian intervention cannot be checked. But there is no doubt that the population of Syria would be absolutely right to go to the aid of their brothers fighting Hussein's reactionary, despotic pro-Western regime and ignore the artificial boundary drawn up by the Western powers as part of the imperialist carve-up after the First World War.

The stories of Syrian intervention are a cover for something far more sinister. Both the Americans and Israel are planning to act if the Palestinians seem close to success.

The United States is talking about preparations to "safeguard its citizens". When such talk has been used before, as in the Congo five years ago, it has been a smokescreen for the US to intervene and tip the balance decisively in the interests of its puppets.

On one side in the present conflict in Jordan stand all the old powers: oil monopolies and feudal sheikhs, Zionist politicians who practise anti-Arab racism and Arab monarchs who thrive on anti-Jewish threats, those who are waging a bitter war against the Vietnamese people and those who put down the workers of Budapest and Prague.

On the other side the Palestinians stand alone. Their only support are the masses in the other Arab countries as they fight for a land free from imperialist domination, where Muslim, Jew and Christian can live and work together.

A minority of the Palestinians see further than this. They recognise that such a democratic state is only possible in the context of a united socialist Middle East.

But in any case, there is no doubt on whose side every socialist and trade unionist should be in the present conflict.

Socialist Worker, 26 September 1970

The prophet and the proletariat

Introduction

The politics of the Middle East and beyond have been dominated by Islamist movements at least since the Iranian revolution of 1978-79. Variously described in the West as "Islamic fundamentalism", "Islamicism", "integrism", "political Islam" and "Islamic revivalism", these movements stand for the "regeneration" of society through a return to the original teachings of the prophet Mohammed. They have become a major force in Iran and the Sudan (where they still hold power), Egypt, Algeria and Tajikistan (where they are involved in bitter armed struggles against the state), Afghanistan (where rival Islamist movements have been waging war with each other since the collapse of the pro-Russian government), the occupied West Bank of the Jordan (where their militancy is challenging the old PLO hegemony over the Palestinian resistance), Pakistan (where they make up a significant portion of the opposition) and most recently Turkey (where the Welfare Party has taken control of Istanbul, Ankara and many other municipalities).

The rise of these movements has been an enormous shock to the liberal intelligentsia and has produced a wave of panic among people who believed that "modernisation", coming on top of the victory of the anti-colonial struggles of the 1950s and 1960s, would inevitably lead to more enlightened and less repressive societies.[1]

Instead they witness the growth of forces which seem to look back to a more restricted society which forces women into purdah, uses terror to crush free thought and threatens the most barbaric punishments on those who defy its edicts. In countries like Egypt and Algeria the liberals are now lining up with the state, which has persecuted and imprisoned them in the past, in the war it is waging against Islamist parties.

But it has not only been liberals who have been thrown into disarray by the rise of Islamism. So too has the left. It has not known how to react to what it sees as an obscurantist doctrine, backed by traditionally reactionary forces, enjoying success among some of the poorest groups in society. Two opposed approaches have resulted.

The first has been to see Islamism as Reaction Incarnate, as a form of fascism. This was, for example, the position taken soon after the Iranian Revolution by the then left wing academic Fred Halliday, who referred to the Iranian regime as "Islam with a fascist face".[2] It is an approach which much of the Iranian left came to adopt after the consolidation of the Khomeini regime in 1981-82. And it is accepted by much of the left in Egypt and Algeria today. Thus, for example, one Algerian revolutionary Marxist group has argued that the principles, ideology and political action of the Islamist FIS "are similar to those of the National Front in France", and that it is "a fascist current".[3]

Such an analysis easily leads to the practical conclusion of building political alliances to stop the fascists at all costs. Thus Halliday concluded that the left in Iran made the mistake of not allying with the "liberal bourgeoisie" in 1979-81 in opposition to "the reactionary ideas and policies of Khomeini".[4] In Egypt today the left, influenced by the mainstream Communist tradition, effectively supports the state in its war against the Islamists.

The opposite approach has been to see the Islamist movements as "progressive", "anti-imperialist" movements of the oppressed. This was the position taken by the great bulk of the Iranian left in the first phase of the 1979 Revolution, when the Soviet-influenced Tudeh Party, the majority of the Fedayeen guerrilla organisation and the left Islamist People's Mujahedin all characterised the forces behind Khomeini as "the progressive petty bourgeoisie". The conclusion of this approach was that Khomeini deserved virtually uncritical support.[5] A quarter of a century before this the Egyptian Communists briefly took the same position towards the Muslim Brotherhood, calling on them to join in "a common struggle against the 'fascist dictatorship' of Nasser and his 'Anglo-American props'".[6]

I want to argue that both positions are wrong. They fail to locate the class character of modern Islamism or to see its relationship to capital, the state and imperialism.

Islam, religion and ideology

The confusion often starts with a confusion about the power of religion itself. Religious people see it as a historical force in its own right, whether for good or for evil. So too do most bourgeois anti-clerical and free thinkers. For them, fighting the influence of religious institutions and obscurantist ideas is in itself the way to human liberation.

But although religious institutions and ideas clearly play a role in history, this does not happen in separation from the rest of material reality. Religious institutions, with their layers of priests and teachers, arise in a certain society and interact with that society. They can only maintain themselves as society changes if they find some way of changing their own base of support. So, for instance, one of the world's major religious institutions, the Roman Catholic church, originated in the late ancient world and survived by adapting itself first to feudal society for 1,000 years and then, with much effort, to the capitalist society that replaced feudalism, changing much of the content of its own teaching in the process. People have always been capable of giving different interpretations to the religious ideas they hold, depending on their own material situation, their relations with other people and the conflicts they get involved in. History is full of examples of people who profess nearly identical religious beliefs ending up on opposite sides in great social conflicts. This happened with the social convulsions which swept Europe during the great crisis of feudalism in the 16th and 17th century, when Luther, Calvin, Munzer and many other "religious" leaders provided their followers with a new world view through a reinterpretation of biblical texts.

Islam is no different to any other religion in these respects. It arose in one context, among a trading community in the towns of 7th century Arabia, in the midst of a society still mainly organised on a tribal basis. It flourished within the succession of great empires carved out by some of those who accepted its doctrines. It persists today as the official ideology of numerous capitalist states (Saudi Arabia, Sudan, Pakistan, Iran, etc), as well as the inspiration of many oppositional movements.

It has been able to survive in such different societies because it has been able to adapt to differing class interests. It has obtained the finance to build its mosques and employ its preachers in turn from the traders of Arabia, the bureaucrats, landowners and merchants of the great empires, and the industrialists of modern capitalism. But at the same time it has gained the allegiance of the mass of people by putting across a message offering consolation to the poor and oppressed. At every point its message has balanced between promising a degree of protection to the oppressed and providing the exploiting classes with protection against any revolutionary overthrow.

So Islam stresses that the rich have to pay a 2.5 percent Islamic tax (the *zakat*) for the relief of the poor, that rulers have to govern in a just way, that husbands must not mistreat their wives. But it also treats the expropriation of the rich by the poor as theft, insists disobedience to a "just" government is a crime to be punished with all the vigour of the law and provides women with fewer rights than men within marriage, over inheritance, or over the children in the event of divorce. It appeals to the wealthy and the poor alike by offering regulation of oppression, both as a bulwark against still harsher oppression and as a bulwark against revolution. It is, like Christianity, Hinduism or Buddhism, both the heart of the heartless world and the opium of the people.

But no set of ideas can have such an appeal to different classes, especially when society is shaken by social convulsions, unless it is full of ambiguities. It has to be open to differing interpretations, even if these set its adherents at each other's throats.

This has been true of Islam virtually from its inception. After Mohammed's death in 632 AD, just two years after Islam had conquered Mecca, dissension broke out between the followers of Abu Bakr, who became the first Caliph (successor to Mohammed as leader of Islam), and Ali, husband of the prophet's daughter Fatima. Ali claimed that some of Abu Bakr's rulings were oppressive. Dissension grew until rival Muslim armies fought each other at the battle of the Camel resulting in 10,000 deaths. It was out of this dissension that the separation of the Sunni and Shia versions of Islam arose. This was but the first of many splits. Groups repeatedly arose who insisted that the oppressed were suffering at the hands of the godless and demanded a return to the original "pure" Islam of the prophet's time. As Akbar S Ahmed says:

> Throughout Islamic history, Muslim leaders would preach a move to the ideal... They gave expression to often vague ethnic, social or political movements... The basis was laid for the entire schismatic gamut in Islamic thought from the Shia, with its offshoots like the Ismailis, to more temporary movements... Muslim history is replete with Mahdis leading revolts against established authority and often dying for their efforts ... Leaders have often been poor peasants and from deprived ethnic groups. Using Islamic idiom has reinforced their sense of deprivation and consolidated the movement.[7]

But even mainstream Islam is not, in its popular forms at least, a homogeneous set of beliefs. The spread of the religion to cover the whole region from the Atlantic coast of northwest Africa to the Bay of Bengal involved the incorporation into Islamic society of peoples who fitted into Islam many of their old religious practices, even if these contradicted some of Islam's original tenets. So popular Islam often includes cults of local saints or of holy relics even though orthodox Islam regards such practices as sacrilegious idolatry. And Sufi brotherhoods flourish which, while not constituting a formal rival to mainstream Islam, put an emphasis on mystical and magical experience which many fundamentalists find objectionable.[8]

In such a situation, any call for a return to the practices of the prophet's time is not in reality about conserving the past but about reshaping people's behaviour into something quite new.

This has been true of Islamic revivalism over the last century. It arose as an attempt to come to terms with the material conquest and cultural transformation of Asia and North Africa by capitalist Europe. The revivalists argued this had only been possible because the original Islamic values had been corrupted by the worldly pursuits of the great medieval empires. Regeneration was only possible by reviving the founding spirit of Islam as expressed by the first four Caliphs (or, for Shiites, by Ali). It was in this spirit that Khomeini, for instance, could denounce virtually the whole history of Islam for the last 1,300 years:

> Unfortunately, true Islam lasted for only a brief period after its inception. First the Umayyids [the first Arab dynasty after Ali] and then the Abbasids who conquered them in 750 AD inflicted all kinds of damage on Islam.
> Later the monarchs ruling Iran continued in the same path; they completely distorted Islam and established something quite diferent in its place.[9]

So, although Islamism can be presented by both defenders and opponents as a traditionalist doctrine, based on a rejection of the modern world, in reality things are more complicated than this. The aspiration to recreate a mythical past involves not leaving existing society intact, but recasting it. What is more, the recasting cannot aim to produce a carbon copy of 7th century Islam, since the Islamists do not reject every feature of existing society. By and large they accept modern industry, modern technology and much of the science on which it is based – indeed, they argue that Islam, as a more rational and less superstitious doctrine than Christianity, is more in tune with modern science. And so the "revivalists" are, in fact, trying to bring about something which has never existed before, which fuses ancient traditions and the forms of modern social life.

This means it is wrong simply to refer to all Islamists as "reactionary", or to equate "Islamic fundamentalism" as a whole with the sort of Christian fundamentalism which is the bastion of the right wing of the Republican Party in the US. Figures like Khomeini, the heads of the rival Mujahedin groups in Afghanistan or the leaders of the Algerian FIS may use traditionalist themes and appeal to the nostalgia of disappearing social groups, but they also appeal to radical currents produced as society is transformed by capitalism. Olivier Roy, referring to the Afghan Islamists, argues:

> Fundamentalism is quite different [to traditionalism]: for fundamentalism it is of paramount importance to get back to the scriptures, clearing away the obfuscation of tradition. It always seeks a return to a former state: it is characterised by the practice of rereading texts and a search for origins. The enemy is not modernity but tradition, or rather, in the context of Islam, of everything which is not the Tradition of the Prophet. This is true reform.[10]

Traditionalist Islam is an ideology which seeks to perpetuate a social order which is being undermined by the development of capitalism – or at least, as with the version promoted by the ruling family in Saudi Arabia, to hark back to this order in order to conceal the transformation of an old ruling class into modern capitalists. Islamism is an ideology which, although it appeals to some of the same themes, seeks to transform society, not to conserve it in the old way. For this reason, even the term "fundamentalism" is not really appropriate. As Abrahamian has observed:

> The label "fundamentalism" implies religious inflexibility, intellectual purity, political traditionalism, even social conservatism and the centrality of scriptural-doctrinal principles. "Fundamentalism" implies rejection of the modern world.[11]

But, in fact, movements like that of Khomeini in Iran have been based on "ideological adaptability and intellectual flexibility, with political protests against the established order, and with socioeconomic issues that fuel mass opposition to the status quo".[12]

Yet there is often a blurring of the differences between Islamism and traditionalism. Precisely because the notion of social regeneration is wrapped in religious language, it is open to different interpretations. It can mean simply ending "degenerate practices" through a return to the forms of behaviour which allegedly preceded the "corruption" of Islam by "cultural imperialism". The stress then is on female "modesty" and the wearing of the veil, an end to "promiscuous" mixing of the sexes in schools and workplaces, opposition to Western popular music and so on. Thus one of the most popular leaders of the Algerian FIS, Ali Belhadj, can denounce the "violence" against Muslims that comes from "cultural invasion":

> We Muslims believe that the most serious form of violence we have suffered is not physical violence, for which we are ready... It is the violence which represents a challenge to the Muslim community by the imposition of diabolical legislation instead of the *sharia*...
>
> Is there any violence worse than that which consists in encouraging that which God has forbidden? They open wine-making enterprises, the work of the demon, and they are protected by the police...
>
> Can you conceive of any violence greater than that of this woman who burns the scarf in a public place, in the eyes of everyone, saying the Family Code penalises women and finding support from the effeminised, the halfmen and the transsexuals...
>
> It is not violence to demand that woman stays at home, in an atmosphere of chastity, reserve and humility and that she only goes out in cases of necessity defined by the legislator...to demand the segregation of sexes among school students and the absence of that stinking mixing that causes sexual violence.[13]

But regeneration can also mean challenging the state and elements of imperialism's political domination. Thus the Iranian Islamists did close down the biggest US "listening" station in Asia and seize control of the US embassy. The Hezbollah in the southern Lebanon and Hamas in the West Bank and Gaza have played a key role in the armed struggle against Israel. The Algerian FIS did organise huge demonstrations against the US war against Iraq – even though these lost them their Saudi funding. Regeneration can even mean, in certain instances, giving support to the material struggles against exploitation of workers and peasants, as with the Iranian Mujahedin in 1979-82.

The different interpretations of regeneration naturally appeal to those from different social classes. But the religious phraseology can prevent those involved recognising their differences with one another. In the heat of the struggle individuals can mix the meanings together, so that the fight against the unveiling of women is seen as the fight against the Western oil companies and the abysmal poverty of the mass of people. Thus in Algeria in the late 1980s, Belhadj:

> made himself the voice of all those with nothing to lose... Conceiving Islam in its most pure scriptural form, he preached strict application of its commandments... Every Friday Belhadj made war against the entire world, Jews and Christians, Zionists, communists and secularists, liberals and agnostics, governments of the East and the West, Arab or Muslim heads of state, Westernised party leaders and intellectuals, were the favourite targets of his weekly preaching. [14]

Yet beneath this confusion of ideas there were real class interests at work.

The class base of Islamism

Islamism has arisen in societies traumatised by the impact of capitalism – first in the form of external conquest by imperialism and then, increasingly, by the transformation of internal social relations accompanying the rise of a local capitalist class and the formation of an independent capitalist state.

Old social classes have been replaced by new ones, although not instantaneously or in a clearcut manner. What Trotsky described as "combined and uneven development" has occurred. Externally, colonialism has retreated, but the great imperialist powers – especially the US – continue to use their military forces as a bargaining tool to influence the production of the Middle East's single major resource, oil. Internally, state encouragement – and often ownership – has led to the development of some large-scale modern industry, but large sectors of "traditional" industry remain, based on vast numbers of small workshops where the owner works with a couple of workers, often from his own family. Land reform has turned some peasants into modern capitalist farmers – but displaced many more, leaving them with little or no land, so forcing them to eke out a livelihood from casual labour in the workshops or markets of sprawling urban slums. A massive expansion of the education system is turning out vast numbers of high school and college graduates, but these then find insufficient job opportunities in the modern sectors of the economy and place their hopes on getting into the state bureaucracy, while ekeing out a living with scraps of work around the informal sector – touting for custom from shopkeepers, acting as guides for tourists, selling lottery tickets, driving taxis and so on.

The crises of the world economy over the last 20 years have aggravated all these contradictions. The modern industries have found the national economy too small for them to operate efficiently, but the world economy too competitive for them to survive without state protection. The traditional industries have not generally been able to modernise without state support and they cannot compensate for the failure of modern industry to provide jobs for the burgeoning urban population. But a few sectors have managed to establish links of their own with international capital and increasingly resent the state's domination of the economy. The urban rich increasingly lap up the luxury goods available on the world market, creating growing resentment among the casual workers and the unemployed.

Islamism represents an attempt to come to terms with these contradictions by people who have been brought up to respect traditional Islamic ideas. But it does not find its support equally in all sections of society. For some sections embrace a modern secular bourgeois or nationalist ideology, while other sections gravitate towards some form of secular working class response. The Islamic revival gets sustenance from four different social groupings – each of which interprets Islam in its own way.

1. *The Islamism of the old exploiters.* First there are those members of the traditional privileged classes who fear losing out in the capitalist modernisation of society – particularly landowners (including clergy dependent on incomes from land belonging to religious foundations), traditional merchant capitalists, the owners of the mass of small shops and workshops. Such groups have often been the traditional sources of finance for the mosques and see Islam as a way of defending their established way of life and of making those who oversee change listen to their voices. Thus in Iran and Algeria it was this group which provided the resources to the clergy to oppose the state's land reform programme in the 1960s and 1970s.

2. *The Islamism of the new exploiters.* Second, often emerging from among this first group, are some of the capitalists who have enjoyed success despite hostility from those groups linked to the state. In Egypt, for instance, the present-day Muslim Brotherhood "wormed their way into the economic fabric of Sadat's Egypt at a time when whole sections of it had been turned over to unregulated capitalism. Uthman Ahmad Uthman, the Egyptian Rockefeller, made no secret of this sympathy for the Brethren". [15]

In Turkey the Welfare Party, which is led by a former member of the main conservative party, enjoys the support of much of middle-sized capital. In Iran among the *bazaaris* who gave support to Khomeini against the Shah were substantial capitalists resentful at the way economic policies favoured those close to the crown.

3. *The Islamism of the poor.* The third group are the rural poor who have suffered under the advance of capitalist farming and who have been forced into the cities as they desperately look for work. Thus in Algeria out of a total rural population of 8.2 million only 2 million gained anything from the land reform. The other 6 million were faced with the choice between increased poverty in the countryside and going to the cities to seek work. [16] But in the cities: "The lowest group are the hard core jobless made up of displaced former peasants who have flooded the cities in search of work and social opportunity...detached from rural society without being truly integrated into urban society". [17]

They lost the certainties associated with an old way of life – certainties which they identify with traditional Muslim culture – without gaining a secure material existence or a stable way of life: "Clear guidelines for behaviour and belief no longer exist for millions of Algerians caught between a tradition that no longer commands their total loyalty and a modernism that cannot satisfy the psychological and spiritual needs of young people in particular". [18]

In such a situation even Islamic agitation against land reform on behalf of the old landowners in the 1970s could appeal to the peasants and ex-peasants. For the land reform could be a symbol of a transformation of the countryside that had destroyed a secure, if impoverished, way of life. "To the landed proprietors and the peasants without land, the Islamists held out the same prospect: the Koran stigmatised the expropriation of things belonging to others; it recommended to the rich and those who ruled according to the Sunna to be generous to others".[19]

The appeal of Islamism grew through the 1980s as economic crisis increased the contrast between the impoverished masses and the elite of about 1 percent of the population who run the state and the economy. Their wealth and their Westernised lifestyles ill fitted their claim to be the heirs of the liberation struggle against the French. It was very easy for the ex-peasants to identify the "non-Islamic" behaviour of this elite as the cause of their own misery.

In Iran likewise the capitalist transformation of agriculture embodied in the Shah's land reform of the 1960s benefited a minority of the toilers, while leaving the rest no better off and sometimes worse off. It increased the antagonism of the rural and recently urbanised poor against the state – an antagonism which did no harm to Islamic forces which had opposed the land reform. So when, for instance, in 1962 the Shah used the forces of the state against Islamic figures, this turned them into a focus for the discontent of very large numbers of people.

In Egypt the "opening up" of the economy to the world market through agreements with the World Bank and the IMF from the mid-1970s onwards substantially worsened the situation of the mass of peasants and ex-peasants, creating enormous pools of bitterness. And in Afghanistan the land reforms which were imposed after the PDPA (Communist Party) coup of 1978 led to a series of spontaneous risings from all sections of the rural population:

> The reforms put an end to the traditional ways of working based on mutual self-interest without introducing any alternative. The landowners who had been dispossessed of their land were careful not to distribute any seed to their sharecroppers; people who traditionally had been willing to provide loans now refused to do so. There were plans for the creation of a bank for agricultural development and for setting up an office to oversee the distribution of seed and fodder, but none of this had been done when the reforms actually took place... So it was the very act of announcing the reforms that cut the peasant off from his seed supplies... The reform destroyed not just the economic structure but the whole social framework of production... It is not surprising, therefore, that instead of setting 98 percent of the people against 2 percent of the exploiting classes, these reforms led to a general revolt of 75 percent of the rural areas. [And] when the new system was seen not to be working even the peasants who had initially welcomed reform felt they would be better off going back to the old system.[20]

But it is not only hostility to the state that makes ex-peasants receptive to the message of the Islamists. The mosques provide a social focus for people lost in a new and strange city, the Islamic charities the rudiments of welfare services (clinics, schooling, etc) which are lacking from the state. So in Algeria the growth of the cities in the 1970s and 1980s was accompanied by a massive increase in the number of mosques: "Everything happened as if the paralysis in education and Arabisation, the absence of structures of culture and leisure, the lack of space for public liberty, the shortage of homes, made thousands of adults, youth and children disposed for the mosques". [21]

In this way, funds which came from those with diametrically opposed interests to the mass of people – from the old landowning class, the new rich or the Saudi government – could provide both a material and a cultural haven for the poor. "In the mosque, everyone – new or old bourgeois, fundamentalist, worker in an enterprise – saw the possibility of the elaboration or realisation of his own strategy, dreams and hopes". [22]

This did not obliterate the class divisions within the mosque. In Algeria, for example, there were innumerable rows in mosque committees between people whose different social background made them see the building of the mosques in different ways – for instance, over when they should refuse to accept donations for the mosque because they came from sinful (*haram*) sources. "It is rare in fact for a religious committee to accomplish its mandate, fixed in principle at two years, with the harmony and agreement recommended by the cult of the unity of the divine which the *muezzins* chant without cease". [23] But the rows remained cloaked in a religious guise – and have not stopped the proliferation of the mosques and the growth in the influence of Islamism.

4. *The Islamism of the new middle class.* However, neither the "traditional" exploiting classes nor the impoverished masses provide the vital element which sustains revivalist, political Islam – the cadre of activists who propagate its doctrines and risk injury, imprisonment and death in confrontation with their enemies.

The traditional exploiting classes are by their very nature conservative. They are prepared to donate money so that others can fight – especially in defence of their material interests. They did so when faced with the land reform in Algeria in the early 1970s; when the Baathist regime in Syria encroached upon the interests of the urban merchants and traders in the spring of 1980s; [24] and when the merchants and small businessmen of the Iranian bazaars felt themselves under attack from the Shah in 1976-78 and threatened by the left in 1979-81. But they are wary of putting their own businesses, let alone their own lives, at risk. And so they can hardly be the force that has torn societies like Algeria and Egypt apart, caused a whole town, Hama, to rise in revolt in Syria, used suicide bombs against the Americans and Israelis in Lebanon – and which caused the Iranian Revolution to take a turn much more radical than any section of the Iranian bourgeoisie expected.

This force, in fact, comes from a fourth, very different stratum – from a section of the new middle class that has arisen as a result of capitalist modernisation right across the third world.

In Iran the cadres of all three of the Islamist movements that dominated the politics of the first years of the revolution came from this background. Thus one account tells of the support for the first postrevolutionary prime minister, Bazargan:

> As Iran's educational system expanded in the 1950s and 1960s, even wider groups of traditional middle class people gained access to the country's universities. Confronted with institutions dominated by the older, Westernised elites, these newcomers to academia felt an urgent need to justify their continued adherence to Islam to themselves. They joined the Muslim Students Associations run by Bazargan etc... Upon entering professional life, the new engineers often joined the Islamic Association of Engineers, also founded by Bazargan. This association network constituted the real organised social support for Bazargan and Islamic modernism... Bazargan's and Taleqani's appeal depended on the way they gave the rising members of the traditional middle classes a sense of dignity which allowed them to affirm their identity in a society politically dominated by what they saw as a godless, Westernised and corrupt elite. [25]

Writing of the People's ujahedin of Iran, Abrahamian comments that many studies of the first years of the Iranian Revolution have talked of the appeal of radical Islam to the "oppressed", but that it was not the oppressed in general who formed the basis of the Mujahedin; rather it was that very large section of the new middle class whose parents had been part of the traditional petty bourgeoisie. He gives breakdowns of the occupations of Mujahedin arrested under the Shah and subject to repression under Khomeini to support his argument. [26]

Although the third Islamist force, the ultimately victorious Islamic

Republican Party of Khomeini, is usually thought of as run by the clergy linked to the traditional *bazaari* merchant capitalists, Moaddel has shown that more than half its MPs were from the professions, teachers, government employees or students – even if a quarter came from *bazaari* families. [27] And Bayat has noted that in their struggle to defeat the workers' organisations in the factories, the regime could rely on the professional engineers who worked there. [28]

Azar Tabari notes that after the downfall of the Shah very large numbers of women in the Iranian cities opted to wear the veil and lined up with the followers of Khomeini against the left. She claims these women came from that section of the middle class that was the first generation to undergo a process of "social integration". Often from traditional petty-bourgeois families – with fathers who were bazaar merchants, tradesmen and so on – they were forced into higher education as traditional opportunities for their families to make money declined with industrialisation. There were openings for them in professions like teaching and nursing. But "these women had to go through the often painful and traumatic experience of first generation adjustment":

> As the young women from such families began to go to universities or work in hospitals, all these traditional concepts came under daily attack from "alien" surroundings, where women mixed with men, wore no veils, and sometimes dressed according to the latest European fashions. Women were often torn between accepted family norms and the pressure of the new environment. They could not be veiled at work, nor could they leave home unveiled.

One widespread response to these contradictory pressures was "a retreat into Islam", "symbolised by deliberately veiled women demonstrators during large mobilisations". Tabari claims this response stood in marked contrast to that of women whose families had been part of the new middle class for two or three generations, and who refused to wear the veil and identified with the liberals or the left. [29] In Afghanistan, Roy notes:

> The Islamist movement was born in the modern sectors of society and developed from a critique of the popular movements that preceded it... The Islamists are intellectuals, the products of modernist enclaves within traditional society; their social origins are what we have termed the state bourgeoisie – products of the government education system which only leads to employment in the state machine... The Islamists are products of the state

educational system. Very few of them have an education in the arts. On the campus they mostly mix with the Communists, to whom they are violently opposed, rather than with the *ulama* [religious scholars] towards whom they have an ambivalent attitude. They share many beliefs in common with the *ulama*, but Islamist thought has developed from contact with the great Western ideologies, which they see as holding the key to the West's technical development. For them, the problem is to develop a modern political ideology based upon Islam, which they see as the only way to come to terms with the modern world and the best means of confronting foreign imperialism. [30]

In Algeria the most important recruitment ground for the FIS has been among Arabic-speaking (as opposed to French-speaking) high school and university students, and that wide section of youth that would like to be students but cannot get college places:

> The FIS draws its membership from three sections of the population: the commercial middle classes, including some who are quite rich, a mass of young people who are unemployed and excluded from higher education, forming the new lumpenproletariat of the streets, and a layer of upwardly mobile Arabic speaking intellectuals. These last two groups are the most numerous and important. [31]

The Islamic intellectuals have made careers for themselves through their domination of the theological and Arabic language faculties of the universities, using these to gain control of many of the positions as imams in the mosques and teachers in the *lycées* (high schools). They form a network that ensures the recruitment of more Islamists to such positions and the inculcation of Islamist ideas into the new generation of students. This in turn has enabled them to exert influence over vast numbers of young people.

Ahmed Rouadia writes that the Islamist groups began to grow from the mid-1970s onwards, receiving support in the universities from Arabic speaking students who found their lack of fluency in French kept them from getting jobs in administration, areas of advanced technology and higher management. [32] Thus, there was, for instance, a bitter conflict with the principal of Constantine university in the mid-1980s, who was accused of impugning the "dignity of Arabic language" and "being loyal to French colonialism" for allowing French to remain the predominant language in the science and technology faculties:[33]

The qualified Arabic speakers find access blocked to all the key sectors, above all in industries requiring technical knowledge and foreign languages... The Arabic speakers, even if they have diplomas, cannot get a place in modern industry. For the most part they end by turning towards the mosque. [34]

The students, the recent Arabic speaking graduates and, above all, the unemployed ex-students form a bridge to the very large numbers of discontented youth outside the colleges who find they cannot get college places despite years spent in an inefficient and underfunded educational system. Thus, although there are now nearly a million students in secondary education, up to four fifths of them can expect to fail the baccalaureate – the key to entry into university – and to face a life of insecurity on the margins of employment: [35]

> Integrism [Islamism] gets its strength from the social frustrations which afflict a large part of the youth, those left out of account by the social and economic system. Its message is simple: if there is poverty, hardship and frustration, it is because those who have power do not base themselves on the legitimacy of *shorah* consultation, but simply on force... The restoration of the Islam of the first years would make the inequalities disappear. [36]

And through its influence over a wide layer of students, graduates and the intellectual unemployed, Islamism is able to spread out to dominate the propagation of ideas in the slums and shanty towns where the ex-peasants live. Such a movement cannot be described as a "conservative" movement. The educated, Arabic speaking youth do not turn to Islam because they want things to stay as they are, but because they believe it offers massive social change. [37]

In Egypt the Islamist movement first developed some 65 years ago, when Hassan al-Banna formed the Muslim Brotherhood. It grew in the 1930s and 1940s as disillusionment set in with the failure of the secular nationalist party, the Wafd, to challenge British domination of the country. The base of the movement consisted mainly of civil servants and students, and it was one of the major forces in the university protests of the late 1940s and early 1950s. [38] But it spread out to involve some urban labourers and peasants, with a membership estimated to have peaked at half a million. In building the movement Banna was quite willing to collaborate with certain figures close to the Egyptian monarchy, and the right wing of the Wafd looked on the Brotherhood as a counter to Communist influence among workers and students. [39]

But the Brotherhood could only compete with the Communists for the support of the impoverished middle classes – and via them to sections of the urban poor – because its religious language concealed a commitment to reform which went further than its right wing allies wished. Its objectives were "ultimately incompatible with the perpetuation of the political, economic and social status quo to which the ruling groups were dedicated". This ensured "the liaison between the Muslim Brotherhood and the conservative rulers would be both unstable and tenuous". [40]

The Brotherhood was virtually destroyed once a new military regime around Abdul Nasser had concentrated full power into its hands in the early 1950s. Six of the Brotherhood's leaders were hanged in December 1954 and thousands of its members thrown into concentration camps. An attempt to revive the movement in the mid-1960s led to still more executions, but then, after Nasser's death, his successors Sadat and Mubarak allowed it to lead a semi-legal existence – provided it avoided any head-on confrontation with the regime. The leadership of what is sometimes called the "Neo-Islamic Brotherhood" has been willing to accept these restraints, following a relatively "moderate" and "reconciliatory" approach, getting large sums of money from members who were exiled to Saudi Arabia in the 1950s and prospered from the oil boom. [41] This has enabled the Brothers to provide "an alternative model of a Muslim state" with "their banks, social services, educational services and...their mosques". [42]

But it has also led them to lose influence over a new generation of radical Islamists which has arisen, as the Brotherhood itself originally did, from the universities and the impoverished section of the "modern" middle class. These are the Islamists who were responsible for the assassination of Sadat in 1981 and who have been waging armed struggle ever since both against the state and against the secular intelligentsia:

> When we speak of the fundamentalists in Egypt, what we mean is a minority group of people who are even against the Muslim Brothers... These groups are composed mainly of youth... They are very pure people, they are prepared to sacrifice their lives, to do anything... And they are used as the spearheads of the different movements because they are able to undertake terrorist actions. [43]

The Islamist student associations which became a dominant force in Egyptian universities during Sadat's presidency "constituted the Islamicist movement's only genuine mass organisations". [44] They grew in reaction to conditions in the universities and to the dismal prospects facing students if they succeeded in graduating:

> The number of students rose from slightly less than 200,000 in 1970 to more than half a million in 1977... In the absence of the necessary resources, providing free high education for the greatest possible number of the country's youth has produced a system of cut-rate education. [45]

Overcrowding represents a particular problem for female students, who find themselves subject to all sorts of harassment in the lecture theatres and overcrowded buses. In response to this situation:

> The *jamaa al islamiyya* [Islamic associations] drew their considerable strength from their ability to identify these problems and to pose immediate solutions – for instance, using student unions funds to run minibuses for female students giving priority to those who wore the veil, calling for separate rows in the lecture theatres for women and men, organising course revision groups which met in the mosques, turning out cheap editions of essential textbooks. [46]

Graduating students do not escape the endemic poverty of much of Egyptian society:

> Every graduate has the right to public employment. This measure is actually the purveyor of massive disguised unemployment in the offices of a swollen administration in which employees are badly paid... He can still manage to feed himself by buying the state-subsidised products, but he is unlikely to rise above the bare level of subsistence... Almost every state employee has a second or a third job... Innumerable employees who sit all morning at desks in one or other of the countless ministry offices spend the afternoon working as plumbers or taxi drivers, jobs they perform so inadequately they might as well be filled by illiterates... An illiterate peasant woman who arrives in the city to land a job as a foreigner's maid will be paid more or less double the salary of a university assistant lecturer. [47]

The only way to get out of this morass for most graduates is to get a job abroad, especially in Saudi Arabia or the Gulf states. And this is not just the only way out of poverty, it is, for most people, the precondition for getting married in a society where premarital sexual relations are rare.

The Islamists were able to articulate these problems in religious language. As Kepel writes of one of the leaders of one of the early

Islamist sects, his position does not involve "acting as a fanatic for a bygone century... He is putting his finger – in his own way – on a crucial problem of contemporary Egyptian society". [48]

As in Algeria, once the Islamists had established a mass base in the universities, they were then in a situation to spread out into a wider milieu – the milieu of the impoverished streets of the cities where the students and ex-students mixed with a mass of other people scrabbling for a livelihood. This began to happen after the regime clamped down hard on the Islamist movement in the universities following the negotiation of the peace agreement with Israel in the late 1970s. "Far from halting the *jamaa*, however, this harassment gave them a second wind...the message of the *jamaa* now began to spread beyond the world of students. Islamicist cadres and agitators went to preach in the poor neighbourhoods". [49]

Radical Islam as a social movement

The class base of Islamism is similar to that of classical fascism and of the Hindu fundamentalism of the BJP, Shiv Sena and RSS in India. All these movements have recruited from the white collar middle class and students, as well as from the traditional commercial and professional petty bourgeoisie. This, together with the hostility of most Islamist movements to the left, women's rights and secularism has led many socialist and liberals to designate the movements as fascist. But this is a mistake.

The petty-bourgeois class base has not only been a characteristic of fascism, it has also been a feature of Jacobinism, of third world nationalisms, of Maoist Stalinism, and Peronism. Petty-bourgeois movements only become fascist when they arise at a specific point in the class struggle and play a particular role. This role is not just to mobilise the petty bourgeoisie, but to exploit the bitterness they feel at what an acute crisis of the system has done to them and so turn them into organised thugs prepared to work for capital to tear workers' organisations apart.

That is why Mussolini's and Hitler's movements were fascist while, say, Peron's movement in Argentina was not. Even though Peron borrowed some of the imagery of fascism, he took power in exceptional circumstances which allowed him to buy off workers' organisations while using state intervention to divert the profits of the large agrarian capitalists into industrial expansion. During his first six years in office a specific set of circumstances allowed real wages to rise by about 60 percent. This was the complete opposite to what would have happened under a genuinely fascist regime. Yet the liberal intelligentsia and the Argentine Communist Party were still capable of referring to the regime as "Nazi Peronism", in much the same way that much of the left internationally refers to Islamism today. [50]

The Islamist mass movements in countries like Algeria and Egypt likewise play a different role to that of fascism. They are not primarily directed against workers' organisations and do not offer themselves to the main sectors of capital as a way of solving its problems at workers' expense. They are often involved in direct, armed confrontation with the forces of the state in a way in which fascist parties rarely have been. And, far from being direct agents of imperialism, these movements have taken up anti-imperialist slogans and some anti-imperialist actions which have embarrassed very important national and international capitalist interests (e.g. in Algeria over the second Gulf War, in Egypt against "peace" with Israel, in Iran against the American presence in the aftermath of the overthrow of the Shah).

The American CIA was able to work with Pakistan intelligence and the pro-Western Middle East states to arm thousands of volunteers from right across the Middle East to fight against the Russians in Afghanistan. But now these volunteers are returning home to discover they were fighting for the US when they thought they were fighting "for Islam", and constituting a bitter hard core of opposition to most of the governments which encouraged them to go. Even in Saudi Arabia, where the ultra-puritan Wahhabist interpretation of the Islamic *sharia* (religious law) is imposed with all the might of the state, the opposition now claims the support of "thousands of Afghan fighters", disgusted by the hypocrisy of a royal family that is increasingly integrated into the world capitalist ruling class. And the royal family is now retaliating, further antagonising some of the very people it encouraged so much in the past, cutting off funds to the Algerian FIS for supporting Iraq in the second Gulf War and deporting a Saudi millionaire who has been financing Islamists in Egypt.

Those on the left who see the Islamists simply as "fascists" fail to take into account the destabilising effect of the movements on capital's interests right across the Middle East, and end up siding with states that are the strongest backers both of imperialism and of local capital. This has, for instance, happened to those sections of the left influenced by the remnants of Stalinism in Egypt. It happened to much of the Iranian left during the closing stages of the first Gulf War, when

American imperialism sent in its fleet to fight on the same side as Iraq against Iran. And it is in danger of happening to the secular left in Algeria, faced with a near civil war between the Islamists and the state.

But if it is wrong to see the Islamist movements as "fascist", it is just as wrong to simply see them as "anti-imperialist" or "anti-state". They do not just fight against those classes and states that exploit and dominate the mass of people. They also fight against secularism, against women who refuse to abide by Islamic notions of "modesty", against the left and, in important cases, against ethnic or religious minorities. The Algerian Islamists established their hold on the universities in the late 1970s and early 1980s by organising "punitive raids" against the left with the connivance of the police, and the first person killed by them was not a state official but a member of a Trotskyist organisation; another of their actions was to denounce *Hard Rock Magazine*, homosexuality, drugs and punk at the Islamic book fair in 1985; in the Algerian towns where they are strongest, they do organise attacks on women who dare to show a little of their skin; the first public demonstration of the FIS in 1989 was in response to "feminist" and "secularist" demonstrations against Islamist violence, of which women were the main victims.[51] Its hostility is directed not just against the state and foreign capital, but also against the more than 1 million Algerian citizens who, through no fault of their own, have been brought up with French as their first language, and the 10 percent of the population who are Berber rather than Arabic speakers.

Similarly, in Egypt, the armed Islamic groups do murder secularists and Islamists who disagree strongly with them; they do encourage communal hatred by Muslims, including pogroms, against the 10 percent of the population who happen to be Coptic Christians. In Iran the Khomeini wing of Islamism did execute some 100 people for "sexual offences" like homosexuality and adultery in 1979-81; they did sack women from the legal system and organise gangs of thugs, the Iranian Hezbollah, to attack unveiled women and to assault left wingers; and they did kill thousands in the repression of the left Islamist People's Mujahedin. In Afghanistan the Islamist organisations which waged a long and bloody war against the Russian occupation of their country did turn their heavy weaponry on each other once the Russians had left, reducing whole areas of Kabul to rubble.

In fact, even when Islamists put the stress on "anti-imperialism", they more often than not let imperialism off the hook. For imperialism today is not usually the direct rule of Western states over parts of the third world, but rather a world system of independent capitalist classes ("private" and state), integrated into a single world market. Some ruling classes have greater power than others and so are able to impose their own bargaining terms through their control over access to trade, the banking system or on occasions crude force. These ruling classes stand at the top of a pinnacle of exploitation, but those just below are the ruling classes of poorer countries, rooted in the individual national economies, also gaining from the system, increasingly linking themselves into the dominant multinational networks and buying into the economies of the advanced world, even if on occasion they lash out at those above them.

The suffering of the great mass of people cannot *simply* be blamed on the great imperialist powers and their agencies like the World Bank and the IMF. It is also a result of the enthusiastic participation in exploitation of the lesser capitalists and their states. It is these who actually implement the policies that impoverish people and wreck their lives. And it is these who use the police and the prisons to crush those who try to resist.

There is an important difference here with what happened under the classic imperialism of the colonial empires, where Western colonists manned the state and directed repression. The local exploiting classes would be pulled two ways, between resisting a state when it trampled on their interests, and collaborating with it as a bulwark against those they themselves exploited. But they were not necessarily in the front line of defending the whole system of exploitation against revolt. They are today. They are part of the system, even if they sometimes quarrel with it. They are no longer its inconsistent opponents. [52]

In this situation any ideology which restricts itself to targeting foreign imperialism as the enemy evades any serious confrontation with the system. It expresses people's bitterness and frustration, but evades focusing it on real enemies. This is true of most versions of Islamism, just as it is true these days of most third world nationalisms. They point to a real enemy, the world system, and on occasions they clash bitterly with the state. But they absolve from responsibility most of the local bourgeoisie – imperialism's most important long-term partner.

A recent study of Khomeinism in Iran by Abrahamian compares it with Peronism and similar forms of "populism":

> Khomeini adopted radical themes... At times he sounded more radical than the Marxists. But while adopting radical themes he remained staunchly committed to the preservation of middle class property. This form of

middle class radicalism made him akin to Latin American populists, especially the Peronists. [53]

And Abrahamian goes on to say:

> By "populism" I mean a movement of the propertied middle class that mobilises the lower classes, especially the urban poor, with radical rhetoric directed against imperialism, foreign capitalism, and the political establishment... Populist movements promise to drastically raise the standard of living and make the country fully independent of outside powers. Even more important in attacking the status quo with radical rhetoric, they intentionally stop short of threatening the petty bourgeoisie and the whole principle of private property. Populist movements thus, inevitably, emphasise the importance, not of economic-social revolution, but of cultural, national and political reconstruction. [54]

Such movements tend to confuse matters by moving from any real struggle against imperialism to a purely ideological struggle against what they see as its cultural effects. "Cultural imperialism", rather than material exploitation, is identified as the source of everything that is wrong. The fight is then not directed against forces really involved in impoverishing people, but rather against those who speak "foreign" languages, accept "alien" religions or reject allegedly "traditional" lifestyles. This is very convenient for certain sections of local capital who find it easy to practice the "indigenous culture", at least in public. It is also of direct material interest to sections of the middle class who can advance their own careers by purging others from their jobs. But it limits the dangers such movements present to imperialism as a system.

Islamism, then, both mobilises popular bitterness and paralyses it; both builds up people's feelings that something must be done and directs those feelings into blind alleys; both destabilises the state and limits the real struggle against the state.

The contradictory character of Islamism follows from the class base of its core cadres. The petty bourgeoisie as a class cannot follow a consistent, independent policy of its own. This has always been true of the traditional petty bourgeoisie – the small shopkeepers, traders and self-employed professionals. They have always been caught between a conservative hankering for security that looks to the past and a hope that they individually will gain from radical change. It is just as true of the impoverished new middle class – or the even more impoverished would-be new middle class of unemployed ex-students

– in the less economically advanced countries today. They can hanker after an allegedly golden past. They can see their futures as tied up with general social advance through revolutionary change. Or they can blame the frustration of their aspirations on other sections of the population who have got an "unfair" grip on middle class jobs: the religious and ethnic minorities, those with a different language, women working in an "untraditional" way.

Which direction they turn in does not just depend on immediate material factors. It also depends on the struggles that occur on a national and international scale. Thus in the 1950s and 1960s the struggles against colonialism and imperialism did inspire much of the aspirant middle class of the Third World, and there was a general feeling that state controlled economic development represented the way forward. The secular left, or at least its Stalinist or nationalist mainstream, was seen as embodying this vision, and it exercised a degree of hegemony in the universities. At that stage even those who began with a religious orientation were attracted by what was seen as the left – by the example of the Vietnamese War against America or by the so called cultural revolution in China – and began to reject traditional religious thinking over, for instance, the women's question. This happened with the Catholic liberation theologists in Latin America and the People's Mujahedin in Iran. And even in Afghanistan the Islamist students

> demonstrated against Zionism during the six-day war, against American policies in Vietnam and the privileges of the establishment. They were violently opposed to important figures on the traditionalist side, to the King and especially his cousin Daoud ... They protested against foreign influences in Afghanistan, both from the Soviet Union and the West, and against the speculators during the famine of 1972, by demanding there should be curbs on personal wealth. [55]

In the late 1970s and 1980s the mood changed. On the one hand there was the beginning of a global wave of disillusionment with the so called "socialist" model presented by the Eastern European states as a result of the killing fields of Cambodia, the mini-war between Vietnam and China, and the move of China towards the American camp. This disillusionment grew in intensity in the later 1980s as a result of the changes in Eastern Europe and the collapse of the USSR.

It was even more intense in certain Middle Eastern countries than elsewhere in the world because the illusions had not merely been a question of foreign policy. The local regimes had claimed to be implementing nationalist versions of "socialism", based to a greater or lesser extent on the East European model. Even those on the left who were critical of their governments tended to accept and identify with these claims. Thus in Algeria the left in the universities volunteered in the early 1970s to go to the countryside to assist in the "land reform", even though the regime had already repressed the left student organisation and was maintaining police control over the universities. And in Egypt the Communists continued to proclaim Nasser as a socialist, even after he had thrown them into prison. So disillusionment with the regime became also, for many people, disillusionment with the left.

On the other hand, there was the emergence of certain Islamic states as a political force – the seizure of power by Gadaffi in Libya, the Saudi-led oil embargo against the West at the time of the Arab-Israeli war of 1973, and then, most dramatically, the revolutionary establishment of the Iranian Islamic Republic in 1979.

Islamism began to dominate among the very layers of students and young people who had once looked to the left: in Algeria, for instance, "Khomeini began to be regarded by layers of young people as Mao and Guevara once had been".[56] Support for the Islamist movements went from strength to strength as they seemed to offer imminent and radical change. The leaders of the Islamist movements were triumphant.

Yet the contradictions in Islamism did not go away, and expressed themselves forcefully in the decade that followed. Far from being an unstoppable force, Islamism has, in fact, been subject to its own internal pressures which, repeatedly, have made its followers turn on one another. Just as the history of Stalinism in the Middle East in the 1940s and 1950s was one of failure, betrayals, splits and repression, so has the history of Islamism been in the 1980s and 1990s.

The contradictions of Islamism: Egypt

The contradictory character of Islamism expresses itself in the way in which it sees "the return to the Koran" taking place. It can see this as through a reform of the "values" of existing society, meaning simply a return to religious practices, while leaving the main structures of society intact. Or it can be seen as meaning a revolutionary overthrow of existing society. The contradiction is to be seen in the history both of the old Islamic Brotherhood of Egypt in the 1930s, 1940s and 1950s, and in the new radical Islamist movements of the 1970s, 1980s and 1990s.

The Muslim Brotherhood grew rapidly in the 1930s and 1940s as it picked up support from those disillusioned by the compromises the bourgeois nationalist Wafd made with the British, as we have seen. It was further aided by the gyrations of the Communist left under Stalin's influence, which went so far as to support the establishment of Israel. By recruiting volunteers to fight in Palestine and against the British occupation of the Egyptian Canal Zone, the Brotherhood could seem to support the anti-imperialist struggle. But just as the Brotherhood reached its peak of support, it began to run into troubles.

Its leadership based themselves on a coalition of forces – recruitment of a mass of petty bourgeois youth, links with the palace, deals with the right wing of the Wafd, plots with junior armed forces officers – which were themselves moving in different directions.

As strikes, demonstrations, assassinations, military defeat in Palestine, and guerrilla warfare in the Canal Zone tore Egyptian society apart, so the Brotherhood itself was in danger of disintegrating. Many members were indignant at the personal behaviour of the general secretary, Banna's brother in law Abadin. Banna himself condemned members of the Brotherhood who assassinated the premier Nuqrashi. After Banna's death in 1949 his successor as "supreme guide" was dismayed to discover the existence of a secret terrorist section. The seizure of power by the military under Nasser in 1952-54 produced a fundamental divide between those who supported the coup and those who opposed it until finally rival groups within the Brotherhood ended up physically battling for control of its offices.[57] "An all-important loss of confidence in the leadership" enabled Nasser eventually to crush what had once been a massively powerful organisation.[58]

But the loss of confidence was not an accident. It followed from the unbridgeable divisions which were bound to arise in a petty-bourgeois movement as the crisis in society deepened. On the one hand, there were those who were drawn to the notion of using the crisis to force the old ruling class to do a deal with them to enforce "Islamic values" (Banna himself dreamt of being involved with the monarchy in establishing a "new Caliphate" and on one occasion gave backing to a government in return for it promising to clamp down on alcohol consumption and prostitution[59]); on the other, there were the radical petty-bourgeois recruits wanting real social change, but only able to conceive of getting it through immediate armed struggle.

The same contradictions run right through Islamism in Egypt today. The reconstituted Muslim Brotherhood began operating semi-legally around the magazine *al-Dawa* in the late 1960s, turning its back on any notion of overthrowing the Egyptian regime. Instead it set its goal as reform of Egyptian society along Islamic lines by pressure from within. The task, as the supreme guide of the Brotherhood had put it in a book written from prison, was to be "preachers, not judges".[60] This meant, in practice, adopting a "reformist Islamist" orientation, seeking an accommodation with the Sadat regime.[61] In return the regime used the Islamists to deal with those it regarded, at the time, as its main enemies – the left: "The regime treated the reformist wing of the Islamist movements – grouped around the monthly magazine *al-Dawa* and on the university campuses by the Islamic Associations – with benevolence, as the Islamicists purged the universities of anything that smelled of Nasserism or Communism".[62]

Egypt was shaken by a wave of strikes, demonstrations and riots in all its 13 main cities in January 1977, in response to the state putting up the price of bread and other main consumption items. This was the largest uprising in the country since the 1919 nationalist revolt against the British. Both the Muslim Brotherhood and the Islamic Associations condemned the rising and sent messages of support to the state against what they called a "Communist conspiracy".

For such Islamist "reformism" what matters is changing the morals of society, rather than changing society itself. The stress is not on the reconstitution of the Islamic community (*umma*) by a transformation of society, but on enforcing certain sorts of behaviour within existing society. And the enemy is not the state or the internal "oppressors", but external forces seen as undermining religious observance – in the case of *al-Dawa* "Jewry", "the crusade" (meaning Christians, including the Copts), "communism" and "secularism". The fight to deal with these involves a struggle to impose the *sharia* (the legal system codified by Islamic jurists from the Koran and the Islamic tradition). It is a battle to get the existing state to impose a certain sort of culture on society, rather than a battle to overthrow the state.

Such a perspective accords neatly with the desires of the traditional social groups who back a certain version of Islamism (the remnants of the old landowning class, merchants), with those who were once radical young Islamists but who have now made good (those who made money in Saudi Arabia or who have risen to comfortable positions in the middle class professions) and to those radical Islamists who have lost heart in radical *social* change when faced with state repression.

But it does not fit at all with the frustrated aspirations of the mass of the impoverished students and ex-students, or with the mass of ex-peasants who they mix with in the poorer parts of the cities. They are easily drawn to much more radical interpretations of what the "return to the Koran" means – interpretations which attack not just extraneous influences in the existing Islamic states, but those states themselves.

Thus a basic text for the Islamists in Egypt is the book *Signposts*, written by one of the Muslim Brothers hanged by Nasser in 1966, Sayyid Qutb. This does not merely denounce the bankruptcies of the Western and Stalinist ideologies, but also insists that a state can call itself Islamic and still be based on anti-Islamic barbarism (*jahiliyya*, the name given by Muslims to the pre-Islamic society in Arabia).[63]

Such a state of affairs can only be rectified by "a vanguard of the *umma*" which carries through a revolution by following the example of the "first Koranic generation"[64] – that is, which withdraws from existing society as Mohammed did when he left Mecca in order to build up a force capable of overthrowing it.

Such arguments went beyond seeing the only enemy as imperialism, and instead, for the first time, attacked the local state directly. They were very embarrassing for the moderates of the neo-Muslim Brotherhood, who are supposed to revere their author as a martyr. But they have inspired many thousands of young radicals. Thus in the mid-1970s one group, al Taktir Wal Higra, whose leader, Shukri Mustafa, was executed for kidnapping a high religious functionary in 1977, rejected as "non-Islamic" existing society, the existing mosques, the existing religious leaders and even the neo-Muslim Brotherhood associated with *Dawa*.[65] Its attitude was that its members alone were genuine Muslims and that they had to break with existing society, living as communities apart and treating everyone else as infidels.

At first the Islamic Associations in the universities were very much under the influence of the moderate Muslim Brotherhood, not only condemning the uprising against the price increases but even disavowing Shukri when he was hanged later in the year. But their attitudes began to shift, particularly when Sadat began the "peace process" with Israel late in 1977. Soon many of the university activists were embracing ideas in some ways more radical than Shukri's: not only did they turn aside from existing society, they began organising to overthrow it, as with the assassination of Sadat by Abd al-Salam Faraj's Jihad group in October 1981.

Faraj spelt out his harsh criticisms of the strategies of different parts of Islamic movement – those sections who restricted themselves to working for Islamic charities, those (the neo-Muslim Brotherhood) who were trying to create an Islamic party which could only give legitimacy to the existing state, those who based themselves on "preaching" and so avoided jihad, those who advocated withdrawal from society on the lines of Shukri's group, and those who saw the priority as fighting against the external enemies of Islam (in Palestine or Afghanistan). Against all of them, he insisted immediate armed struggle, "jihad against the iniquitous prince", was the duty of all Muslims:

> The fight against the enemy at home takes priority over the fight against the enemy abroad... The responsibility for the existence of colonialism or imperialism in our Muslim countries lies with these infidel governments. To launch a struggle against imperialism is therefore useless and inglorious, a waste of time. [66]

Faraj's argument led straight to a perspective of insurrection against the state. But this did not stop there being significant differences within his own group between the Cairo section, built round the prime objective of destroying the infidel state, and the other section in the middle Egyptian city of Asyut, who "considered Christian proselytism the main obstacle to the propagation of Islam".[67]

In practice this meant the Asyut group directed most of its fire against the Coptic minority (mostly poor peasants) – a policy which had already been followed with horrific success by the *jamaa* students earlier in the year, when it ignited murderous inter-communal fighting first in the middle Egypt town of Minya and then in the Cairo neighbourhood of Al-Zawiyya al-Hamra: "The *jamaa* did not hesitate to fan the flames of sectarian tension in order to place the state in an awkward position and to demonstrate they were prepared to supplant the state, step by step, so to speak".[68]

The Asyut section of *jihad* was, then, following a tried and proven method of gaining local popular support through a strategy of encouraging communal hatreds. This enabled it briefly to seize control of Asyut in the aftermath of the assassination of Sadat. By contrast, the Cairo activists, with their stress on the state as the enemy, "enjoyed no networks of complicity or sustenance, and their isolated act – the assassination of Sadat – was not followed by the uprising of the Muslim population of Cairo so ardently sought by Faraj and his friends".[69]

Instead of the assassination leading to the Islamists being able to seize state power, the state was able to take advantage of the confusion created by the assassination to crush the Islamists. As thousands were arrested and many leaders executed, repression significantly weakened the movement. However, the causes which had led so many young people to turn to the Islamists did not disappear. By the end of the 1980s the movement had regained confidence and was starting to grow rapidly in some quarters of Cairo and Alexandria. This was coupled with an effective terrorist campaign against the police and the security forces.

Then in December 1992 the state launched a new and unprecedented campaign of repression. Slum areas in Cairo, such as Imbaba, were occupied by 20,000 troops with tanks and armoured cars. Tens of thousands were arrested and death squads set out to kill those activists who escaped. The main mosques used by the radical Islamists were blocked with concrete. Parents, children and wives of activists were arrested and tortured.

Again as in the early 1980s the campaign of state terror was successful. The Islamist movement was not able to, and did not even try to, mobilise support in the form of demonstrations. Instead, it moved to a totally terrorist strategy which did not seriously shake the Mubarak regime, even if it did virtually destroy the tourist industry.

Meanwhile, the Muslim Brotherhood has continued to behave like a loyal opposition, negotiating with the regime over the gradual introduction of the *sharia* into the state legal code and holding back from protests at the repression.

The contradictions of Islamism: Algeria

The story of the rise and radicalisation of Islamism in Algeria is similar in many ways to that in Egypt. The Algerian dictator of the late 1960s and 1970, Boumediène, encouraged moderate Islamism as a counterbalance to the left and to his historic opponents within the liberation movement that had ended French colonialism.

In 1970 the state initiated an Islamisation campaign under Mouloud Kassim, minister of education and religion, which denounced the "degradation of morals" and "Western influences" behind "cosmopolitanism, alcoholism, the snobbism that consists in always following the West and dressing half naked".[70] The Islamicists were able to climb on this bandwagon to increase their own influence, getting money from landowners worried about the agrarian reform to propagate a message which could appeal to the most impoverished layers in society:

> The theme of the integrists' propaganda was that Islam was menaced by atheistic and communist intrusion of which the agrarian reform was the

bearer... The integrists...spread their own ideas in the most unfavoured neighbourhoods, after building improvised mosques which were later made into solid constructions. Untouched by the agrarian revolution, workers and unemployed, discontented by their conditions, listened to the integrists.[71]

Then in the mid-1970s they got support from sections of the regime to undermine the left in the colleges: "Between 1976 and 1980 the integrists succeeded, with the connivance of the regime, in reducing to nothing the influence of the Marxists".[72]

In the early 1980s a section of the regime continued to look towards the more "moderate" versions of Islamism to bolster itself. The minister of religious affairs until 1986, Chibane, hoped to build such an Islamist tendency, and to this end helped the Islamists to get money for building mosques from industrialists and commercial interests.[73] But this could not stop the development of radical interpretations of Islam which rejected the regime. Thus in the city of Constantine, one study tells:

> Integrism replaces among large sections of Constantine opinion the traditional conceptions by the popularity of a new Islamic vision standing for a resurgence of the Community of the Prophet. This integrism gets its strength from the social frustrations which afflict a large part of the youth, those left out of account by the social and economic system.[74]

The strength of this interpretation of Islam was such as to be able to force the ministry of religious instruction to employ its people as *imams* (preachers) in the mosques rather than those who accepted "moderate" views.

The regime was losing control of the very mechanism it had encouraged to deal with the left. Instead of controlling the masses for the regime, Islamism was providing a focus for all their bitterness and hatred against those leaders who harked back to the liberation struggle of the 1960s but who had grown into a comfortable ruling class. The economic crisis which hit Algerian society in the mid-1980s deepened the bitterness – just as the ruling class turned back to the Western capitalists it had once denounced in an effort to come to terms with the crisis. And the Islamist agitation against those who spoke French and were "corrupted by Western morals" could easily become an attack on the interests of "the small but influential stratum of highly educated technocrats who constitute the core of a new salaried and bureaucratised class".[75]

The regime began to turn against the Islamists imprisoning certain of their leaders in the mid-1980s, with the regime's head, Chadli, accusing the imams of "political demagogy".[76] The effect, however, was not to destroy the Islamists, but to increase their standing as *the* opposition to the regime.

This became clear in October 1988. All the bitterness against the ruling class and the regime exploded in upheaval very similar to that which was to take place in Eastern Europe a year later. The movement, beginning as a series of spontaneous strikes in the Algiers area, soon turned into massive street clashes between young people and the police: "The people, like a freed prisoner, rediscovered their own voices and their sense of liberty. Even the power of the police no longer frightened them."[77] "The insurrection of October 1988 was above all a revolt of young people against their conditions of life after a quarter of a century of military dictatorship".[78]

The revolt shook the regime to its core. As in Eastern Europe all sorts of political forces that had been repressed now came out into the open. Journalists wrote freely for the first time, intellectuals began to speak openly about the real condition of Algerian society, exiled politicians of both left and right returned from abroad, a women's movement emerged to challenge the regime's Islamic family law, which gave women fewer rights than men. But it soon became clear that outside the Berber-speaking areas the Islamists were the hegemonic force among the opposition. Their influence was in many ways like that of the "democrats" in Eastern Europe and the USSR in the following year. The tolerance shown to them by sections of the regime in the past, and the support they continued to get from some powerful foreign states (for instance, finance from Saudi Arabia) combined with their ability to articulate a message that focused the bitterness of the mass of the population:

> By their number, their network of mosques, and their tendency to act spontaneously as a single man, as if obeying the orders of a secret central committee, the Islamists appeared as the only movement capable of mobilising the masses and influencing the course of events. It was they who would come forward as the spokesmen of the insurgents, able to impose themselves as future leaders of the movement... Not knowing who to talk to, after quietening its machine guns, the regime was looking for "leaders", representatives capable of formulating demands and controlling a crowd as violent as they were uncontrollable. So Chadli received Madani, Belhadj and Nahnah [the best-known Islamist figures].[79]

So influential did the Islamist movement, now organised as the FIS, become in the months that followed that it was able to win control of the most important municipalities in the June 1990 local elections and then the biggest share of the votes in the general elections of December 1991, despite being subject to severe repression. The Algerian military annulled the elections in order to stop the Islamists forming a government. But this did not stop the massive support for the Islamists creating near civil war conditions in the country, with whole areas falling under effective control of Islamist armed groups.

Yet the rise of Islamist influence was accompanied by growing confusion as to what the FIS stood for. While it was in control of the country's major municipalities between June 1990 and May 1991:

> the changes it brought about were modest: the closing of bars, the cancellation of musical spectacles, campaigns, at times violent, for "feminine decency" and against the ubiquitous satellite dishes that "permitted reception of Western pornography"... Neither Madani [the FIS's best-known leader] nor its consultative assembly drew up a true politico-social programme or convened a congress to discuss it. Madani limited himself to saying that this would meet after they had formed a government.[80]

What the FIS did do was show opposition to the demands of workers for improved wages. In these months it opposed a dust workers' strike in Algiers, a civil servants' strike and a one-day general strike called by the former "official" union federation. Madani justified breaking the dust workers' strike in a newspaper interview, complaining that it was forcing respectable people like doctors and professional engineers to sweep up:

> The dustmen have the right to strike, but not the right to invade our capital and turn our country into a dustbin. There are strikes of trade unions that have become terrains for action by the corrupters, the enemies of Allah and the fatherland, communists and others, who are spreading everywhere because the cadre of the FLN have retreated... We are reliving the days of the OAS.[81]

Such a respectable stance fitted neatly with the interests of the classes who had financed the Islamists from the time of the land reform onwards. It also suited those successful members of the petty bourgeoisie who were part of the FIS – the professors, the established imams and the grammar school teachers. And it appealed to those in the countryside whose adhesion to the former ruling party, the FLN, had enabled them to prosper, becoming successful capitalist farmers or small businessmen. But it was not enough either to satisfy the impoverished urban masses who looked to the FIS for their salvation or to force the ruling class and the military to sit back and accept an FIS government.

At the end of May 1991, faced with threats by the military to sabotage the electoral process rather than risk a FIS victory, the FIS leaders turned round and "launched an authentic insurrection which recalled October 1988: molotov cocktails, tear gas, barricades. Ali Belhadj, the charismatic Imam, launched tens of thousands of demonstrators onto the streets. [82] For a time the FIS took control of the centre of Algiers, supported by vast numbers of young people to whom Islam and the jihad seemed the only alternative to the misery of the society the military were defending.

In reality, the more powerful the FIS became, the more it was caught between respectability and insurrectionism, telling the masses they could not strike in March 1991 and then calling on them to overthrow the state two months later in May.

The same contradictions have emerged within the Islamist movement in the three years since, as guerrilla warfare has grown in intensity in both the cities and the countryside. "The condemnation of Abasi Madani and Ali Belhadj to 12 years in prison...provoked a major radicalisation of the FIS and a fragmentation of its rank and file. The detention of thousands of members and sympathisers in camps in the Sahara spread urban terrorism and rural guerrilla warfare".[83] Two armed organisations emerged, the Armed Islamic Movement (MIA, recently renamed AIS) and the Armed Islamic Groups (GIA), which were soon getting the support of armed bands right across the country. But the underground movements were characterised by "internal dissension":[84]

> As against the presumed "moderation" of the MIA, which "only" executes the representatives of the "impious regime", the GIA opposes an extreme jihad, whose chosen victims are journalists, writers, poets, feminists and intellectuals...since November 1993 killing 32 moderate Islamic imams and unveiled women...
>
> Fratricidal fights between the MIA and the GIA have led to dozens of casualties...the deaths of seven terrorists are imputed to these quarrels by some people, but to the death squads of the police by others.[85]

The GIA accuses the historical leaders of the FIS of opportunism, treachery and abandoning their programme of the complete application of the *sharia*.[86]

Splitting two ways

The experience of Islamism in Egypt and Algeria shows how it can split over two different questions: first over whether to follow the course of more or less peaceful reform of the existing society or to take up arms; second over whether to fight to change the state or to purge society of "impiety".

In Egypt the present-day Muslim Brotherhood is based on a policy of reform directed at the state. It attempts to work within existing society building up its strength so as to become a legal opposition, with MPs, a press of its own, control over various middle class professional organisations and influence over wider sections of the population through the mosques and the Islamic charities. It also tends to stress the fight to impose Islamic piety through campaigning for the existing regime to incorporate the *sharia* into the legal code.

This is a strategy which also seems to appeal to a section of the imprisoned or exiled leadership of the FIS in Algeria. In the first few months of 1994 there were reports of negotiations between them and a section of the regime, with a perspective of sharing power and implementing part of the *sharia*. Thus *The Guardian* could report in April 1994 that Rabah Kebir, an exiled leader of FIS, welcomed the appointment of a new prime minster for Algeria, the "technocrat", Redha Malek, as "a positive act"[87] – only two days after the FIS had denounced the latest package agreed between that government and the IMF.[88]

Some perceptive commentators see such a deal as providing the best way for the Algerian bourgeoisie to end the instability and preserve its position. Thus Juan Goytisolo argues that the military could have saved itself a lot of trouble by allowing the FIS to form a government after the 1991 elections:

> The conditions in which it acceded to power would have limited in a very effective way the application of its programme. The indebtedness of Algeria, its financial dependence on its European and Japanese creditor, the economic chaos and the hostile reservations of the Armed Forces would have constituted a difficult obstacle for a FIS government to overcome... Its

inability to fulfil its electoral promises were fully predictable. With a year of a government so tightly constrained by its enemies, the FIS would have lost a good part of its credibility. [89]

"Islamist reformism" fits the needs of certain major social groups – the traditional landowners and merchants, the new Islamic bourgeoisie (like those of the Muslim Brotherhood who made millions in Saudi Arabia) and that section of the Islamic new middle class who have enjoyed upward mobility. But it does not satisfy the other layers who have looked to Islamism – the students and impoverished ex-students, or the urban poor. The more the Muslim Brotherhood or the FIS look to compromise, the more these layers look elsewhere, seeing any watering down of the demand for the installation of Islam of the Koranic years as betrayal.

But their reaction to this can be in different directions. It can remain passive in the face of the state, urging a strategy of withdrawal from society, in which the stress is on preaching and purifying the Islamic minority, rather than on confrontation. This was the original strategy of the Shukri group in Egypt in the mid-1970s, and it is the approach of some of the radical preachers who are aware of the power of the state today.

Or it can turn to armed struggle. But just as peaceful struggle can be directed against the state or against impiety alone, so armed struggle can be armed struggle to overthrow the state, or armed actions against "the enemies of Islam" among the population at large – the ethnic and religious minorities, unveiled women, foreign films, the influence of "cultural imperialism" and so on. The logic of the situation might seem to push people towards the option of armed struggle *against the state*. But there is a powerful counter-logic at work, which is rooted in the class composition of the Islamist following.

As we have seen, the sections of the exploiting classes which back Islamism are naturally drawn to its more reformist versions. Even where they find little choice but to take up arms, they want to do so in ways which minimise wider social unrest. They look to coups d'état rather than mass action. And if this erupts despite them, they seek to bring it to an end as quickly as possible.

The impoverished new petty bourgeoisie can move much further towards a perspective of armed action. But its own marginal social position cuts it off from seeing this as developing out of mass struggles like strikes. Instead it looks to conspiracies based on small armed groups – conspiracies that do not lead to the revolutionary change their instigators want, even when, as with the assassination of Sadat, they achieve their immediate goals. It can cause enormous disruption to existing society but it cannot revolutionise it.

This was the experience of the populists in Russia before 1917. It was the experience of a generation of students and ex-students right across the third world who turned to Guevarism or Maoism in the late 1960s (and whose successors still fight on in the Philippines and Peru). It is the experience of armed anti-state Islamists in Egypt and Algeria today.

The only way out of this impasse would be for the Islamists to base themselves on the non-marginal groups among the urban poor today – among the workers in medium and large-scale industry. But the basic notions of Islamism make this all but impossible since Islam, in even its most radical form, preaches the return to a community (*umma*) which reconciles the rich and the poor, not an overthrow of the rich. Thus the economic programme of the FIS puts forward as an alleged alternative to "Western capitalism" a blueprint for "small business" producing for "local needs" which is virtually indistinguishable from the electoral propaganda of innumerable conservative and liberal parties right across the world.[90] And its attempt to create "Islamic unions" in the summer of 1990 laid stress on the "duties of workers", because, it was claimed, the old regime gave them too many rights and "accustomed the workers to not working". The class struggle, it insisted, "does not exist in Islam", for the sacred texts do not speak of it. What is needed is for the employer to treat his workers in the same way the Koran tells the faithful to treat their domestic slaves – as "brothers".[91]

It is not surprising that nowhere have any of the Islamist groups ever succeeded in building a base in the factories even one tenth as strong as they built up in the neighbourhoods. But without such a base they cannot of their own accord determine the direction of social change, even if they do succeed in bringing about the collapse of an existing regime. Those on the margins of society can occasionally provoke a great crisis within an already unstable regime. They cannot determine how the crisis is resolved.

The Islamist groups may be able to provoke such a crisis in one of the existing regimes and so force out its existing leaders. But that will not prevent an outcome in which the ruling class, which has prospered beneath these leaders, does a deal with the less militant Islamists to hold on to power. And short of such a crisis the militant Islamists themselves face an enormous toll of deaths at the hands of the state.

It is this pressure from the state which encourages some of them to turn away from direct assault on the regime to the easier task of assaulting the "impious" and the minorities – an approach which in turn can bring them back closer to the mainstream "moderate" reformist Islamists.

There is, in fact, a certain dialectic at work within Islamism. Militant anti-state Islamists, after bearing the brunt of unsuccessful armed struggle, learn the hard way to keep their heads down and instead turn to fighting to impose Islamic behaviour either directly or through Islamic reformism. But neither imposing Islamic behaviour nor reforms can deal with the immense dissatisfaction of the social layers that look to Islamism. And so new militants are continually arising who split off to return to the path of armed action, until these too learn the hard way the limitations of armed actions which are cut off from an active social base.

There is no automatic progression from seeing the limitations of Islamic reformism to moving to revolutionary politics. Rather the limitations of reformism lead either to the terrorism and guerrillaism of groups that try to act without a mass base, or in the direction of a reactionary attack on scapegoats for the problems of the system. And because each of the approaches expresses itself in the same religious language, there is often an overlap between one and the other. People who do want to attack the regime and imperialism do attack the Copts, the Berbers and unveiled women. People who have an instinctive hatred of the whole system do fall into the trap of wanting to negotiate over the imposition of the *sharia* by the state. And where there are divisions between rival groups – sometimes so bitter that they start killing each other as "apostates" (renegades from true Islam) – the divisions are expressed in ways which obscure the real social causes behind them. If one upwardly mobile Islamist abandons the struggle, that only proves that he personally is a "bad Muslim" (or even an apostate); it does not in itself prevent another upwardly mobile Islamist from being a "good Muslim".

The Iranian experience

The Islamic regime in Iran dominates discussions on Islamic revivalism, much as the record of Stalinism dominates discussions on socialism. And often, even on the left, very similar conclusions are drawn. The Islamists are seen, much as the Stalinists were once seen, as the most dangerous of all political forces, able to impose a totalitarianism that will prevent any further progressive development. In order to stop them it is necessary for the left to unite with the liberal section of the bourgeoisie,[92] or even to support non-democratic states in their repression of the Islamist groups.[93] It is a view that overrates the cohesion of Islamism and ascribes to it an ability to dictate historical events which in reality it does not have. And it rests on an erroneous understanding of the role of Islam during and after the Iranian Revolution of 1979.

That revolution was not a product of Islamism, but of the enormous contradictions that arose in the Shah's regime in the mid to late 1970s. Economic crisis had heightened the deep divisions which existed between sections of modern capital associated with the state and other, more "traditional", sections centred around the bazaar (which was responsible for two thirds of wholesale trade and three quarters of retail trade) at the same time as deepening the discontent of the mass of the workers and the vast numbers of recent ex-peasants who had flooded into the cities. Protests of intellectuals and students were joined by the disaffected clergy and spread to involve the urban poor in a series of great clashes with the police and army. A wave of strikes paralysed industry and brought the all-important oil fields to a standstill. And then early in February 1979 the left wing guerrillas of the Fedayeen and the left-Islamist guerrillas of the People's Mujahedin succeeded in fomenting large-scale mutinies in the armed forces, so bringing about a revolutionary collapse of the old regime.

Much of the rising movement had identified with the exiled Islamist Ayatollah Khomeini. His name had come to symbolise opposition to the monarchy, and his residence outside Paris had been the point of contact between representatives of the different forces involved – the *bazaaris* and the clergy who were close to them, the liberal bourgeois opposition, the professional associations, the students and even the left guerrillas. On his return to Tehran in January 1979 he became the symbolic leader of the revolution.

Yet at this stage he was far from controlling events, even though he had an acute sense of political tactics. The key events that brought the Shah down – the spread of the strikes, the mutiny inside the armed forces – occurred completely independently of him. And in the months after the revolution Khomeini was no more able to impose a single authority over the revolutionary upheaval than anyone else. In the cities various local committees (*komitehs*) exercised de facto power. The universities were in the hands of the left and the Mujahedin. In the factories *shoras* (factory councils) fought for control with man-

THE PROPHET AND THE PROLETARIAT 339

agement, often forcing out those associated with the Shah's regime and taking over the organisation of production themselves. In the regions inhabited by ethnic minorities – Kurdistan in the northwest and Khuzistan in the Arab-speaking southwest – movements began to fight for self-determination. And at the top, overseeing this process, was not one body but two. The provisional government was run by Bazargan, a "moderate" Islamist linked to modern sections of the bourgeoisie (he had founded the Islamic students' associations in the 1950s and then the Islamic Engineers Association). But next to it, acting as an alternative centre of authority, was a revolutionary council nominated by Khomeini, around which coalesced a group of clerics and Islamist intellectuals with links with the bazaars.

The group around Khomeini were eventually able to establish near total power for themselves and their Islamic Republican Party (IRP). But it took them two and a half years of manoeuvring between different social forces which could easily have overwhelmed them. For most of 1979 they collaborated with Bazargan in an effort to clamp down on the *shoras* within the factories and the separatist nationalist movements. They used Islamic language to mobilise behind them sections of the lumpenproletariat into gangs, the Hizbollah, which would attack the left, enforce Islamic "morality" (for instance, against women who refused to wear the veil) and join the army in putting down the separatist revolts. There were instances of brutal repression (the execution of about a hundred people for "sexual crimes", homosexuality and adultery, the killing of some left wing activists, the shooting down of protesters belonging to the national minorities), as in any attempt to restore bourgeois "normality" after a great revolutionary upheaval. But the overall balance sheet for the IRP was not very positive in the early autumn of 1979. On the one hand, those successes they had enjoyed in checking the revolution had strengthened the position of the grouping around Bazargan with whom they were increasingly at odds. As a study of Bazargan's movement has put it:

> One year after the fall of the Shah it was becoming clear that the better-educated middle classes and the political forces they were supporting [i.e. Bazargan] were rapidly expanding their influence, being dominant in sensitive positions in the mass media, state organisations and especially educational institutions ... With the disintegration of the unity of the Islamic forces, the Islamic committees were not capable of having a large majority of the employees of the organisations behind them.[94]

On the other, there was a growing ferment that threatened to escape from the Khomeiniites' control, leading to a massive growth of both the secular left and the Islamic left. The left was dominant among the students, despite the first wave of repression against it in August 1979. The *shoras* in the factories had been weakened by this same repression, but many remained intact for another year,[95] and the workers' willingness to struggle was certainly not destroyed – there were 360 "forms of strikes, sit-ins and occupations" in 1979-80, 180 in 1980-81 and 82 in 1981-82.[96]

The IRP could only regain control itself by making a radical shift in November 1979 – organising the minority of students who followed its banner rather than that of the Fedayeen or People's Mujahedin to seize the US Embassy and hold its staff hostage, provoking a major confrontation with the world's most important imperialist power. Another study of this period says, "The fundamentalist student of the 'Islamic Associations' who a few weeks earlier had been looked on by their rivals as reactionaries and fanatics, were now posing as super-revolutionaries and were cheered by masses of people whenever they appeared at the gate of the Embassy to be interviewed by reporters."[97]

The shift to an apparently radical anti-imperialist stance was accompanied by radicalisation of the IRP's policies in the workplaces. From defending many of the old managers it moved to agitating for their removal – although not for their power to be taken over by the factory councils, but by "Islamic managers" who would collaborate with Islamic councils from which the left and the Mujahedin were automatically excluded as "infidels".

This radical turn gave new popularity to the IRP. It seemed to be putting into effect the anti-imperialism which the group around Bazargan had propagated during their long years of opposition to the Shah but which they were now abandoning as they sought to cement a new relationship between Iran and the US. It was also acting in accord with some of the main and most popular slogans raised in the months since the revolution by the growing forces of both the secular and Islamic left:

> The taking over of the American Embassy helped the fundamentalists to overcome some of their difficulties... The outcome helped those groups that advocated the sovereignty of the clergymen to implement their polices and take over the sensitive organisations that were manned and controlled by the better educated middle class. When the students who were loyal to the clergymen invaded the gates of the US Embassy, those who had been

identified as "reactionaries" re-emerged as the leading revolutionaries, capable of dumping the modernist and secularist forces altogether... It was the beginning of a new coalition in which certain clergy and their *bazaari* associates were the leaders and large groups from the lower middle class and the urban lower class were the functionaries.[98]

The group around Khomeini was not just gaining in popularity; it was also creating a much wider base for itself as it displaced, or at least threatened to displace, the old "non-Islamic" managers and functionaries. In industry, the media, the armed forces, the police, a new layer of people began to exercise control whose careers depended on their ability to agitate for Khomeini's version of Islamism. And those who remained from the old hierarchies of power rushed to prove their own Islamic credentials by implementing the IRP line.

What the group around Khomeini succeeded in doing was to unite behind it a wide section of the middle class – both the traditional petty bourgeoisie based in the bazaar and many of the first generation of the new middle class – in a struggle to control the hierarchies of power. The secret of its success was its ability to enable those who followed it at every level of society to combine religious enthusiasm with personal advance. Someone who had been an assistant manager in a foreign-owned company could now run it under state control and feel he was fulfilling his religious duty to serve the community (*umma*); someone who had lived in deep poverty among the lumpenproletariat could now achieve both material security and a sense of self-achievement by leading a hizbollah gang in its attempts to purify society of "indecency" and the "infidel Communists".

The opportunities open to those who opted for the Khomeini line were enormous. The flight from the country of local and foreign managers and technicians during the early months of revolutionary upheaval had created 130,000 positions to be filled.[99] The purging of "non-Islamic" managers, functionaries and army officers added enormously to the total.

The interesting thing about the method by which the group around Khomeini ousted their opponents and established a one-party regime was that there was nothing specifically Islamist about it. It was not, as many people horrified by the religious intolerance of the regime contend, a result of some "irrational" or "medieval" characteristic of "Islamic fundamentalism". In fact, it was very similar to that carried through in different parts of the world by parties based on sections of the petty bourgeoisie. It was the method used, for instance, by the weak Communist Parties of much of Eastern Europe to establish their control after 1945.[100] And a prototype for the petty-bourgeois who combines ideological fervour and personal advance is to be found in Balzac's Pére Goriot – the austere Jacobin who makes his fortune out of exploiting the shortages created by the revolutionary upheaval.

A political party based on organising a section of the petty-bourgeoisie around the struggle for positions cannot take power in just any circumstances. Most such attempts come to nothing, because the petty bourgeois formations are too weak to challenge the power of the old ruling class without a mobilisation of the mass of society which they then cannot control. Thus in the Portuguese Revolution of 1974-75 the Communist Party's attempts to infiltrate the hierarchies of power fell apart in the face of a resistance coordinated by the major Western capitalist powers on the one hand and of an upsurge of workers' militancy from below on the other. Such attempts can only work if, for specific historical reasons, the major social classes are paralysed.

As Tony Cliff put it in a major piece of Marxist analysis, if the old ruling class is too weak to hang on to power in the face of economic crisis and insurgency from below, while the working class does not have the independent organisation to allow it to become the head of the movement, then sections of the intelligentsia are able to make a bid for power, feeling that they have a mission to solve the problems of society as a whole:

> The intelligentsia is sensitive to their countries' technical lag. Participating as it does in the scientific and technical world of the 20th century, it is stifled by the backwardness of its own nation. This feeling is accentuated by the "intellectual unemployment" endemic in these countries. Given the general economic backwardness, the only hope for most students is a government job, but there are not nearly enough of these to go round.
>
> The spiritual life of the intellectuals is also in a crisis. In a crumbling order where the traditional pattern is disintegrating, they feel insecure, rootless, lacking in firm values.
>
> Dissolving cultures give rise to a powerful urge for a new integration that must be total and dynamic if it is to fill the social and spiritual vacuum, that must combine religious fervour with militant nationalism. They are in search for a dynamic movement which will unify the nation and open up broad vistas for it, but at the same time will give themselves power...

> They hope for reform from above and would dearly love to hand the new world over to a grateful people, rather than see the liberating struggle of a self-conscious and freely associated people result in a new world for themselves. They care a lot for measures to drag their nation out of stagnation, but very little for democracy... All this makes totalitarian state capitalism a very attractive goal for intellectuals.[101]

Although these words were written about the attraction of Stalinism, Maoism and Castroism in third world countries, they fit absolutely the Islamist intelligentsia around Khomeini in Iran. They were not, as many left wing commentators have mistakenly believed, merely an expression of "backward", bazaar-based traditional, "parasitic", "merchant capital".[102] Nor were they simply an expression of classic bourgeois counter-revolution.[103] They undertook a revolutionary reorganisation of ownership and control of capital within Iran even while leaving capitalist relations of production intact, putting large-scale capital that had been owned by the group around the Shah into the hands of state and parastate bodies controlled by themselves – in the interests of the "oppressed", of course, with the corporation that took over the Shah's own economic empire being named the Mustafazin ("Oppressed") Foundation. As Bayat tells:

> The seizure of power by the clergy was a reflection of a power vacuum in the post-revolutionary state. Neither the proletariat nor the bourgeoisie was able to exert their political hegemony. The reason for their inability must be sought in their historical development which is a testimony to the weakness of both.[104]

Or, as Cliff put it of the intelligentsia in third world countries, "Their power is in direct relation to the feebleness of other classes and their political nullity".[105]

It was because they depended on balancing between the major social classes to advance their own control over the state and a section of capital that the Khomeini group had to hit first at the left organisation and then at the established bourgeois organisations (Bazargan etc) before being able to consolidate their own power. In 1979 this meant working with Bazargan against the left to subdue the revolutionary wave, and then making certain gestures to the left at the time of the seizure of the US Embassy to isolate the established bourgeoisie. During the 1980s it meant another zigzag, allowing another Islamic figure linked to the established bourgeoisie, Bani

Sadr, to take the presidency and then working with him to smash the bastion of the left, the universities. When the IRP suggested sending the Islamic gangs, the Hizbollah, into the universities to purge them of "anti-Islamic elements", Bani Sadr was happy to comply:

> Both the IRP leaders and the liberals agreed to the idea of cultural revolution through direct action by the people who were mobilised to march on university campuses... For the liberals it was a means to get rid of the leftist agitators in the public institutions, the factories and the rural areas, so that economic and political stability could be restored to the country...
>
> The gangs of the Hizbollah invaded the universities, injured and killed members of the political groups who were resisting the cultural revolution, and burned books and papers thought to be "un-Islamic". The government closed all universities and colleges for three years, during which university curricula were rewritten.[106]

Yet even at this time the Khomeiniites continued to preserve part of their own "left" image, using anti-imperialist language to justify what they were doing. They insisted the fight to impose "Islamic values" was essential in the struggle against "cultural imperialism", and that, because the left resisted this, it was in reality working for imperialism.

External events helped them to get away with these arguments. These were the months of the abortive US attempt to recapture the embassy by sending in armed helicopters (which crashed into each other in the desert), of Shiite demonstrations against the government of Bahrin, of pro-Khomeini riots in the oil-rich Saudi province of Hasa, of the seizure of the Grand Mosque in Mecca by armed Sunni Islamists, and of the attempt by Saddam Hussein of Iraq to ingratiate himself with the US and the Arab Gulf sheikhdoms by launching an invasion of Iran. The Khomeiniites could proclaim, rightly, that the revolution was under attack from forces allied to imperialism and, wrongly, that they alone could defend it. No wonder Khomeini himself referred to the attack as a "godsend". The need for all-out mobilisation against the invading forces in the winter of 1980-81 allowed his supporters to justify increasing their control, at the expense of both the left and the Bani Sadr group, until in June-July 1981 they were able to crush both, establishing a near-totalitarian structure.

But why were the left not able to deal with the advance of the IRP?

In retrospect, it is often argued that the fault lies with the failure of the left to understand in time the need for an alliance with the "progressive", "liberal" bourgeoisie. This is Halliday's argument.[107] But, as we have seen, the liberal bourgeoisie under Bazargan and then Bani Sadr were united with Khomeini in the campaign against the *shoras* in the factories and the campaign to purge the universities. What divided them was who was going to get the fruits of their successes against the left. It was only when he finally found that he had lost out that Bani Sadr (but not, interestingly, Bazargan, whose party continued to operate legally but ineffectively) joined with the left Islamists of the People's Mujahedin in an abortive attempt to overthrow the regime.

The Khomeiniites were able to outmanoeuvre the allegedly "liberal" section of the bourgeoisie because, after beating the left, they were then able to use anti-imperialist rhetoric to mobilise sections of the urban poor against the established bourgeoisie. They could play on the obvious gap between the miserable lives of the masses and the "un-Islamic" lifestyles of the well-to-do. The left could not resist this manoeuvre by lining up with the well-to-do Westernised section of the bourgeoisie.

The key to genuinely undercutting the Khomeiniites lay in mobilising workers to fight on their own behalf. This would have thrown both the allegedly "liberal" section of the bourgeoisie and the IRP onto the defensive.

The workers' struggles played a central role in the overthrow of the Shah, and in the aftermath there were major struggles in the large factories between the factory councils and the management. But once the Shah was removed, the workers' struggles rarely went beyond the confines of individual factories to contest the leadership of all the oppressed and exploited. The factory councils never became *workers' councils* on the pattern of the soviets of Russia in 1905 and 1917.[108] And because of that failing they did not succeed in attracting behind them the mass of casual labourers, self-employed, artisans and impoverished tradesmen – the "lumpenproletariat" – who the Khomeiniites mobilised against the left under religious slogans.

This weakness of the workers' movement was partly a result of objective factors. There was a division within the working class between those in the modern sector of large factories and those in the traditional sector of small workshops (many operated by family members or their owners). The areas that workers lived in were often numerically dominated by the impoverished sectors of the petty bourgeoisie: there were 750,000 "merchants, middlemen and small traders" in Tehran in 1980, as against about 400,000 workers in large industrial enterprises.[109] Very large numbers of workers were new to industry and had few traditions of industrial struggle – 80 percent came from a rural origin and every year 330,000 more ex-peasants flooded into the towns.[110] Only a third were fully literate and so able to read the left's press, although 80 percent had televisions. Finally, the scale of repression under the Shah meant that the number of established militants in the workplaces was very small.

But the inability of the workers' movement to take the leadership of the wider mass movement was not just a result of objective factors. It was also a result of the political failings of the considerable left wing forces that existed in the post-revolutionary months. The Fedayeen and People's Mujahedin boasted of meetings many thousands strong, and the Mujahedin picked up a quarter of the votes in Tehran in the elections of the spring of 1980. But the traditions of the Fedayeen and the Mujahedin were guerrillaist, and they paid little attention to activity round the factories. Their bastions of support were the universities, not the factory areas. Thus the People's Mujahedin had five "fronts" of activity: an underground organisation for preparing "armed struggle", a youth front, a women's front, a *bazaari* front and, clearly not the top priority, a workers' front.

What is more, the large left organisations had little to say, even when worker activists did join them. In the vital first eight months of the revolution they made only limited criticisms of the new regime and these consisted mainly of its failure to challenge imperialism. The People's Mujahedin, for instance:

> scrupulously adhered to a policy of avoiding confrontations with the clerical shadow government. In late February when the Fedayeen organised a demonstration of over 80,000 at Tehran university demanding land reform, the end of press censorship and the dissolution of the armed forces, the Mujahedin stayed away. And early in March, when Western educated women celebrated international women's day by demonstrating against Khomeini's decrees abrogating the Family Protection Law, enforcing the use of the veil in government offices, and pushing the "less impartial gender" from the judiciary, the Mujahedin warned that "imperialism was exploiting such divisive issues". In late March when zealous club wielders attacked the offices of the anti-clerical paper *Ayandegan*, the Mujahedin said nothing. They opposed a boycott of the referendum over the Islamic republic and Kurdish struggle for autonomy. If the nation did not remain united behind Imam Khomeini, the Mujahedin emphasised, the imperialists would be tempted to repeat their 1953 performance.[111]

In August the Mujahedin kept silent when armed gangs attacked the Fedayeen headquarters, and they avoided challenging IRP candidates in the 1979 elections for the Assembly of Experts.

After the occupation of the American Embassy, the left became even less critical of Khomeini than before. Khomeini:

> was able to split the left opposition completely. Khomeini now declared that all problems arising in the factories, among women and among national minorities were due to US imperialism. It was US imperialism that was fighting the government in Kurdistan, in Tabriz, in Torkamansahra and in Khuzistan. Women opposing Islamic laws were US and Zionist agents. Workers resisting *shoras* were imperialist agents.
>
> The Tudeh party fell in behind Khomeini's argument and backed his line. The biggest left organisations – the Fedayeen, the Mujahedin and the Paykar – also broke away from the struggle, abandoning the militant workers, the women and the national minorities, among whom they had some significant presence.[112]

The Tudeh (pro-Russian Communist) Party and the majority of the Fedayeen continued to support Khomeini until he had fully consolidated his power in 1982, whereupon he turned on them.

As time went on, the left compounded one mistake with another. While the majority of the Fedayeen dropped all criticism of the regime after the takeover of the US Embassy, the People's Mujahedin eventually moved in the opposite direction, coming out in open opposition to the regime by the end of 1980 (after the regime's attack on its supporters in the universities). But its guerrilla strategy then led it to play straight into the regime's hands by joining with Bani Sadr to launch a direct struggle for power which was not rooted at all in the day-to-day struggles of the mass of people. When mass demonstrations failed to bring the regime down, its leaders fled into exile, while its underground activists launched armed attacks on key figures in the regime: "The bombing of the IRP's headquarters in June 1981, which resulted in the death of Ayatollah Beheshti [IRP chairman] and many other leaders and cadres of the IRP, provided the *ulama* [i.e. clergy] with the excuse to unleash a reign of terror against the opposition unheard of in contemporary Iranian history".[113]

The left was uniting with a representative of the established bourgeoisie in a campaign of assassinations directed against figures who the mass of people saw as playing an anti-imperialist role. It was hardly surprising that the impoverished petty-bourgeois and lumpen supporters of the IRP identified with its leaders in the onslaught against the left. These leaders found it easy to portray the left as working hand in hand with imperialist opponents of the revolution – an argument which gained even greater credibility a couple of years later when the People's Mujahedin joined in the onslaught against Iran waged by the Iraqi army.

In fact, the Mujahedin was displaying all the faults which characterise the radical new petty bourgeoisie in many third world countries, whether it is organised in Islamist, Maoist or nationalist parties. It sees the political struggle as dependent upon a minority acting as a "vanguard" in isolation from the struggle of the masses. The battle for power is reduced to the armed coup on the one hand and the alliance with existing bourgeois forces on the other. With "leadership" such as this, it is not surprising that the most radical workers were not able to build the militant struggles in individual factories into a movement capable of uniting behind it the mass of urban poor and peasants, and so left a vacuum which the IRP was able to fill.

Not all the left were as bad as the Mujahedin, the Fedayeen majority or the Tudeh Party. But these constituted the major forces to which those radicalised by the revolutionary experience looked. Their failings were a very important factor in allowing the Khomeini group to retain the initiative and to rebuild a weakened state into a powerful instrument capable of the most bloody repression.

Finally, even those on the left who did not make mistakes on the scale of the Mujahedin, Fedayeen and Tudeh Party made mistakes of their own. They had all been brought up on Stalinist or Maoist traditions which made them search for a "progressive" section of the bourgeoisie or petty bourgeoisie to lead the struggle. If they decided a certain movement was of the "progressive" or "anti-imperialist" petty-bourgeoisie, then they would dampen down any criticism. If, on the other hand, they decided a certain movement was not of the "progressive petty bourgeoisie", then they concluded it could never, ever engage in any conflict with imperialism. They had no understanding that again and again in third world countries bourgeois and petty-bourgeois leaders who are pro-capitalist and extremely reactionary in their social attitudes have, despite themselves, been drawn into conflicts with imperialism. This was, for instance, true of Kemal Ataturk in Turkey, of Grivas and Makarios in Cyprus, of Kenyatta in Kenya, of Nehru and Gandhi in India, and most recently of Saddam Hussein in Iraq. This has often given them a popularity with those they are intent on exploiting and oppressing.

The left cannot undercut that either by extolling them as "progressive, anti-imperialist" heroes, or by pretending that the confrontation with imperialism does not matter. Instead the left has at all costs to preserve its own political independence, insisting on public criticism of such figures both for their domestic policies and for their inevitable failings in the struggle with imperialism, while making it clear that we want imperialism to be defeated much more than they do.

Unfortunately, virtually the whole of the Iranian left flipflopped from one mistaken position to another, so that they ended up taking a neutral stand in the final months of the first Gulf War when the US fleet intervened directly to tilt the balance against Iran. They did not understand that there were ways of taking an anti-imperialist stance that would have strengthened the fight against the Iranian regime at home (denouncing the refusal of the regime to make the rich pay for the war, criticising the barbaric and futile "human wave" tactics of sending lightly armed infantry into frontal attacks on heavily defended Iraqi positions, condemning the failure to put forward a programme that would arouse the Iraqi workers and minorities to rise against Saddam Hussein, denouncing the call for war reparations as making the Iraqi people pay for their rulers crimes, and so on). Instead, they adopted a position which cut them off from anyone in Iran who remembered what imperialism had done to the country in the past and who could see that it would do so again if it got the chance.

The victory of Khomeini's forces in Iran was not, then, inevitable, and neither does it prove that Islamism is a uniquely reactionary force against which the left must be prepared to unite with the devil (or rather, the Great Satan) of imperialism and its local allies. It merely confirms that, in the absence of independent working class leadership, revolutionary upheaval can give way to more than one form of the restabilisation of bourgeois rule under a repressive, authoritarian, one-party state. The secret ingredient in this process was not the allegedly "medieval" character of Islam, but the vacuum created by the failure of the socialist organisations to give leadership to an inexperienced but very combative working class.

The contradictions of Islamism: Sudan

Iran is not the only country in which Islamists have exercised power. In the last few years the Sudanese Islamic Brotherhood, the *Ikhwan al*

Muslimin, has become the decisive influence in a military government through the National Islamic Front (NIF).

The Sudanese Brotherhood began in the 1940s as an offshoot of Banna's Muslim Brotherhood in Egypt, but took on a life of its own with its own doctrines, after the crushing of the parent organisation by Nasser in the 1950s. The organisation originated in Khartoum University, where it battled with the Communists for influence over the students. This led to its first leadership emphasising the radical elements in Islamism. But in the 1960s a new leadership, under Hassan al-Turabi, succeeded in widening the base of the organisation, adding thousands of newcomers to its 2,000 hardcore members. "The membership also witnessed a significant diversification by the involvement of *ulama*, mosque imams, merchants, Sufi leaders and others, although the proportion of nonmodern educated elements remained small in the active membership".[114] In the 1980s it grew further, aided by the emergence (under state encouragement) of an "Islamic" financial sector: "The employment policy of the Islamic Bank, which favoured religious people, was helpful to *Ikhwan*." The Islamic institutions led to "the evolution of a totally new class of businessmen who became rich overnight" and "opened up avenues of economic mobility for many who would otherwise have been, at most, higher civil servants". The Brotherhood did not own the Islamic banks – they were financed by a combination of Saudi money and local capital. But it exerted enormous power by its ability "to influence loans and other advances to customers".[115] This translated itself into support for the Brotherhood among some of the new rich and within the state machine itself: "The movement continued to be based on a hard core of activists, mostly modern educated professionals, but a significant contingent of businessmen (or professionals turned executives) started to acquire prominence".[116]

In the 1986 elections after the overthrow of the Nimeiry dictatorship the Brotherhood's front, the NIF, won only 18.5 percent of the total vote, most votes going to the traditional parties. But it picked up no fewer than 23 out of 28 of the seats elected by university graduates only, and it soon became clear it had enough support among a section of the urban middle classes and businessmen to be the natural ally of key figures in the armed forces. A coup in 1989 gave power to General Bashir, but effective power seemed to be in the hands of the NIF. And since then Khartoum has become one of the centres of the international Islamist movement, a pole of attraction to rival Tehran and Riyadh for the activists.

Yet the Sudanese Brotherhood's rise to power has not been an easy one. It has repeatedly come close to losing many members and much of its support. And its tenure in power is not likely to be secure.

Turabi has sought to build the Brotherhood's influence when his rivals have been in government by agitating among the students, the middle class and, to some extent, the workers – but he has then seized every chance of participating in government himself so as to increase the Brotherhood's influence within the hierarchies of the state. This he first did in the early 1960s. The Brotherhood's agitation among students helped precipitate the October 1964 revolution of students, middle class professionals and workers. It then used its position in the new government to dampen down the wave of radicalisation and to push for the banning of the Communists – so winning to it some of the conservative privileged groups.

It followed the same manoeuvre again after a military coup put General Gaafar al-Nimeiry in power in May 1969. He repressed the Brotherhood along with the traditional parties for a period. But its spell in opposition allowed it to rebuild some of the popular support it had lost while in government, taking the lead in agitation over student conditions and leading an unsuccessful student rising against the regime in 1973. Then in the late 1970s it seized on an offer from Nimeiry of "National Reconciliation" to join his regime, with Turabi becoming attorney general "in charge of the review of laws to make them conform to the sharia".[117] It was during this time that it used the development of the Islamic financial sector to get roots among the owners of capital. It was also during this period that it began to win over certain army officers.

Yet these manoeuvres created continual tensions within the Brotherhood and repeatedly threatened its wider base of support. The original cadres of the Brotherhood from the early 1950s were not at all happy with its leader's cultivation of sections of the traditional elite and of the new rich. Turabi's methods did not seem at all to fit the original notion of an Islamic vanguard which they had held as radical students in the 1940s. He seemed, to them, to be watering down Islamic ideas in order to gain respectability – especially when he set out to recruit women, supported them having the vote and produced a pamphlet asserting that "genuine" Islam should give them the same rights as men.[118] To the dissidents it seemed that he was simply out to pander to the secular middle classes. On top of this Nimeiry was someone who was notorious for his non-Islamic behaviour – particularly his drinking. A group of older members preferred the radicalism of someone like

Qutb, and finally split away to form an organisation of their own linked to the Egyptian Muslim Brotherhood.[119]

Collaboration with an increasingly unpopular regime began to undercut the Brotherhood's wider support. The early 1980s saw a growing wave of popular agitation against Nimeiry, with student demonstrations in 1981-82, a strike by rail workers in 1982, mutinies by southern troops in 1983 followed by strikes of judges and doctors. Through this period the Brotherhood became the only force outside the regime itself supporting Nimeiry, and began to fear being destroyed alongside the dictator when he eventually fell.

Then Nimeiry took a last gamble. He announced the immediate introduction of the sharia into law. The Brotherhood had no choice but to throw their weight behind him. For more than 30 years the "return to the sharia" had been their answer to all of Sudan's problems. It was the single, simple slogan which connected their brand of reform with the Islamic traditions of the mass of people outside the urban middle class. And so they began agitation to support implementation of the sharia, in the face of resistance from the judges and much of the legal system. A million people joined a Brotherhood demonstration for an international conference on the implementation of the sharia, and Brotherhood members helped man the special sharia courts set up by Nimeiry.

This increased the Brotherhood's pull among certain traditionalist circles, especially when the courts began to pick upon certain prominent people and expose their corruption. And the new power it exercised increased its attraction to those in the state machine looking for promotion. But while making the Brotherhood popular among some traditionalist sections of the population and more influential among those who ran the state, the measures also massively increased resentment against them elsewhere. It upset those who were secularist or supporters of non-Islamic religions (the majority of the population in the south of the country) without being, in reality, able to improve the conditions of the Islamic masses. The myth of the sharia was that of a new legal system which would end all injustices. But this could not be brought about by any reform that was merely a legal reform, and least of all one introduced by a corrupt and unpopular regime. So all the new law really meant was a resort to sharia punishments, the hudud – amputation for theft, stoning for adultery, and so on.

In the 1960s the Brotherhood had been able to build itself among the urban intelligentsia in part because it downplayed this aspect of the sharia. The Islamic orthodoxy accepted by Turabi was to "skirt the issue by insisting the hudud was only applicable in an ideal Islamic society from which want had been completely banished".[120] Now, however, the most tangible evidence that the sharia was changing the legal system became the use of such punishments, and Turabi did a 180-degree turn, attacking those who claimed you could not impose morality on people by legislation".[121]

Associated with resentment against the sharia courts was resentment against the Islamic financial sector. This had enabled some members of the middle class to move upwards into important business sectors. But it necessarily left many, many more disappointed:

> Resentment was created in the business community and among thousands of aspirants who believed the main reason they were deprived of the benefits of the new system was Ikhwan favouritism... In the end, allegations about Ikhwan's abuse of the Islamic banking system were the single most damaging liability that emerged from the Nimeiry era and discredited them in the eyes of large sections of the population.[122]

Finally, the Brotherhood's alliance with Nimeiry over the sharia forced it to excuse everything else he did, at a time when there was a growing agitation against him. Even though Nimeiry, under US pressure, finally moved against the Brotherhood just before a popular rising overthrew him, it was too late for the Brotherhood to be identified in any sense with the revolution.

It survived, to take greater power than ever into its hands within four years, because it offered to those army officers who had finally turned against Nimeiry something no one else had – thousands of active members prepared to back them in their bitter civil war against non-Muslim rebels in the south of the country and in their repression of discontent in the towns of the north. The coalition of secular forces that had led the uprising against Nimeiry were paralysed by their opposed class interests, unable either to focus the discontent into a movement for a complete transformation of society, including massive redistribution of wealth and the granting of self-determination to the south, or to crush it. This allowed the Brotherhood increasingly to offer itself to the army officers as the only force capable of imposing stability, showing its strength visibly by organising a large demonstration against any concessions to the southern rebels. So it was that in 1989 when the military seized power once more, in order to pre-empt a proposed peace agreement between the government and the rebels, it connived with the Brotherhood.

In power, however, the Brotherhood has known only one answer to the problems that face the regime – increasingly severe repression wrapped in religious terminology. In March 1991 the sharia was reintroduced together with the hudud punishments. The war in the south has now been matched by repression against other non-Arab communities, including the Fur and the Nuba, despite Turabi's claims, when in opposition, to oppose any form of Islam based on Arab chauvinism. Typical of the repression against those who oppose the war in the south were the death sentences handed out two years ago to a group of people in Dafur for "inciting war against the state and possessing weapons". One man was sentenced to be hanged and then his body to be publicly crucified.[123] In the run-up to elections in trade union and professional bodies there were reports of intimidation, arrests and torture.[124] Even some of the traditionalists who supported the campaign of Islamisation are now on the receiving end of repression. The regime has been tightening its grip on Sufi sects "whose sermons are believed to be nurturing popular discontent",[125] and most people blame the regime and the Brotherhood for a bomb attack on a Sufi mosque earlier this year which killed 16 people.

Repression has not, however, provided more than temporary stability to the regime. There were a series of riots in the towns two years ago as a result of shortages and price increases. Initial gestures of defiance to the IMF have been followed by an Economic Salvation Programme based upon "economic liberation" which "involves many policies previously advocated by the fund",[126] leading to new negotiations with the IMF. This has led to a sharp decline in living standards, further discontent and further riots.

Meanwhile, the regime is isolated internationally from the other major Islamic regimes: the Brotherhood fell out with Iran by lining up against it in the first Gulf War, and with Saudi Arabia by supporting Iraq in the second Gulf War. Presumably because of this it has tried to present itself as a pole of attraction to Islamists elsewhere who are disaffected with these two countries and with the Egyptian Muslim Brotherhood – even though Turabi's own policies have been, for 30 years, a long way from the radicalism these Islamist groups espouse.

Yet the Sudanese Brotherhood itself is under enormous pressure. "There are rumours that the NIF might split in two, with the zealots being sidelined and the relatively more moderate faction joining the conservative wings of the Umma Party and the DUP [the two main traditional parties]. There are divisions between the NIF's older generation who are prepared to accommodate with the secular parties and the younger and uncompromising zealots".[127]

One final point is worth making about Sudan. The rise of the Brotherhood to power there has not been because of any magic powers on its own part. Rather the cause lies in the failure of other political forces to provide the way out of the progressively deeper impasse in the country. In the 1950s and the 1960s the Communist Party was a stronger force than the Brotherhood. It had competed with the Brotherhood for influence among the students and built up a following among urban trade unionists. But in 1964 and 1969 it chose to use this influence, not to present a revolutionary programme for change, but to enter non-revolutionary governments, which then turned on it once it had calmed down the wave of popular agitation. It was, in particular, its support for Nimeiry in his first years that gave the Brotherhood the chance to take the lead in university agitation and undercut the Communists' base.

Conclusions

It has been a mistake on the part of socialists to see Islamist movements either as automatically reactionary and "fascist" or as automatically "anti-imperialist" and "progressive". Radical Islamism, with its project of reconstituting society on the model established by Mohammed in 7th century Arabia, is, in fact, a "utopia" emanating from an impoverished section of the new middle class. As with any "petty-bourgeois utopia"[128], its supporters are, in practice, faced with a choice between heroic but futile attempts to impose it in opposition to those who run existing society, or compromising with them, providing an ideological veneer to continuing oppression and exploitation. It is this which leads inevitably to splits between a radical, terrorist wing of Islamism on the one hand, and a reformist wing on the others. It is also this which leads some of the radicals to switch from using arms to try to bring about a society without "oppressors" to using them to impose "Islamic" forms of behaviour on individuals.

Socialists cannot regard petty-bourgeois utopians as our prime enemies. They are not responsible for the system of international capitalism, the subjection of thousands of millions of people to the blind drive to accumulate, the pillaging of whole continents by the banks, or the machinations that have produced a succession of horrific wars since the proclamation of the "new world order". They were not responsible for the horrors of the first Gulf War, which began with an attempt by Saddam Hussein to do a favour for the US and the Gulf sheikhdoms, and ended with direct US intervention on Iraq's side. They were not to blame for the carnage in Lebanon, where the Falangist onslaught, the Syrian intervention against the left and the Israeli invasion created the conditions which bred militant Shiism. They were not to blame for the second Gulf War, with the "precision bombing" of Baghdad hospitals and the slaughter of 80,000 people as they fled from Kuwait to Basra. Poverty, misery, persecution, suppression of human rights, would exist in countries like Egypt and Algeria even if the Islamists disappeared tomorrow.

For these reasons socialists cannot support the state against the Islamists. Those who do so, on the grounds that the Islamists threaten secular values, merely make it easier for the Islamists to portray the left as part of an "infidel", "secularist" conspiracy of the "oppressors" against the most impoverished sections of society. They repeat the mistakes made by the left in Algeria and Egypt when they praised regimes that were doing nothing for the mass of people as "progressive" – mistakes that enabled the Islamists to grow. And they forget that any support the state gives to secularist values is only contingent: when it suits it, it will do a deal with the more conservative of the Islamists to impose bits of the sharia – especially the bits which inflict harsh punishment on people – in return for ditching the radicals with their belief in challenging oppression. This is what happened in Pakistan under Zia and the Sudan under Nimeiry, and it is apparently what the Clinton administration has been advising the Algerian generals to do.

But socialists cannot give support to the Islamists either. That would be to call for the swapping of one form of oppression for another, to react to the violence of the state by abandoning the defence of ethnic and religious minorities, women and gays, to collude in scapegoating that makes it possible for capitalist exploitation to continue unchecked providing it takes "Islamic" forms. It would be to abandon the goal of independent socialist politics, based on workers in struggle organising all the oppressed and exploited behind them, for a tail-ending of a petty-bourgeois utopianism which cannot even succeed in its own terms.

The Islamists are not our allies. They are representatives of a class which seeks to influence the working class, and which, insofar as it succeeds, pulls workers either in the direction of futile and disastrous adventurism or in the direction of a reactionary capitulation to the existing system – or often to the first followed by the second.

But this does not mean we can simply take an abstentionist, dismissive attitude to the Islamists. They grow on the soil of very large social groups that suffer under existing society, and whose feeling of revolt could be tapped for progressive purposes, providing a lead came from a rising level of workers' struggle. And even short of such a rise in the struggle, many of the individuals attracted to radical versions of Islamism can be influenced by socialists – provided socialists combine complete political independence from all forms of Islamism with a willingness to seize opportunities to draw individual Islamists into genuinely radical forms of struggle alongside them.

Radical Islamism is full of contradictions. The petty bourgeoisie is always pulled in two directions – towards radical rebellion against existing society and towards compromise with it. And so Islamism is always caught between rebelling in order to bring about a complete resurrection of the Islamic community, and compromising in order to impose Islamic "reforms". These contradictions inevitably express themselves in the most bitter, often violent, conflicts within and between Islamist groups.

Those who treat Islamism as a uniquely reactionary monolith forget that there were conflicts between the different Islamists over the attitude they should take when Saudi Arabia and Iran were on opposite sides during the first Gulf War. There were the arguments that led the FIS in Algeria to break with its Saudi backers, or Islamists in Turkey to organise pro-Iraqi demonstrations from Saudi-financed mosques during the second Gulf War. There are the bitter armed battles which wage between the rival Islamist armies in Afghanistan. Today there are arguments within the Hamas organisation among Palestinians about whether or not they should compromise with Arafat's rump Palestinian administration – and therefore indirectly with Israel – in return for its implementing Islamic laws. Such differences in the attitude necessarily arise once "reformist" Islam does deals with existing states that are integrated into the world system. For each of these states is in rivalry with the others, and each of them strikes its own deals with the dominant imperialisms.

Similar differences are bound to arise every time there is a rise in the level of workers' struggle. Those who finance the Islamist organisations will want to end such struggle, if not break it. Some of the radical young Islamists will instinctively support the struggle. The leaders of the organisations will be stuck in the middle, muttering about the need of the employers to show charity and the workers forbearance.

Finally, the very development of capitalism itself forces the Islamist leaders to do ideological somersaults whenever they get close to power. They counterpose "Islamic" to "Western values". But most so-called

Western values are not rooted in some mythical European culture, but arise out of the development of capitalism over the last two centuries. Thus a century and a half ago the dominant attitude among the English middle class to sexuality was remarkably similar to that preached by the Islamic revivalists today (sex outside of marriage was forbidden, women were not supposed to bare even their ankles, illegitimacy was a taint people could not live down), and women had fewer rights in some respects than most versions of Islam grant them today (inheritance was to the eldest son only, while Islam gives the daughter half the son's portion; there was no right at all to divorce, while Islam grants women that right in very restricted circumstances). What changed English attitudes was not something inbuilt into the Western psyche or any alleged "Judeo-Christian values", but the impact of developing capitalism – the way in which its need for women's labour power forced it to change certain attitudes and, more importantly, put women in a situation where they could demand even greater changes.

That is why even in countries where the Catholic church used to be immensely strong, like Ireland, Italy, Poland and Spain, it has had to accept, reluctantly, a diminution in its influence. The countries where Islam is the state religion cannot immunise themselves from the pressure for similar changes, however hard they try.

This is shown by the experience of Iranian Islamic Republic. Despite all the propaganda about women's main role being as mothers and wives and all the pressure to drive them out of certain professions like the law, the proportion of women in the workforce has grown slightly and they continue to make up 28 percent of government employees, the same as at the time of the revolution.[129] Against this background, the regime has had to shift its stance on birth control, with 23 percent of women using contraceptives,[130] and on occasions to relax the strict enforcement of the veil. Although women are denied equal rights with men when it comes to divorce and family law, they retain the vote (there are two women MPs), attend school, get a quota of places in university in all disciplines and are encouraged to study medicine and to receive military training.[131] As Abrahamian notes of Khomeini:

> His closest disciples often mocked the "traditionalists" for being "old fashioned". They accused them of obsessing over ritual purity; preventing their daughters from going to school; insisting that young girls should be veiled even when no men were present; denouncing such intellectual pursuits as art, music and chess playing; and, worst of all, refusing to take advantage of newspapers, radios and televisions.[132]

None of this should really be surprising. Those who run Iranian capitalism and the Iranian state cannot dispense with female labour power in key sections of the economy. And those sections of the petty bourgeoisie who have formed the backbone of the IRP started sending their daughters to university and to seek employment in the 1970s precisely because they wanted the extra salaries – to enlarge the family income and to make their daughters more marriageable. They have not been willing in the 1980s to write these off in the interests of religious piety.

Islamism cannot freeze economic and therefore social development any more than any other ideology can. And therefore again and again tensions will arise within it and find expression in bitter ideological disputes between its proponents.

The Islamist youth are usually intelligent and articulate products of modern society. They read books and newspapers and watch televisions, and so know all the divisions and clashes within their own movements. However much they may close ranks when faced with "secularists", whether from the left or from the bourgeoisie, they will argue furiously with each other – just as the pro-Russian and pro-Chinese wings of the apparently monolithic world Stalinist movement did 30 years ago. And these arguments will begin to create secret doubts in the minds of at least some of them.

Socialists can take advantage of these contradictions to begin to make some of the more radical Islamists question their allegiance to its ideas and organisations – but only if we can establish independent organisations of our own, which are not identified with either the Islamists or the state.

On some issues we will find ourselves on the same side as the Islamists against imperialism and the state. This was true, for instance, in many countries during the second Gulf War. It should be true in countries like France or Britain when it comes to combating racism. Where the Islamists are in opposition, our rule should be, "with the Islamists sometimes, with the state never".

But even then we continue to disagree with the Islamists on basic issues. We are for the right to criticise religion as well as the right to practise it. We are for the right not to wear the veil as well as the right of young women in racist countries like France to wear it if they so wish. We are against discrimination against Arab speakers by big business in countries like Algeria – but we are also against discrimination against the Berber speakers and those sections of workers and the lower middle class who have grown up speaking French. Above all, we are against any action which sets one section of the exploited and oppressed against another section on the grounds of religion or ethnic origin. And that means that as well as defending Islamists against the state we will also be involved in defending women, gays, Berbers or Copts against some Islamists.

When we do find ourselves on the same side as the Islamists, part of our job is to argue strongly with them, to challenge them – and not just on their organisations' attitude to women and minorities, but also on the fundamental question of whether what is needed is charity from the rich or an overthrow of existing class relations.

The left has made two mistakes in relation to the Islamists in the past. The first has been to write them off as fascists, with whom we have nothing in common. The second has been to see them as "progressives" who must not be criticised. These mistakes have jointly played a part in helping the Islamists to grow at the expense of the left in much of the Middle East. The need is for a different approach that sees Islamism as the product of a deep social crisis which it can do nothing to resolve, and which fights to win some of the young people who support it to a very different, independent, revolutionary socialist perspective.

First published in *International Socialism* 64, autumn 1994

Notes

Women's liberation and revolutionary socialism

1. This assertion caused more argument among people to whom I showed the first draft of this article than virtually any other. It was suggested to me that anthropology had, in fact, shown that male supremacy and women's oppression exists in all societies. People like Godelier were quoted, to the effect that "however meagre our historical and anthropological sources...it seems at the moment reasonable to suppose that men have so far dominated power in the last analysis... In all societies, including the most egalitarian, there is a power hierarchy, with the top places occupied by men."

Such assertions have been very much the established wisdom in academic anthropology for the last half century and more, and because anthropology, like its related discipline of sociology, claims the status of a "science" – even many Marxists have accepted them. But in fact anthropology is little more than the collation of the observations of visitors from advanced capitalist societies to various precapitalist societies. And these observations cannot be taken at face value as providing information about what society was like before the development of classes for two reasons.

(i) The anthropologists who made these observations almost all shared the prejudices of the capitalist societies from which they came. They viewed the "primitive" peoples through these stereotypes, interpreting their behaviour in terms which would be used to explain behaviour under capitalism. (For an excellent account of the prejudices of anthropologists like Malinowski, Evans-Pritchard and Lévi-Strauss, see Karen Sacks, *Sisters and Wives*, pp.1-67).

Thus anthropologists have seen the nuclear family as an invariant feature of all societies where couples produce children – even though the role the man-woman relationship plays in, say, hunter-gatherer societies is markedly different to that played in modern Britain. Again, Lévi-Strauss and his followers refer to "exchange of women" in societies where women from one kin lineage marry into another kin lineage which they go and live with. But the term "exchange" can only be used in its normal sense when you are talking about what goes on in commodity-producing societies. Giving and taking has a quite different significance in non-commodity-producing societies. The point is proved by existence of societies where the men have to marry out of their own kin lineage and to live with their wives' families; does this amount to "exchange of men"? But Lévi-Strauss virtually ignores these. As Eleanor Leacock has pointed out, of the 400 or so pages of his *Elementary Structures of Kinship*, only one and a half pages deal with such "matrilineal-matrilocal" societies – and these pages contain four basic factual errors!

These crudities have not stopped people like Godelier accepting Lévi-Strauss's arguments at their face value. But then this former colleague of Althusser's believes that he himself disproved the labour theory of value by showing it did not apply in a precapitalist society, the Baruya of New Guinea (see "Salt currency and the circulation of commodities among the

Baruya of New Guinea", in *Studies in Economic Anthropology*, 1971; for a feminist critique of Godelier, see Barbara Bradby, "Male Rationality in Economies', in *Critique of Anthropology*, double issue 9-10, 1977).

(ii) Present-day "primitive" societies cannot be simply equated with the societies all human beings lived in until the growth of class societies about 6,000 years ago. They have all changed themselves over the years since, in part due to the impact of the class societies they have come into contact with. Some at least of them are "pseudo-archaic" – they were once at a higher stage of social development, and were caused by circumstance to regress, for instance from being agricultural societies to gathering and hunting. (For examples, see Lévi-Strauss, "The concept of Archaism in Anthropology", in *Structural Anthropology*, p.101 *et seq.*)

You cannot see existing hunter-gatherer societies as identical with the societies of the old stone age. As Rayna Rapp Reiter has noted:

"We cannot literally interpret the lives of existing foraging peoples – such as the !Kung bushmen of the Kalahari, the Eskimos, the Australian Aborigines – as exhibits and replications of processes we speculate to have occurred in the Paeleolithic. Neither can we assume that the decimated, marginalised existence of peoples pushed to the edges of their environment by thousands of years of penetration will exhibit original characteristics". (*"The search for origins"*, in *Critique of Anthropology*, **op. cit.**).

The expansion of capitalism into a world system has reshaped all the precapitalist societies it has come in contact with. Pre-class gatherer-hunter and horticultural societies today are involved to a greater or lesser degree in transactions with the wider capitalist world (buying and selling goods, supplying labour and so on). These have produced fundamental changes in their internal organisation. And at the same time outside agencies (governments, churches, school systems) have attempted to impose on them "civilised" norms of conduct (like capitalist property laws, capitalist forms of marriage, and so on). It is not surprising under such circumstances if many features of the oppression of women to be found in "advanced" societies are also found in surviving "primitive" societies.

The way the impact of capitalism has distorted the features of these societies; makes it all the easier for anthropologists to apply social categories from our society (like "hierarchy", "subordination", "power" and 'the nuclear family') to them. Eleanor Leacock has attempted to show how this has happened in two significant cases, that of the Montagnais-Naskapi and Iroquois Indians of North America. (See "Women's Status in Egalitarian Societies", *Current Anthropology*, vol.10 no.2, June 1978, and *Myths of Male Dominance*, New York 1981).

These obscuring influences have been so great as to make some authorities doubt whether we can know anything about what the situation of women was like before the rise of class societies (see the comments of Judith K. Brown on Leacock's argument in *Women's Status etc.*, *op. cit.*).

But we can learn something: that there have been societies in which women's position vis-à-vis men is so different to that in our own (or any other class society) as to rule out any talk of the oppression of women in these societies. Thus in hunter-gatherer societies like the Montagnais-Naskapi, the !Kung and the Mbuti, women participated in all the major decision making until fairly recently, controlled their own sexuality, and led an existence based upon mutual cooperation with other women and men. (See Leacock, *op. cit.*).

There is much debate about other hunter-gatherer societies. While Eleanor Leacock will argue women once had a high status in all such societies, others like Ernestine Friedl differentiate between hunter-gatherer societies dependent upon gathering (mainly done by women) for the great bulk of their food and those, like the Eskimos and Australian Aborigines, in which hunting (mainly done by men) is important. In the latter, she says, men tend to be more highly esteemed than women. (*Women and Men, An Anthropologist's View*, New York 1975).

Yet Friedl also points out that even in those hunter gatherer societies where men's activities are evaluated more highly than women's, nothing exists comparable to the systematic oppression of women you get in class societies. Women always play some part in major decision making and are free to leave husbands they cannot abide any more.

"Individual decisions are possible for both men and women with respect to their daily routines ... Men and women alike are free to decide how they will spend each day: whether to go hunting or gathering, and with whom."

What applies to hunter-gatherer societies also applies to some 'horticultural' societies ie societies where crops are cultivated using the hoe and digging stick rather than the plough. Although almost all these are today integrated into the world capitalist system, producing crops for sale, in the recent past women played a role in them quite at variance with that in class societies.

The most famous case is that of the Iroquois. From the time of Morgan (whose *Ancient Society* inspired Engels to write the *Origins of the Family*) observers have been struck by the influence women exercised over decision making.

Women seem to have a relatively high standing in all 'matrilineal-matrilocal' societies (i.e. societies where kinship is reckoned along the female line, and men go to live with their wives' kin). It is wrong to describe these societies as 'matriarchies' (the point is that neither sex exercises the same sort of dominance in them as men do in patriarchal societies), but they do stand in sharp contrast to societies where power is monopolised by a minority of males.

Archaeologists like Gordon Childe (see *Man Makes Himself* and *What Happened in History*) have argued, following Engels, that all societies were like this at the beginnings of the period of 'barbarism' (the term used by Morgan, Engels and Childe for the early horticultural societies). Karen Sacks has distinguished between a lower stage of these societies where 'communal production' prevailed, and a higher stage in which control was in the hands of 'kin corporations'. Here leadership was with 'big men', who would increase their control by marrying several women and getting control of their labour. But even at this stage, Sacks argues, women themselves gained as they got older, becoming 'controllers of labour and productive means, as sisters who control their brothers' children's lineage affairs and as mothers who control their own children and their children's productive means...' And women themselves could, on occasion become the 'big men', even entering into marriage as 'husbands' to other women so as to get control of their labour (op. cit., pp.117-121).

So even in these societies, women's position was quite different from complete subordination you find once you get the division into classes.

Eleanor Leacock cannot be faulted when she writes:

"Such patrilineal elements as might have existed in horticultural society would be altogether different from patrilineality as it developed in societies with class structures, private property and political organisation... The patriarchal family, in which the individual male could have complete control over a household of wives, children and servants or slaves, has no parallel in the pre-political world."

(For further discussion on these issues see: Carolyn Fluer-Lobban, "A Marxist Reappraisal of Matriarchy", in *Current Anthropology*, June 1979; Ala Singer, "Marriage Payments and the Exchange of People", *Man* 8:80-92, 1971; Martin K. White, "The Status of Women in Pre-Industrial Society", *Critique of Anthropology*, special issue 8-9, 1977. Evelyn Reed's *Women's Evolution* is better known than these sources. But despite the fact that she is very good at tearing apart the way anthropologists have imposed capitalist categories on pre-class societies, she ruins her case by wild speculation based upon a jumbling together of misunderstood data from a range of widely differing societies. For a full critique of her, see Eleanor Leacock's review in *Myths of Male Dominance*, op. cit.).

2. See Engels, *The Origins of the Family, Private Property and the State*. For attempts to update Engels, see Leacock, op. cit., Sacks op. cit., Fluer-Lobban, op. cit.

3. This is essentially the argument of Engels which was taken up by Gordon Childe, op. cit. Some recent anthropological evidence tends to back this view. Thus Aberle notes that: "In general matriliny is associated with horticulture, in the absence of major activities carried on and coordinated by males, of the type of cattle raising or extensive public works. It tends to disappear with plough culture, and vanish with industrialisation." (David F. Aberle, *Matrilineal Descent in Cross Cultural Perspective*, in David Schneider and Kathleen Gough (eds), Matrilineal Kinship.) Although matriliny cannot be identified with matriarchy, it does tend to exist in societies where women have a relatively high standing. The same view is implicit in Sacks' work. She stresses the way the subordination of women coincides with the 'subversion' of 'kin corporations' by the rise of classes and the state. Leacock emphasises the development of commodity production as undermining kin lineages which give influence to women. This explains what happens in some cases – but not in others, where classes develop through the differentiation out of a layer of state officials or a priestly ruling group, without the development of commodity production.

4. This was true of medieval Europe, see, for example, Susan Cahn, "Patriarchal Ideology and the Rise of Capitalism", *International Socialism* 2:5.

5. Where women control trade, as in some West African societies, they have a very high status. And the same has, from time to time, been true of parts of Europe. Walter Scott noted the high status of women (which he called 'gyneocracy') in some Scottish fishing villages, where they sold the fish and controlled the family incomes because their husbands were mostly at sea. ("Them that sell the goods guide the purse, them that guide the purse rule the house", *The Antiquary*, London 1907, p.304.) Feminist anthropologists have more recently noticed similar phenomenon in some villages in Galicia in north west Spain.

6. For the working class family in the mid 19th century, see Ivy Pinchbeck, *Women Workers and the Industrial Revolution*, and Janet Humphries, *The Persistence of the Working Class Family*.

7. See Ruth Milkman, "Women's work and economic crisis: Some lessons of the Great Depression", *Review of Radical Political Economy*, 1976.

8. See the section, "Labour Power in the Long Boom", in my book *Explaining the Crisis*, London 1984.

9. For an excellent account of the women's movements in Britain and the US, see Tony Cliff, *Class Struggle and Women's Liberation*, London 1984.

10. As Karen Sacks has noted, these feminists share the presuppositions of male supremacists who see the subordination as an 'innate' feature of all societies: "Much feminist thought has been shaped by...an innatist approach... Accepting the innatist world view, but altering it to accommodate equal rights for

women by exempting women from blameworthy traits...underlies some contemporary radical feminism.' (Sacks, op. cit., p.25).
11. See her article in *New Statesman*, January 1980, reprinted in the collection, *No Turning Back*.
12. Lindsey German, "Theories of Patriarchy", *International Socialism* 2:12.
13. Heidi Hartmann, "The Unhappy Marriage of Marxism and Feminism", *Capital and Class*, no.8, Summer 1979.
14. I use the word 'reproduce' in the narrowest sense here, meaning the physical reproduction of the individual members of the species. There is a wider sense, of course, meaning the reproduction of the fully socialised adult, capable of carrying through necessary social tasks. There are certainly changes from society to society in the way this is accomplished. But that does not alter the fundamental argument. For these changes are a result of other social factors, and do not develop according to a dynamic of their own. The same applies to the way in which in certain societies women control their own fertility through periods of sexual abstinence etc. For a discussion on these matters, see Friedl, op. cit., p.8.
15. *Women's Consciousness, Men's World*, Harmondsworth 1973, pp.59-66. Despite its misplaced theory, this book is far better than almost anything produced by the remnants of the women's movement today (including the present writings of Sheila Rowbotham).
16. *International Socialism* 1:100.
17. *International Socialism* 1:68.
18. *International Socialism* 2:1.
19. *International Socialism* 2:3.
20. *International Socialism* 1:104.
21. For an account of the effects of these defeats on the women's movement, see Cliff, op. cit.
22. The great mistake of revolutionary socialists in the early 1970s was not to understand this, and to assume that, regardless of the state of the class struggle, women revolutionaries could only organise women workers. This was the error Kath Ennis slipped into her excellent 1973 article, and it was repeated in my own piece in the Socialist Workers Party Internal Bulletin in February 1979, "*Women's Voice*, Some of the Issues at Stake". We should have paid more attention to the experience of the great women revolutionaries!
23. "Socialism needs feminism", *International Socialism* 2:14.
24. Lindsey German, op. cit.
25. Review of *Brothers* in *Socialist Review*, no.61.
26. The formulae quoted here are from Barbara Winslow's pamphlet, *Revolutionary Feminism*, and from Joan Smith's various articles. But they weren't the only attempts to square the circle in the 1970s – see the discussion over the issue of *Women's Voice* in the *IS* and Socialist Workers Party Internal Bulletins of 1977-82.

Party and Class

1. Leon trotsky, *The First Five Years of the Communist International*, Vol.1, New York 1977; p.98.
2. Karl Kautsky, *The Erfurt Program*, Chicago 1910, p.8.
3. ibid.
4. ibid., p.43.
5. ibid., p.85.
6. ibid., p.198.
7. ibid., p.198.
8. ibid., p.198.
9. Karl Kautsky, *The Road to Power*, Chicago 1910, p.24.
10. See Karl Kautsky, *Social Revolution*, p.45. Also Carl E. Schorske, *German Social Democracy 1905-1917*, Cambridge, Mass 1955, p.115.
11. Karl Kautsky, op. cit., p.47.
12. Karl Kautsky, *The Erfurt Program*, p.188.
13. ibid., p.188.
14. ibid., p.189.
15. Karl Kautsky, *The Road to Power*, p.95.
16. Leon Trotsky in Nashe Slovo, 17th October 1915. Quoted in Leon Trotsky, *Permanent Revolution*, London 1962, p.254.
17. e.g. Although these are referred to as "organs of revolutionary rule", in an important article on perspectives in *Sotsial-democrat* in 1915, they receive very little emphasis – references to them accounting for only five or six lines in an article of four pages.
18. cf. both *Organisational Questions of the Russian Social-Democracy* (published by her epigones under the title *Leninism or Marxism*), and *The Mass Strike, the Political Party and the Trade Unions*.
19. Rosa Luxemburg, *Leninism or Marxism*, Ann Arbor, 1962, p.82. Interesting enough, Lenin, in his reply, does not concentrate on the question of centralism in general, but on factual mistakes and distinctions in Luxemburg's article.
20. Rosa Luxemburg, *The Mass Strike*, p.57.
21. ibid.
22. Rosa Luxemburg, *Leninism or Marxism*, p.92.
23. ibid., p.85.
24. ibid., p.94.
25. ibid., p.93.
26. ibid., p.93.
27. Leon Trotsky, "Results and Prospects" (1906), in *The Permanent Revolution and Results and Prospects*, London 1962, p.246.
28. Quoted in I. Deutscher, *The Prophet Armed*, London 1954, pp.92-93.
29. ibid.
30. Unfortunately there is no room here to deal with Trotsky's later discussion on these matters.
31. V.I. Lenin, "Revolutionary Days" (31 January 1905) in *Collected Works*, Vol.VIII, p.104.
32. V.I. Lenin, *Revolutionary Army and Revolutionary Government*, ibid., p.564.
33. Quoted in Raya Dunyevskaya, *Marxism and Freedom*, New York 1958, p.182.
34. ibid.
35. V I Lenin, "The Collapse of the

Second International", in *Collected Works*, Vol.XXI, pp.257-8.
36. Leon Trotsky, *History of the Russian Revolution*, London 1965, p.981.
37. V.I. Lenin, *Collected Works*, Vol. XXVI, pp.57-58.
38. V.I. Lenin, *What is to be Done?*, Moscow, n.d., p.25.
39. q.v. V.I. Lenin, *Collected Works*, Vol.VII, p.263.
40. V.I. Lenin, *Collected Works*, Vol. VI, p.491.
41. ibid., Vol.VII, p.265.
42. ibid., Vol.VIII, p.157.
43. ibid., Vol.VIII, p.155.
44. Antonio Gramsci, *Passato e Presente*, Turin 1951, p.55.
45. Antonio Gramsci, *The Modern Prince and other Essays*, London 1957, p.59.
46. ibid., pp.66-67.
47. Antonio Gramsci, *Il Materialismo storico e la filosofia di Benedetto Croce*, Turin 1948, p.38.
48. Antonio Gramsci, *The Modern Prince and other Essays*, p.67.
49. V.I. Lenin, *Collected Works*, Vol. VII, p.117.
50. ibid., Vol.VIII, p.145.
51. ibid., Vol.VIII, p.196.
52. V.I. Lenin, *What is to be Done?*, p.11.
53. V.I. Lenin, *Collected Works*, Vol. VIII, p.154.
54. ibid., Vol.VII, p.116.
55. For a naïve statement of the opposite view see "An Open Letter to IS Comrades", *Solidarity Special*, September 1968.
56. Some confusion creeps into the argument because of the experience of Russia after 1918. The Important point, however, is that it is not the *form* of the party that produces party as opposed to Soviet rule, but the decimation of the working class. (See C Harman, "How the Revolution Was Lost", *IS* 1:30) Cliff makes this point in "Trotsky on Substitutionism", but for some unaccountable reason, also says that in Trotsky's early claims that Lenin's theory of organisation was "substitutionist", "one can see his prophetic genius, his capacity for looking ahead, to bring into a unified system every facet of life".
57. T Cliff, *Rosa Luxemburg*, London 1959, p.54. Here again Cliff's desire to honour a great revolutionary seems to overcome a genuine scientific evaluation.

How the revolution was lost

1. Trotsky, *The Russian Revolution*, p.72.
2. Martov to Axelrod, 19 November 1917, quoted in Israel Getzler, *Martov*, Cambridge, 1967.
3. Israel Getzler, op. cit., p.183.
4. Ibid., p.199.
5. See Trotsky, *Hue and Cry over Kronstadt*.
6. Quoted in Max Shachtman, *The Struggle for the New Course*, New York, 1943, p.150.
7. Lenin, *Collected Works*, Vol.32, p.24.
8. See Lenin's response to Riazanov's demand that the habit of different groups within the Party putting forward "platforms" be prohibited: "We cannot deprive the Party and the members of the central committee of the right to appeal to the Party in the event of disagreement on fundamental issues. I cannot imagine how we can do such a thing!" Lenin, *Collected Works*, Vol.32, p.261.
9. Appendix to E.H. Carr, *The Interregnum*, p.369.
10. Quoted in Shachtman, op. cit., p.172.
11. E.H. Carr, op. cit., p.39.
12. Ibid.
13. Cf. Stalin, *Lenin and Leninism*, Russian ed. 1924, p40: "Can the final victory of socialism in one country be attained without the joint efforts of the proletariats of several advanced countries? No, this is impossible." (Cited by Trotsky, *The Third International after Lenin*, p.36.)
14. We do not deal here with the earlier oppositions, e.g. the Workers' Opposition and the Democratic Centralists. Although these arose as a response to the early bureaucratisation and degeneration of the revolution, they were also partly a utopian reaction against objective reality as such (i.e. the real strength of the peasants and the real weakness of the working class). What survived and mattered in the Workers' Opposition eventually became part of the Left Opposition, while its leaders, Kollontai and Shlyapnikov, capitulated to Stalin.

The Eastern Bloc

1. Martov to Axelrod, 19 November 1917. Quoted in G Getzler, *Martov* (Cambridge, 1967).
2. L Trotsky, *History of the Russian Revolution* (London, 1965), p812.
3. S M Schwartz, quoted in Max Schachtman, *The Bureaucratic Revolution* (NewYork, 1962), p69.
4. Trotsky, op cit, p55.
5. For details see Chris Harman, *How the Revolution was Lost*, London, 1969 (to a certain extent this whole section in a précis of that pamphlet), and T Cliff, 'Trotsky on Substitutionism', *International Socialism* 2.
6. Trotsky, op cit, p1147.
7. Lenin, *Collected Works*, quoted in M Lewin, *Lenin's Last Struggle* (London, 1969), p12.
8. Over the question of Georgia, see Lewin, op cit, pp91 et seq.
9. At the 17th Party Congress in 1934 40% of the delegates had been in the party since before the revolution and 80% from 1919 or earlier; by the 18th Congress of 1939 only 5% had been members since before the revolution and only 14% since before 1919. Again in 1939, although it has been estimated that something approaching 200,000 members of the Bolshevik Party of 1918 must have been alive, there were only 20,000 or 10% of them left in the party. See Schwartz, op cit.
10. For fuller information of this whole section see T Cliff, *Russia: A Marxist Analysis* (London, nd), chapter 1.
11. For a full account of wage bargaining in these years see E H Carr and R W Davies, *Foundations of a Planned Economy*, vol 1 (London, 1969), chapter 19.
12. See one estimate in Cliff, op cit, p36.
13. See E H Carr and R W Davies, op cit, sections A and B, also I Deutscher, *Stalin* (London, 1961), pp328 et seq.
14. E H Carr and R W Davies, op cit, p563.
15. Regulations quoted in Cliff, op cit, p25.
16. For estimates see Cliff, ibid. For a differing estimate for 1928-33 see E H Carr and R W Davies, op cit, p342.
17. Cliff, op cit, pp30-1.
18. E H Carr and R W Davies, op cit, pxii.
19. Ibid, p277.
20. Kuibishev, quoted in ibid, p277.
21. Ibid, p313.
22. Cf Cliff, op cit, p33.
23. Stalin, "Problems of Leninism", p356, quoted in Deutscher, op cit, p328.
24. Stalin, quoted in Carr and Davies, op cit, p327.
25. Marx, *Capital* I, pp648-52.
26. Although Engels writes quite clearly "until 1865 the stock-exchange was still a secondary element in the capitalist system" ('Afterword', *Capital* III, p884).
27. For such an identification see E Mandel, *The Inconsistencies of State Capitalism* (London, 1969).
28. Again, see ibid.
29. K Marx, *Fondements de la Critique de l'Economie Politique* (Paris, 1967), p147.
30. Ibid.

31. Marx, *Capital* I, p592.
32. Ibid.
33. R Hilferding, *Das Finanzkapital* (Vienna, 1910), p286.
34. Lenin, *Works* (in Russian), vol XXV, p51, quoted in T Cliff, op cit, p153.
35. Trade between the USSR and the West, although increasing, accounts for only about 1% of total Russian production. This has, however, been of decisive importance at certain points in Russian development. For instance, the drop in the price of agricultural produce on the world market in the early 1930s forced Stalin to sell much greater quantities abroad in order to buy machinery needed for industrialisation, and therefore to extract a much greater surplus through 'collectivisation' than would otherwise have been the case. With some other Stalinist states the direct pressure of trade competition has been greater - eg Czechoslovakia, Cuba.
36. Marx, *1844 Manuscripts* (Moscow, 1959), p70.
37. In the early 1930s Stalin seems to have needed the personnel of the various oppositions in so far as he lacked capable, educated, manpower. It was not until after 1930 that these began to be produced by the Stalinised educational system. But between 1928 and 1940 the number of specialists increased 77-fold. This made it possible for Stalin to eliminate physically some of his opponents and make others politically impotent.
38. Above all by Trotsky.
39. Also in North Korea, but not in Yugoslavia or Albania, where the regimes resulted from purely indigenous movements.
40. See, eg, Harrison Salisbury, *The Coming War between Russia and China* (London, 1969), or, for a much earlier account, Ygael Gluckstein, *Mao's China* (London, 1957), pp394 et seq, and for Yugoslavia, M Djilas, *Conversations with Stalin* (London, 1967), pp11-14.
41. Many supporters of Trotsky who took seriously his definition of the Stalinist parties as "counter-revolutionary".
42. Even at world market prices less developed countries are exploited by more developed ones. See, for instance, Popovic, *On Economic Relations Between Socialist Countries* (London, 1950).
43. Borba, quoted in Y Gluckstein, *Stalin's Satellites in Europe* (London, 1952), p245. For further details see H Draper, "The Economic Drive Behind Tito", *New International*, October 1948, and A Sayer, "Between East and West", *International Socialism* 41,
44. *Peking Review*, 8 May 1964. Marxists in the West had been aware of this exploitative relationship long before - see Gluckstein, op cit, p167.
45. *Financy*, SSR 28/69.
46. For the best account of this period see J Kuron and K Modzelewski, "A Revolutionary Socialist Manifesto (An Open Letter to the Party)", *IS*, London, nd. For documents from 1956 to 1957 see J J Marie and B Nagy (eds), *Pologne-Hongrie, 1956* (Paris, 1966).
47. For example the "virgin lands scheme" and the organisation of industry through Sovnarkhozy.
48. The only one to refuse to confess, Krestinsky, relented under pressure.
49. Op cit, p54.
50. For a much longer account of Trotsky's analysis see Cliff op cit.
51. Trotsky, *The Workers' State and the Question of Thermidor and Bonapartism* (London, nd), p8.
52. Trotsky, *The Revolution Betrayed* (London, 1957), p59.
53. Trotsky, *The Workers' State and the Question of Thermidor and Bonapartism*, p19.

54. Trotsky, *The Revolution Betrayed*, op cit.
55. Trotsky, *The Class Nature of the Soviet State* (London, 1967), p13.
56. Trotsky, *The Workers' State and the Question of Thermidor and Bonapartism*, p4.
57. Trotsky, *The Revolution Betrayed*, p235.
58. Trotsky, *Problems of the Development of the USSR* (New York, 1931), p36.
59. Trotsky, *The Revolution Betrayed*, p249.
60. Ibid.
61. Trotsky, *USSR and The War*.

The crisis of bourgeois economics

1. See P.A. Samuelson, *Economics*, R.G. Lipsey's *Introduction to positive economics*.
2. N.G. Mankiw and D. Romer, *New Keynesian Economics*, Vol.1: *Imperfect competition and sticky prices*.
3. A. Crosland, *The future of socialism* (London 1956), and J. Strachey, *Contemporary Capitalism* (London 1956).
4. The marginalists differed among themselves over a number of points, but shared a common general approach. For a reasonably accessible discussion on their differences see E. Roll, *A History of Economic Thought* (London 1962), chapters 8 and 9, and for critical overview of their ideas, M. Dobb, *Political Economy and Capitalism* (London 1946), ch.1 and 5. There is a marginalist attack on Marxism with a reply by one of the most eminent Marxist economists in E. Boehm Bawerk and R. Hilferding, *Karl Marx and the Close of His System*. Nicolai Bukharin's *Economic Theory of the Leisure Classes* is a brilliant demolition of the 'Austrian' version of marginalism, but is sometimes difficult to follow since it assumes an acquaintance with Boehm Bawerk's own formulations, which are somewhat different to the version of marginalism usually taught in Britain.
5. The so called 'transformation problem' which Marx takes up in Volume III of *Capital*.
6. J.S. Mill, *Principles of Political Economy* (London 1911), p.339.
7. See, for example, A. Marshall, *Principles of Economics* (8th edition, London 1936), pp.140-141. See also the very useful discussion on this in M. Dobb, *Political economy and capitalism*, op. cit.
8. For fuller summaries of Boehm Bawerk's views see M. Dobb, op. cit., pp.151-156; E. Roll, op. cit., pp.404-406.
9. Some marginalists qualified this by recognising that costs of production could fall as output increased up to a certain point – but then insisted that at a later point they would inevitably start rising, so that the cost curve would be J shaped. This was one of the problems that worried Marshall. But none of them let the problem disturb their basic view that there was only one equilibrium point – or that if the cost of production of a certain commodity rose (for instance because of union pressure on wages or a minimum wage law) this would lead to a fall in the demand for it.
10. See L. Walras, *Elements of Pure Economics* (1889, trans. London 1954), but don't try reading it unless you want to get an insufferable headache.
11. A. Marshall, *The Principles of Economics*, op. cit., p.62.
12. Ibid., p.109.
13. Ibid., p.368.
14. L. Walras, op. cit., p.242.
15. Ibid., p.317.
16. Ibid., p.381.
17. Pareto's phraseology, adopted by most other neo-classical

18. economists. The formulation of one English populariser of marginalism, Lord Robbins.
19. Von Mises, quoted in M. Dobb, op. cit., p.177.
20. Julian Bell, quoted in R. Skidelsky, *John Maynard Keynes*, Vol.2, (London 1994), p.515.
21. Ibid. p.341.
22. J.M. Keynes, *General Theory of Employment, Interest and Money*, (London 1960), p.19-20.
23. Ibid., p.28.
24. Quoted in R. Skidelsky, op. cit., p.535.
25. J.M. Keynes, op. cit., p.156.
26. Ibid., p.159.
27. Ibid., p.33.
28. Ibid., pp.261-262.
29. Ibid., p.262.
30. Ibid., p.267.
31. Ibid., p.504.
32. Ibid., p.12.
33. Ibid., pp.8-9 and p.14.
34. A. Leijonhufvud, *On Keynesian Economics* (London 1968), p.37.
35. P. Mattick, *Marx and Keynes* (Boston 1969), p.7.
36. J.M. Keynes, op. cit., p.264.
37. J. Robinson, *Further Contributions to Economics* (Oxford 1980), p.34.
38. Ibid.
39. Quoted in R. Skidelsky, op. cit., p.477-478.
40. J.M. Keynes, op. cit., p.376.
41. Ibid., p.377.
42. Ibid., p.164.
43. Ibid., p.164.
44. Ibid., p.378.
45. Ibid., p.378.
46. Ibid., p.378.
47. Quoted in R. Skidelsky, op. cit., p.515.
48. Ibid., p.517.
49. Ibid., p.521.
50. Ibid., p.511.
51. J. Strachey, op. cit., p.235.
52. Ibid., p.239.
53. Ibid., p.353.
54. R. Skidelsky, op. cit., pp.188-189.
55. Ibid., p.193.
56. Ibid., p.191.
57. Ibid., p.394.
58. Ibid., p.394.
59. Quoted in ibid., p.394.
60. Ibid., p.394.
61. Quoted in ibid., p.488.
62. Ibid., p.605.
63. Summary of article, with quotes, in R. Skidelsky, op. cit., p.629.
64. Estimate given in R. Middleton, *Towards the Managed Economy* (London 1985), pp.176-177.
65. Estimated by S. Glynn and P.G.A. Howells, quoted in ibid., p.178.
66. These points are well made in G. Pilling, *The Crisis of Keynesian Economics* (London 1986), pp.50-51
67. Arndt, quoted in R. Middleton, op. cit., p.179.
68. Kindelberger, *The World in Depression 1929-34* (London 1973), p.272.
69. A.D.H. Kaplan, *The Liquidation of War Production* (New York 1944), p.91.
70. Quoted by R. Skidelsky, op. cit., p.491.
71. P. Mattick, op. cit., pp.161-163. For a very similar mistaken analysis see D. Yaffe and R. Schmiede, *State Expenditure and the Marxian Theory of Crisis* (London 1972).
72. R.C.O. Matthews, *Why has Britain had full employment since the war?*, Economic Journal, September 1968, p.556.
73. Ibid., p.556.
74. Ibid., p.560.
75. Figures in J. Tomlinson, *The "Economics of Politics" and Public Expenditure: a Critique*, in Economy and society, vol.10, no.4, November 1981, p.390.
76. Budget deficit figures given in Independent on Sunday, 19 November 1995.
77. See, for example, M.C. Sawyer, *The Economics of Michal Kalecki* (London 1985), pp.78-79 and p.132.
78. Ibid., p.132.
79. Ibid., p.135.
80. Summary of Sraffa's letter to

Keynes cited in R. Skidelsky, op. cit., p.290.
81. J.H. Hicks, *Value and Capital* (Oxford 1939), p.82.
82. Quoted in R. Skidelsky, op. cit., p.604.
83. Ibid., p.290.
84. 'Two sets of incommensurable collections of miscellaneous objects cannot in themselves provide the material for a quantitative analysis', J.M. Keynes, op. cit., p.39.
85. Ibid.
86. Although it is Malthus's version, in which the wage is the measure of value, rather than Ricardo's version, in which it is labour performed.
87. J.M. Keynes, op. cit., p.41.
88. Ibid., pp.213-214.
89. Quoted in R. Skidelsky, op. cit., p.603.
90. J.M. Keynes, op. cit., p.149.
91. Ibid., p.157.
92. Ibid., p.164.
93. Ibid., p.162.
94. Ibid., p.161-162.
95. Ibid., p.219.
96. Ibid., p.219.
97. Ibid., p.221. For Keynes's account of the 'marginal efficiency of capital' and its tendency to 'diminish' see pp.135-136 and p.214.
98. J.M. Keynes, op. cit., p.221.
99. J. Robinson, op. cit., p.13.
100. R. Skidelsky, op. cit., p.811.
101. Ibid., p.613.
102. J. Robinson, op. cit., p.34.
103. Ibid.
104. Ibid.
105. A. Leijonhufvud, op. cit., pp.6-7.
106. Ibid., p.37.
107. For a readily accessible discussion on the similarities and differences between the 'orthodox' Keynesians and the monetarists, see J.A. Trevithick, *Inflation, a guide to the crisis in economics* (Harmondsworth 1977).
108. J. Robinson, op. cit., p.36.
109. Quoted in *The Guardian*, 15 September 1994.
110. English translations are to be found in the first articles in M. Kalecki, *Selected essays on the dynamics of the capitalist economy* (Cambridge 1971).
111. See the account by Rosa Luxemburg of how different economists dealt with the issue, in her *The Accumulation of Capital* (London 1963).
112. M.C. Sawyer, op. cit., p.162. Sawyer does, however, point to a work by Kalecki in 1945 which seems to imply a theory of the falling rate of profit – see pp.85-86.
113. Ibid., p.64. Kalecki's account shows considerable similarities with two other theories of long term stagnation. See J. Steindl, *Maturity and Stagnation in American Capitalism* (London 1953) and P. Baran and P. Sweezy, *Monopoly Capital* (London 1973). For a critique of their views, see my *Explaining the Crisis* (London 1984), pp.148-154.
114. M.C. Sawyer, op. cit., p.136.
115. J. Robinson, op. cit., pp.148-149.
116. For a series of articles discussing this problem and the failure of different marginalist economists to deal with it, see J. Eatwell, M. Millgate and P. Newman, (eds.), *Capital Theory* (London 1990). The article by L.L. Pasinetti and R. Scazzieri, *Capital Theory: Paradoxes*, pp.136-147, provides a useful and relatively accessible summary of the arguments.
117. Joan Robinson, *Economic Philosophy* (London, 1962), p.68.
118. J. Robinson's discussion on this question can be found in *Further Contributions to Economics*, op. cit., p.21. A long, rather opaque, account of the argument is to be found in P. Garegnani, *Quantity of Capital*, in J. Eatwell et al., op. cit., pp.1-78.
119. P. Garegnani, *Quantity of capital*, ibid., pp.70-71.

120. J. Robinson, *Further Contributions to Economics*, op. cit., p.101.
121. Ibid., p.xii.
122. Quoted in J.P. Potier, *Piero Sraffa* (London, 1991), p.73.
123. J. Robinson, *Further Contributions to Economics*, op. cit., footnote on p.188.
124. This was the argument of I. Steedman, *Marx after Sraffa* (London 1977) and was more or less accepted by Joan Robinson, who had always rejected the labour theory of value and the falling rate of profit, see J. Robinson, op. cit.
125. A. Glyn and B. Sutcliffe, *British Capitalism, Workers and the Profits Squeeze* (Harmondsworth 1972). For the 'neo-Ricardian' arguments against Marx that led to this conclusion, see, for example, A Glyn in *The Bulletin of Socialist Economists*, Autumn 1973.
126. J.R. Schumpeter, *Capitalism, Socialism and Democracy* (London 1950), p.103.
127. Ibid., p.104.
128. Ibid., pp.77 and 93.
129. Ibid., and J.K. Gailbraith, op. cit. J. Robinson, *Further Contributions to Economics*, op. cit., p.56.
130. N.G. Mankiw & D. Romer, op. cit., p.1.
131. M. Skousen, *Free Market Response to Keynesian Economics*, in M. Skousen (ed.), *Dissent on Keynes*, p.30.
132. J.B. Egger, *Fiscal stimulus*, in ibid.
133. Quoted favourably in H.H. Happe, *The Misesian case against Keynes*, in ibid., p.200.
134. Quoted (unfavourably) in *Interview with Kenneth Arrow*, in C.R. Feiwel (ed.), *Joan Robinson and Modern Economics* (London 1989), p.164.
135. See R.W. Garrison, *Is Milton Friedman a Keynesian?*, in M. Skousen (ed.), op. cit., p.131.
136. H.H. Happe, op. cit., p.209.
137. J. Robinson, *Further Contributions to Economics*, op. cit., p.2.
138. R. Blackburn, *Fin de siécle: socialism after the crash*, New Left Review 185, Jan-Feb 1991.
139. From *The Constitution of Liberty* (London 1970), reprinted in F.A. Hayek, *A Tiger by the Tail* (London 1972), pp.73 and 84. See also his 1967 argument along the same lines in the same collection, p.64.
140. See, for instance, ibid., p.56: 'The main cause of recurrent waves of unemployment', he wrote, was that 'during each boom period a greater quantity of factors of production is drawn into the capital goods industry than can be permanently employed there'. This is 'the cause of the collapse which has regularly followed a boom'.
141. J. Tomlinson, *Hayek and the Market* (London 1990), pp.2, 8.
142. F.A. Hayek, *Competition as a discovery process*, in C. Nishijypama and K.R. Leube, *The Essential Hayek*, p.259
143. F.A. Hayek, *Profits, interest and investment* (London 1939), p.138.
144. F.A. Hayek, *Prices and Production* (London 1935), p.103-4.
145. F. Hayek, *Competition as a discovery process*, in C. Nishijypama & K.R. Leube, op. cit. p.255.
146. Ibid., p.258.
147. Letter to *The Guardian*, 29 February 1996.
148. F.A. Hayek, *The pure theory of capital* (London 1941), section reprinted in F.A. Hayek, *A tiger by the tail*, op. cit., p.3.
149. Ibid., p.3.
150. A passage from 1967, reprinted in ibid., p.57.
151. F.A. Hayek, *Competition as a discovery process*, in C. Nishijypama & K.R. Leube, op. cit., p.262.

152. *Ibid.*, p.262.
153. J. Tomlinson, op. cit., p.110.
154. J.R. Schumpeter, op. cit., p.66. Schumpeter was pessimistic in that he thought the capitalist system he supported was doomed. But this was because he thought people would reject its harsh logic, not because of inbuilt economic contradictions.
155. See their two volume work, *New Keynesian Economics*.
156. J.E. Stiglitz, *Whither socialism?* (Cambridge 1995), p.x.
157. D. Card and A.B. Kreuger, *Myth and Measurement: the new economics of the minimum wage* (Princeton 1995).
158. W. Hutton, op. cit., pp.245-247.
159. B. Arthur, quoted in M. Mitchell Waldrop, *Complexity* (London 1994), p.139.
160. A. Medio, *Chaotic dynamics: theory and application to economics*, p.11.
161. P. Smith, *The Guardian*, 29 October 1990.
162. Interview with Kenneth J. Arrow, in G.R. Feiwel (ed.), *Joan Robinson and macroeconomic theory* (London 1989), pp.147-148
163. Ibid., pp.165 and 168.
164. P. Ormerod, *The Death of Economics* (London 1994).
165. O. Hart, *A model of imperfect competition with Keynesian features*, in N.G. Mankiw and D. Romer, op. cit., pp.337-338.
166. These are effectively the arguments of E. Stiglitz's *Whither Socialism?*, op. cit.
167. P. Ormerod, op. cit., p.207.
168. *The Guardian*, 29 February 1996.

Notes to Appendix:

1. As Robinson admits: 'The model presents a strictly one technique economy. In the system of equations, each input used up in one period is replaced in kind as production goes on. This entails the same technique is going to be used in the new period... Sraffa blurs the point by introducing changes into his self repeating story..' J. Robinson, *Further Contributions to Economics*, op. cit., p.65. Sungar Savron has argued that even with simple reproduction Sraffa's equations do not allow for any change in distribution between wages and profits, and so fail to fulfil Sraffa's own aim. See S. Savron, "On the Theoretical Consistency of Sraffa's Economics", *Capital and Class*, issue 7 (London, 1979).
2. Ibid., p.65.
3. Ibid., p.86.
4. For further details, see my two part article, "Where is capitalism going?", in *International Socialism 58* (Spring 1993) and *International Socialism 60* (Autumn 1993).

The rate of profit and the world today

1. This article is based on research for a forthcoming book on capitalism in the 21st century. I would appreciate suggestions and constructive criticism. [Published as *Zombie Capitalism* (Bookmarks, 2009)]
2. Marx, *Grundrisse* (Penguin, 1973), p.748.
3. Marx, *Capital* vol III (Moscow, 1962), pp.236-237.
4. Ibid.
5. Ibid, p.245.
6. The organic composition of capital was depicted algebraically by Marx by the formula c/v, where c = constant capital, and v = variable capital.
7. P Clarke, "Issues in the Analysis of Capital Formation and Productivity Growth", *Brookings Papers on Economic Activity*, volume 1979, number 2, p.427. See also the comment by M.N. Bailey, p.433-436. For a graph showing the long term rise of the capital-labour ration, see G Duménil and D Lévy, *The Economics of the Profit Rate* (Edward Elgar, 1993), p.274.
8. I Steedman, *Marx After Sraffa* (Verso, 1985), p.64; compare also pp.128-129.
9. For Marx's argument with a numerical example, see Marx, *Capital* vol I (Moscow, 1965), pp.316-317.
10. For more on this argument, with a simple numerical example of my own, see C Harman, *Explaining the Crisis: A Marxist Reappraisal* (Bookmarks, 1984), pp.29-30.
11. This point was made by Robin Murray in a reply to an attempt by Andrew Glyn to use a "corn model" to disprove the falling rate of profit (Murray, *CSE Bulletin*, spring 1973), and was taken up by Ben Fine and Lawrence Harris in *Rereading Capital* (Macmillan, 1979). It now stands at the centre of the arguments put forward by the "temporal single-system interpretation" of Alan Freeman and Andrew Kliman. See, for instance Freeman and Carchedi, *Marx and Non-equilibrium Economics* (Edgar Elgar, 1996), and A Kliman, *Reclaiming Marx's Capital: A Refutation of the Myth of Inconsistency* (Lexington, 2007).
12. B Fine and L Harris, *Rereading Capital* (Macmillan, 1979), p.64. The argument is also accepted by Andrew Kliman, see Kliman, op cit, pp.30-31.
13. See the figures in Harley, *Cotton Textiles and the Industrial Revolution Competing Models and Evidence of Prices and Profits*, Department of Economic, University of Western Ontario, May 2001.
14. R Allen, *Capital Accumulation, Technological Change, and the Distribution of Income during the British Industrial Revolution*, Department of Economics, Oxford University, 2005.
15. M Flamant and J Singer-Kérel, *Modern Economic Crises* (Barrie and Jenkins, 1970), p.18.
16. Hence Kidron's description of present day capitalism as "ageing capitalism", rather than the term

"late capitalism" popularised by Ernest Mandel.
17. The latter term is misleading, since it equates mass production methods of exploitation, rising consumer spending and state intervention in industry, as if someone set out to produce all three; rather than the logic of the concentration and centralisation of capital working itself out. The term "post-Fordism" is even more confusing, since mass production methods remain in many sectors of the economy, and there is everywhere a complex interaction between states and capitals.
18. Different measures of profit rates give slightly different pictures in these decades.
19. Mike Kidron ascribed this to the role of arms spending in his two books, *Western Capitalism Since the War* (Pelican, 1970), and *Capitalism and Theory* (Pluto, 1974), a view which I endorsed in *Explaining the Crisis*. More on this question later in this article.
20. Kidron, "The Wall Street Seizure", *International Socialism* 44, first series (July-August 1970), p.1.
21. Harman, "Arms, State Capitalism and the General Form of the Current Crisis", *International Socialism* 26 (spring 1982), p.83. This article was reprinted, with minor changes, as chapter three of *Explaining the Crisis*.
22. P Alemi and D Foley, *The Circuit of Capital, US Manufacturing and Non-financial Corporate Business Sectors, 1947-1993*, manuscript, September 1997.
23. Duménil and Lévy, *The Real and Financial Components of Profitability* (2005), p.11.
24. T Michl, "Why Is the Rate of Profit Still Falling?", *The Jerome Levy Economics Institute Working Paper number 7* (September 1988).
25. E Wolff, "What's Behind the Rise in Profitability in the US in the 1980s and 1990s?", *Cambridge Journal of Economics*, volume 27, number 4 (2003), pp.479-499.
26. Brenner, *The Economics of Global Turbulence* (Verso, 2006), p.7.
27. F Moseley, *The Rate of Profit and the Future of Capitalism*, May 1997.
28. G Duménil and D Lévy, "The Profit Rate: Where and How Much Did it Fall? Did It Recover? (USA 1948-1997)" (2005).
29. F Moseley, 1991, op cit, p.96.
30. K Mastroianni, *The 2006 Bankruptcy Yearbook & Almanac*, chapter 11 available from www.bankruptcydata.com/Ch11History.htm
31. J Stiglitz, *The Roaring Nineties: Why We're Paying the Price for the Greediest Decade in History* (Penguin, 2004).
32. G Dale, *Between State Capitalism and Globalisation* (Peter Lang, 2004), p.327.
33. See Harman, "Poland: Crisis of State Capitalism", *International Socialism* 93 and 94, first series (November/December 1976, January 1977), and "The Storm Breaks", *International Socialism* 46 (spring 1990).
34. It took repeated comments by Ken Muller to make me even begin to try to think this through.
35. "In a rare emotional appeal to the House of Representatives, Speaker Tip O'Neill brought a hush to the chamber as he recalled the dark days of the Great Depression and warned that failure to save Chrysler would result in worker layoffs large enough to trigger a new depression. Said he: 'We won't be able to dig ourselves out for the next ten years'." *Time* magazine, 31 December 1989.
36. O Leiva, "The World Economy and the US at the Beginning of the 21st Century", *Latin American Perspectives*, vol.134, no.1, 2007, p12.
37. See OECD, "Government Policies Towards Financial Markets" (1996), available from www.olis.

38. oecd.org/olis/1996doc.nsf/ See the chapter "Waste US: 1970" in Kidron, 1974, op cit. See also my discussion of this in *Explaining the Crisis*, op cit.
39. F Moseley, *The Falling Rate of Profit in the Post War United States Economy* (Macmillan, 1991), p.126. He mistakenly underestimates the amount of productive and unproductive labour by excluding the public sector from the capitalist economy, see p.35.
40. A Sheikh and E Tonak, *Measuring the Wealth of Nations* (Cambridge University Press, 1994), p.110.
41. S Mohun, "Distributive Shares in the US Economy, 1964-2001", *Cambridge Journal of Economics*, vol 30, no 3 (2006), figure 6.
42. Kidron, 1974, op cit, p.56.
43. Kidron, "Failing Growth and Rampant Costs: Two Ghosts in the Machine of Modern Capitalism", *International Socialism* 96 (Winter 2002), p.87.
44. However, Duménil and Lévy do not accept that unproductive expenditures necessarily lower the rate of profit. They contend that unproductive expenditures can help the rate of profit through the impact of increased managerial supervision on productivity. They claim this explains the rise in the rate of profit which occurred between the 1920s and the late 1940s. Their argument is doubly wrong. The most obvious cause of that rise was the destruction of capital in slump and war. And increased productivity in itself cannot increase the rate of profit, since its effect, once it takes place right across the system, is to lower the socially necessary labour required to produce, and hence the value of, each unit of output. Their position follows from their inversion of Marx's relationship between productivity and value, which in effect abandons the labour theory of value by denying it is possible to use values as a basis for prices. See my review of their *Capital Resurgent*, "Half-explaining the Crisis", *International Socialism* 108 (Autumn 2005).
45. F Moseley, 1991, op cit, p.104.
46. Shaikh and Tonak, op cit, p.124.
47. One fault with Moseley's analysis is that he does not see this, but looks for other factors to explain the rising level of waste.
48. It was a mistake on my part to use such a formulation in 1982 – although I think excusable as we faced only the second real recession my generation had experienced and did so a mere four years after the end of the first.
49. Leiva, op cit, p.11.
50. *Financial Times*, 5 September 2001.
51. *The Economist*, 23 June 2001.
52. Leiva, op cit, p.11.
53. Riley, op cit.
54. All figures on British profit rates are from Barell and Kirkby, "Prospects for the UK economy", *National Institute Economic Review*, April 2007.
55. O'Hara, op cit.
56. For much more on this, see Harman, "China's economy and Europe's crisis", *International Socialism 109* (Winter 2006).

The summer of 1981: a post-riot analysis

1. Ilene Melish, *Guardian*, 31 July 1981.
2. *Guardian*, 7 July 1981.
3. *Guardian*, ibid.
4. Reply to Questionnaire sent to SWP branches a fortnight after riots; Liverpool reply. In future these replies will simply be referred to as Questionnaire, Liverpool etc.
5. Questionnaire, Manchester.
6. Ibid.
7. *Financial Times*, 10 July 1981.
8. Questionnaire, Handsworth.
9. Questionnaire, Southall.
10. Questionnaire, Leeds.
11. Questionnaire, Bolton.
12. Questionnaire, Luton.
13. Questionnaire, Leicester.
14. Questionnaire, Nottingham.
15. Questionnaire, Hackney.
16. Questionnaire, Hull.
17. Questionnaire, Gloucester.
18. Questionnaire, Hull.
19. Questionnaire, Walthamstow.
20. Questionnaire, Woolwich.
21. Questionnaire, Handsworth.
22. Questionnaire, Southall.
23. See the chart of arrests and police injuries, *Socialist Worker*, 18 July 1981.
24. Bob Holton, *British Syndicalism 1910-14*, London 1976, pp.81-82.
25. Ibid., p.99.
26. Ibid., p.100.
27. Quoted ibid.
28. Ibid., p.100.
29. Max Beer, *History of British Socialism*, Vol.II, London 1940, p.260.
30. Gareth Stedman Jones, *Outcast London*, Harmondsworth 1976, pp.291-2. For other accounts see Beer, op. cit.; Yvonne Kapp, *Eleanor Marx*, Vol.II, New York 1976, pp.77-79; E.P. Thompson, *William Morris*, London 1977, p.486.
31. See quotations in Yvonne Kapp, op. cit.
32. Stedman Jones, op. cit., p.294.
33. Kapp, op. cit., pp.225-4.
34. Beer, op. cit., p.262.
35. Wal Hannington, *Unemployed Struggles*, London 1977, p.223.
36. Ibid, p.226.
37. All detail from Some Merseyside Militants by Tony Lane, in H.H. Hikins, ed. *Building the Union*, Liverpool 1973.
38. Ibid.
39. Hannington, op. cit., pp.248-9.
40. *Kerner Report* (The US National Advisory Committee on Civil Disorders, 1967).
41. Nathan Cohen, ed., *The Los Angeles Riots*, New York 1970, p.3.
42. *Kerner Report*, op. cit.
43. Ibid.
44. Joseph Boskin, *Urban Racial Violence*, Los Angeles 1969, p.59.
45. Bayard Rustin, quoted in Boskin, op. cit., p.105
46. F.J. Hacker, writing on Watts, quoted in Boskin, op. cit., p.90
47. *Newsweek*, 7 August 1967, reprinted in Boskin, op. cit., p.133. In Newark 21 of the 23 deaths were of blacks, (ibid., p.125), in Detroit 32 of the 40 deaths (ibid., p.133).
48. Cohen, op. cit., p.12.
49. *Newsweek*, op. cit.
50. Figures given by Baran & Sweezy, *Monopoly Capital*, Harmondsworth 1973, p.252.

51. Ibid, p.255.
52. *Kerner Report*, op. cit.
53. R.M. Egelson, quoted in A. Platt, *The Politics of Riot Commissions*, New York 1971, p.313.
54. *Kerner Report*, op. cit.
55. Tyrone, a black SWP member in Brixton, quoted in *Socialist Worker*, 18 April 1981.
56. Micky, another black SWP member in Brixton, interviewed in *Socialist Review* 1981:5.
57. Johnny Evans, *Socialist Worker*, 12 April 1980.
58. *Guardian*, 4 May 1981.
59. Questionnaire, Southall.
60. Questionnaire, Toxteth; see also Ilene Melish, op. cit.
61. *Guardian*, 19 August 1981.
62. Questionnaire, Wood Green.
63. Questionnaire, Handsworth.
64. Questionnaire, Woolwich.
65. Questionnaire, Leeds.
66. Questionnaire, Bolton.
67. Questionnaire, Halifax.
68. For details of all these trends, see Stedman Jones, op. cit., pp.19-159.
69. *Department of Employment Gazette*, August 1979, p.746.
70. Because of underregistration by women, the male figures give a better indication of average trends than do the figures for all unemployed.
71. Figures given in Friend and Metcalfe, *Slump City*, London 1981, p.118.
72. Quoted in ibid., p.118.
73. Quoted in *Guardian*, 1 July 1981.
74. Figures from *Department of Employment Gazette*, July 1981, table 2.5.
75. For details of the pattern of black employment, see The Runnymede Trust and the Radical Statistics Group, *Britain's Black Population* London 1980, pp.55-63; and Smith, *Racial Disadvantage in Britain*, Harmondsworth 1977, pp.65-95.
76. The most important conclusion of both accounts is that black people are more concentrated in manual work than white (about the same proportion being skilled manual workers, but a much lower proportion being in white collar jobs and a much higher proportion in semi-skilled and unskilled manual jobs), were twice as likely to work shifts and earnt an average of about 11% less in the case of men (although 'there are no such inequalities among women', possibly because women are already discriminated against because of their sex).
77. Smith, op. cit., p.68. What the Department of Employment call 'minority groups' are people from Africa, India, Pakistan, Bangladesh, the West Indies and 'other Commonwealth territories' and those with one or more parents from these places.
78. Ibid., p.69.
79. Runnymede Trust etc., op. cit., p.66.
80. *Department of Employment Gazette*, June 1981, table 2.17.
81. For instance, see Runnymede Trust etc., p.66.
82. Ibid., p.76.
83. Smith, op. cit., p.96.
84. Runnymede Trust etc., p.67.
85. *Guardian*, 7 July 1981.
86. Rex and Tomlinson, *Colonial Immigrants in a British City*, London 1979, p.217. Interestingly, the *Kerner Report* on the US riots of 1967 finds 'unemployment and underemployment' to be second in the list of black grievances, just behind police practice and ahead of inadequate housing.
87. For a dismissal as 'pure impressionism' of a claim that youth unemployment in Handsworth was "25 per cent" in the mid-70s, see Rex and Tomlinson, op. cit., p.235.
88. I don't intend here to go into the argument as to whether this is simply a response to economic hardship, or as some 'deviancy' sociologists argue, a sort of pre-

political protest against society – see for instance, Michael Pratt, *Mugging as a Social Problem*, Ken Pryce, *Endless Pressure*, Harmondsworth 1979.
89. What is surprising is that so far this only applies to Afro-Caribbean youth, not to Asian youth who commit less than average crime. According to police arrest figures (which will of course be distorted by police racism) in Lambeth in 1977, West Indians, who were 10% of the population, were responsible for 28% of robberies (but only 10% of shop lifting and 14% of burglaries) while Asians were responsible for less than 2% or robberies and 1% of burglaries.
90. For a much more prolonged discussion of this question, see Stuart Hall and others, *Policing the Crisis*, London 1978.
91. Figures from Pratt, op. cit., p.152.
92. Brown, *Shades of Grey*, quoted in Rex and Tomlinson, op. cit., p.234.
93. Rex and Tomlinson, op. cit.; for the small amounts robbed in 'muggings' see Pratt, op. cit.
94. *Memorandum to the Select Committee on Race Relations and Immigration*, quoted in Pratt, op. cit., p.135.
95. Quoted in Friends and Metcalfe, op. cit., p.150.
96. Reported in *Guardian*, 30 June 1981.
97. Interview in the *Leveller*, 21 August 1981.
98. Richmond, *Migration and Race Relations in an English City*, London 1973, p.81.
99. Rex and Tomlinson, op. cit., p.78.
100. Richmond, op. cit., p.188. Cf. also Pearson, *Race, Class and Political Activism*, Farnborough 1981, p.116.
101. Rex and Tomlinson, op. cit., pp.80 and 116.
102. *Guardian*, 7 July 1981
103. *Guardian*, 24 July 1981.
104. See, for instance, W.J. Wetherby, *Guardian*, 24 August 1981.
105. See, for instance, the otherwise excellent article by a university research worker in race relations, Ilene Melish, *Guardian*, 31 July 1981.
106. Rex and Tomlinson, op. cit., p.229.
107. Almost certainly, from the description of it, Highfields in Leicester.
108. Pearson, op. cit.
109. Ken Pryce, op cit., p.156
110. One of the defendants in the 1976 Leeds Bonfire trial, interviewed in *Race Today*, September 1976.
111. Rex and Tomlinson, op. cit., p.225.
112. *Race Today*, March 1978.
113. *Race Today*, Nov-Dec 1977.
114. *Race Today*, July-August 1978.
115. *Race Today*, November 1980.
116. Ibid., The argument has been taken up by those who should know better. Quoting copiously from interviews with black teenagers in *Race Today* (April 1975), Tony Bogues has insisted: 'Black youth have no interest in shit work. For them it is both lack of work and the nature of work. In other words, a rejection of the capitalist labour process ...' As total unemployment goes up: 'the tendency not to take part in the capitalist labour process is strengthened ...' from this it follows that black youth cannot 'accept the notion of "the right to work"'. The way to organise the 'rejection of the capitalist labour process' is not through workplace or unemployed struggles, but by defence campaigns over police harassment: 'with the increasing scale of harassment by the police, the Defence campaigns will become vehicles by which mass organisations of the black community can be built.' (*International Socialism*, old series, 101, Oct 1977).
117. This neither fits in with the findings of numerous surveys of black

youth – that the overwhelming majority are as interested in getting jobs as white youth – or with the experience of 'mass defence campaigns' which rarely involve large numbers of people for more than one or two demonstrations.
118. Bradford speech. *Race Today*, March 1978.
119. *Race Today*, Nov.-Dec. 1974.
120. Laurie and Sy Landy, *International Socialism* (old series) 48.
121. A particular feature of these is the demand for 'public inquiries' of one sort or another – see for instance *Black Voice*, vol.12, account of a meeting of the New Cross Massacre Action Committee where 'it was unanimously decided that an Independent International Commission of Inquiry would be set up ...'
122. *Race Today*, June 1978.
123. From a forthcoming paper on Black Nationalism.
124. Beer, op. cit., p.203.
125. Figures given in Pierre Frank, *Histoire de l'Internationale Communiste*, Paris 1979, vol. II, p.634.
126. I owe this information to Mike Millotte, who is working on a book on the history of Communism in Ireland.
127. *Guardian*, 19 August 1981.
128. Runnymede Trust etc., op. cit., p.60.
129. Smith, op. cit., pp.25 and 67.
130. Figures given in Hall and others, op. cit., p.341.
131. Rex and Tomlinson, op. cit.
132. Which is why it is mistaken as well as trite to denounce those socialists who insist on relating to industrial and lower grade white collar workers, for having 'stereotype of the class' as 'white and male' – that stereotype actually applies to the higher grade white collar layers from which most of those who repeat that denunciation usually come.

1. Thus a perceptive study of the Egyptian Muslim Brotherhood could conclude in 1969 that the attempt at the revival of the movement in the mid-1960s "was the predictable eruption of the continuing tensions caused by an ever dwindling activist fringe of individuals dedicated to an increasingly less relevant Muslim 'position' about society." R.P. Mitchell, *The Society of the Muslim Brothers* (London, 1969), p.vii.
2. Article in the *New Statesman* in 1979, quoted by Fred Halliday himself in "The Iranian Revolution and its Implications", *New Left Review*, 166 (November/ December 1987), p.36.
3. Interview with the Communist Movement of Algeria (MCA) in *Socialisme Internationale* (Paris, June 1990). The MCA itself no longer exists.
4. F. Halliday, op. cit., p.57.
5. For an account of the support given by different left organisations to the Islamists see P. Marshall, *Revolution and Counter Revolution in Iran* (London, 1988), pp.60-68 and pp.89-92; M. Moaddel, *Class, Politics and Ideology in the Iranian Revolution* (New York, 1993), pp.215-218; V. Moghadam, "False Roads in Iran", *New Left Review*, p.166.
6. Pamphlet quoted in R.P. Mitchell, op. cit., p.127.
7. A.S. Ahmed, *Discovering Islam* (New Delhi, 1990), pp.61-64.
8. For an account of Afghan Sufism, see O. Roy, *Islam and Resistance in Afghanistan* (Cambridge, 1990), pp.38-44. For Sufism in India and Pakistan, see A.S. Ahmed, op. cit., pp.90-98.
9. I. Khomeini, *Islam and Revolution* (Berkeley, 1981), quoted in A.S. Ahmed, op. cit. p.31.
10. O. Roy, op. cit., p5. A leading Islamist, Hassan al-Turabi, leader of the Sudanese Islamic Brotherhood, argues exactly the same, calling for an Islamicisation of society because "religion can become the most powerful motor of development", in *Le nouveau reveil de l'Islam, Liberation* (Paris, 5 August, 1994).
11. E. Abrahamian, *Khomeinism* (London, 1993), p.2.
12. Ibid.
13. *Who is responsible for violence?* in *l'Algerie par les Islamistes*, edited by M. Al Ahnaf, B. Botivewau and F. Fregosi (Paris, 1990), pp.132ff.
14. Ibid., p.31.
15. G. Kepel, *The Prophet and the Pharoah, Muslim Extremism in Egypt* (London, 1985), p.109.
16. See, for example, K. Pfeifer, *Agrarian Reform Under State Capitalism in Algeria* (Boulder, 1985), p.59; C Andersson, *Peasant or Proletarian?* (Stockholm, 1986), p.67; M. Raffinot and P. Jacquemot, *Le Capitalisme d'état Algerien* (Paris, 1977).
17. J.P. Entelis, *Algeria, the Institutionalised Revolution* (Boulder, 1986), p.76.
18. Ibid.

19. A. Rouadia, *Les Freres et la Mosque* (Paris, 1990), p.33.
20. O. Roy, op. cit., pp.88-90.
21. A. Rouadia, op. cit., p.82.
22. Ibid., p.78.
23. Ibid.
24. For an account of these events, see D. Hiro, *Islamic Fundamentalism* (London, 1989), p.97.
25. H.E. Chehabi, *Iranian Politics and Religious Modernism* (London, 1990), p.89.
26. E. Abrahamian, *The Iranian Mojahedin* (London, 1989), pp.107, 201, 214, 225-226.
27. M. Moaddel, op. cit., pp.224-238.
28. A. Bayat, *Workers and Revolution in Iran* (London, 1987), p.57.
29. A. Tabari, *Islam and the Struggle for Emancipation of Iranian Women*, in A. Tabari and N. Yeganeh, *In the Shadow of Islam: the Women's Movement in Iran*.
30. O. Roy, op. cit., pp.68-69.
31. M. Al-Ahnaf, B Botivewau and F. Fregosi, op. cit.
32. A. Rouadia, op. cit.
33. Ibid.
34. Ibid.
35. In 1989, of 250,000 who took exams, only 54,000 obtained the bac, ibid., p.137.
36. Ibid., p.146.
37. Ibid., p.147.
38. See R.P. Mitchell, op. cit., p.13.
39. See ibid., p.27.
40. Ibid., p.38.
41. M. Hussein, *Islamic Radicalism as a Political Protest Movement*, in N. Sa'dawi, S. Hitata, M. Hussein and S. Safwat, *Islamic Fundamentalism* (London, 1989).
42. Ibid.
43. S. Hitata, *East West Relations*, in N. Sa'dawi, S. Hitata, M. Hussein and S. Safwat, op. cit., p.26.
44. G. Kepel, op. cit., p.129.
45. Ibid., p.137.
46. Ibid., pp.143-44.
47. Ibid., p.85.
48. Ibid., p.95-96.
49. Ibid., p.149.
50. For an account of this period see, for example, A. Dabat and L. Lorenzano, *Conflicto Malvinense y Crisis Nacional* (Mexico, 1982), pp.46-8.
51. M. Al-Ahnaf, B. Botivewau and F. Fregosi, op. cit., p.34.
52. Phil Marshall's otherwise useful article, "Islamic Fundamentalism – Oppression and Revolution", in *International Socialism 40*, falls down precisely because it fails to distinguish between the anti-imperialism of bourgeois movements faced with colonialism and that of petty bourgeois movements facing independent capitalist states integrated into the world system. All his stress is on the role these movements can play as they "express the struggle against imperialism". This is to forget that the local state and the local bourgeoisie are usually the immediate agent of exploitation and oppression in the Third World today – something which some strands of radical Islamism do at least half recognise (as when Qutb describes states like Egypt as "non-Islamic").
53. It also fails to see that the petty bourgeoisie limitations of Islamist movements mean that their leaders, like those of movements like Peronism before them, often use rhetoric about "imperialism" to justify an eventual deal with the local state and ruling class while deflecting bitterness into attacks on those minorities they identify as local agents of "cultural imperialism". Marshall is therefore mistaken to argue that revolutionary Marxists can follow the same approach to Islamism as that developed by the early, pre-Stalinist Comintern in relation to the rising anti-colonial movements of the early 1920s. We must certainly learn from the early Comintern that you can be

on the same side as a certain movement (or even state) in so far as it fights imperialism, while at the same time you strive to overthrow its leadership and disagree with its politics, its strategy and its tactics. But that is not at all the same as saying that the bourgeois and petty bourgeois Islamism of the 1990s is the same as the bourgeois and petty bourgeois anti-colonialism of the 1920s.
54. Otherwise we can fall into the same mistake the left in countries like Argentina did during the late 1960s and early 1970s, when they supported the nationalism of their own bourgeoisie on the grounds that they lived in "semi-colonial states".
55. As A. Dabat and L. Lorenzano have quite rightly noted, "The Argentine nationalist and Marxist left confused ... the association (of their own rulers) with the interests of the imperialist bourgeoisie and their diplomatic servility in the face of the US army and state with political dependency ('semi-colonialism', 'colonialism'), which led to its most radical and determined forces to decide to call for an amid struggle for 'the second independence'. In reality, they were faced with something quite different. The behaviour of any government of a relatively weak capitalist country (however independent its state structure is) is necessary 'conciliatory', 'capitulationist' when it comes to meeting its own interests...in getting concessions from imperialist governments or firms...or consolidating alliances... with these states. These types of action are in essence the same for all bourgeois governments, however nationalist they consider themselves. This does not affect the structure of the state and its relationship with the process of self-expansion and reproduction of capital on the national scale (the character of the state as a direct expression of the national dominant classes and not as an expression of the imperialist states and bourgeoisies of other countries)." *Conflicto Malvinense y Crisis Nacional*, op. cit., p.70.
56. E. Abrahamian, *Khomeinism*, op. cit., p.3.
57. Ibid., p.17.
58. O. Roy, op. cit., p.71.
59. M. Al-Ahnaf, B. Botivewau and F. Fregosi, op. cit., pp.26-27.
60. R.P. Mitchell, op. cit., p.145.
61. Ibid., p.116.
62. Ibid., p.40.
63. Book by Hudaybi, quoted in G. Kepel, op. cit., p.61.
64. Ibid., p.71.
65. Ibid.
66. See quote in ibid., p.44.
67. Ibid., p.53.
68. For details, see ibid., p.78.
69. For a long account of Faraj's views in his book, *The Hidden Imperative*, see ibid., pp.193-202.
70. Ibid., p.208.
71. Ibid., p.164.
72. Ibid., p.210.
73. A. Rouadia, op. cit., p.20.
74. Ibid., pp.33-4.
75. Ibid., p.36.
76. Ibid., p.144.
77. Ibid., p.145-146.
78. J.P. Entelis, op. cit., p.74.
79. A. Rouadia, op. cit., p.191.
80. Ibid., p.209.
81. M. Al-Ahnaf, B. Botivewau and F. Fregosi, op. cit., p.30.
82. Ibid.
83. J. Goytisolo, *Argelia en el Vendava*, in *El Pais*, 30 March, 1994.
84. *El Salaam*, 21 June 1990, translated in M. AI-Ahnaf, B. Botivewau and F. Fregosi, op. cit., pp.200-202.
85. See the account of these events in J. Goytisolo, op. cit., 29 March 1994. This is now the course recommended by the British big business daily, the *Financial*

86. J. Goytisolo, op. cit., 30 March 1994.
87. Ibid.
88. Ibid.
89. Ibid., 3 April 1994.
90. *Guardian*, 15 April 1994.
91. *Guardian*, 13 April 1994.
92. J. Goytisolo, op. cit., 29 March 1994.
93. See the translation on economic policy in M. Al-Ahnaf, B. Botivewau and F. Fregosi, op. cit.
94. Ibid., p.109.
95. This is the view put forward by F. Halliday, op. cit. It was the view put forward in relation to Stalinism by Max Shachtman and others. See M. Shachtman, *The Bureaucratic Revolution* (New York, 1962), and, for a critique, T. Cliff, "Appendix 2: The theory of Bureaucratic Collectivism", in *State Capitalism in Russia* (London, 1988).
96. The position of much of the left today in both Algeria and Egypt.
97. H.E. Chehabi, op. cit., p.169.
98. For details, see A. Bayat, op. cit., pp.101-102, 128-129.
99. Figures given in ibid., p.108.
100. M.M. Salehi, *Insurgency through Culture and Religion* (New York, 1988), p.171.
101. H.E. Chehabi, op. cit., p.169.
102. The figure is given in D Hiro, op. cit., p.187.
103. See ch.3 of my *Class Struggles in Eastern Europe, 1945-83* (London, 1983).
104. T Cliff, "Deflected Permanent Revolution", *International Socialism*, 1:12 (Spring, 1963), reprinted in *International Socialism*, 1:61. Unfortunately, this very important article is not reprinted in the selection of Cliff's writings, *Neither Washington nor Moscow*, but it is available as a pamphlet from Bookmarks.
105. Still less did they represent, as Halliday seems to contend, "the strength of pre-capitalist social forces", op. cit., p.35. By making such an assertion Halliday is only showing how much his own Maoist-Stalinist origins have prevented him understanding the character of capitalism in the present century.
106. As P. Marshall seems to imply in an otherwise excellent book *Revolution and Counter Revolution in Iran*, op. cit.
107. A. Bayat, op. cit., p.134.
108. T. Cliff, op. cit.
109. M. Moaddel, op. cit., p.212.
110. F. Halliday, op. cit., p.57.
111. Maryam Poya is mistaken to use the term "workers' councils" to translate "shoras" in her article, "Iran 1979: Long Live the Revolution ... Long Live Islam?" in *Revolutionary Rehearsals* (Bookmarks, London, 1987).
112. According to M. Moaddel, op. cit., p.238.
113. A. Bayat, op. cit., p.42.
114. E. Abrahamian, *The Iranian Mojahedin*, op. cit., p.189.
115. M Poya, op. cit.
116. M. Moaddel, op. cit., p.216.
117. Abdelwahab el-Affendi, *Turabi's revolution, Islam and power in Sudan* (London, 1991), p.89.
118. Ibid., pp.116-117.
119. Ibid., p.117.
120. Ibid., p.115.
121. For his position on women, see summary of his pamphlet in *Ibid.*, p.174. See also his article, *Le Nouveau Reveil de l'Islam*, op. cit..
122. Affendi, op. cit., p.118.
123. Ibid., p.163.
124. Ibid., pp.163-164.
125. Ibid., p.116.
126. Amnesty International report, quoted in *Economist Intelligence Unit Report, Sudan*, 1992:4.
127. Ibid.
128. *Economist Intelligence Unit Report, Sudan*, 1993:3
129. *Economist Intelligence Unit, Country Profile, Sudan*, 1993-4. Turabi himself has been keen to

insist that "the Islamic awakening is no longer interested in fighting the West ... The West is not an enemy for us". *Le nouveau Reveil de l'Islam*, op. cit.
130. *Economist Intelligence Unit Report, Sudan*, 1993:1.
131. This was the quite correct description of the ideas of the People's Mojahedin provided by the section of the leadership and membership who split away in the mid-1970s to form the organisation that later took the name Paykar. Unfortunately, this organisation continued to base itself on guerrillaism and Maoism rather than genuine revolutionary Marxism.
132. V. Moghadam, "Women, Work and Ideology in the Islamic Republic", *International Journal of Middle East Studies*, 1988, p.230.
133. Ibid., p.227.
134. Ibid.
135. E. Abrahamian, *Khomeinism*, op. cit., p.16.